THE APOSTOLIC FATHERS AND PAUL

D1565825

PAULINE AND PATRISTIC SCHOLARS IN DEBATE

SERIES EDITORS

Todd D. Still
George W. Truett Theological Seminary, Baylor University
and
David E. Wilhite
George W. Truett Theological Seminary, Baylor University

VOLUME TWO
THE APOSTOLIC FATHERS AND PAUL

edited by
Todd D. Still
and
David E. Wilhite

t&tclark

LONDON · NEW YORK · OXFORD · NEW DELHI · SYDNEY

BR
60
.A65
A65
2018

T&T CLARK
Bloomsbury Publishing Plc
50 Bedford Square, London, WC1B 3DP, UK
1385 Broadway, New York, NY 10018, USA

BLOOMSBURY, T&T CLARK and the T&T Clark logo are
trademarks of Bloomsbury Publishing Plc

First published in Great Britain 2017
Paperback edition first published 2018

Library of Congress Cataloging-in-Publication Data
Names: Still, Todd D., editor.
Title: The Apostolic Fathers and Paul / edited by Todd D.Still and David E. Wilhite.
Description: New York : Bloomsbury Academic, 2016- |Series: Pauline and
Patristic Scholars in Debate ; VOLUME TWO Contents: VOLUME ONE.
Identifiers: LCCN 2016050131 | ISBN 9780567672292 (volume1 : hardback))
Subjects: LCSH: Apostolic Fathers–History and criticism.| Bible. Epistles
Of Paul–Criticism, interpretation, etc. | Bible. Epistles of Paul–Theology.
Classification: LCC BR60.A65 A65 2016 | DDC227/.609–dc23
LC record available at https://lccn.loc.gov/2016050131

ISBN: HB: 978-0-56767-229-2
PB: 978-0-56768-261-1
ePDF: 978-0-56767-230-8

Series: Paul and Patristic Scholars in Debate, Volume 2

Typeset by Forthcoming Publications (www.forthpub.com)

To find out more about our authors and books visit
www.bloomsbury.com and sign up for our newsletters.

CONTENTS

ACKNOWLEDGEMENTS

This volume has been a long time in the making. We began this series with a volume on Tertullian's reading of Paul. The reason for such an asynchronous ordering is that we as editors thought it would be a stand-alone book. After we presented the idea for the initial volume to Dominic Mattos, Publisher at Bloomsbury T&T Clark, however, he suggested that we expand the project and produce a series of volumes on the reception of Paul among early Christian writers. We thank him for his encouragement and support.

Since we had already lined up the contributors for the Tertullian volume, we went forward with that project. Subsequently, we found backtracking from Tertullian to the Apostolic Fathers, ostensibly the earliest Christian writings after the New Testament texts, more difficult than we had imagined. Since many excellent studies have analyzed the reception of New Testament writers in the Apostolic Fathers, a volume that focused solely on Paul's reception required us to find scholars who were willing to take on the task of retreading some well-worn paths while still offering something new to the discipline. The contributors are to be thanked for their diligent work and their patience with us as we worked to define the task of a volume such as this.

We would also like to extend our gratitude for the institutional support we received from Baylor University's Truett Theological Seminary. Our school was generous in providing the assistance needed to bring this volume to fruition. Three different graduate assistants helped us with this project, namely, Jeremy Crews, Andy Stubblefield, and Joshua Thiering. We are most grateful for their hard work and for taking such care with countless details.

Lastly, but most importantly, we would like to thank our wives, Amber Wilhite and Carolyn Still, for their unwavering support. Their love, if we may be permitted our own form of reception of Paul, is "patient" and "bears all things." May it "never end" (1 Cor 13:4-8).

Todd D. Still and David E. Wilhite
Baylor University, George W. Truett Theological Seminary, Waco, Texas
All Saints' Day 2015

ABBREVIATIONS

AB	Anchor Bible
ABD	*Anchor Bible Dictionary.* Edited by D. N. Freedman. 6 vols. New York, 1992
ABRL	Anchor Bible Reference Library
ACNT	Augsburg Commentaries on the New Testament
ACW	Ancient Christian Writers
AnBib	Analecta biblica
ANTC	Abingdon New Testament Commentaries
AThR	*Anglican Theological Review*
AYB	Anchor Yale Bible
BDAG	Bauer, W., F. W. Danker, W. F. Arndt, and F. W. Gingrich. *Greek-English Lexicon of the New Testament and Other Early Christian Literature.* 3rd ed. Chicago, 1999
BECNT	Baker exegetical commentary on the New Testament
BETL	Bibliotheca ephemeridum theologicarum lovaniensium
BHT	Beiträge zur historischen Theologie
Bib	*Biblica*
BibScRel	*Biblioteca di scienze religiose*
BRAH	*Boletín de la Real Academia de la Historia*
BZHT	Beiträge zur historischen Theologie
CBQ	*Catholic Biblical Quarterly*
DLNT	*Dictionary of the Later New Testament and Its Developments.* Edited by R. P. Martin and P. H. Davids. Downers Grove, 1997
DTT	*Dansk teologisk tidsskrift*
ECIL	Early Christianity and Its Literature
ETL	*Ephemerides theologicae lovanienses*
ExpTim	*Expository Times*
HAnt	*Hispania Antigua*
HCSB	Holman Christian Standard Bible
HNT	Handbuch zum Neuen Testament
HTR	*Harvard Theological Review*
ICC	International Critical Commentary
IP	*Instrumenta patristica*
ITQ	*Irish Theological Quarterly*
IVPNTC	The IVP New Testament commentary series
JBL	*Journal of Biblical Literature*
JECS	*Journal of Early Christian Studies*

JRS	*Journal of Roman Studies*
JSNT	*Journal for the Study of the New Testament*
JSNTSup	Journal for the Study of the New Testament: Supplement Series
JTS	*Journal of Theological Studies*
KAV	Kommentar zu den Apostolischen Vätern
KEK	Kritisch-exegetischer Kommentar über das Neue Testament (Meyer-Kommentar)
KFA	Kommentar zu frühchristlichen Apologeten
LCC	Library of Christian Classics. Philadelphia, 1953–
LCL	Loeb Classical Library
LNTS	Library of New Testament Studies
LSJ	Liddell, H. G., R. Scott, H. S. Jones, *A Greek–English Lexicon.* 9th ed. with revised supplement. Oxford, 1996
LXX	Septuagint
MT	Masoretic text
MTSR	*Method and Theory in the Study of Religion*
NCB	New Century Bible
Neot	*Noetestamentica*
NIBC	New International Biblical Commentary
NICNT	New International Commentary on the New Testament
NIGTC	New International Greek Testament Commentary
NovT	*Novum Testamentum*
NovTSup	Novum Testamentum Supplements
NPNF	*Nicene and Post-Nicene Fathers*, Series 2
NTG	New Testament Guides
NTS	*New Testament Studies*
OAF	Oxford Apostolic Fathers
PAST	Pauline Studies
PFES	Publications of the Finnish Exegetical Society
PG	Patrologia graeca [= Patrologiae cursus completus: Series graeca]. Edited by J.-P. Migne. 162 vols. Paris, 1857–86
PNTC	Pelican New Testament Commentaries
PRSt	*Perspectives in Religious Studies*
PTS	Patristische Texte und Studien
RBén	*Revue bénédictine*
RECM	Routledge Early Church Monographs
RelSRev	*Religious Studies Review*
RHPR	*Revue d'histoire et de philosophie religieuses*
SEÅ	*Svensk exegetisk årsbok*
SBL	Sources for Biblical Study
SBLMS	Society of Biblical Literature Monograph Series
SBLSymS	Society of Biblical Literature Symposium Series
SC	Sources chrétiennes. Paris: Cerf, 1943–
SHAW	Sitzungen der heidelberger Akademie der Wissenschaften
SNTIW	Studies of the New Testament and its world
SNTSMS	Society for New Testament Studies Monograph Series
StPatr	Studia patristica

TNTC	Tyndale New Testament Commentaries
TU	Texte und Untersuchungen
TUGAL	Texte und Untersuchungen zur Geschichte der altchristlichen Literatur
TynBul	*Tyndale Bulletin*
WGRWSup	Writings from the Greco-Roman World. Supplements
VC	*Vigiliae christianae*
VCSup	Supplements to *Vigiliae christianae*
WBC	Word Biblical Commentary
WSA	Works of Saint Augustine
WTJ	*Westminster Theological Journal*
WUNT	Wissenschaftliche Untersuchungen zum Neuen Testament
ZAC	*Zeitschrift für Antikes Christentum/Journal of Ancient Christianity*
ZKG	*Zeitschrift für Kirchengeschichte*

Contributors

L. Stephanie Cobb
George and Sallie Cutchin Camp Professor of Bible
University of Richmond
Richmond, VA

David J. Downs
Associate Professor of New Testament Studies
Fuller Theological Seminary
Pasadena, CA

David L. Eastman
Associate Professor of Religion
Ohio-Weslyan University
Delaware, Ohio

Paul Foster
Senior Lecturer in New Testament
University of Edinburgh
Edinburgh, Scotland

Andrew Gregory
Chaplain at University College
Oxford University
Oxford, England

Paul Hartog
Vice President for Academic Service and Dean of the College
Faith Baptist Bible College and Theological Seminary
Ankeny, Iowa

CLAYTON N. JEFFORD
Professor of Scripture
Saint Meinrad Seminary & School of Theology
St Meinrad, IN

HARRY O. MAIER
Professor of New Testament and Early Christian Studies
Vancouver School of Theology
Vancouver, Canada

JAMES CARLETON PAGET
Lecturer in New Testament Studies
University of Cambridge
Cambridge, England

CLARE K. ROTHSCHILD
Professor of Theology
Lewis University
Romeoville, IL

TODD D. STILL
Dean & William M. Hinson Chair of Christian Scriptures
George W. Truett Theological Seminary
Baylor University
Waco, Texas

DAVID E. WILHITE
Associate Professor of Theology
George W. Truett Theological Seminary
Baylor University
Waco, Texas

INTRODUCTION

David E. Wilhite

"One might write a history of dogma as a history of the Pauline reactions in the Church," according to Adolf von Harnack.[1] Part of writing such a history, however, would mean defining what is "Pauline" and understanding what constitutes a "reaction," two items which are still debated a century after Harnack. The present volume is the second in a series devoted to the reception of Paul. The essays herein are offered as forays which explore how (and even if) Paul was received in the collection of works known as the Apostolic Fathers, which represent some of the earliest generations to follow Paul's time.

The study of the Apostolic Fathers in one sense has never been far removed from Pauline scholarship, and yet in another sense the distance between the two has often been great. The Apostolic Fathers represent texts from the latter days of *Urchristentum* or "primitive Christianity," to use a now outdated concept. That is to say, they represent some of the latest sources for "Christian origins." In such a view, Paul belongs to the earliest sources, if not the earliest days, of the Christian community. Scholars easily sketched a linear development from Paul's charismatic communities to the birth of the hierarchical church with its high Christology found in the corpus of the Apostolic Fathers. While certain developments are obvious, making this general approach one to be valued, there is also room for much nuance in this depiction of early Christian development.[2] The current volume attempts to foster an approach that brings Paul and the Apostolic Fathers back into conversation, without denying the historical distance between the two.

---

1. Adolf von Harnack, *The History of Dogma*, 3rd ed., trans. Neil Buchanan (New York: Dover, 1961), 1:135.

2. Larry W. Hurtado, "Interactive Diversity: A Proposed Model of Christian Origins," *JTS* 64, no. 2 (2013): 445–62.

There is a growing trend among Paul scholars to study how Paul was read by succeeding generations.[3] Recent doctoral dissertations focusing on Paul must now account for Paul's reception as much as his own context. This trend is a good thing in that our contemporary reading of Paul has inevitably been shaped by centuries of interpretation. Being able to appreciate the various readings that have gone before us, even those with which we disagree, enhances our ability to "hear" Paul, that is, to sift through the important and unavoidable historical minutiae without allowing the historical debates about Paul to drown out Paul's voice. Scholars are finding how earlier readings of Paul, be they from Barnabas or Bultmann, can present old questions afresh.

In this Gadamerian approach, one possible benefit is to overcome the impasse in debates about the "real" Paul. Instead of debating Pauline authorship, which has its place, this new trend in scholarship readily admits that the Paul who inspired Christian epistles, such as Ignatius's, and the Paul who inspired Christian virtues, such as found in *1 Clement*, can all be understood as the "real" Paul, at least to these early readers. While future studies will perennially need to revisit Pauline authorship, the study of Paul (without inverted commas) can proceed fruitfully. After all, the Paul read by later audiences is the only one we have. The future study of Paul will have to appreciate him as the Apostle read by countless Christians who followed in his steps (cf. 1 Cor 11:1).

Alongside this trend in Pauline studies, there are a few developments in the study of the Apostolic Fathers.[4] At the methodological level, rhetorical analysis has been used for some time in understanding the structure and aims of this body of literature. Those insights offer especially promising prospects since they can now be correlated with the rhetorical analysis of Paul, popular at least since Professor Betz's seminal commentary on Galatians.[5]

3. For biblical studies in general, see Robert Evans, *Reception History, Tradition and Biblical Interpretation Gadamer and Jauss in Current Practice* (London: Bloomsbury T&T Clark, 2014).

4. For an introduction into the secondary literature about the Apostolic Fathers, see Wilhelm Pratscher, ed., *The Apostolic Fathers: An Introduction* (Waco, TX: Baylor University Press, 2010).

5. Hans Dieter Betz, *Galatians: A Commentary on Paul's Letter to the Churches in Galatia*, Hermeneia (Philadelphia: Fortress, 1979). For more general discussion and bibliography, see Stanley E. Porter and Thomas H. Olbricht, eds., *Rhetoric and the New Testament*, JSNTSup 90 (Sheffield: Sheffield Academic, 1993); and J. Paul Sampley and Peter Lampe, eds., *Paul and Rhetoric* (London: T&T Clark, 2010).

Another trend has to do with the reception of the New Testament in the Apostolic Fathers. This trend is not so much new as it is one where there is additional development and new resources. The Oxford Committee, appointed by the Society of Historical Theology, produced its findings in 1905, and that work has now been updated and given renewed analysis in the volumes edited by Andrew Gregory and Christopher Tuckett (2005).[6] This has further been supplemented by the Oxford Apostolic Fathers series which is providing new critical editions and commentaries on this corpus (2012–), and so far each editor has carefully discussed the reception of Paul along with other New Testament writers.

In addition to these resources and trends, there is also a tension in current scholarship regarding how best to understand the Apostolic Fathers in relation to the New Testament. The notion of a corpus of "Apostolic Fathers" is largely a modern category dating to 1672, when J. B. Cotelier published his two-volume collection. Since Cotelier, scholars have often debated whether certain texts belong to this corpus.[7] However, the tension lies in the fact that the earliest reception and use of these texts belongs in the same literary stream as the New Testament texts themselves. The New Testament as a collection did not exist at the time the Apostolic Fathers were penned, and so most recent approaches have proceeded to under-stand neither body of literature as codified canons but both as belonging to fluid streams of reception history within early Christianity. Both collec-tions represent later attempts to categorize what were initially texts from the same array of early Christian literature, and scholarly awareness of this fact has helped to break down the barrier between New Testament studies and Patristics as separate fields of inquiry.[8]

Although these disciplinary boundaries will not go away anytime soon, they are more commonly subsumed under the general category of Early Christian Studies. To be sure, even in first and second centuries, observers noted degrees of difference, such as an apostle's own authority and the at best derived authority of texts we call the Apostolic Fathers. On the other

6. A Committee of the Oxford Society of Historical Theology, *The New Testament in the Apostolic Fathers* (Oxford: Clarendon, 1905); Andrew F. Gregory and Christo-pher M. Tuckett, eds., *The New Testament and the Apostolic Fathers*, 2 vols. (Oxford: Oxford University Press, 2005).

7. For a brief introduction to these issues, see Michael W. Holmes, *The Apostolic Fathers*, 3rd ed. (Grand Rapids: Baker, 2007), 5–6.

8. Elizabeth A. Clark, "From Patristics to Early Christian Studies," in *The Oxford Handbook to Early Christian Studies*, ed. Susan Ashbrook Harvey and David G. Hunter (Oxford: Oxford University Press, 2008), 7–41.

hand, there were also instances where Apostolic Fathers were deemed in some sense canonical according to later recollection.[9] Therefore, historians must study these texts in tandem with earlier writings, like those of Paul, analyzing both the continuities and discontinuities.

It is also worth noting one trope within the study of the Apostolic Fathers that is not at all new: the relationship between Christianity and Judaism on the one hand and the relationship between Christianity and Greco-Roman culture on the other.[10] While we are unlikely to say anything altogether new about such important topics, they are topics that must ever be present in scholarly analysis of texts such as these which represent some of our earliest evidence about how Christian communities first emerged from its Jewish roots into the wider Mediterranean world. The "parting of the ways" question, moreover, is one that was already present in Paul's time, and therefore his reception by the next generations of writers is an important point of focus in contemporary scholarship since his views were accommodated in numerous ways that shaped later trajectories.[11]

In terms of how Paul was received specifically within the writings known as the Apostolic Fathers, we should note three ways in which "reception" can be understood. First, there is still work to be done in determining when Paul is actually cited or referenced, which raises the question of what counts as a citation and what criteria one would use to establish said citation.[12] It should be noted that no standard set of criteria was prescribed for the contributors of this volume; instead, the authors establish their own rationale if and as such a need arose.

---

9. See Robert M. Grant, "The Apostolic Fathers' First Thousand Years," *Church History* 57 (1988): 20–28.

10. Helmut Koester, "The Apostolic Fathers and the Struggle for Christian Identity," *ExpTim* 117, no. 4 (2006): 133–39.

11. The secondary literature on this topic is now vast. A still helpful starting point is Judith Lieu, "'The Parting of the Ways': Theological Construct or Historical Reality?," *JSNT* 56 (1994): 101–19; and James D. G. Dunn, *The Parting of the Ways: Between Christianity and Judaism and Their Significance for the Character of Christianity*, 2nd ed. (London: SCM, 2006).

12. For criteria used to establish reception in general, see Andrew F. Gregory and Christopher M. Tuckett, "Reflections on Method: What Constitutes the Use of the Writings That Later Formed the New Testament in the Apostolic Fathers?," in *The New Testament and the Apostolic Fathers*. Vol. 1, *The Reception of the New Testament in the Apostolic Fathers*, ed. Andrew F. Gregory and Christopher M. Tuckett (Oxford: Oxford University Press, 2005), 61–82. However, there is still much debate about what constitutes citation, parallels, allusions, echoes, etc.

Second, beyond specific citations, there is still debate as to what constitutes reception in general of a certain author by another, or conversely
rejection of one author by another. For Paul in particular and his reception
(or rejection) by the Apostolic Fathers, this question touches on the debate
about whether the so-called catholic writers ever shied away from Paul
because of his reception by the so-called heretics.[13] Third, even if one
were to establish any sort of positive reception of Paul the question arises
as to what items are classified as Pauline.[14] In other words, scholars must
sill debate whether certain Pauline teachings were received, rejected, or
ignored, and this returns us to the question about what constitutes the
"real" or "essential" Paul.[15]

The following essays were arranged generally so that each text from
the corpus of the Apostolic Fathers received attention. Several texts
have little to no direct citation of Paul but still deserve attention when
thinking about Pauline reception. Other texts are so indebted to Paul
that they merit several essays (if not an entire collection). Then, there
are overarching questions about Paul's reception that transcend any one
text, such as his role as author, church planter, and martyr. Even though
none of these essays individually nor the collection as a whole can claim
to be exhaustive, in what follows some of the ongoing questions about
Paul's reception in the writings known as the Apostolic Fathers have been
addressed, and they aim to foster additional work in this area.

13. A notion rejected by Andreas Lindemann, *Paulus im ältesten Christentum. Das
Bild des Apostels und die Rezeption der paulinischen Theologie in der frühchristlichen Literatur bis Marcion*, BHT 58 (Tübingen: Mohr, 1979), but which still lingers
in some circles. See further discussion in Mark W. Elliott, "The Triumph of Paulinism
by the Mid-Third Century," in *Paul and the Second Century*, ed. Michael F. Bird and
Joseph R. Dodson, LNTS 412 (London: T&T Clark, 2011), 244–56.

14. See the famous example of Thomas F. Torrance, *The Doctrine of Grace in
the Apostolic Fathers* (Edinburgh: Oliver & Boyd, 1948), who claimed that Paul's
teaching on justification by grace through faith was all but forgotten in the time of
the Apostolic Fathers. Of course, much has changed in how scholars understand Paul
on this isse since Torrance; see especially Michael R. Whitenton, "After ΠΙΣΤΙΣ
ΚΡΙΣΤΟΥ: Neglected Evidence from the Apostolic Fathers," *JTS* 61, no. 1 (2010):
82–109.

15. E.g. Markus Vinzent, *Christ's Resurrection in Early Christianity and the
Making of the New Testament* (Farnham and Burlington: Ashgate, 2012), 77–192.
Furthermore, the differing kinds of reception can be outlined; e.g. Daniel Marguerat,
"Paul après Paul: une histoire de reception," *NTS* 54 (2008): 317–37; François
Bovon, 'Paul as Document and Paul as Monument', in *New Testament and Christian
Apocrypha: Collected Studies II*, ed. Glenn E. Snyder, WUNT 237 (Tübingen: Mohr
Siebeck), 307–17.

David Eastman surveys material from across the Apostolic Fathers about Paul as a martyr. Eastman is able to discuss the many details available in these texts and place them into conversation with what else can be known about Paul's reception from other sources. In so doing, Eastman begins this collection by reminding us how Pauline reception often involved more than simple questions about citation.

Paul Hartog, like Eastman, takes more of a bird's-eye view to examine Paul's role as interpreted in more than one text, namely *1 Clement* and Polycarp's letter to the Philippians. Paul as church planter and letter writer influenced the way in which these later writers interpreted him. Moreover, Hartog argues that later writers' attention to how Paul's formative role in particular churches, such as Rome and Philippi, can inform other areas in New Testament studies, such as the dating of Revelation.

The next three essays address texts in which no direct citation of Paul can be found. Clayton Jefford attempts to answer why Paul is "missing" in certain texts. He reviews in particular the *Didache*, the *Shepherd of Hermas*, *Papias*, the *Martyrdom of Polycarp*, and the *Epistle to Diognetus*. As opposed to past theories that postulate a single reason for numerous authors "rejecting" or "avoiding" Paul, Jefford finds that each case requires its own explanation, and Jefford surveys the possibilities for each and offers several conclusions about how best to understand these texts in relation to Paul, including the fact that Paul is more present in these texts than is often acknowledged.

Paul Foster takes on the question about the absence of the apostle, in this case with *2 Clement*. There are numerous verbal and conceptual parallels between Paul and *2 Clement*, and Foster meticulously analyzes them to asses any possible relationship between the two. No direct literary dependence can be established since so many of these belong to a common Christian repertoire. In contrast to the writings of Justin Martyr, too little is known about the context of *2 Clement* to allow for conjectures as to why Paul is absent – which may not be the same thing as saying Paul is rejected.

Next, James Carleton Paget revisits the question about whether or not the author of *Barnabas* knows Paul and can be read as Pauline. Despite any direct citations of Paul or allusions to the apostle himself, Paget does see evidence that *Barnabas* is influenced by Paul's letters, even if he takes the argument in directions that Paul himself did not. This does not necessarily mean opposition to Paul, for Paget, as some have argued. Instead, Paul's influence can best be detected at the "doctoral" level, wherein Paul's teachings have influenced the author of *Barnabas* even if this later author adapted them for a later context.

The rest of the essays then examine individual authors or texts and their reception of Paul. Clare Rothschild analyzes *1 Clement* in what could be described as at the macro-level (while still devoting serious attention to micro-level details). That is to say, instead of simply assessing what citations can be found from Paul, she compares *1 Clement* with Paul in terms of rhetorical structure as well. The result is the impression that the author of *1 Clement* took Paul's blueprint from 1 Corinthians and constructed a letter that addresses a new occasion, but in a very Pauline way. Rothschild, therefore, classifies *1 Clement* not as pseudonymous (because she is leaving aside Clementine authorship), but as a pseudepigraphon because the text invokes all the authority of Paul's letter without having pretense to Paul's identity.

In turning to Ignatius of Antioch, Todd Still traces the bishop's own comparison with Paul. Both Paul and Ignatius speak about their own possible imminent deaths. Contrary to some, Still finds that Ignatius and Paul went about describing a noble death in very different tones and with very different assumptions. In short, both the reason for living and the eschatological vision that includes death differ greatly between the two, despite Ignatius's attempt to cast himself in a Pauline mold.

In another essay devoted to Ignatius's reading of Paul, David Downs looks specifically at the concept of union with Christ in each author. As with Paul, Ignatius frequently uses the phrases "in Christ," "in Jesus Christ," and "in Christ Jesus." For both Paul and Ignatius, such a phrase includes an array of implications. Ignatius does not always align with Paul in these implications, even if he does share much in common philologically. Despite some differences, Downs still finds Ignatius to share a fairly high level of conceptual correspondence with Paul's teachings on this issue.

The third and last essay on Ignatius is by Harry Maier, who explores the notion of space in both authors. In particular, Maier looks at references to geographical spaces used by early Christians (i.e. "house-churches"), but he uses the socio-philosophical concept of Thirdspace as a paradigm for comparing the two authors. Ignatius aligns most closely with the Pastoral Epistles when it comes to how he imagines the new Christian space.

Stephanie Cobb likewise devotes an essay to Ignatius, only this is to Pseudo-Ignatius, who has all but disappeared from scholarly study of the Apostolic Fathers – if not late antiquity – since the consensus of scholars concluded that the middle recension of Ignatius's letters was the authentic version. Cobb examines the longer recension corpus, which is in a sense "authentic," to find that the author invoked Paul as a proponent of marriage, since marriage itself was being challenged in fourth-century

Syrian Christianity. The claim to Ignatius's authority was also, in Cobb's reading, a claim to Paul's authority.

My own contribution to this project places rhetorical analysis into conversation with the study of Pauline reception in Polycarp's letters. When the results of each are compared, one observes Polycarp's need to switch from Pauline material to Johannine at a crucial moment in the rhetorical structure. Polycarp's statement about docetism in this reading appears to be a negative contrast with the audience who have suffered from the monetary infidelity of a certain Valens, but they have nevertheless retained their faith which they share with Paul and the rest of the martyrs who have renounced "the world."

Finally, Andrew Gregory has generously offered to complete this volume with an afterword. Gregory reviews these essays and places them into further dialogue with scholarship on the reception of the New Testament in general and Paul in particular. He especially focuses on the methodologies involved in these studies, and he offers insights into possible ways forward for future studies.

The study of the Apostle Paul and the Apostolic Fathers is one that will continue for the foreseeable future, and it is hoped that this volume will benefit future scholars who engage these topics.

Chapter 1

PAUL AS MARTYR IN THE APOSTOLIC FATHERS

David L. Eastman

Introduction

The writings of the Apostolic Fathers represent a critical stage in the development of Christian identity. Early leaders were seeking to establish some parameters for the authority within, and the future development of, the communities of Jesus followers. In this formative period the apostle Paul stood as a towering example through his writings and his manner of life. Of the various ways in which Christians remembered Paul, they had special affinity for the memory of him as a martyr. In the post-Constantinian period, this image would dominate the visual representations of the apostle; yet even in the era before iconography, the martyred Paul cast a long shadow over the Christian conceptual landscape. In the Apostolic Fathers, appeals to Paul as a martyr serve significant rhetorical functions at crucial moments in several texts, particularly when authors are attempting to exert and expand influence, to encourage those suffering or potentially about to suffer persecution, or to establish an idealized model for Christian identity.

1 Clement

Discussions of Paul in the Apostolic Fathers invariably begin with a much-disputed passage from the text traditionally known as *1 Clement*. Written probably around the end of the first century or in the first few decades of the second century CE,[1] this is a letter from the leaders of the Roman church

---

1. The traditional dating of 1 Clement assigns it to the time of the emperor Domitian, ca. 95 CE. See, e.g., Adolf von Harnack, *Einführung in die alte kirchengeschichte. Das schreiben der Römischen Kirche an die Korinthische aus der*

to a group of young upstarts in Corinth[2] who have challenged the authority of the older leaders of the church and threaten to split the community. The Roman leaders chastise the dissidents, warning that their actions could even bring the Corinthian church into danger of intervention by the government. In the early part of the text, the authors present a series of biblical examples of the disastrous outcomes of jealousy. Using the terms ζῆλος, φθόνος, and ἔρις interchangeably, they begin with seven examples from the Hebrew Bible. The first three specifically involve brothers turning against one another: Cain and Abel, Jacob and Esau, and Joseph and his brothers. One of these examples results in a murder, and the other two lead to at least threats of fratricide. The next three examples center around Moses: Moses and the fellow Israelite after he kills the Egyptian, the opposition to Moses by Aaron and Miriam, and the rebellion led by Dathan and Abiram. Here again, the consequences are dire. After being confronted by his fellow Israelite, Moses flees into the desert. Miriam is struck leprous and cast outside the camp, and Dathan and Abiram are swallowed up along with their households. In the seventh example David suffers jealousy from foreigners and from King Saul, who, as we know, attempted to kill David on many occasions. Of the seven examples, therefore, four involve conflicts within families, and the other three represent Israelites turning against one another. All seven are examples of intramural disputes in which one person or faction turns against another out of jealousy, because the rival receives special favor or claims special authority. The potential implications for the

---

zeit Domitians (I. Clemensbrief) (Leipzig: Hinrichs, 1929); Elio Peretto, *Clemente Romano: Lettera ai Corinzi* (Bologna: Dehoniane, 1999), 34–36; Andreas Lindemann, *Die Clemensbriefe*, HNT 17 (Tübingen: Mohr Siebeck, 1992), 12–13; Horacio E. Lona, *Der erste Clemensbrief*, KAV 2 (Göttingen: Vandenhoeck & Ruprecht, 1998), 75–78. Cf. Laurence L. Welborn, "The Preface to 1 Clement: The Rhetorical Situation and the Traditional Date," in *Encounters with Hellenism: Studies on the First Letter of Clement*, ed. Cilliers Breytenbach and Laurence L. Welborn (Leiden: Brill, 2004), 197–216. Welborn questions the connection with Domitian and suggests a broader range of possible dates, 80–140 CE. More recently, Otto Zwierlein has argued for a date of 120–125 CE. See Otto Zwierlein, *Petrus in Rom: Die literarischen Zeugnisse*, 2nd ed. (Berlin: de Gruyter, 2010), 245–331. He contends that the authors of *1 Clement* know some of the later epistles in the New Testament, thus pushing the date of the letter into the third decade of the second century. The parallels that he offers, however, are unconvincing.

2. Tradition ascribes the letter to a certain Clement, who is elsewhere identified as one of Peter's successors in the Roman episcopal line. But these are later traditions, and the text itself purports to be from a collective group of Roman leaders.

divided Corinthian community are obvious, if the younger rivals do not put aside their aspirations in the interest of concord.[3]

The authors do not stop with cautionary tales from the Hebrew Bible, however, but turn their attention to more recent examples:

> But so that we may cease with the ancient examples, let us come to the athletes who are nearest to us, and let us take up the examples from our time. On account of jealousy and envy the greatest and most righteous pillars were persecuted and fought to the death. Let us place before our eyes the noble apostles. Because of unjust jealousy Peter endured hardships, and not once or twice but many times. Thus, after bearing witness he went to the place of glory that was due him. On account of jealousy and conflict Paul pointed the way to the prize for perseverance. After he had been bound in chains seven times, driven into exile, stoned, and had preached in both the East and in the West, he received the noble glory for his faith, having taught righteousness to the whole world and having gone even to the limit of the West. When he had borne witness before the rulers, he was thus set free from the world and was taken up to the holy place, having become the greatest example of perseverance.[4]

Here the leading roles belong to Peter and Paul. They are described as "athletes" (ἀθλητάς) and "pillars" (στῦλοι),[5] who contend to the death. We might expect some explicit reference to the manner of those deaths to follow. Instead, the subsequent passage is rather elusive in its details. The authors deal briefly with Peter, summarily stating that he suffered persecution, bore witness (μαρτυρήσας[6]), and then died. They say nothing specific concerning the manner or location of his death and even speak of it only euphemistically: "he went to the place of glory that was due him."

The focus then turns to Paul in a more extended passage. This section has been the subject of considerable study and debate over the years, but for the sake of our inquiry, I will limit myself to four points.

---

3. I treated this list and its implications in greater detail in David L. Eastman, "Jealousy, Internal Strife, and the Deaths of Peter and Paul: A Reassessment of *1 Clement*," *ZAC* 18, no. 1 (2014): 34–53.

4. *1 Clem.* 5.2–7 (A. Jaubert, ed., *Clément de Rome: Épître aux Corinthiens*, SC 167 [Paris: Cerf, 1971], 106–8). All translations are my own.

5. Cf. Gal 2:9; Rev 3:12.

6. The verb μαρτυρέω did not yet have the technical meaning *to die as a martyr*, as argued by Boudewijn Dehandschutter, "Some Notes in 1 Clement 5, 4–7," *IP* 19 (1989): 83–89.

(1) The text strongly suggests that Paul died as a martyr. This may seem obvious in retrospect, but it must be stated that *1 Clement* is the earliest evidence for this tradition. The authors are no doubt drawing upon Pauline imagery to make this point. In Phil 3:12–14 Paul employs athletic language and says that he is striving to win the prize (βραβεῖον) for which God has called him, and in 1 Cor 9:24–27 he admonishes the Corinthians to compete so that they may win the prize (βραβεῖον), which is a crown (στέφανος), just as he himself does. According to *1 Clement* Paul has now "pointed the way to the prize (βραβεῖον) for perseverance," suggesting that he has reached his goal. The reference to Paul's impending death and receipt of a "crown" from the Lord in 2 Tim 4:7–8 could also be relevant, but because the authorship and date of 2 Timothy are disputed, we cannot firmly establish this connection.[7] What is certain is that *1 Clement* makes a significant contribution to later conceptions of Paul, particularly in Rome, where he is often shown receiving a martyr's prize from Christ in the form of a crown. For example, numerous gold glass pieces from the fourth and fifth centuries have been found in the subterranean burial grounds of Rome. These pieces were originally the bottoms of cups, and many preserve scenes of Peter and Paul being crowned by Christ. As I have demonstrated elsewhere, these cups were probably used at banquets in honor of the apostles, as pilgrim tokens, and perhaps as gifts, so they served important liturgical, cultic, and mimetic functions.[8] The crowning scenes reinforced the image of Paul as a triumphant martyr, an image already portrayed in this passage in *1 Clement*. Beyond the language of prizes and crowns, the authors also make the point about Paul's death by stating that he "received the noble glory for his faith" and "was thus set free from the world and was taken up to the holy place." As in the reference to Peter, they avoid any direct reference to death, opting for euphemisms – yet not particularly opaque ones. Thus, the text leaves little doubt that Paul has died as a martyr.

(2) Paul suffered many hardships prior to his death, and these resulted from opposition to his preaching. Here the authors mimic a letter that Paul had written to the Corinthians themselves in which he outlined many of his trials:

7. The dating of disputed Pauline epistles makes any study of this type challenging, because even among those who deny Pauline authorship of 2 Timothy, the proposed dates vary from the late first century to the late second century. I am most convinced by arguments for a date at the end of the first century and will therefore suggest, with all due caution, that *1 Clement* and those after could have known this text.

8. David L. Eastman, *Paul the Martyr: The Cult of the Apostle in the Latin West*, WGRWSup 4 (Atlanta: Society of Biblical Literature; Leiden: Brill, 2011), 79–81.

Five times I received at the hands of the Judeans forty lashes less one. Three times I was beaten with rods. Once I was stoned. Three times I was shipwrecked; a night and a day I was adrift at sea; on frequent journeys, in danger from rivers, danger from robbers, danger from my own people, danger from Gentiles, danger in the city, danger in the wilderness, danger at sea, danger from false brothers; in toil and hardship, through many a sleepless night, in hunger and thirst, often without food, in cold and exposure. (2 Cor 11:24–27)

The lists are of course not identical. *1 Clement* omits many of the details from 2 Corinthians yet adds that Paul had been "driven into exile" and "bound in chains seven times." The source of the former is not obvious. Perhaps the authors have in mind Paul's three-year hiatus in Arabia (i.e. Nabatea) between his calling and his first trip to Jerusalem to meet Peter and James.[9] Acts states that Paul had to flee for his life from Damascus after he had begun preaching Jesus as the Messiah.[10] The authors of *1 Clement* might be conflating these elements, but this connection to Acts is quite uncertain.[11] As for Paul's being in chains (δεσμά), Phil 1:13–14 seems to be a crucial passage. There Paul states that his fetters (δεσμούς in 1:13, δεσμοῖς in 1:14)[12] have actually led to the advance of the gospel, for many have heard of his imprisonment, and the others spreading the message now speak more boldly. His very next comment in Philippians is concern over rival teachers, some of whom preach "because of jealousy and envy" (διὰ φθόνον καὶ ἔριν), two of the same terms used in *1 Clement*.[13] Thus, the jealousy of which Paul speaks in Philippians followed him throughout his life, according to *1 Clement*, and I have argued elsewhere that even Paul's death may have been precipitated by this same internal strife, rather than

---

9. Gal 1:17–18. The chronological details of Paul's life present an ongoing challenge to scholars. For a treatment of the main issues, see David L. Eastman, "Paul: An Outline of His Life," in *All Things to all Cultures: Paul among Jews, Greeks, and Romans*, ed. Mark Harding and Alanna Nobbs (Grand Rapids: Eerdmans, 2013), 34–56.

10. Acts 9:23–25. Paul's three years in Arabia would occur between 9:25 and 9:26.

11. If one accepts some of the latest revisionist dating of Acts, then Ignatian dependence on Acts would be even more unlikely. Richard I. Pervo, for example, dates Acts to ca. 115 CE. See Richard I. Pervo, *Acts: A Commentary*, Hermeneia (Minneapolis: Fortress, 2009), 5 n. 26.

12. The base meaning of δεσμός is *fetter* or *bond*, but in the context of ancient prisons this certainly refers to being in chains.

13. This connection was first noted by Oscar Cullmann, *Peter: Disciple, Apostle, Martyr: A Historical and Theological Study*, 2nd ed., trans. Floyd V. Filson (London: SCM, 1962), 105–6.

by outside opponents.[14] In Philemon, another of the "Prison Epistles," Paul again makes explicit reference to his bonds, twice referring to himself as δέσμιος ("enchained").[15] The other references to Paul's fetters come from the disputed Pauline epistles, so their possible influence on *1 Clement* is less secure; nevertheless, there are multiple sources from which the authors of 1 Clement could derive the image of Paul in chains.[16]

(3) Paul traveled to "the limit of the West" and bore witness "before the rulers" prior to his death. What do these claims tell us about the circumstances of Paul's death? The reference to "the limit of the West" likely preserves the Roman memory of a Pauline voyage to Spain, as the apostle hoped for in Rom 15:23–28. According to multiple authors writing between the first century BCE and the second century CE, Spain was the western limit of the known world. Diodorus Sicilus notes that Gades (modern Cádiz) "is situated at the end of the inhabited world."[17] The geographer Strabo, who had spent time in Rome, refers to the Pillars of Heracles and the Sacred Cape (St. Vincent) as the "the most westerly point not only of Europe, but of the entire inhabited world."[18] Similarly, the Roman historian Velleius Paterculus places the city of Gades "in the farthest district of Spain, at the extreme end of our world,"[19] while Philostratus states that "the city of Gades lies at the extreme end of Europe."[20] For the authors of *1 Clement*, writing from Rome during this same period, "the limit of the West" would almost certainly refer to Spain.[21] This would suggest a Roman tradition that Paul did not die at the

14. Eastman, "Jealousy."

15. Phlm 1, 9.

16. Col 4:18 (μνημονεύετέ μου τῶν δεσμῶν), 2 Tim 1:8 (τὸν δέσμιον αὐτοῦ), and 2 Tim 2:9 (μέχρι δεσμῶν) include the same terminology, while in Eph 6:20 (ἐν ἁλύσει) and 2 Tim 1:16 (τήν ἅλυσίν μου) the more specific term for chain (ἅλυσις) appears.

17. Diodorus Sicilus, *Bibl. hist.* 25.10.1: εἰς τὰ ἔσχατα τῆς οἰκουμένης (Francis R. Watson, ed., *Diodorus Siculus: Library of History*, LCL 409 (Cambridge, MA: Harvard University Press, 1957], 11:154).

18. Strabo, *Geogr.* 2.1.1; 2.4.3; 3.1.2; 3.5.5; 3.1.4 (quoted): τὸ δυτικώτατον οὐ τῆς Εὐρώπης μόνον ἀλλὰ καὶ τῆς οἰκουμένης ἁπάσης σημεῖον (Stefan Radt, ed., *Strabons Geographika* [Göttingen: Vandenhoeck & Ruprecht, 2002], 1:338).

19. Velleius Paterculus, *Hist. Rom.* 1.2.3: "in ultimo Hispaniae tractu, in extremo nostri orbis termino...Gadis condidit" (William Smith Watt, ed., *Vellei Paterculi Historiarum ad M. Vinicium Consulem libri duo* [Stuttgart: Teubner, 1998], 2).

20. Philostratus, *Vit. Apoll.* 5.4; 4.47: τὰ δὲ Γάδειρα κεῖται μὲν κατὰ τὸ τῆς Εὐρώπης τέρμα (C. L. Kayser, ed., *Flavii Philostrati Opera* [Leipzig: Teubner, 1870], 1:166–67).

21. For further discussion, see Eastman, *Paul the Martyr*, 145–46; Lona, *Der erste Clemensbrief*, 165; Angel Custudio Vega, "La venida de San Pablo a Espana y los Varones Apostólicos," *BRAH* 154 (1964): 17; Zacarías García Villada, *Historia*

end of Acts but had been released from prison and traveled farther west to Spain. That Paul bore witness "before the rulers" (μαρτυρήσας ἐπὶ τῶν ἡγουμένων) has typically been read as support for the traditional account of a Roman martyrdom. From this perspective, the authors of *1 Clement* do not need to make explicit the place of Paul's death, because the Corinthians would have already known this. Alternatively, it is possible that this is an allusion to Acts 9:15, where the Lord says that Paul is "my chosen instrument for carrying my name before the Gentiles [or nations] and kings and the sons of Israel." If Acts is the source of this comment in *1 Clement*, then a specifically Roman connection need not be assumed. Because *1 Clement* is not more explicit on the circumstances of Paul's death, we cannot be conclusive in our analysis of this detail. Reading this as a reference to Paul's Roman martyrdom may be the correct implication to draw, but it must be said that the authors are not explicit about who these "rulers" are or where they are located.

(4) Paul's example should serve as a model for others. Through his suffering and death Paul "pointed the way to the prize for perseverance" and established himself as "the greatest example of perseverance." Despite the various trials that he faced, he endured and did not cease preaching "in both the East and in the West." He did not back down even when facing the "rulers," and the Roman church remembers him, therefore, as the "greatest example" – yes, greater than even Peter himself, who was laudable but *not* the "greatest."

1 Clement stands as an important monument to the reception of Paul as martyr in the period of the Apostolic Fathers. It marks the first reference to Paul as a martyr, highlights how his death followed numerous other experiences of suffering, may provide information on the circumstances of his death, and emphasizes his status as the ultimate example of one who witnessed to Christ even unto death.

Ignatius of Antioch

Another important source for Pauline reception is Ignatius, bishop of Antioch in Syria. For reasons unknown to us, Ignatius was sentenced to death and sent to Rome to meet his fate. The general scholarly consensus dates Ignatius's journey and death to the latter part of the reign of the

eclesiástica de España (Madrid: Compañía Ibero-americana de Publicaciones, 1929), 1:122–29; A. González Blanco, "Alusiones a España en las obras de san Juan Crisóstomo," *HAnt* 4 (1974): 352–62; Roger D. Aus, "Paul's Travel Plans to Spain and the 'Full Number of the Gentiles' of Rom XI 25," *NovT* 21, no. 3 (1979): 242–46.

emperor Trajan (ca. 110–117 CE), although a martyrdom during Hadrian's reign (117–138 CE) has been suggested.[22] As he was traveling through Asia Minor, Ignatius wrote a series of letters that survive in three forms. (1) The middle recension is almost universally considered to be the most authentic. It includes seven letters: six to churches and one to Polycarp, the bishop of Smyrna. A Greek edition was first published in 1646. The consensus in favor of this recension has been challenged several times, but to this point these challenges have not altered scholarly opinion.[23] (2) The long recension includes expanded versions of the seven authentic letters and six additional but spurious letters. This recension is probably the work of an Arian redactor of the fourth century CE.[24] (3) The short recension contains abridged, Syriac versions of the letters to the Ephesians, the Romans, and to Polycarp.[25]

In the authentic letters, Ignatius is particularly concerned with the destructive effects of false teachers within the church, with maintaining church unity and organization (particularly through following the bishop), and with his own role as one dying for his faith, which he embraces with an enthusiasm that at times borders on the macabre. In this section I will focus on a particular element of Ignatius's self-understanding as a martyr, namely the way in which he is following the Pauline model.

22. See, e.g., Michael W. Holmes, *The Apostolic Fathers: Greek Texts and English Translations*, 3rd ed. (Grand Rapids: Baker, 2007), 170–73.

23. Notable works supporting the authenticity of the middle recension have included John Pearson, *Vindiciae epistolarum S. Ignatii* (Cambridge: Hayes, 1672); Theodor Zahn, *Ignatius von Antiochen* (Gotha: Perthes, 1873); Adolf van Harnack, *Die Zeit des Ignatius und die Chronologie der antiochenischen Bischöfe bis Tyrannus nach Julius Africanus und den späteren Historikern* (Leipzig: J. C. Hinrichs, 1878); J. B. Lightfoot, *The Apostolic Fathers. Part 2, S. Ignatius; S. Polycarp*, 3 vols. (London: Macmillan, 1885); Andreas Lindemann, "Antwort auf die 'Thesen zur echtheit und Datierung der sieben Briefe des Ignatius von Antiochien,'" *ZAC* 1, no. 2 (1997): 185–94; Mark J. Edwards, "Ignatius and the Second Century: An Answer to R. Hübner," *ZAC* 2, no. 2 (1998): 214–26.

24. Lightfoot includes editions of the middle and long recensions in *The Apostolic Fathers*, Part 2. On the fourth-century date and Arian connections in the longer recension, see Dieter Hagedorn, *Der Hiobkommentar des Arianers Julian*, PTS 14 (Berlin: de Gruyter, 1973), xli–lvi. Cf. Jack W. Hannah, "The Setting of the Ignatian Long Recension," *JBL* 79, no. 3 (1960): 221–38, who dates the long recension to around 140 CE.

25. William Cureton, *The Ancient Syriac Version of the Epistles of Saint Ignatius to Saint Polycarp, the Ephesians, and the Romans* (London: Rivingtons, 1845).

One obvious connection between Paul and Ignatius is that both tradi-tionally were arrested in the East and sent to Rome, where they eventually died. Ignatius celebrates this connection, writing in his letter to the Ephesians, "For when you heard that I was coming from Syria bound for the sake of our common name and hope, and that I was hoping by your prayer to be permitted to fight with the beasts in Rome – so that by doing this I might be able to become a disciple – you hurried to see me."[26] Later in the same letter he reiterates, "Pray for the church in Syria, from where I am being led bound to Rome – I who am the least of the faithful there."[27] Ignatius seems to take great pride in the fact that he will die in Rome in a way that will link him to Paul's death, for he later tells the Ephesians, "You are the highway of those being killed for God. You are fellow initiates of the mysteries with Paul, the one who was sanctified, who was well attested (μεμαρτυρημένου),[28] who is worthy of blessing. May I be found in his footsteps when I attain to God."[29] Although they had not taken the same path from the East to get to Rome – Paul went by sea, while Ignatius crossed Asia Minor by land – Ignatius is describing

26. Ign. *Eph.* 1.2 (all Ignatius texts are from Holmes, *Apostolic Fathers*).

27. Ign. *Eph.* 21.2. Ignatius's rhetorical self-effacement in describing himself as the "least of the faithful" may be an echo of Paul's description of himself as "the least of the apostles" in 1 Cor 15:9. Similar language also appears in Eph 3:8, where Paul (or "Paul") calls himself "the least of all the saints." Assuming that at least one of these epistles was known in Asia Minor in Ignatius's time, then the Ephesians likely would have understood this comparison between the condemned bishop and the apostle. Ignatius employs this rhetoric again in his letter to the Smyrnaeans, where he calls himself "the least of those" in the church of Antioch (Ign. *Smyrn.* 11.1). But as Matthew W. Mitchell has pointed out, "Ignatius' pattern of using language filled with humility and near self-denigration, while yet giving directions and commands, bears a strong resemblance to Paul's writings. Mitchell, "In the Footsteps of Paul: Scriptural and Apostolic Authority in Ignatius of Antioch," *JECS* 14, no. 1 (2006): 36.

28. The verb could also be rendered "martyred," but it is unclear if μαρτυρέω had the technical sense of dying for one's faith by the time of Ignatius, so I have opted for this more philologically conservative translation. For an argument that such use is attested as early as *1 Clement*, Acts, and Revelation, see Robert F. Stoops, "If I Suffer... Epistolary Authority in Ignatius of Antioch," *HTR* 80, no. 2 (1987): 165–67. Cf. Thomas A. Robinson, *Ignatius of Antioch and the Parting of the Ways: Early Jewish–Christian Relations* (Grand Rapids: Baker Academic, 2009), 156–57, who argues that the terms "martyr" and "martyrdom" developed only in the mid- to late second century.

29. Ign. *Eph.* 12.2.

his own journey and impending martyrdom as an imitation of Paul.[30] He hopes quite literally to walk in Paul's footsteps as he approaches Rome and his own death.

In Ignatius's letter to the Roman church, he again makes much of his desire to die in Rome: "Having prayed to God I have managed to see your godly faces, receiving even more than I asked, for having been bound for Christ Jesus I hope to greet you, if it is his will that I should be found worthy to reach this goal."[31] Following this declaration, he immediately begins to plead with them not to hinder his path to martyrdom in Rome. He seems concerned that either he will not be found worthy of suffering in Rome, or that the Roman Christians themselves will intervene and frustrate his plans. On the contrary, he seeks their proactive support in bringing about his death: "Pray to the Lord on my behalf, so that through these instruments[32] I may be found as a sacrifice to God. I am not giving you orders like Peter and Paul did. They were apostles, while I am a convict. They were free, while up to now I am a slave. But if I suffer, I will be a freedman of Jesus Christ and will rise again free in him."[33] On the surface, Ignatius is contrasting himself with Paul and Peter, but closer inspection reveals that he is actually forecasting an even closer association with the apostles. Yes, they are apostles, and he is a convict. But they *were* convicts in Rome, just as he *will be*. They *are* free, which he is not but *will be* following his suffering. Thus, his martyrdom will bring him even closer to the apostles, for while he may literally follow in Paul's footsteps by coming to Rome, he will also symbolically follow in the apostles' footsteps through Roman imprisonment to ultimate freedom. Ignatius's seeming humility is in fact a rhetorical device for elevating his own status as an authoritative figure in the line of Paul (and in this case Peter, as well).[34]

---

30. James W. Aageson has argued that Ignatius's letter to the Ephesians may form an implicit connection to Paul's farewell visit with the Ephesian elders in Acts 20:11–38. Aageson, *Paul, the Pastoral Epistles, and the Early Church* (Peabody, MA: Hendrickson, 2008), 124–25.

31. Ign. *Rom.* 1.1.

32. That is, the various instruments of torture and execution used by the imperial officials.

33. Ign. *Rom.* 4.2–3.

34. Carl B. Smith has commented, "It may be intimated from this passage that the authority of the pair of apostles was further enhanced by the fact that they were martyrs, an end that Ignatius sought with perhaps its attending authority as well as freedom. This may be the reason Ignatius chose to single out these particular apostles and may indicate that he knew traditions related to their deaths in Rome, the city of

Ignatius also presents himself in Pauline fashion through his emphasis on his chains or bonds. We have already seen examples of this imagery in the Pauline corpus, and Ignatius uses it freely. In his letter to the Ephesians he writes, "Let nothing appeal to you except the one for whom I bear these chains, which are spiritual pearls. By them may I rise again by your prayer, and may I also share in them, so that I may be found in the number of the Ephesian Christians, who always have agreed with the apostles in the power of Jesus Christ."[35] Ignatius specifies that his chains (τὰ δεσμά) connect him with the Ephesians and, through them, with the apostles themselves; but the bishop's larger concern is building a direct link between himself and Paul, the most famous "bound" apostle. He ties himself to Paul through his chains in his letter to the Smyrnaeans, as well. There he comments, "Let my spirit be your ransom, and also my chains, which you did not despise, and of which you were not ashamed."[36] Ignatius was not the only author to link imprisonment in Rome with the provocation of shame. In 2 Tim 1:16–17, the author states, "May the Lord give mercy to the house of Onesiphorus, because often he refreshed me and was not ashamed of my imprisonment (ἅλυσιν). But when he came to Rome, he looked eagerly for me and found me." Onesiphorus had come (apparently from Ephesus) to Rome and sought out Paul, not being afraid to associate with a man in chains. Similarly, the Smyrnaeans recognize Ignatius, a condemned man in chains on his way to Rome. They are perhaps new versions of Onesiphorus, remaining faithful to the bishop from Antioch, just as Onesiphorus had done to the apostle.[37] Ignatius makes several other references to being in chains, and on two occasions he states that he is in this state for Christ.[38] Here we may detect yet another Pauline connection to Phil 1:13: "It has become clear throughout the entire praetorium and to everyone else that I am in chains for Christ." While current scholarly

---

address in this letter." Smith, "Ministry, Martyrdom, and Other Mysteries: Pauline Influence on Ignatius of Antioch," in *Paul and the Second Century*, ed. Michael F. Bird and Joseph R. Dodson, LNTS 412 (London: T&T Clark, 2011), 39. Smith is too timid in his argument here, for martyrdom was certainly connected to apostolic authority at least as early as *1 Clement*. This follows the connection of suffering and authority in the Pauline epistles, as discussed by, e.g., James A. Kelhoffer, "Suffering as Defense of Paul's Apostolic Authority in Galatians and 2 Corinthians 11," *SEÅ* 74 (2009): 127–43. I have shown in *Paul the Martyr* how this connection grew exponentially in the early centuries of Christianity.

35. Ign. *Eph.* 11.2.

36. Ign. *Smyrn.* 10.2.

37. Here again, questions of dating require me to suggest this influence tentatively.

38. Ign. *Phld.* 7.2; *Trall.* 12.2.

consensus is divided on the provenance of Philippians, until the nineteenth century Rome was the general assumption.[39] If Ignatius shared this assumption, then it would be wholly appropriate and Pauline for him to describe his chains on the way to Rome as being "for Christ," in the same way that Paul had been "in chains for Christ" in Rome. Here again, the bishop was in some sense retracing the steps of the apostle.

Ignatius also employs Pauline imagery in describing his own likely fate. In his letter to the Romans he writes, "Permit me nothing more than to be poured out as an offering (σπονδισθῆναι) to God, while the altar is still prepared."[40] His use of the verb σπένδω is reminiscent of two passages in which the apostle also looks forward to a likely end. In Phil 2:16 Paul writes, "But if I am being poured out as a drink offering (σπένδομαι) upon the sacrifice and service of your faith, then I am glad and rejoice together with all of you." As Paul faces the possible end of his life, he describes himself as a sacrifice on behalf of the Philippians. This language appears again in the other Pauline passage most closely tied to the apostle's death, 2 Tim 4:6, where the author (Paul or "Paul") writes, "I am already being poured out as a drink offering (σπένδομαι), and the time of my departure has come." The use of σπένδω links the two passages within the Pauline tradition, even if the authorship of the latter example is doubted. Ignatius paints his future with a Pauline brush by applying this same verb (whether taken from Philippians or 2 Timothy or both) to his own future, if the Romans will oblige him by not interfering.[41]

Ignatius seems quite certain that he is following the Pauline model in some regards, but he seems less certain about whether or not this imitation would include his manner of death. In his letter to the Smyrnaeans, he writes, "Why, then, have I given myself over to death, to fire, to the sword,

---

39. Contemporary theories of provenance favor Ephesus, Caesarea Maritima, or Corinth against the traditional view placing it in Rome. For a summary of the positions with select bibliography, see John Reumann, *Philippians: A New Translation with Introduction and Commentary*, AYB (New Haven: Yale University Press, 2008), 13–15.

40. Ign. *Rom.* 2.2.

41. Smith ("Ministry," 55) notes this connection but is again too hesitant in assessing its implications: "While these parallels do not prove Ignatius's dependence, they do provide a strong argument for the Jewish orientation of the concepts under-girding early Christian theology of martyrdom, a world that our bishop shared with Paul." Ignatius's employment of the same verb as Paul in speaking of impending death is not accidental. Moreover, it is not clear how Ignatius could have arrived at such particular usage from a general "Jewish orientation," given that Judaism's most famous martyr story – that of the Maccabees – does not use this verb.

to the beasts? But the one near the sword is near to God; and the one with the beasts is with God. Only let it be in the name of Jesus Christ, so that I might suffer with him."[42] Ignatius identifies three possible means of execution in Rome and then highlights the latter two of these. Death by the sword certainly would have put Ignatius directly in the Pauline line, yet he stops short of making this connection. He simply does not know how he will die; yet however he dies, he knows that he will be with God and suffering with Christ. When Ignatius writes to the Romans, he focuses more on the possibility of facing the wild beasts, which he will force to attack him if they are timid. Yet he still reflects on the possibility that his end could come through a variety of means: "Fire and cross, combats with the beasts, mutilations, ripping apart, the wrenching of bones, the cutting off of body parts, the grinding up of my whole body, the wicked torments of the devil – let them come upon me. Only let me reach Jesus Christ."[43] Ignatian hyperbole is not in short supply when he comes to discussing his own death, which he – rhetorically, at least – eagerly anticipates. It does appear, however, that his morbid enthusiasm for the moment of death is directed not only at an apostolic model, but also at a Christological one. He had told the Smyrnaeans that he was hoping to suffer with Christ, and in his appeal to the Romans *not* to help him, he pleads, "Allow me to be an imitator of the passion of my God."[44] Anyone who is in Christ, he continues, will understand this desire.[45] Ignatius hopes to imitate Christ in substance, even if not in form, for he anticipates dying in the arena, not on a cross. In this regard perhaps Ignatius hopes to be very much like Paul, who was "crucified with Christ"[46] but only symbolically. Indeed, in 2 Cor 4:8–11, where Paul lists various trials experienced by followers of Christ, he links these directly to the death of Jesus:

42. Ign. *Smyrn.* 4.2.
43. Ign. *Rom.* 5.3.
44. Ign. *Rom.* 6.3.
45. As Candida Moss has noted, "This passage is illustrative of the way in which Ignatius sees the life of the Christian generally, and the death of the martyr particularly, as modeled on the pattern of Christ crucified. This may be the only instance in which the imitation of Christ is connected with his own suffering and death, but it is strikingly unambiguous in viewing the death of the believer as an imitation of the death of Christ." Moss, *The Other Christs: Imitating Jesus in Ancient Christian Ideologies of Martyrdom* (New York: Oxford University Press, 2010), 43. Smith ("Ministry," 54) also points out that Ignatius's concept of martyrdom is based on the stories of Jesus, Paul, and Peter.
46. Gal 2:20.

In every way we are afflicted, but not beaten down; perplexed, but not in despair; persecuted but not abandoned; cast down but not destroyed. We always carry the death of Jesus in our body, so that the life of Jesus may be made manifest in our body. For we who are alive are always being handed over to death for the sake of Jesus, so that the life of Jesus may be made manifest in our mortal flesh.[47]

For Paul, one does not need to die on a cross to emulate the death of Jesus. In a similar way, Ignatius advocates for an *imitatio Christi* that transcends the actual form of the suffering experienced.

Polycarp to the Philippians

Polycarp, bishop of Smyrna, was a recipient of one of the letters from Ignatius and was deeply influenced by the Ignatian model. It is not surprising, therefore, that he echoes Ignatius's Pauline references in his own letter to the Philippians, who had, after all, received a letter from the apostle himself about a century earlier. Immediately following his opening greeting, Polycarp comments, "I rejoice greatly with you in our Lord Jesus Christ, for you received the examples of true love and sent forth, as the opportunity came to you, those bound in chains, which are suitable for the saints and are diadems for those truly chosen by God and our Lord."[48] The Philippians' reputation was based on their care for Christians "in chains" – Ignatius among them – and Polycarp cites Ignatius alongside Paul as models of perseverance for them to follow:

I encourage you all, then, to obey the teaching about righteousness discipline yourselves with all the endurance that you saw with your own eyes – not only in the blessed men Ignatius, Zosimus, and Rufus, but also in others from among your number, and in Paul himself, and in the other apostles. Be assured that all of these did not run in vain, but in faith and righteousness, and that they are in the place that is due them in the presence of the Lord, with whom they suffered. For they did not love the present age but the one who died for us and was raised again by God for our sake.[49]

---

47. Smith, "Ministry," 52, also links Ign. *Rom.* 5.3 with 2 Cor 11:23–32 and Heb 11:32–40.

48. Pol. *Phil.* 1.1 (all Polycarp texts are from Paul Hartog, ed., *Polycarp's* Epistle to the Philippians *and the* Martyrdom of Polycarp: *Introduction, Text, and Commentary*, OAF [Oxford: Oxford University Press, 2013]).

49. Pol. *Phil.* 9.1–2.

Zosimus and Rufus presumably accompanied Ignatius on his journey to martyrdom, although Ignatius never mentions them in his letters. The Philippians should emulate them along with the example who those men had followed in going bravely to their deaths in Rome, namely Paul. Polycarp thus affirms the connection between Ignatius and Paul, which the former had claimed in his letters, and calls upon the Philippians to place themselves in that line, as well. Polycarp's reference to Paul is particularly noticeable in comparison to his silence on another apostle, namely Peter.[50] Peter had traditionally died in Rome at around the same time as Paul,[51] yet Polycarp mentions only Paul. This is no doubt a result of the historical connection between the Philippians and Paul and of Ignatius's emphasis on the Pauline model, rather than the Petrine one.

Polycarp further highlights Paul as a model of perseverance by referring here to two passages from the Pauline epistles, both of which allude to Paul's (at least potential) impending death. The examples whom Polycarp mentions "did not run in vain" (οὐκ εἰς κενὸν ἔδραμον), an allusion to Phil 2:16, where Paul encourages the Philippians to hold fast to the faith, "so that I may have reason to boast on the day of Christ, because I did not run in vain (οὐκ εἰς κενὸν ἔδραμον) nor toil in vain."[52] As Paul faces the possibility that his "race" may be nearly complete, he fears that his work may have been in vain and calls upon the Philippians to ensure that it will

50. After making this observation, I discovered that it was also mentioned by Andreas Lindemann, *Paulus im ältesten Christentum. Das Bild des Apostels und die Rezeption der paulinischen Theologie in der frühchristlichen Literatur bis Marcion*, BHT 58 (Tübingen: Paul Siebeck, 1979), 89.

51. Among the patristic authors who link the deaths of Peter and Paul directly, some claim that they died on the exact same day: Jerome, *Vir. ill.* 5; *Tract. Ps.* 96.10; Maximus of Turin, *Serm.* 1.2; 2.1; 9.1; and implied by Dionysius of Corinth according to Eusebius, *Hist. eccl.* 2.25.8. A similar passage credited to Damasus of Rome is spurious, as shown by Cuthbert H. Turner, ed., *Ecclesiae occidentalis monumenta iuris antiquissima* (Oxford: Clarendon: 1899–1939), 1.2:157. Other authorities claim that they died on the same date but a year apart: Ambrose of Milan, *Virginit.* 19.124; Augustine, *Serm.* 295.7; 381.1; Prudentius, *Perist.* 12.5, 21–22; Gregory of Tours, *Glor. mart.* 28; and Arator, *Act. apost.* 2.1247–49. Sorting out the timing of the apostolic deaths among these sources and the various martyrdom accounts is the focus of a separate project in process.

52. For a discussion of previous acceptance or rejection of this parallel, see Michael W. Holmes, "Polycarp's *Letter to the Philippians* and the Writings That Later Formed the New Testament," in *The New Testament and the Apostolic Fathers*. Vol. 1, *The Reception of the New Testament in the Apostolic Fathers*, ed. Andrew F. Gregory and Christopher M. Tuckett (Oxford: Oxford University Press, 2005), 212 n. 108.

not be so. The fact that the Philippians remain faithful a century later is proof to Polycarp that Paul's desire was fulfilled. Polycarp also refers to the other Pauline passage most closely tied to the apostle's death, 2 Tim 4. After predicting his impending death, as we saw earlier, in language that echoes Philippians (2 Tim 4:6–8), Paul/"Paul" speaks of a certain Demas, who had abandoned him because "he loved this present age" (ἀγαπήσας τὸν νῦν αἰῶνα). Demas and Paul, therefore, stand as polar opposites in 2 Timothy, because the former had fled (probably Rome in the text) to protect himself, while the latter was staying to face his possible demise.[53] Demas provides for Polycarp the ideal foil, the very picture of what Paul, Ignatius, and the others did *not* do when they faced persecution in Rome. These exemplary figures are worthy of honor and imitation because, unlike Demas, they did not love this current age (οὐ γὰρ τὸν νῦν ἠγάπησαν αἰῶνα).[54] Polycarp's choice of these two Pauline allusions is focused and intentional. Ignatius and the others most clearly follow Paul in that they persevered as he did before dying in Rome. They were most like Paul when they came closest to their own deaths, which they faced with Pauline resolve. The Philippians should do likewise, thus placing themselves in the lineage of the martyred apostle.

53. Rome is the traditional setting for 2 Timothy, although scholars still debate whether this imprisonment is meant to be in Rome or in Caesarea Maritima. For a summary of the main points on both sides, see Martin Dibelius and Hans Conzelmann, *The Pastoral Epistles*, ed. Helmut Koester, trans. Philip Buttolph and Adela Yarbro, Hermeneia (Philadelphia: Fortress, 1972), 126–27.

54. I diverge from many scholars on the question of Polycarp's knowledge of the Pastoral Epistles. The claim that Polycarp did not know the Pastoral Epistles is sometimes employed against Pauline authorship of these letters, but this seems to be a specific reference by Polycarp to 2 Tim 4:10. My argument does not address all the issues related to Pauline authorship of the Pastorals, but the notion that Polycarp was ignorant of at least this letter stands on questionable ground. See, e.g., Kenneth Berding, "Polycarp of Smyrna's View of the Authorship of 1 and 2 Timothy," *VC* 53 (4 1999): 349–60; Paul Hartog, *Polycarp and the New Testament*, WUNT 2/134 (Tübingen: Mohr Siebeck, 2002), 228–35; Holmes, "Polycarp's *Letter to the Philippians*," 217–18. I would not, however, go as far as suggesting that Polycarp actually wrote or commissioned the Pastorals, as did Hans von Campenhausen, "Polykarp von Smyrna und die Pastoralbriefe," in *Aus der Frühzeit des Christentums* (Tübingen: Mohr Siebeck, 1963), 196–252.

2 Clement

Two final examples of appeals to Paul as a martyr come from *2 Clement*. Dated to around the middle of the second century,[55] this anonymous text of unknown provenance – which, like *1 Clement*, has no demonstrable connection to anyone named Clement – is a general sermon that covers a wide variety of topics, including the importance of remaining faithful amid persecution. Early in the text the author encourages the audience, "Therefore, brothers [and sisters], after leaving aside the temporary residence of this world, let us do the will of the one who called us. And let us not fear to leave this world, for the Lord says, 'You will be like lambs among wolves.' Peter answered him and said, 'What, then, if the wolves tear apart the lambs?' And Jesus said to Peter, 'The lambs will not fear the wolves after they die.' "[56] Jesus then explains to Peter that he should fear eternal, not physical death, so the author has at this point introduced the potential for martyrdom into the text. Just a few lines later, the preacher returns to the topic and encourages the audience with imagery taken especially from 2 Tim 4:6–8:

> Let us compete, knowing that the competition is close at hand. Many travel to the earthly (φθαρτούς)[57] competitions, but not all are crowned – only those who have trained hard and competed well. Let us compete, then, so that we may all be crowned. Let us run the straight course, the incorruptible (ἄφθαρτον) competition; and let many of us set out for it and compete, so that we may be crowned. But if we cannot all be crowned, then let us come near to the crown. (*2 Clem.* 5.1–4)[58]

The key terms are shared with 2 Timothy: ἀγών (competition or struggle), its verbal equivalent ἀγωνίζομαι (to struggle or compete in the games), and στέφανος (crown). The author of *2 Clement* is peering into the future and sees for his audience the likelihood of a fight to the death, just as Paul/"Paul" sees for himself in 2 Tim 4:6–8, and the prize for being victorious is a crown. The author returns to the theme of crowning later in this sermon: "We are struggling in a trial for the living God, and we are being trained in this life, so that we may be crowned (στεφανωθῶμεν) in the life to come."[59] But the passage in 2 Timothy is not the only place

---

55. Holmes, *Apostolic Fathers*, 133–35.

56. Christopher Tuckett, ed., *2 Clement: Introduction, Text, and Commentary*, OAF (Oxford: Oxford University Press, 2012), 92.

57. Literally, "corruptible."

58. *2 Clem.* 7.1–3.

59. *2 Clem.* 20.2.

in which athletic imagery appears in the Pauline corpus,[60] and *2 Clement* also has specific echoes of 1 Cor 9:24–25: "Do you not know that in the stadium all the runners run, but only one receives a prize (βραβεῖον)? Run, therefore, so that you may receive it. Everyone competing disciplines himself in all things. They do it to receive a crown (στέφανον) that is perishable, but we do it to receive one that is imperishable." In describing the rewards for those who are faithful to death, Paul refers to a crown (στέφανος) and a contrast between what is corruptible (φθαρτός) and incorruptible (ἄφθαρτος).[61] Thus, the author of *2 Clement* has likely taken some inspiration from 1 Corinthians, as well, but the dependence on 2 Timothy remains clear, even primary.[62] As "Clement" is preparing his listeners for the possibility of having to "leave this world" for their faith, he particularly highlights "Paul's" example from 2 Timothy.

Conclusion

The impact of Paul's mission, example, and eventual death left distinctive marks on the development of earliest Christianity. Paul's importance as an apostle and theologian were undeniable, yet his role as a martyr played an especially powerful role in the establishment of ecclesiastical authority and the promotion of an example for others to follow. The leaders in Rome appealed to Paul's martyrdom as a warning to the upstart Corinthians, while also lifting up the apostle as "the greatest example of perseverance." Ignatius styled himself an heir to the Pauline legacy and desired to be "found in his footsteps," for Ignatius too was being sent to Rome to face his death. Yet in constructing his authoritative voice, the Antiochene bishop

60. In Phil 3:12–14, Paul describes himself as straining (ἐπεκτείνω) to receive a reward (βραβεῖον), but the particular vocabulary has no overlap with *2 Clement*.

61. Many scholars believe Paul is using the imagery of the prizes earned at the Isthmian Games near Corinth.

62. Cf. Andrew F. Gregory and Christopher M. Tuckett, "*2 Clement* and the Writings That Later Formed the New Testament," in Gregory and Tuckett, eds., *The Reception of the New Testament in the Apostolic Fathers*, 279–89. Gregory and Tuckett claim concerning the author of *2 Clement* that "at no point did he make conscious and deliberate reference either to Paul or to his writing, and that no direct citations of, or allusions to, Paul's letters are to be found in *2 Clement*." They ascribe possible parallels as "already part of the common discourse of early Christianity" (279). Regarding the possible parallel with 1 Cor 9, they comment, "The metaphor of a race is a common one, and therefore insufficient to demonstrate dependence on Paul" (283). I have attempted to show, however, that the density and specificity of shared vocabulary significantly weakens their position.

also highlighted, even exaggerated, his desire to die in imitation of Pauline rhetoric in which suffering granted authority.[63] One of Ignatius's protégés, Polycarp of Smyrna, perpetuated Ignatius's self-presentation and held him up with Paul as models of those who underwent torment and death, rather than loving "the present age." And Pauline language appears at the center of the encouragement to "compete" for a "crown" in *2 Clement*. In receiving and propagating this aspect of the Pauline heritage, these early bishops and church leaders were contributing to the incipient stages of a Pauline cult that later spread across the Christian world and resulted in the development of even more stories about Paul, of monumental architecture, of pilgrimage sites, and of many other practices that celebrated, amplified, and constantly re-created the image of Paul as a model martyr.[64]

63. These Pauline connections are expanded and intensified by the anonymous authors of the additions to the long recension of the Ignatian corpus, the six additional spurious letters that accompany the long recension, and the *Martyrdom of Ignatius*. For more on what I have labeled "second order reception," see David L. Eastman, "Ignatius, pseudo-Ignatius, and the Art of Pauline Reception," *Early Christianity* 7 (2016): 1–16.

64. For a detailed study of this cult in the West, see my *Paul the Martyr*.

Chapter 2

THE IMPLICATIONS OF PAUL AS EPISTOLARY
AUTHOR AND CHURCH PLANTER IN *1 CLEMENT*
AND POLYCARP'S *PHILIPPIANS*

Paul Hartog

Introduction

Both *1 Clement* and Polycarp's one extant epistle were written to Pauline churches (in Corinth and Philippi, respectively). More particularly, *1 Clem.* 47 and Polycarp's *Phil.* 11–12 parallel each other in multiple ways, and together the passages offer distinct insights into the early reception of Paul. A comparison of these two passages offers a complementary understanding of Paul's church-planting and letter-writing ministries "in the beginning." Moreover, the chronological distancing in Polycarp's *Philippians* between Paul's church-planting and letter-writing ministries and the later formation of the Smyrnaean church has not been sufficiently integrated into New Testament scholarship (including relevant facets of the interpretation of Acts 19 and Rev 2).

Comparison of 1 Clement *47 and Polycarp,* Philippians *11–12*
Some have reasoned that *1 Clement* served as a direct model for Polycarp.[1] B. H. Streeter believed that Polycarp knew *1 Clement* almost "by heart," adding that Polycarp's *Philippians* was "more influenced by the language of Clement than by any book of the New Testament, except perhaps 1 Peter."[2] Robert Grant declared that Polycarp's *Philippians* alludes to

---

1. Cf. the two letter openings; Otto Bardenhewer, *Geschichte der altkirchlichen Literatur*, 2nd ed. (Freiburg: Herder, 1913), 1:166; A. M. Ritter, "De Polycarpe à Clément: Aux origines d'Alexandrie chrétienne," in *ΛΛΕΞΛΝΔΡΙΝΛ: Hellénisme, judaïsme et christianisme à Alexandrie*, ed. P. Claude Mondésert (Paris: Cerf, 1987), 152–53.

2. B. H. Streeter, *The Four Gospels* (London: Macmillan, 1924), 528; B. H. Streeter, *The Primitive Church* (London: Macmillan, 1929), 159.

1 Clement "throughout," and Michael Holmes has maintained that Polycarp was "particularly familiar with" *1 Clement* (and 1 Peter).[3] Kenneth Berding examined the cluster of Clementine materials bundled in *Phil.* 4.2–3.[4] More recently, Berding has re-examined Polycarp's use of *1 Clement*, reaching modest conclusions: "Polycarp knew and used *1 Clement*, but his familiarity with this early Christian document should not be exaggerated."[5] Although one cannot establish any literary dependence of Polycarp's *Phil.* 11–12 upon *1 Clem.* 47, there are interesting parallels.[6]

1 Clement 47 states,

> Take up the epistle of the blessed Paul the apostle. What did he first write to you in the beginning of the gospel? Truly he wrote to you in the Spirit about himself and Cephas and Apollos, because even then you had split into factions. Yet that splitting into factions brought less sin upon you, for you were partisans of highly reputed apostles and of a man approved by them. In contrast now think about those who have perverted you and diminished the respect due your renowned love for others. It is disgraceful, dear friends, yes, utterly disgraceful and unworthy of your conduct in Christ, that it should be reported that the well-established and ancient church of the Corinthians, because of one or two persons, is rebelling against its presbyters. And this report has reached not only us but also those who differ from us, with the result that you heap blasphemies upon the name of the Lord because of your stupidity, and create danger for yourselves as well.[7]

3. Robert M. Grant, "Polycarp of Smyrna," *AThR* 28 (1946): 141; Michael W. Holmes, "Polycarp of Smyrna," *DLNT*, 936.

4. Kenneth Berding, *Polycarp and Paul*, VCSup 62 (Leiden: Brill, 2002), 151–53. Berding mentions the use of *1 Clem.* 1.3; 21.6–8; 41.2; and 21.3, although the latter does not appear in his list on p. 202.

5. Kenneth Berding, "Polycarp's Use of *1 Clement:* An Assumption Reconsidered," *JECS* 19 (2011): 139. Berding earlier listed three "probable" and seven "possible" dependences of Polycarp's *Philippians* upon *1 Clement* (Berding, *Polycarp and Paul*, 202). See also D. B. Capelle, "La 1ᵃ Clementis et l'épitre de Polycarpe," *RBén* 37 (1925): 283–87; J. B. Lightfoot, *Apostolic Fathers* (London: Macmillan, 1889), 1.1:149–52; James Donaldson, *The Apostolical Fathers: A Critical Account of their Genuine Writings and of their Doctrines* (London: Macmillan, 1874), 231; Horacio E. Lona, *Der erste Clemensbrief*, KAV 2 (Göttingen: Vandenhoeck & Ruprecht, 1998), 90–92; Ritter, "De Polycarpe," 151–72; Johannes Baptist Bauer, *Die Polykarpbriefe*, KAV 5 (Göttingen: Vandenhoeck & Ruprecht, 1995), 28–30.

6. Berding finds a "possible influence from *1 Clem.* 37.5" upon Pol. *Phil.* 11.4 (Berding, *Polycarp and Paul*, 114–15, 202).

7. Unless noted otherwise, English translations of the Apostolic Fathers come from Michael W. Holmes, *The Apostolic Fathers: Greek Texts and English Translations*, 3rd ed. (Grand Rapids: Baker, 2007).

Polycarp's *Phil.* 11.1–12.1 states,

> I am exceedingly grieved for Valens, who at one time was made an elder
> among you, that he should so disregard the position which was given to
> him. Therefore, I admonish [you] to keep yourselves from avarice and to
> be pure [and] truthful. Keep yourselves from every evil. Moreover, if one
> is unable to control himself in these matters, how [can] he decree this to
> another? If anyone has not kept himself from avarice, he will be defiled by
> idolatry and will be judged as though among the Gentiles, who are ignorant
> of the judgment of the Lord. Or are we unaware that the saints will judge
> the world, as Paul teaches? But I have neither observed nor heard such a
> thing among you, in whose midst the blessed Paul labored, being in the
> beginning – in his letters.[8] Indeed he boasts about you in all the churches,
> which alone had known God at that time. We, however, had not yet known
> [him]. Therefore, brothers, I am very grieved for him and for his wife – may
> the Lord grant them genuine repentance. So be temperate also yourselves
> in this matter, and do not esteem such ones as enemies, but restore them as
> ailing and wandering members, in order that you may heal your entire body.
> Indeed I am confident that you are well trained in the sacred writings, and
> nothing escapes you. But to me it has not been granted. Only, as it has been
> said in these Scriptures, "Be angry and refuse to sin," and "Let not the sun
> set upon your wrath." Blessed [is] the one who remembers [this], which I
> myself believe to be [the case] with you.[9]

Both *1 Clement* and Polycarp's *Philippians* call for repentance in the
face of ecclesiastical troubles in Pauline-founded churches. In the case
of *1 Clement*, congregational factionalism had erupted in the Corinthian
assembly, in the form of "rebelling" against the elders. In the case of
Polycarp's *Philippians*, the avarice of an elder and his wife had apparently led to communal instability.[10] Both the Clementine and Polycarpian
passages caution that the name of the Lord could be blasphemed among
the Gentiles because of the moral lapses.[11] Both texts mention the Apostle

---

8. For an in-depth examination of this problematic phrase and interpretive options,
see the discussion below.

9. Adapted from Paul Hartog, *Polycarp's Epistle to the Philippians and the
Martyrdom of Polycarp*, OAF (Oxford: Oxford University Press, 2013), 93.

10. *1 Clem.* 46.5–7; 47.3–6; 51.1; Pol. *Phil.* 11.1, 4. See Paul Hartog, *Polycarp
and the New Testament*, WUNT 134 (Tübingen: Mohr Siebeck, 2002), 106–8, 136–39;
idem, "The Relationship Between Paraenesis and Polemic in Polycarp, *Philippians*,"
StPatr (2012): 27–38; H. O. Maier, "Purity and Danger in Polycarp's Epistle to the
Philippians: The Sin of Valens in Social Perspective," *JECS* 1 (1993): 229–47.

11. *1 Clem.* 47.7; Pol. *Phil.* 10.2–3.

Paul by name and label him as "the blessed Paul."[12] Both passages may harken back to Paul's ministry "in the beginning."[13] *1 Clement* 47.6 specifically praises the "the well-established and ancient church of the Corinthians," a sentiment paralleled in Polycarp's epistle, which speaks of the Philippians' "established root" of faith, "which has been proclaimed from earliest times."[14] By contrast, Polycarp's *Philippians* emphasizes that the Smyrnaeans "had not yet come to know" the Lord "at that time" (11.3; cf. 3.2), forming a definite chronological separation between the inceptions of the two churches.

Both the Clementine and Polycarpian passages particularly highlight the letter-writing ministry of Paul.[15] *1 Clement* 47 and Polycarp's *Phil.* 11–12 both allude to or quote 1 Corinthians specifically, as well as echoing other Pauline materials.[16] *1 Clement* 47.1 approvingly references "the epistle of the blessed Paul the apostle," which (in this context) obviously refers to Paul's letter now titled 1 Corinthians.[17] Andrew Gregory maintains, "Such clear testimony to 1 Corinthians means that this conclusion is secure, even without any significant verbatim parallels at this point."[18] *1 Clement* 47.2 then echoes 1 Cor 1:12, calling both Paul and Cephas (Peter) "highly reputed apostles" and labeling Apollos as "a man approved by them."[19] And a short phrase in *1 Clem.* 47.1 resembles Phil 4:15 ("beginning of the gospel"), causing some to posit dependence.[20] Polycarp's *Phil.* 11 possibly alludes to 1 Tim 3:5; 2 Thess 1:4, and 2 Thess 3:15, and it definitely quotes 1 Cor 6:2.[21] Moreover, the next chapter begins with a quotation

12. *1 Clem.* 47.1; Pol. *Phil.* 11.3.
13. *1 Clem.* 47.2; Pol. *Phil.* 11.3.
14. *1 Clem.* 47.6; Pol. *Phil.* 1.2 (English translation mine); cf. 3.2.
15. *1 Clem.* 47.1–3; Pol. *Phil.* 11.3; cf. 3.2.
16. *1 Clem.* 47.2–3; Pol. *Phil.* 11.2.
17. Donald Alfred Hagner, *The Use of the Old and New Testaments in Clement of Rome* (Leiden: Brill, 1973), 195–96. Andrew Gregory surmises that the author of *1 Clement* knew 1 Corinthians because "there were ongoing relationships between the churches in the imperial capital and in one of its major colonies." Andrew F. Gregory, "*1 Clement* and the Writings That Later Formed the New Testament," in *The New Testament and the Apostolic Fathers*. Vol. 1, *The Reception of the New Testament in the Apostolic Fathers*, ed. Andrew F. Gregory and Christopher M. Tuckett (Oxford: Oxford University Press, 2005), 157. See also Horacio E. Lona, "'Petrus in Rom' und der erste Clemensbrief," in *Petrus und Paulus in Rom*, ed. Stefan Heid (Freiburg: Herder, 2011), 221–46.
18. Gregory, "*1 Clement* and the Writings," 144.
19. Cf. 1 Cor 3:22.
20. Cf. Hagner, *Use of the Old and New Testaments*, 226.
21. Hartog, *Polycarp and the New Testament*, 177–79.

of Eph 4:26.[22] There are also complementary features in the ways that *1 Clement* and Polycarp's *Philippians* treat these Pauline materials. For example, *1 Clement* speaks of Paul writing 1 Corinthians πνευματικῶς ("in the Spirit" or "spiritually"),[23] and Polycarp's *Philippians* seems to refer to Ephesians as "scripture."[24]

Exposition of Polycarp, Philippians 11.3

In the extant Latin, Pol. *Phil.* 11.3 states: *in quibus laboravit beatus Paulus, qui estis in principio epistulae eius.*[25] The phrase in context appears thus: "But I have neither observed nor heard such a thing among you, *among whom the blessed Paul labored, who are his letters in the beginning* [or *who are in the beginning of his letter*]. For he boasts about you in all the churches, which alone had known God at that time. We, however, had not yet known him."[26] Clearly the general sentiment draws from Paul's laboring among the Philippians and his letter-writing. The specific Latin phrase in question, however, remains problematic. William Schoedel identified it as "One of the most difficult phrases in the letter," and P. T. Camelot described the material as "resisting every explanation."[27] Kenneth Berding muses that "something was lost or altered either in translating from Greek to Latin or in the Greek or Latin process of transmission."[28]

Scholars have amassed a variety of solutions.[29] One cluster of options takes ἐν ἀρχῇ (behind the Latin *in principio*) in a locative sense of "in the

---

22. See Paul Hartog, "Polycarp, Ephesians, and 'Scripture,'" *WTJ* 70 (2008): 255–75.

23. *1 Clem.* 47.3; cf. 1 Cor 7:40.

24. Pol. *Phil.* 12.1. See Hartog, "Polycarp, Ephesians, and 'Scripture,'" 255–75. Cf. Pol. *Phil.* 12:3 with Phil 3:18.

25. Chapter 11 of Polycarp's *Philippians* is only extant in Latin translation (see Hartog, *Polycarp's Epistle to the Philippians*, 26–27).

26. Adapted from Hartog, *Polycarp's Epistle to the Philippians*, 93.

27. William R. Schoedel, *Polycarp, Martyrdom of Polycarp, Fragments of Papias*, The Apostolic Fathers: A New Translation and Commentary 5 (New York: Nelson, 1967), 32; P. T. Camelot, *Ignace d'Antioche, Polycarpe de Smyrne: Lettres, Martyre de Polycarpe*, 4th ed., SC 10 (Paris: Cerf, 1998), 190 n. 2; cf. Michael W. Holmes, "A Note on the Text of Polycarp *Philippians* 11,3," *VC* 51 (1997): 207.

28. Berding, *Polycarp and Paul*, 111; cf. Holmes, "Note," 207.

29. Portions of the next two paragraphs are a re-worked summarization of Hartog, *Polycarp's Epistle to the Philippians*, 144–47. Cf. Schoedel, *Polycarp*, 32–33; Berding, *Polycarp and Paul*, 111–13.

beginning of his epistle."[30] Thus Theodor Zahn reconstructs the original Greek as οἵτινές ἐστε ἐν ἀρχῇ τῆς ἐπιστολῆς αὐτοῦ.[31] Interpreters with this view have often added a word, such as "praised" or "mentioned" or "addressed."[32] For example, with *laudati* supplied, the phrase becomes "who are praised in the beginning of his epistle" (cf. Phil 1:3–11).[33] In many instances, such views are combined with 2 Thess 1:4 (which mentions Paul's boasting of the Thessalonians among the churches).[34] Interpreters have deduced that Polycarp mistakenly assumed 2 Thess 1:4 was addressed to the Philippians, due to a memory lapse;[35] or he

30. Schoedel, *Polycarp*, 32–34; Bauer, *Die Polykarpbriefe*, 64–67; Bart Ehrman, *The Apostolic Fathers*, LCL 24 (Cambridge, MA: Harvard University Press, 2003), 1:349. Gustav Volkmar believed the Latin originally had *qui est testis* ("who testifies"), a translation of ὅς μαρτυρεῖ. The omission of a letter T from QUIEST-TESTIS resulted in QUIESTESTIS (as found in Adolf Hilgenfeld, *Ignatii Antiocheni et Polycarpi Smyrnaei epistulae et martyria* [Berlin: Schwetschke, 1902], 326–27).

31. Theodor Zahn, *Ignatii et Polycarpi: Epistulae, martyria, fragmenta*, Patrum Apostolicorum Opera (Leipzig: Hinrichs, 1876), 126.

32. Cf. PG vol. 62, 503, line 35; PG vol. 62, 179, line 23; PG 75, 581, line 31; PG vol. 82, 313, line 52. See James A. Kleist, *The Didache; the Epistle of Barnabas; the Epistles and the Martyrdom of St. Polycarp; the Fragments of Papias; the Epistle to Diognetus*, ACW 6 (Westminster: Newman, 1948), 81; Cyril C. Richardson, ed., *Early Christian Fathers*, LCC 1 (London: SCM, 1953), 136 n. 94; Kenneth J. Howell, *Ignatius of Antioch and Polycarp of Smyrna*, rev. ed., Early Christian Fathers Series 1 (Zanesville: CHResources, 2009), 156.

33. Cf. Henning Paulsen, *Die Briefe des Ignatius von Antiochia und der Brief des Polykarp von Smyrna*, HNT: Apostolischen Väter 2 (Tübingen: Mohr Siebeck, 1985), 124; Andreas Lindemann, *Paulus im ältesten Christentum*, BHT 58 (Tübingen: Mohr Siebeck, 1979), 90; idem, "Paul in the Writings of the Apostolic Fathers," in *Paul and the Legacies of Paul*, ed. W. S. Babcock (Dallas: Southern Methodist University Press, 1990), 42; Walter Bauer, *Die Briefe des Ignatius von Antiochia und der Polykarpbrief*, HNT: Apostolischen Väter 2 (Tübingen: Mohr Siebeck, 1920), 295. Pol. *Phil.* 3.2 refers to Paul writing "letters" (plural) to the Philippians, but see Hartog, *Polycarp and Paul*, 223–28; idem, *Polycarp's Epistle to the Philippians*, 113–14.

34. Berding contends that the parallels to 2 Thess 1:4 "are obvious" (Berding, *Polycarp and Paul*, 112). Eduard Schweizer even suggested that 2 Thessalonians was originally addressed to the Philippians, so that 2 Thess 1:4 concerned them directly (Eduard Schweizer, "Der zweite Thessalonicherbrief ein Philipperbrief?," *TZ* 1 [1945]: 90–105). Holmes, however, categorizes the use of 2 Thess 1:4 with a "D" rating. Michael W. Holmes, "Polycarp's *Letter to the Philippians* and the Writings That Later Formed the New Testament," in Gregory and Tuckett, eds., *The Reception of the New Testament in the Apostolic Fathers*, 214.

35. A Committee of the Oxford Society of Historical Theology, *The New Testament in the Apostolic Fathers* (Oxford: Clarendon, 1905), 95.

applied the text to the Philippians as fellow Macedonians;[36] or he was acquainted with a collection of Macedonian letters;[37] or he regarded all of Paul's letters as written to all of his churches;[38] or he drew from 2 Thess 1:4 while being further influenced by Paul's praise of the "Macedonian" churches in Rom 15:26; 2 Cor 8:1–2, and 11:9; or he merged the spirit of 2 Thess 1:3–4 with Phil 1:3–5 and 1 Thess 1:2–10.[39] According to the creative and careful work of Michael Holmes, Polycarp originally wrote something like τοῖς ἐπαινουμένοις ἐν ἀρχῇ τῆς ἐπιστολῆς αὐτοῦ ("who are praised in the beginning of his letter").[40] A copyist jumped from the last three letters of τοῖς to the last three letters of ἐπαινουμένοις (an example of "homoeoteleuton").[41] Thus the participle was removed from the Greek text prior to Latin translation.[42]

A second cluster of proposals takes the original behind in principio (usually reconstructed as ἐν ἀρχῇ) in some temporal sense. (1) The original was "who were his letters in the beginning," perhaps in the sense of "who in the beginning were his letters [of commendation]" (an allusion to 2 Cor 3:2–3).[43] Such an emendation interprets the Latin qui estis (present tense) as "a mistranslation of a temporally ambiguous participle (τοῖς οὖσιν, 'being')," as in τοῖς οὖσιν ἐν ἀρχῇ ἐπιστολαῖς αὐτοῦ.[44] The Latin version recurrently includes similarly loose (and even misleading)

---

36. The following verse (Pol. Phil. 11.4) alludes to 2 Thess 3:15.

37. See Adolf von Harnack, Die Pfaff'schen Irenäus-Fragmente als fälschungen Pfaffs nachgewiesen, TUGAL 5/3 (Leipzig: Hinrichs, 1900), 86–93; A. E. Barnett, Paul Becomes a Literary Influence (Chicago: University of Chicago Press, 1941), 178–79. Harnack mentions similar conflations of the Philippian and Thessalonian correspondence in Tertullian, Scorp. 13 and Clement of Alexandria, Protrept. 9.87.

38. Cf. Ign. Eph. 12.2, which states that Paul "in every letter remembers you in Christ Jesus."

39. Bauer, Die Polykarpbriefe, 66.

40. Holmes, "Note," 208. Harnack suggested οἵτινες αἰνεῖσθε, but Holmes responds that early Christian literature only uses αἰνέω with God as the object, while ἐπαινέω is more often used with humans (ibid., 210 n. 16).

41. Holmes maintains that "The similarity of the following letters (i.e., ΕΠΑ, ΕΝΑ) would have made this common slip even easier to commit" (ibid., 208).

42. Ibid., 207–10.

43. Lightfoot, Apostolic Fathers, 2.3:342–43. While 2 Cor 3:2 uses a singular "letter," Holmes maintains that "the transformation of a singular into a plural under the influence of the plural 'you' reflects just the kind of adaptation found elsewhere in Polycarp's use of written documents" (Holmes, "Note," 208).

44. Lightfoot, Apostolic Fathers, 2.3:342–43; Kirsopp Lake, The Apostolic Fathers, LCL 24 (Cambridge, MA: Harvard University Press, 1912), 1:297 n. 1. Holmes, "Note," 209 n. 4.

renditions elsewhere.[45] (2) The text originally said "who were in the beginning of the church," as found in one manuscript.[46] (3) The Greek had "who were in the beginning of his apostolate" (cf. Gal 2:8), and the original ἀποστολῆς was misread as ἐπιστολῆς.[47] (4) The text stated, "who were in the beginning of the gospel" (cf. Phil 4:15; *1 Clem.* 47.2), and "gospel" was altered into "epistle."[48] (5) The original was an inelegant "But I have neither observed nor heard such a thing among you (ἐν ὑμῖν), in whose midst (ἐν οἷς) the blessed Paul labored, being in the beginning – in his letters (τοῖς οὖσιν ἐν ἀρχῇ – ἐν ἐπιστολαῖς αὐτοῦ)."[49] (6) The original included an adjectival ἀρχαίᾳ, similar to the adjectival usage in Pol. *Phil.* 1.2 (ἐξ ἀρχαίων χρόνων) and *1 Clem.* 47.6 (τὴν ἀρχαίαν ἐκκλησίαν), and thus a construction akin to τοῖς ἐν τῇ ἀρχαίᾳ ἐπιστολῇ αὐτοῦ ("those in his ancient letter").[50] By initially anticipating or supposing the more common ἐν τῇ ἀρχῇ instead of ἐν τῇ ἀρχαίᾳ, a loose or careless Latin translation resulted.[51]

45. Hartog, *Polycarp and the New Testament*, 161–62; idem, *Polycarp's Epistle to the Philippians*, 158–59.

46. Concerning proposals (2), (3), and (4) as listed here, Holmes notes that "they share a conviction that the problem lies in the noun at the end of the phrase, but each results in a clause that is somewhat awkward with respect to syntax and somewhat obscure with respect to content – hardly characteristics of a compelling emendation" (Holmes, "Note," 208).

47. Cf. the confusion between ἀποστέλλω and ἐπιστέλλω in the transmission of various LXX passages and Acts 21:25. But Holmes counters, "the proposal envisions the interchange not only of ἀ/ἐ but also ο/ι (ἀποστ- versus ἐπιστ-)" (Holmes, "Note," 210 n. 9).

48. Gustav Krüger, "Briefe des Ignatius und Polykarp," in *Handbuch zu den neutestamentlichen Apokryphen*, ed. Edgar Hennecke (Tübingen: Mohr Siebeck, 1904), 203. Cf. *1 Clem.* 47.1–2. Some have hypothesized that an alteration occurred after being translated into Latin, so that *in principio apostolatus* (or *in principio evangelii*) was read as *in principio epistulae*. See D. K. Rensberger, "As the Apostle Teaches: The Development of the Use of Paul's Letters in Second-Century Christianity" (PhD diss., Yale University, 1981), 115.

49. By dropping the second ἐν through oversight, the wording reverts to the Greek of option (1) above, through which Lightfoot and Lake meant to explain the resultant Latin translation. For the anarthrous ἐν ἐπιστολαῖς, see PG 51, 189, line 36; PG 39, 628, line 8. Admittedly, option (5) is awkward, although an improvement upon the faulty explanation (and assessment of Lightfoot) found in Hartog, *Polycarp's Epistle to the Philippians*, 147.

50. See PG vol. 110, 217 line 29 (cf. PG vol. 45, 236, line 8).

51. As with many of the options, the logical flow would be enhanced if a Greek καὶ γάρ stood behind the Latin *etenim* of the second sentence (see Holmes, "Note," 210 n. 13): "But I have neither observed nor heard such a thing among you, in whose

Several evidences could be used to support a temporal notion behind *in principio* as reflected in the various temporally oriented proposals above, including option (1) – the most commonly held of such temporal readings and one that easily bridges into Latin translation (although the allusion to 2 Cor 3:2–3 seems rather subtle).[52] The overall sentiment of Pol. *Phil.* 11.3 is temporally oriented, as Polycarp engages in "exhortation based on appeals to the ancient reputation of the church in Philippi (as in 3:2)."[53] A temporal use of ἐν ἀρχῇ would resemble *1 Clem.* 47.1–2: "Take up the epistle of the blessed Paul the apostle. What did he first write to you in the beginning (ἐν ἀρχῇ) of the gospel?" (cf. Phil 4:15).[54] *1 Clement* 47.6 speaks of the "established and ancient (βεβαιοτάτην καὶ ἀρχαίαν) church of the Corinthians," and Polycarp similarly tells the Philippians, "I also rejoice because of the established (βεβαία) root of your faith, renowned from the earliest (ἀρχαίων) times" (Pol. *Phil.* 1.2).[55] Moreover, Pol. *Phil.* 3.2 describes the ministry of Paul, "being among you in the presence of the people of that time," adding that he "wrote you letters" while absent. And Pol. *Phil.* 11.3 itself goes on to contrast the churches intertwined with Paul's ministry ("that at that time had come to know the Lord") with the Smyrnaean congregation ("for we had not yet come to know him"). Consequently a temporal notion behind *in principio*, if accepted, could nicely suit both the immediate context and other passages in Polycarp's *Philippians*, and could be corroborated by similar material in *1 Clem.* 47.

midst the blessed Paul labored, those [mentioned] in his ancient letter. For indeed he boasts about you in all the churches which alone had known God at that time. We, however, had not yet known him." Option (6) would involve a careless rendering from the Greek to the extant Latin. For the loose rendering of the Latin in general, see Lightfoot, *Apostolic Fathers*, 2.1:551.

52. Compare the more direct use of 2 Cor 3:2 in Patrick, *Confession* 11: "we who are, in the words of Scripture, a letter of Christ for salvation to the ends of the earth, …written on your hearts not with ink but with the Spirit of the living God" (English translation from R. P. C. Hanson, *The Life and Writings of the Historical Saint Patrick* [New York: Seabury, 1983], 83–84). Option (1) is held by Lightfoot, *Apostolic Fathers*, 2.3:342–43; Francis X. Glimm, Joseph Marie-Felix Marique, and Gerald Groveland Walsh, *The Apostolic Fathers*, FC 1 (New York: Cima, 1947), 142; Maxwell Staniforth and Andrew Louth, *Early Christian Writings: The Apostolic Fathers*, rev. ed. (London: Penguin, 1987), 123; Richardson, *Early Christian Fathers*, 136; Berding, *Polycarp and Paul*, 111; Mark Galli, *The Apostolic Fathers* (Chicago: Moody, 2009), 131. Holmes argues that this option would "require [Polycarp's] readers to infer so much of his train of thought" (Holmes, "Note," 207).

53. Schoedel, *Polycarp*, 34.

54. *1 Clem.* 47.1–2.

55. English translation adapted from Holmes, *Apostolic Fathers*, 281.

More importantly, if one reasonably prefers a locative notion tied to an original ἐν ἀρχῇ in Pol. *Phil.* 11.3 instead (as in Holmes's emendation above), these same collected evidences still demonstrate that the "ancient" nature of the Philippian church is sustained by Polycarpian materials elsewhere, as in 1.2 and 3.2 (and parallels the description of the "ancient" Corinthian church in *1 Clem.* 47). Furthermore, in returning to *terra firma*, it must be stressed that no matter what emendation or interpretation one may hold regarding this problematic Latin phrase (involving either a temporal or locative understanding of the original Greek behind *in principio*), the next sentence in Pol. *Phil.* 11.3 *clearly* points toward a chronological separation between the inceptions of the Philippian and Smyrnaean congregations.[56] "For he boasts about you in all the churches – the ones that at that time had come to know the Lord, for we had not yet come to know him."[57] This subsequent sentence in Pol. *Phil.* 11.3 establishes a definite, temporal separation between the founding of the Philippian church (which had come to know the Lord in the era of Paul's correspondence) and the congregation of Smyrnaeans (who had not yet come to know the Lord). The early fame of the Philippian congregation is confirmed by Pol. *Phil.* 1.2 ("your firmly rooted faith, renowned from the earliest times") and is reinforced by 3.2 ("in the presence of the people of that time").[58]

Polycarp's *Phil.* 11.3 explicitly mentions "*all* the churches – the ones that at that time had come to know the Lord."[59] Thus Polycarp, as leader of the Smyrnaean church, chronologically distanced the founding of his own ecclesial community from that of the various churches appearing in Paul's letters (like the Philippian congregation). Polycarp's mere mention of

56. According to Charles Torrey, who understands ἐν ἀρχῇ in a locative manner, "[Polycarp] refers expressly to the beginning of Paul's Epistle (Phil. 1:5), and adds: We, the church of Smyrna, did not exist at the time when you of Philippi were already praised by Paul, as he went about among the earliest of the churches (referring to Phil. 4:15f.)." Torrey, *The Apocalypse of John* (New Haven: Yale University Press, 1958), 78–79.

57. Paul boasted of some churches with others, especially when seeking to motivate his readers (cf. 2 Cor 9:1–5). The "Macedonians" are mentioned or praised in various Pauline epistles (Rom 15:26; 2 Cor 8:1–2; 11.9; Phil 4:15). Phil 4:15 narrows Paul's praise of the Macedonians to the Philippians alone, and the other texts could be read in this light.

58. "For neither I nor another like me can keep pace with the wisdom of the blessed and glorious Paul. When he was with you in the presence of the people of that time (τῶν τότε ἀνθρώπων), he accurately and reliably taught the word concerning the truth. And when he was absent he wrote you letters" (Pol. *Phil.* 3.2).

59. The Latin MSS vary between *deum solae tunc* and *solae tunc dominum*.

the temporal separation implies there would be no question or confusion concerning his chronological assessment. Polycarp simply assumed that the Philippians would readily accept the temporal distance between Paul's letter-writing and the foundation of the Smyrnaean church. Therefore, the *tenor* of the passage implies a straightforward, chronological separation between Paul's ministry, correspondence, and life on the one hand and the founding of the Smyrnaean church on the other.[60]

Polycarp, Philippians *11.3 and Acts 19*

Scholars have not yet fully integrated these materials in Pol. *Phil.* 11.3 with Pauline and broader New Testament studies. Numerous scholars have assumed that a Christian congregation in Smyrna was established during Paul's Ephesian stay as reflected in Acts 19. Acts 19:10 states, "This continued for two years, so that all the residents of Asia heard the word of the Lord, both Jews and Greeks."[61] Verse 26 adds, "And you see

---

60. Note the emphasis upon Paul's death in Pol. *Phil.* 9. Chronological reconstructions might be further enhanced by bringing Pol. *Phil.* 6.3 into the discussion, with its reference to "the apostles who preached the gospel to us." Charles Hill reasons, "If we may believe Irenaeus, Polycarp would have heard this oral preaching personally; perhaps the 'us' in 'preached the gospel to us' is meant not only collectively of all Christians, but personally, to him as well." Hill, *Who Chose the Gospels? Proving the Great Gospel Conspiracy* (Oxford: Oxford University Press, 2010), 194. Pol. *Phil.* 7.2 exhorts, "let us return to the word delivered to us from the beginning" (cf. 1 John 1:1–4). Denis Farkasfalvy connected "the word delivered to us from the beginning" in 7.2 with "the gospel" which was preached "to us" in 6.3. Farkasfalvy, "'Prophets and Apostles': The Conjunction of the Two Terms before Irenaeus," in *Texts and Testaments*, ed. W. Eugene March and Stuart Dickson Currie (San Antonio: Trinity University Press, 1980), 133 n. 45. If Pol. *Phil.* 6.3 and 7.2 connect Polycarp himself into the beginnings of the Smyrnaean church (a reading that must remain conjectural), and if *Mart. Pol.* 9.3 can be used to place Polycarp's birth eighty-six years prior to his martyrdom (and this too is debated), then the Smyrnaean church *could not* have been founded before AD 70. This reasoning builds upon disputed readings and conjectures, however, and thus cannot serve as a trustworthy foundation of confidence. One should note that some manuscripts of 6.3 substitute "you" for "us."

61. English translations of the New Testament come from the ESV, unless noted otherwise. Although some scholars question the historicity of this two-year Ephesian residence, Gerd Lüdemann concedes, "It could well be true that Paul worked for two years in Ephesus, and since the indicated place is linked with a reliable indication of time, one may reasonably suspect that it, too, has historical validity." Lüdemann, *The Acts of the Apostles: What Really Happened in the Earliest Days of the Church* (Amherst: Prometheus, 2005), 256.

and hear that not only in Ephesus but in almost all of Asia this Paul has persuaded and turned away a great many people, saying that gods made with hands are not gods."

By integrating Acts 19 with Rev 2–3, many commentators have declared that "perhaps" or "probably" some or all of the seven churches of Rev 2–3 can be traced to Paul's Ephesian residency.[62] For example, F. F. Bruce asserted, "Perhaps all seven of the churches of Asia addressed in the Revelation of John were also founded about this time. The province was intensively evangelized, and remained one of the leading centers of Christianity for many centuries."[63] R. Kent Hughes firmly declares, "Luke tells us that everyone in Asia (the area around modern-day Turkey) 'heard the word of the Lord.' It was during this time that the seven churches named in Revelation 2–3, as well as many others, came into being. By any estimate, what happened in those two years is amazing."[64]

Congruent with this line of thinking, various scholars have conjectured that the Smyrnaean congregation in particular was founded during Paul's Ephesian stay.[65] Colin Hemer has reasoned, "In any case there were probably some Christians resident in Smyrna from an early date, and the city must have been a primary objective in the evangelism of Asia during Paul's Ephesian residency (Acts 19.10). We can thus be confident that a church became established there in the period c. 52–55, if not earlier."[66]

62. Philip A. Bence, *Acts* (Indianapolis: Wesleyan Publishing House, 1998), 189; Darrell L. Bock, *Acts*, BECNT (Grand Rapids: Baker, 2007), 601; Homer A. Kent, *Jerusalem to Rome: Studies in the Book of Acts* (Grand Rapids: Baker, 1972), 151; William J. Larkin, Jr., *Acts*, IVPNTC (Downers Grove: InterVarsity, 1995), 275; Paul W. Walaskay, *Acts*, Westminster Bible Companion (Louisville: Westminster John Knox, 1998), 178; David J. Williams, *Acts*, NIBC (Peabody, MA: Hendrickson, 1990), 332. See also Richard S. Ascough, *Religious Rivalries and the Struggle for Success in Sardis and Smyrna*, Studies in Christianity and Judaism 15 (Waterloo: Wilfrid Laurier University Press, 2005), 8.

63. F. F. Bruce, *Book of the Acts*, rev. ed., NICNT (Grand Rapids: Eerdmans, 1988), 366.

64. R. Kent Hughes, *Acts: The Church Afire*, Preaching the Word (Wheaton, IL: Crossway, 1996), 255.

65. George Eldon Ladd, *A Commentary on the Revelation of John* (Grand Rapids: Eerdmans, 1972), 42; Robert H. Mounce, *The Book of Revelation*, rev. ed., NICNT (Grand Rapids: Eerdmans, 1997), 74; Lightfoot, *Apostolic Fathers*, 2.3:343; Robert W. Wall, *Revelation*, NIBC 18 (Peabody, MA: Hendrickson, 1991), 72.

66. Colin J. Hemer, *The Letters to the Seven Churches of Asia in their Local Setting* (Sheffield: JSOT, 1986), 66. Hemer grasps for the *Vita Polycarpi* as corroboration of a Pauline foundation to the Smyrnaean church, even while admitting its unreliability. Although Berding states, "there are no ancient sources that connect the

David Aune is more guarded: "It is possible that during Paul's two year
stay at Ephesus (Acts 19:10), the Christian community at Smyrna was
founded (cf. Acts 19:26), though it must be admitted that nothing concrete
is known about the founding of the Christian community at Smyrna."[67]

Caution is in order, however, so that the Lukan statement is not
over-read. Luke's generalization must be interpreted within the overall
purposes and style of Acts.[68] The passage's context (including the use of
"all") provides pointers to the generalizing nature of the Lukan report. In
Acts 19:13–17, the seven sons of Sceva were overpowered by evil spirits
in a botched exorcism. According to v. 17, "And this became known to
all the residents of Ephesus, both Jews and Greeks. And fear fell upon
them all, and the name of the Lord Jesus was extolled." The following
verses describe the Christian burning of magic materials. According to
v. 19, "And a number of those who had practiced magic arts brought their
books together and burned them in the sight of all." In v. 27, Artemis
is described as "she whom all Asia and the world worship." An angry
crowd subsequently gathered in the theatre. And according to v. 34, "for
about two hours they all cried out with one voice, 'Great is Artemis of the
Ephesians!'"

One might add that the generalized statement in Acts 19:10 is framed in
a Lukan manner to fit Lukan purposes. Thus Jacob Jervell calls it another
occurrence of a Lukan "success message" ("eine Erfolgsmeldung").[69]
Proclaiming the "word of the Lord" is shorthand for evangelistic mission,
as paralleled elsewhere in Acts (4:4, 31; 6:2, 7; 8:4, 14, 25; 11:1; 12:24;
13:5, 49; 15:7, 36; 16:32; 18:11).[70] The text emphasizes that those who
heard were both "Jews and Greeks," a Lukan theme.[71] As Hans Conzelmann

person or writings of Paul to Polycarp," the untrustworthy *Vita Polycarpi* does so.
Berding, "John or Paul? Who Was Polycarp's Mentor," *TynBul* 59 (2008): 140; cf.
137 n. 9.

67. David E. Aune, *Revelation 1–5*, WBC 52A (Dallas: Word, 1997), lviii.

68. I. Howard Marshall, *Acts*, TNTC 5 (Downers Grove: InterVarsity, 2008), 328.
Ben Witherington views Acts 19:10 as speaking "somewhat hyperbolically," and he
highlights the spreading of the word in the Lycus Valley but does not explicitly refer
to the founding of churches. Witherington III, *The Acts of the Apostles: A Socio-Rhetorical Commentary* (Grand Rapids: Eerdmans, 1998), 576.

69. Jacob Jervell, *Die Apostelgeschichte*, KEK 3 (Göttingen: Vandenhoeck &
Ruprecht, 1998), 481.

70. Luke Timothy Johnson, *The Acts of the Apostles*, Sacra Pagina 5 (Collegeville:
Liturgical Press, 1992), 339.

71. Johnson, *Acts of the Apostles*, 339. Jervell, *Die Apostelgeschichte*, 481
believes the Ἕλληνας in this verse is a reference to Godfearing Gentiles (see 14:1;
17:4; 18:4). But see Acts 19:17 in context.

points out, Luke (in line with his purposes) underscores Paul's personal role in the dissemination of the gospel, rather than mission work carried out by fellow workers of Paul.[72] The next verse even highlights the miraculous work of Paul ("And God was doing extraordinary miracles by the hands of Paul").[73] Beverly Gaventa further notes, "This large hearing in turn sets the stage for the eruption of vv. 23–41, when response to the gospel prompts deadly envy."[74]

Gerhard Krodel argues an additional, particular point: "Luke did not speak of a mass conversion of the people of the province of Asia, but that they heard the word of the Lord."[75] Acts 19 states that "all the residents of Asia heard the word of the Lord, both Jews and Greeks" (v. 10), and "a great many people" "in almost all of Asia" were persuaded by Paul and turned away from the gods (v. 26).[76] Thus v. 10 claims that "all" the residents of Asia "heard" the word of the Lord, but it does not claim that they necessarily believed it (although a great many did, according to v. 26).

It is true that "hearing" the word can be used synonymously with belief in some Lukan instances ("the Holy Spirit fell on all who heard the word" in Acts 10:44). And elsewhere, the two notions can be closely associated: "the Gentiles should hear the word of the gospel and believe" (Acts 15:7). Nevertheless, although associated, hearing and believing can be conceptually distinguished. Acts 4:4 does not use the terms as full equivalents: "But many of those who had heard the word believed." In Acts 13:7, Sergius Paulus "sought to hear the word of God," and after he saw the blinding of Elymas, he subsequently "believed" in Acts 13:12. Acts 13:44 also employs "hearing" without necessarily "believing": "The next Sabbath almost the whole city gathered to hear the word of the Lord" (Acts 13:44).[77] Within the context of ch. 19 itself, the attendees of the Ephesian synagogue heard the message as Paul spoken boldly for three

---

72. Hans Conzelmann, *Acts of the Apostles*, Hermeneia (Philadelphia: Fortress, 1987), 163.

73. See Jervell, *Die Apostelgeschichte*, 481.

74. Beverly Roberts Gaventa, *The Acts of the Apostles*, ANTC (Nashville: Abingdon, 2003), 266.

75. Gerhard Krodel, *Acts*, ACNT (Minneapolis: Augsburg, 1986), 361. Krodel compares this with the "sowing" of Luke 8:11–15.

76. Perhaps, for example, the Laodicean church originated in this two-year period. See Mounce, *Book of Revelation*, 108; Robert L. Thomas, *Revelation 1–7: An Exegetical Commentary* (Chicago: Moody, 1992), 299; cf. David G. Peterson, *The Acts of the Apostles*, PNTC (Grand Rapids: Eerdmans, 2009), 536.

77. Interestingly, Acts 13:44 is another "generalizing" Lukan statement.

months (v. 8), but "some became hardened and would not believe" (v. 9).[78] Furthermore, Acts 19:26 qualifies the "great many people" who were persuaded as residing "in almost all of Asia," thus allowing for pocketed unreached areas as well.

If we accept Polycarp's own witness to the founding of his own church, he implies that the Smyrnaeans had not yet believed when Paul engaged in ministry among the churches of "that time," exemplified by his letter-writing.[79] Even if one narrows the focus upon Paul's epistle to the Philippians alone, that epistle was written ca. AD 54–55 in an Ephesian provenance view, ca. 57–59 in a Caesarean view, and ca. 60–62 in a Roman view.[80] The Roman and Caesarean views, when combined with Polycarp's claim, do not fit with the Smyrnaean church being founded between 52 and 55 (Paul's Ephesian ministry, as reconstructed from Acts), and an Ephesian view hardly does so.

Furthermore, the tenor of Polycarp's declaration (dropping the mere fact without anticipation of confusion) argues against the Philippians being expected to engage in precise mathematical calculating (i.e., Paul wrote in AD 54, but the Smyrnaean church was not founded until 55). Rather, the tenor seems to portray the Philippian church as existing in the era of Paul's letter-writing or general ministry as a whole, and the Smyrnaean church as not originating from this time of his correspondence and life of ministry.[81] Based upon Pol. *Phil.* 11.3, Leon Morris concluded that "the church at Smyrna does not seem to have been in existence in the time of Paul," and Grant Osborne concurs that the Smyrnaean church "may not have existed in the 60s."[82]

78. English translation from the HCSB.
79. That is, if Polycarp was not simply confused or mistaken.
80. Aune puts forward two placements of Paul's Philippians, one from Ephesus in 53 to 55 and another from Caesarea in 56 to 58 (Aune, *Revelation 1–5*, lviii). He does not mention the third (and more traditional) provenance of Rome in 61 or 62. See Paul Hartog, "Philippians" in *The Blackwell Companion to the New Testament,* ed. David E. Aune, *Blackwell Companions to Religion* (Chichester: Wiley-Blackwell, 2010), 475–77.
81. Note the emphasis upon Paul's death in Pol. *Phil.* 9. If Polycarp's citation of Paul's praise of the Philippians refers to the apostle's praise of the Macedonians in Romans and 2 Corinthians, then the composition of those letters (ca. 55–57) becomes particularly relevant as well.
82. Leon Morris, *Revelation*, 2nd ed., TNTC 20 (Downers Grove: InterVarsity, 1987), 40; Grant R. Osborne, *Revelation*, BECNT (Grand Rapids: Baker, 2002), 9.

Polycarp, Philippians *11.3 and Revelation*

The description of Paul's ministry in Polycarp's *Phil.* 11 yields important though neglected evidence relevant to the interpretation of not only Acts but also of Revelation. Within biblical scholarship, the date of the composition or completion of Revelation is no settled matter.[83] As George Beasley-Murray summarizes, "two chief possibilities present themselves, namely, the end of the reign of Nero, c. A.D. 68, or the end of Domitian's reign, c. A.D. 95."[84] Between these two options, the majority of contemporary scholars seem to prefer the mid-90s,[85] while a strong minority prefers the late 60s.[86]

83. Heinz Giesen, *Die Offenbarung des Johannes*, Regensburger Neues Testament (Regensburg: Pustet, 1997), 41–42. For an overview, see G. K. Beale, *The Book of Revelation: A Commentary on the Greek Text*, NIGTC (Grand Rapids: Eerdmans, 1999), 4–27.

84. G. R. Beasley-Murray, *The Book of Revelation*, NCB (London: Oliphants, 1974), 37. See also Wall, *Revelation*, 5. For a survey of scholarly opinions up to forty years ago, see Pierre Prigent, "Au temps de l'Apocalypse," *RHPR* 54 (1974): 455–83; 55 (1975): 215–35, 341–63.

85. For examples, see Beasley-Murray, *Book of Revelation*, 37–38; G. B. Caird, *The Revelation of St. John* (Peabody, MA: Hendrickson, 1993), 6; Hemer, *Letters to the Seven Churches of Asia*, 3; Helmut Koester, *Introduction to the New Testament* (Philadelphia: Fortress, 1982), 2:250–51; A. C. Isbell, "The Dating of Revelation," *Restoration Quarterly* 9 (1966): 107–17; James H. Charlesworth, *The Old Testament Pseudepigrapha and the New Testament* (Cambridge: Cambridge University Press, 1985), 87; J. P. M. Sweet, *Revelation* (Philadelphia: Westminster, 1979), 27; Leonard L. Thompson, *The Book of Revelation: Apocalypse and Empire* (New York: Oxford University Press, 1990), 13–15; Mounce, *Book of Revelation*, 15–21.

86. Karl August Eckhardt, *Der Tod des Johannes als Schlüssel zum Verständnis der Johanneischen Schriften* (Berlin: de Gruyter, 1961); Kenneth L. Gentry, *Before Jerusalem Fell: Dating the Book of Revelation* (Tyler: Institute for Christian Economics, 1989); John W. Marshall, "Parables of the War: Reading the Apocalypse within Judaism and during the Judaean War," 2 vols. (PhD diss., Princeton University, 1997); C. Van der Waal, "The Last Book of the Bible and the Jewish Apocalypses," *Neot* 12 (1981): 111–32; R. C. Sproul, *The Last Days According to Jesus* (Grand Rapids: Baker, 1998), 141–45; David Chilton, *The Days of Vengeance: An Exposition of the Book of Revelation* (Fort Worth: Dominion, 1987), 3–4; John A. T. Robinson, *Redating the New Testament* (Philadelphia: Westminster, 1976), 221–53; E. Lipiński, "L'apocalypse et le martyre de Jean à Jérusalem," *NovT* 11 (1969): 225–32; Christopher Rowland, *The Open Heaven: A Study in Apocalyptic in Judaism and Early Christianity* (New York: Crossroad, 1982), 403–13; idem, *Revelation*, Epworth Commentaries (London: Epworth, 1993), 16; J. Christian Wilson, "The Problem of the Domitianic Date of Revelation," *NTS* 39 (1993): 587–605; Albert A. Bell, Jr., "The Date of John's Apocalypse: The Evidence of Some Roman Historians Reconsidered," *NTS* 25 (1978): 93–102.

Other proposals exist, of course. Some commentators have dated the composition during the reigns of Claudius (AD 41–54), Galba (AD 68–69), Vespasian (AD 69–79), Titus (AD 79–81) or Trajan (AD 98–117).[87] André Feuillet maintained that the author wrote in Domitian's time, but like other apocalyptic writers antedated his work.[88] Others have suggested complex composition proposals.[89] For example, Robert Moberly speculated that the bulk of the Apocalypse (chs. 4–22) was conceived on the Isle of Patmos in the fall of AD 69 and was written during that winter, but the seven letters (chs. 2 and 3) were written or updated after John returned to the mainland upon the death of Domitian.[90] Martin Hengel theorized that Revelation may have been composed directly after the Neronian persecution and possibly reworked in the early part of Trajan's reign.[91] John Court similarly hypothesized that the book was begun in earlier contexts of persecution but was completed under Domitian (or perhaps Trajan).[92] David Aune also has argued that the book went through stages of composition, so that traditions incorporated within the Apocalypse date from the 60s or earlier, but the final edition was completed late in Domitian's reign or early in Trajan's rule.[93]

---

87. See Jan Stolt, "Om dateringen af Apokalypsen," *DTT* 40 (1977): 202–7; Martin Karrer, *Die Johannesoffenbarung als Brief* (Göttingen: Vandenhoeck & Ruprecht, 1986), 18 n. 6; Austin Farrer, *The Revelation of St. John the Divine* (Oxford: Clarendon, 1964), 37; Steven J. Friesen, *Imperial Cults and the Apocalypse of John* (Oxford: Oxford University Press, 2001), 150.

88. André Feuillet, *L'Apocalypse: état de la question* (Paris: Desclée, 1963), 93.

89. Cf. Margaret M. Barker, *The Revelation of Jesus Christ* (Edinburgh: T&T Clark, 2000), 75–81. J. Massyngberde Ford proposed a composite theory stretching from John the Baptist's ministry through at least the 60s, involving three distinct authors. Massyngberde Ford, *Revelation*, AB 38 (Garden City: Doubleday, 1975), 50–57. But see the declarations of Rev 1:1–11.

90. Robert B. Moberly, "When Was Revelation Conceived?," *Bib* 73 (1992): 376–93.

91. Martin Hengel, *The Johannine Question* (London: SCM, 1989), 80–81.

92. John M. Court, *Revelation*, NTG (Sheffield: Sheffield Academic, 1999), 95–101; cf. John M. Court; *Myth and History in the Book of Revelation* (London: SPCK, 1979), 125–38.

93. Aune, *Revelation 1–5*, lviii. R. H. Charles believed that the letters to the seven churches were written earlier than the rest of the book and had already been sent to the seven churches prior to the book's composition. Charles, *A Critical and Exegetical Commentary on the Revelation of St. John*, ICC (Edinburgh: T&T Clark, 1920), 1:46–47; cf. lxxxvii–xci. See also David L. Barr, *Tales of the End: A Narrative Commentary on the Book of Revelation* (Santa Rosa: Polebridge, 1998), 21.

Aune's extensive commentary on the Apocalypse discusses the Polycarpian material as the first relevant evidence in his discussion of the dating of Revelation.[94] Aune declares, "Polycarp, writing to the Philippians before AD 155 (the year of his martyrdom), claims that when Paul wrote Philippians, no Smyrnaeans had yet been evangelized (Pol. *Phil.* 5:3, *non autem nondum cognoveramus*, 'we had not yet known him [i.e., the Lord]'). This bit of information, if true, suggests a *terminus a quo* for the composition of Revelation."[95] Yet a few clarifications are required.[96] First, the passage cited comes from Pol. *Phil.* 11.3 rather than 5.3. Second, Polycarp obviously wrote *Philippians* prior to his martyrdom (as stated by Aune), but most scholars would go further and date the epistle decades before his execution, often between AD 110 and 135.[97] Third, Aune claims that Polycarp places the Smyrnaeans' belief after Paul's writing of his own epistle to the Philippians, but the tenor of the passage seems to go further. The Polycarpian material seems to distance the Smyrnaeans' belief from the church-planting and epistle-writing ministry of Paul *as a whole* (as argued above).

If Polycarp rightly distances the Smyrnaean congregation from Paul's ministry, this information could help narrow the dating range of the composition or completion of Revelation.[98] The material addressed to the Smyrnaean church would have to be placed after Paul's martyrdom in the mid-60s or latter years of Nero's reign (who died in 68).[99] Moreover,

94. Joseph Mangina affirms that Aune "explored this question perhaps more thoroughly than any other scholar." Mangina, *Revelation*, Brazos Theological Commentary on the Bible (Grand Rapids: Brazos, 2010), 33.

95. Aune, *Revelation 1–5*, lviii.

96. Even the date of Polycarp's martyrdom is highly debated. Although 155 is commonly favored (as cited by Aune), a reasonable range of dates may perhaps stretch from 155 to 161. For an overview, see Hartog, *Polycarp's Epistle to the Philippians*, 191–200.

97. See Holmes, *Apostolic Fathers*, 170, 275–76; idem, "Polycarp of Smyrna, Epistle to the Philippians," in *The Writings of the Apostolic Fathers*, ed. Paul Foster (London: T&T Clark, 2007), 123–24. For my own placement of Polycarp's epistle in a Trajanic (probable) or early Hadrianic (possible) setting, see Hartog, *Polycarp's Epistle to the Philippians*, 40–45.

98. As long as the recipients of Rev 2:8–11 were not a Christian congregation entirely unrelated to the church led by Polycarp.

99. Scholars tend to date Paul's martyrdom between 64 and 68. Representing an early placement, Harry Tajra situated Paul's martyrdom in late 63 or early 64. Tajra, *The Martyrdom of St. Paul: Historical and Judicial Context, Traditions, and Legends*, WUNT 2/67 (Tübingen: Mohr Siebeck, 1994), 31, 199. The latest possible date is 68, the year of Nero's death, and some scholars date Paul's martyrdom as late as 67

Rev 2:8–11 reflects a reasonably established congregation in Smyrna. The church had raised the opposition of "those who say that they are Jews and are not, but are a synagogue of Satan" (Rev 2:9).[100] And the Smyrnaean congregation is paralleled with similar churches in Asia Minor (Rev 2:11), some of which were declining.[101] Such developments would apparently take some time, so that several years at the least would probably be required past the initial founding of the church (which did not occur until *after* Paul's ministry, based upon the Polycarpian evidence). When one combines the materials of Rev 2 with Polycarp's evidence, a Neronian composition of Rev 2 seems hard-pressed.

Although the Polycarpian evidence does not pinpoint the composition or completion of the Apocalypse, it might help to narrow the window of possibilities. While commenting upon the date of Revelation, Adela Yarbro Collins nodded at the Polycarpian evidence. Although initially dismissive, she guardedly surmised that the Polycarpian material favors a post-70 composition of Revelation (or at least of the material addressed to the Smyrnaean church): "Polycarp bishop of Smyrna in the first half of the second century, implies that the congregation in Smyrna was founded later than the one in Philippi. Some commentators argue on this basis that the message to Smyrna, and thus Revelation as a whole, could not have been written as early as the 60s. This argument is not compelling, but Polycarp's remark does favor a date after 70 for Revelation."[102]

Over ninety years ago, R. H. Charles concluded that Polycarp's letter showed that Rev 2:8–11 "may have been written in the closing years of Vespasian (75–79) but hardly earlier."[103] Charles argued that Polycarp's material suggests that several years may have elapsed between AD 64 and the founding of the Smyrnaean church. Moreover, Charles reasoned that the description of the Smyrnaean church in Rev 2:8–11 presupposes

---

or 68; see John B. Polhill, *Paul and His Letters* (Nashville: Broadman & Holman, 1999), 438–40.

100. Cf. the community tensions reflected in the *Martyrdom of Polycarp* and the *Martyrdom of Pionius*.

101. According to Mounce, *Book of Revelation*, 19, "the spiritual decline at Ephesus, Sardis, and Laodicea would require an extended period of time." Beale, *Book of Revelation*, 16, agrees: "It is plausible that such spiritual deterioration took a significant period of time to develop." Some scholars have further noted that the "Nicolaitans" seem to have been a defined, established group (cf. Morris, *Revelation*, 41). See Rev 2:6, 15.

102. Collins, *Crisis and Catharsis: The Power of the Apocalypse* (Philadelphia: Westminster, 1984), 75.

103. Charles, *Critical and Exegetical Commentary*, 1:xciv.

"a development of apparently many years to its credit." Combining these suppositions, Charles reached AD 75–79 as the earliest possible date of composition for the Apocalypse. After re-investigating the relevant data, we find Charles' reasoning to be essentially sound in its general inclination, although sliding "the earliest possible date" over half a decade earlier.

Polycarp's subtle yet important evidence cannot be summarily dismissed (as J. A. T. Robinson attempted to do).[104] Polycarp's assertions in Pol. *Phil.* 11.3 would seem to place Paul's martyrdom (in the mid-60s or latter years of Nero's reign) as the earliest *terminus a quo* for the formation of the Smyrnaean church. The *tenor* of Pol. *Phil.* 11.3, however, seems to push the Smyrnaean church's foundation past Nero's reign altogether. Polycarp lays out a clear chronological distinction between the founding of the Smyrnaean church and Paul's ministry (focused on his letter-writing), without expecting the Philippians to engage in the exactitudes of calculations. Moreover, as noted above, the description of the Smyrnaean church in Rev 2 seems to imply that the congregation had been around for some time.

Therefore, although some Patristic authors (and a few modern commentators) have placed the composition of Revelation in the reign of Claudius, such a date is *decidedly* ruled out by the evidence of Polycarp's *Philippians*.[105] And the tenor of the Polycarpian material in tandem with the description of the established Smyrnaean congregation in Rev 2 leans toward moving the *terminus a quo* of composition beyond Nero's reign altogether. Furthermore, Polycarp's material may do more than simply help date the book of Revelation. Polycarp indicates that the Smyrnaean congregation (at least the one he represented) was not Pauline in its origins. Interestingly, facets of Rev 2 also seem to point away from a Pauline milieu (as reflected in scholarly comparisons of 1 Cor 8–10 with

---

104. Robinson, *Redating the New Testament*, 229–30; see also Cecil John Cadoux, *Ancient Smyrna* (Oxford: Blackwell, 1938), 310 n. 2. Robinson favored a Neronian date, partly based upon the "intense experience" implied by the work. Collins, *Crisis and Catharsis*, 69 (cf. 77), responds, "Robinson makes a large assumption and seems to forget how relative 'an intense experience' can be." Notwithstanding, Robinson's dismissal of the Polycarpian evidence has attracted an array of scholars; cf. Donald Guthrie, *New Testament Introduction*, rev. ed. (Downers Grove: InterVarsity, 1990), 954–55; Gentry, *Before Jerusalem Fell*, 323–24; Hemer, *Letters to the Seven Churches of Asia*, 66; Torrey, *Apocalypse of John*, 78.

105. For such Patristic placements in the reign of Claudius, see Gary DeMar and Francis X. Gumerlock, *The Early Church and the End of the World* (Powder Springs, GA: American Vision, 2006), 129–30.

Rev 2:14 and 2:20).[106] In their historical reconstructions, scholars must consider how a non-Pauline founded church came to be represented by an ecclesiastical leader so fond of Paul (as Polycarp evidently was).[107]

Conclusion

It seems natural to bring Acts 19 and Rev 2–3 together, as various commentators have done.[108] Nevertheless, contemporary scholars have neglected a third strand of tradition, the relevant materials in Polycarp's epistle. Polycarp's *Phil.* 11 describes Paul's letter-writing and church-planting ministries "at that time" (perhaps paralleling a temporal notion behind *in principio* in the previous sentence), in a manner that corresponds with other Polycarpian passages and resembles *1 Clem.* 47. Although many scholars have theorized that the Smyrnaean church was founded during Paul's Ephesian residency reflected in Acts 19, one is cautioned that Acts 19:10 and 19:26 are generalized statements befitting the context, style, and purposes of Lukan composition. Polycarp suggests that his Smyrnaean congregation did not exist in the era of Paul's letter-writing ministry, a datum that interpreters of Rev 2 should consider further. Based upon the tenor of Polycarp's material and the nature of the established churches in Rev 2, the earliest possible date for the completion of the Apocalypse seems oriented toward a post-Neronian date.

106. See C. K. Barrett, "Things Sacrificed to Idols," in *Essays on Paul* (Philadelphia: Westminster, 1982), 41–42. Elaine Pagels uses the differences for her wider purposes in *Revelations: Visions, Prophecy, and Politics in the Book of Revelation* (New York: Viking, 2012), 37–72.

107. Cf. Pol. *Phil.* 3.2. See Berding, *Polycarp and Paul*, 126–41. While the (unreliable) *Vita Polycarpi* ties Polycarp directly into a Pauline succession, other Patristic traditions claim a Johannine or "apostolic" pedigree for Polycarp (see Hartog, *Polycarp's Epistle to the Philippians*, 11–16).

108. See C. K. Barrett, *The Acts of the Apostles: A Shorter Commentary* (London: T&T Clark, 2002), 292; and idem, *Critical and Exegetical Commentary on the Acts of the Apostles*, ICC (Edinburgh: T&T Clark, 1998), 2:906.

Chapter 3

Missing Pauline Tradition in the Apostolic Fathers? *Didache, Shepherd of Hermas*, Papias, the *Martyrdom of Polycarp*, and the *Epistle to Diognetus*

Clayton N. Jefford

Introduction

In his 1990 essay on the influence of the apostle Paul in the Apostolic Fathers,[1] Andreas Lindemann offers several comments concerning texts in which the presence of the apostle is not found. The first of these appears in reference to four specific writings within the collection, as follows:

> At any rate, and for whatever reason, this work [i.e., the *Didache*] shows no contact with Paul or with Pauline theology... The author [of *Barnabas*] probably did make use of traditions in which Pauline ideas were reflected, but it seems to me that he does not himself show any interest in Pauline theology or in Pauline texts, whether he knew them or not... The *Second Letter of Clement* shows no connection to Paul; and the same is true of the last of the writings included in the apostolic fathers, the apocalyptic (and paraenetic) *Pastor Hermae*.[2]

Lindemann continues with the general observation that, though Paul's name is not used nor his letters employed anywhere in the Apostolic Fathers apart from the writings of *1 Clement* or letters of Ignatius and Polycarp, this should not be seen "as an indication of open (or hidden)

1. Andreas Lindemann, "Paul in the Writings of the Apostolic Fathers," in *Paul and the Legacies of Paul*, ed. W. S. Babcock (Dallas: Southern Methodist University Press, 1990), 25–45.
2. Ibid., 27.

hostility toward Paul" nor viewed "as a reaction of the church against the use of Pauline texts by (Gnostic or other) heretics."[3] Instead, as he concludes, we should understand the situation as such:

> ...it is clear that they [i.e., the Apostolic Fathers] show no signs of interest in extended use of Paul – his letters or his theology – "in his own right"; nor do they have any interest in what we would call "critical discussion" of Pauline theology (e.g., the writing of commentaries or the drawing of systematic conclusions from Pauline themes). Pauline texts and Pauline ideas were simply employed as needed (so to speak) or where the writer thought it important to call on an apostolic authority in support of his own argumentation.[4]

These observations may be easily extracted from an overview of the literature, and they would suggest that it is only within a narrow "school" of authors throughout the Apostolic Fathers that Paul's legacy held any real meaning. But this raises the question of whether the remainder of the collection may be so readily culled into a single category of writers who simply did not "need" Pauline tradition to make their argument (as Lindemann suggests)[5] or, more likely, that each represents a unique situation deserving of exploration.

In the essay that follows I will speak briefly to the state of five different authors within the corpus for whom Pauline tradition ostensibly has no role. Two of these are mentioned by Lindemann in his comments (the *Didache* and *Shepherd of Hermas*); two others are not cited there (Papias of Hierapolis and the *Martyrdom of Polycarp*). These latter were not considered by Lindemann at the time of writing and thus were never placed under the light of examination. The situations of *Barnabas* and *2 Clement* certainly deserve singular attention with respect to this question, but they are treated elsewhere in this volume in the essays of James Carleton Paget (on *Barnabas*) and Paul Foster (on *2 Clement*). These works will thus not be considered here. Otherwise, I will review only one additional text, that is, the final two chapters of the *Epistle to Diognetus*, a passage that I believe to be secondary to the writing as it now stands and, even though a clear quotation of Paul appears there, I do not consider to have originally reflected any interest in Pauline tradition.

---

3. Ibid.

4. Ibid., 44–45.

5. This is how Berding sees the comments of Lindemann here ("those who did not use Paul were mostly apologists for whose purposes Paul was not germane"), though this conclusion may be slightly unwarranted, as I will argue below. See Kenneth Berding, *Polycarp and Paul*, VCSup 62 (Leiden: Brill, 2002), 189 n. 7.

The Didache

A potential key to missing Pauline tradition in the *Didache* may be associated with how one assigns a date to the work. Various views have been offered since the publication of the only known manuscript in 1883, but a majority of approaches have favored some placement no earlier than the beginning of the second century, primarily due to the presumption that the Didachist was familiar with the Gospel of Matthew and refers to it (or its tradition) as "the gospel" (τό εὐαγγέλιον).[6] To the extent that scholars maintain this view, there is no easy way by which to explain why the *Didache* does not reflect Pauline perspectives apart from the author's conscious choice not to include such materials.[7]

Yet to argue that the Didachist simply did not know Pauline traditions is complicated by various fleeting parallels that appear throughout the text. There are not so many of these however, and they may be explained in a variety of ways. For example, certain equivalents may simply be secondary to the task at hand, with the Didachist having focused on sources that Paul himself employed. Thus, *Did.* 1.2 ("love of neighbor")

---

6. Cf. *Did.* 8.2; 15.3, 4. This view concerning the second century is still prevalent among distinguished scholars of the *Didache* today, as evidenced in the work of Vicky Balabanski, *Eschatology in the Making*, SNTSMS 97 (Cambridge: Cambridge University Press, 1997), 208; Kurt Niederwimmer, *The Didache*, Hermeneia, trans. Linda M. Maloney (Minneapolis: Fortress, 1998), 52–54; and Joseph Verheyden, "Eschatology in the Didache and the Gospel of Matthew," in *Matthew and the Didache*, ed. Huub van de Sandt (Assen: Van Gorcum; Minneapolis: Fortress, 2005), 193–215.

7. The options were certainly available to the author. E.g., while the Didachist made use of literature parallel to Matt 24:10, 24; Joel 2:2; 1 Pet 1:7; and Zech 13:8–9 at 16:4–5 ("And then the deceiver of the world will appear as a son of God and perform signs and wonders, and the earth will be handed over into his hands, and he will do such atrocities as have never existed before. Then all humanity will come to the fire of testing, and many will fall away"), the author of the *Apostolic Constitutions*, who otherwise employs the *Didache* as a framework for Book 7, turns to 2 Thess 2:8–9 at *Ap. Con.* 7.32.2 ("And then the deceiver of the world will appear – the enemy of truth, the prince of lies, 'whom the Lord Jesus will destroy by the spirit of his mouth,' who destroys the ungodly with his lips – and many will fall away"). Milavec certainly is correct when he offers that the author of the *Apostolic Constitutions* either no longer understood the focus of the Didachist's argument or wished to approach the topic from another perspective. See Aaron Milavec, "The Saving Efficacy of the Burning Process in *Didache* 16.5," in *The* Didache *in Context*, ed. Clayton N. Jefford, NovTSup 77 (Leiden: Brill, 1995), 131–55. Regardless, one must necessarily assume that the Didachist had the option of 2 Thessalonians available at the time of writing.

has a clear parallel at Gal 5:14, but Lev 19:18 is the obvious basis for both; 4.10 ("do not give orders…when you are angry") suggests Eph 6:9, with Sir 4:30 as their likely roots; 12.1 ("anyone who comes in the name of the Lord shall be welcomed") echoes Rom 12:13, both of which reflect Ps 118:26; and, 13.1 ("any true prophet…is worthy of their share") mirrors 1 Cor 9:14 and 1 Tim 5:18, the last of which specifically cites the "teaching of the Lord" as its basis, which is likely the same source for the others.[8] Elsewhere the Didachist appeals to commonly known wisdom teachings that Paul also would have employed: so *Did.* 3.1 ("run from each kind of evil") and 1 Thess 5:22; and 3.6 ("do not be a grumbler") and Phil 2.14; also 4.11 ("be obedient to [your] masters") and Eph 6:5–8/Col 3:22–25;[9] then 12.3 ("let them work and eat") and 2 Thess 3:7–12; and, 16.5–7 on the parousia of the Lord and 1 Cor 3:13 and 15:52, 1 Thess 3:13 and 4:16. A third category for consideration is the text of *Did.* 1.5 ("Woe to the one who receives"), which has as its likely parallel the admonition of 2 Thess 3:10. But this material falls within the interpolation of 1.3b–2.1 (the so-called *sectio evangelica*) and likely should be assigned to a later hand with different concerns and influences.[10] Thus, it may be unfair to assign this instance to the hand of the Didachist when in fact it belongs to a subsequent editor. In result, it is incorrect to say that the *Didache* does *not* reflect any knowledge of materials known elsewhere from Paul, since certain thematic parallels do indeed exist.[11] It may be better to say that counterparts to Pauline tradition may be explained as either dependent on alternative sources, drawn from common wisdom tradition, or the result of secondary interpolation. One must look elsewhere to explain the absence of a direct Pauline connection here.

A recent explanation for the absence of Pauline influence may be gathered from the argument of those who maintain that the *Didache* was composed prior to Matthew. Two figures are most prominent in this respect: Aaron Milavec and Alan J. P. Garrow. Milavec contends that the text should be read holistically, derived from oral performance, rehearsed

---

8. Cf. Matt 10:10/Luke 10:7.

9. These materials fall within the commonly used household codes of antiquity.

10. See already the early discussion of Bentley Layton, "The Sources, Date and Transmission of *Didache* 1.3b–2.1," *HTR* 61 (1968): 343–83; and Niederwimmer, *The Didache*, 68–72.

11. Hagner draws attention to parallels from Romans, 1 Corinthians, and 1 Thessalonians specifically, but taking the traditionalist view observes, "The Didache is a product of Jewish Christianity and it may well be for this reason, rather than a supposed decline in the popularity of Paul's epistles, that Paul's influence upon this treatise is negligible." See Donald Alfred Hagner, *The Use of the Old and New Testaments in Clement of Rome*, NovTSup 34 (Leiden: Brill, 1973), 285.

in the earliest years of Christian development, and was in evidence prior to the composition of the Matthean gospel.[12] Garrow is less concerned for a unified reading of the *Didache*, arguing instead that it represents a combination of ancient Christianity's traditions and views, which then served as a specific source for the author of Matthew.[13] In both cases the question of priority has been turned around with the suggestion that the *Didache*, having formalized early traditions in an arrangement that predated Matthew, may represent an approach that either operated prior to or alongside of the general circulation of Paul's letters and the establishment of his authority. Though these opinions have yet to be widely accepted among scholars, many readers have found them to offer provocative modifications for how one might see the formation of the text.[14] If either of these views may be accepted, this would explain why the teachings of Paul are not otherwise represented in the *Didache*.

One may perhaps take a less draconian approach by espousing the view that the Didachist and the author(s) of Matthew lived and wrote within the same literary community. My own suggestion for this location would be Antioch, primarily because this city has been so often suggested as a provenance for the gospel.[15] The more important consideration is whether traditions circulated freely within some larger community out of which both the *Didache* and Matthew were subsequently constructed. The former likely was formulated from otherwise well-known local materials; the latter probably reflects the influence of a combination of written and oral sources that became available from beyond indigenous resources known to the gospel's initial audience.[16] This would explain many similarities, while providing a sufficiently large context within which the struggling forces of conservative Christian Judaism (so the *Didache*), the dominance of Pauline tradition (so bishop Ignatius of Antioch), and the

12. See especially his *The Didache* (New York: Newman, 2003).

13. His principle work in this regard is *The Gospel of Matthew's Dependence on the* Didache, JSNTSup 254 (London: T&T Clark, 2004). Likewise, he argues that some of these same traditions may have influenced Paul's own writings, see his "The Eschatological Tradition behind 1 Thessalonians: *Didache* 16," *JSNT* 32 (2009): 191–213.

14. Milavec's approach, for example, clearly stands behind the recent introductions of William Varner, *The Way of the Didache* (Lanham, MD: University Press of America, 2007); and Thomas O'Loughlin, *The Didache* (Grand Rapids: Baker; London: SPCK, 2010).

15. I have supported this view in various forms since the publication of my dissertation, *The Sayings of Jesus in the Teachings of the Twelve Apostles*, VCSup 11 (Leiden: Brill, 1989).

16. One thinks here of the Gospel of Mark and the Q source, for example.

synthesizing efforts of gospel tradition (so the Gospel of Matthew) may
have arisen as representatives of local, evolving, ecclesiastical trends.[17]
If this perspective is acceptable, then the *Didache* would not represent
an author ignorant of Paul and his teachings but, instead, one who
purposefully avoided them as contrary to the core of a more conservative
Christian Jewish perspective.[18]

Three logical alternatives thus remain: the *Didache* was written at the
time of Paul and thus without Pauline influence by default;[19] the *Didache*
was written in a community setting in which Pauline teachings were
rejected by choice; or, the *Didache* was written after the formation of
Matthew and subsequently was either ignorant of Paulinism, in opposition
to it, or under the view that Paul's writings were irrelevant for issues at
hand. There is little available evidence to make a conclusive case for any
of these positions, though each carries its own values.

17. My stance on this approach is developed under several titles to date:
"Reflections on the Role of Jewish-Christianity in Second-Century Antioch," in
Actes du colloque international, ed. Simon C Mimouni with F. Stanley Jones, Lectio
Divina, Hors Série (Paris: Cerf, 2001), 147–67; "Conflict at Antioch: Ignatius and the
Didache at Odds," *StPatr* 36 (2001): 262–69; "The Milieu of Matthew, the Didache,
and Ignatius of Antioch: Agreements and Differences," in van de Sandt, ed., *Matthew
and the Didache*, 35–47; and "Social Locators as a Bridge between the Didache and
Matthew," in *The New Testament and the Apostolic Fathers*. Vol. 2, *Trajectories
through the New Testament and the Apostolic Fathers*, ed. Andrew F. Gregory and
Christopher M. Tuckett (Oxford: Oxford University Press, 2005), 245–64. See also
the contributions of Magnus Zetterholm, *The Formation of Christianity in Antioch*,
RECM (London: Routledge, 2003), 185–224; and "The Didache, Matthew, James –
and Paul: Reconstructing Historical Developments in Antioch," in *Matthew, James,
and Didache*, ed. Huub van de Sandt and Jürgen K Zangenberg, SBLSymS 45
(Atlanta: Society of Biblical Literature, 2008), 73–90.

18. Henry Chadwick asserts that "[p]ossibly the Didachist led a faction opposed
by Ignatius," so Chadwick, *The Church in Ancient Society*, OHCC (Oxford: Oxford
University Press, 2001), 84 n. 1. Proximity to the local Matthean tradition, which itself
is essentially neutral toward Paul, may also help to explain why a similar impression
was left on the Didachist at the time of writing. See Ernst Dassmann, *Der Stachel im
Fleisch* (Munster: Aschendorff, 1979), 98–108.

19. Lindemann himself takes this position elsewhere when he says, "Es ist aber
doch wahrscheinlich, daß Did tatsächlich von Paulus (und von seiner Mission) nichts
weiß; für diese Annahme spricht das Fehlen von parallelen bei verwandten oder
identischen Themen Die Annahme, Paulus werde von der Did bewußt totgeschiegen,
läßt sich jedenfalls nicht begründen": so Andreas Lindemann, *Paulus im ältesten
Christentum*, BHT 58 (Tübingen: Mohr Siebeck, 1979), 177 (for his complete discussion on the *Didache*, see pp. 174–77).

Papias

Not all early collections of literature of the Apostolic Fathers include the materials of Papias of Hierapolis, though more recent editors have incorporated traditions both by and about the bishop among those writings,[20] and thus one might consider him briefly here as well. It is clear that Papias was a forceful personality among second-century Christians, a leader whose ideas both memorialized the early teachings of Jesus of Nazareth and furthered theological speculation within the church.[21]

The primary problem is that so little remains from his writings, and what survives is in second- and third-hand sources. Furthermore, virtually nothing from the bishop's hand addresses either the teachings or traditions of Paul apart from a general tendency toward apocalypticism, which finds its expression specifically in a chiliastic form.[22] Ulrich Körtner sees the issues here to be quite clear, finding no evidence of any particular anti-Pauline tendency in Papias but, instead, a certain "un-Pauline" attitude.[23] This is perhaps surprising, since Paul traveled in regions of Asia Minor with which Papias (being in Hierapolis) undoubtedly was quite familiar. There can thus be little question that the bishop was familiar with the apostle's legacy and influence.[24] Yet, this view is derived from no true evidence.[25]

20. Ulrich H. J. Körtner observes that this has been true since the nineteenth century, though following the limited corpus of J. B. Cotelier in 1672, has not been the traditional view. See Körtner, *Papias von Hierapolis* (Göttingen: Vandenhoeck & Ruprecht, 1985), 43–44. For more recent collections that feature Papias, see Andreas Lindemann and Henning Paulsen, *Die Apostolischen Väter* (Tübingen: Mohr Siebeck, 1992), 286–303; Bart Ehrman, ed. and trans., *The Apostolic Fathers*, 2 vols., LCL 25 (Cambridge, MA: Harvard University Press, 2003), 2:86–119; and Michael Holmes, ed., *The Apostolic Fathers*, 3rd ed. (Grand Rapids: Baker, 2007), 722–67.

21. For a succinct, if traditional, view of the literary character and theological tendencies of Papias and his writings, see already Philipp Vielhauer, *Geschichte der urchristlichen Literatur* (Berlin: de Gruyter, 1975), 759–65.

22. Two instances are preserved in Holmes, *Apostolic Fathers*, 762–67, featuring fragments 24 and 27, the former taken from Andrew of Caesarea, *On the Apocalypse*, at Rev 12:7–9 and John of Dârâ, *On the Resurrection of Bodies* 2.13. For further consideration of the former witness, see Folker Siegert, "Unbeachtete Papiaszitate bei armenischen Schriftstellern," *NTS* 27 (1981): 605–14. See also Charles E. Hill, *Regnum Caelorum*, 2nd ed. (Grand Rapids: Eerdmans, 2001), 22–23.

23. Körtner, *Papias von Hierapolis*, 223–24. Also in support of this view is Charles E. Hill, "Papias of Hierapolis," *ExpTim* 117 (2006): 312.

24. Though Hill ("Papias of Hierapolis," 312) may be correct when he notes, "Any Pauline references therefore would most likely have been illustrative or corroborative."

25. See the review of David K. Rensberger, "As the Apostle Teaches: The Development of the Use of Paul's Letters in Second-Century Christianity" (PhD diss., Yale

Perhaps as important is the question of whether Papias chose to socialize in Pauline circles at all. As with the situation of the *Didache* discussed previously, Papias may not have been an ardent disciple of the apostle to the nations. If such were the case, there would be no reason to pursue evidence of Paulinism in the witness of Papias, unlike his contemporaries and fellow bishops Ignatius and Polycarp. His primary concerns would have been directed toward the recollection of the sayings of Jesus[26] and not necessarily those of the apostle Paul.[27]

But there may be a further need to understand the role of Papias with respect to the evolution of Paul's own sources. In recent days Dennis MacDonald has offered additional consideration to the possible role of the bishop in the acquisition and enlargement of various gospel materials related to the teachings of Jesus.[28] MacDonald's thesis focuses on the *logoi* of Jesus as a foundation for various gospel sources known by later authors of Christian antiquity, including Irenaeus and the elders John and Aristion. If one can indeed make the case that there is some legitimate reason to believe ancient accounts of these *logoi* served as a widely circulating source known to the New Testament evangelists, would this not provide added reason to envisage that Paul himself may have had such a source available during his ministry? In the light of various other traditions and teachings that Paul accumulated during his work,[29] seen now scattered throughout his writings, this source may indeed have been a

University, 1981), 198–201. He concludes that "Papias tells us nothing one way or the other about attitudes to Paul" (p. 201).

26. Hence the production of his, now lost, five-volume work entitled *Interpretations of the Sayings of the Lord*.

27. Paul himself makes only limited use of Jesus' teachings, though scholars sometimes have sought to argue otherwise. See David L. Dungan, *The Sayings of Jesus in the Churches of Paul* (Philadelphia: Fortress; Oxford: Blackwell, 1971); Dale C. Allison, "The Pauline Epistles and the Synoptic Gospels: The Pattern of the Parallels," *NTS* 28 (1982): 1–32; Michael B. Thompson, *Clothed with Christ*, JSNTSup 59 (Sheffield: JSOT, 1991); and Larry W. Hurtado, *Lord Jesus Christ* (Grand Rapids: Eerdmans, 2003), 235–38.

28. Dennis R. MacDonald, *Two Shipwrecked Gospels*, ECIL 8 (Atlanta: Society of Biblical Literature, 2012).

29. Cf., e.g., Paul's use of hymns, creeds, and sayings that likely were already in circulation among the earliest Christian communities (so Rom 1:1–5; 1 Cor 13:1–8; Phil 2:6–11; Titus 1:12). An additional argument may be made for a pre-Pauline tradition behind Paul's eschatological comments in 1 Cor 15:20–28. See Walter Schmithals, "The Pre-Pauline Tradition in 1 Corinthians 15:20–28," *PRSt* 20 (1993): 357–80.

foundation for his teachings and theological speculation.[30] Unfortunately, the evidence for such materials is not so easily found, and thus such a presumption must remain simply that – a presumption – either to be accepted or rejected without further empirical evidence.[31]

Shepherd of Hermas

Unlike the situation of Papias, the text of *Hermas* remains in its entirety and leaves no need to offer an argument from silence. Subsequently, the perceived absence of Pauline parallels here is perplexing for a number of reasons. In the first instance, the work likely derives from the mid-second century, a time when Pauline traditions and teachings were already circulating widely among other authors of the period. Secondly, the provenance of the writing purports to be Rome, a city to which Paul had already written and whose community would have been familiar with his ministry from the time when he was imprisoned there.[32] This is the same location from which *1 Clement* derives, whose author is seemingly quite familiar with the apostle and thereby serves as a witness to the presence of the Pauline legacy in that region.[33] Finally, a number of images and themes that appear in *Hermas* find ready parallel within the Pauline letters[34] and therefore should have been seen as useful material for the construction of the author's argument. If the author of *Hermas* was aware of these texts,

---

30. This was already the focus of much scholarly debate prior to MacDonald, evidenced, e.g., in the earlier work of D. Alfred Resch, *Der paulinismus und die Logia Jesu*, TUGAL 27, Bd 12 (Leipzig: Hinrichs, 1904); and W. D. Davies, *Paul and Rabbinic Judaism* (London: SPCK, 1948; repr., Philadelphia: Fortress, 1980), 136–46. Davies states with conviction here, "in addition to any traditional material that Paul used he had also the words of Jesus to which he turned for guidance" (141), though the evidence for this conjecture is tenuous at best.

31. So too Lindemann, *Paulus*, 290–92.

32. Herm. *Vis.* 1.1 ("in Rome"); 1.2 ("in the Tiber river"); 1.3 ("going to Cumae"); and 4.1 ("by the Via Campania"). This assumes, of course, that the opening "vision" of the work is a reliable marker for the writing's context.

33. For *1 Clement*, see 5.5–7, in addition to the numerous Pauline words and phrases that appear throughout. Yet the nature of this knowledge is not secure, since one observes that the author of *1 Clement* has chosen to rely on Old Testament figures as models of leadership for the Corinthians rather than Paul (or even Peter; see 5.4).

34. One imagines here by way of example: Herm. *Vis.* 1.8 (evil ideas within a righteous person), cf. Rom 7:14–25; Herm. *Vis.* 3.2 (suffering for the name), cf. Rom 5:3–5; 2 Cor 1:3–11; Eph 3:13; Herm. *Mand.* 1.2 and 2.4 (putting on righteousness and reverence), cf. Eph 6:10–17; Herm. *Mand.* 4.4–11 (on impurity in marriage), cf. 1 Cor 7:1–16; etc.

it might be considered peculiar that those resources were not incorporated as a means by which to reinforce the authority of the message. Otherwise, one envisages that the writer composes this text simply under the aegis of personal prophecy (presumably recognized already by the intended audience) and not under the established prominence of apostolic tradition.

With these three elements in mind, one perhaps does well to give more careful reflection to possible Pauline parallels within the text. Indeed, the situation may not be quite as clearly determined as is typically assumed by scholars. This is easily demonstrated through use of a limited table of potential parallels drawn merely from Paul's letter to Rome:[35]

Hermas	Topic	Paul
Vis. 3.6.2	adhering and detaching	Rom 12:9 (cf. 1 Cor 6:16)
Vis. 3.8.9	renewal of spirit / mind	Rom 12:2 (cf. 2 Cor 4:16; Col 3:10)
Vis. 3.12.1–3	new life through inheritance	Rom 8:18 (cf. Gal 3:29)
Vis. 4.1.8	faith in the Lord as armor	Rom 13:12 (cf. Eph 6:11, 14; 1 Thess 5:8)[36]
Mand. 7.4–5	two types of fear	Rom 13:3–4, 7
Mand. 10.3.2	lawlessness of sin	Rom 6:19 (cf. Titus 2:14)
Mand. 12.4–5	obedience to God's power	Rom 10:3; 13:1 (cf. Eph 5:21)
Sim. 4.4	destruction of sinners	Rom 1:20–21
Sim. 9.13.7	having the same mind	Rom 12:16 (cf. 2 Cor 13:11; Phil 2:2; 4:2)[37]
Sim. 9.16.1–4	language of death	Rom 6:1–11[38]

---

35. Numerous lesser parallels are evident that undoubtedly reflect common usage beyond Paul, e.g., "spirits of the world" – Hermas *passim* (Rom 8:15; 1 Cor 2:12; Gal 5:16–25; etc.); "righteous / holy ones" – *Vis.* 1.1.8; 1.4.2; 2.2.5; *Sim.* 3.2; 4.2; 8.9.1 (cf. Rom 1:1; 1 Cor 1:2; Phil 1:1); "God creator of all" – *Mand.* 1.1 (Rom 4:17; Eph 3:9); "fear the Lord" – *Mand.* 1.2 (Rom 3:18; 2 Cor 5:11); "simplicity" – *Mand.* 2.1 (Rom 12:8; 2 Cor 8:2; 9:11, 13; 11:3; Eph 6:5; Col 3:22); "God as rock / Christ as cornerstone" – *Sim.* 9.2.1–2 (Rom 9:33; Eph 2:20); "hospitality to the needy" – *Sim.* 9.27.2–3 (Rom 12:13; 1 Tim 5:4–5); etc.

36. Cf. also Herm. *Sim.* 9.13.1–2.

37. The phrase "to have the same mind" (τὸ αὐτὸ φρονεῖν) that Hermas employs here is a virtual quotation of the language that Paul himself uses in these parallels, and is seemingly a preferred Pauline expression.

38. Though as Osiek correctly observes here: "The language of death and life is similar to Pauline language but is not exactly the same: here, death is the pre-baptismal state, not the dying process that is symbolically enacted in the course of baptism." See Carolyn Osiek, *The Shepherd of Hermas*, Hermeneia (Minneapolis: Fortress, 1999), 238.

What is immediately evident from this brief overview of elements is that, though *Hermas* does not appeal directly to the authority of Paul or to the distinction of his correspondence, there is in fact much reliance on Pauline terminology and phraseology that is not likely coincidental. One might argue with some justification that such language already circulated widely in the middle of the second century, and thus the text of Hermas may simply reflect what was popular as Christian speech during those decades. The concentration of such language throughout the whole of the writing (and not only in individual tropes or pericopae), however, suggests that some more conscious employment is at work in the mind of the author, and consideration of this aspect implies that the text falls within the broader spectrum of the apostle's influence.[39]

There is little of a definitive nature to be concluded from this analysis perhaps, except that it is roundly untrue to assert that the author of *Hermas* was wholly unaware of Pauline tradition.[40] One must suppose instead that, being aware of that legacy and having incorporated phraseology from its ranks, it was considered the wiser choice neither to quote Paul directly nor to make allusion to his authority. In this respect one might argue against the conclusions of Lindemann concerning this text here, not only with respect to the author's lack of knowledge of things Pauline, but even more so that no hostility is at work against their trajectory.[41] At the same time, there is no particular reason to imagine that

39. At the same time, of course, the random usage of Pauline parallels suggests that the author of Hermas did not choose to follow either the structure or argument of any particular epistle (here demonstrated by comparison with Romans) as a model for the work's composition Hagner states, "The allusions are quite free, often amounting to an appropriation of some idea or phraseology recalled from the Pauline epistles by memory." See Hagner, *Use*, 285.

40. James Drummond had already suggested some foundation for a refutation of this position in his brief review of *Hermas* in 1905, finding parallels with Romans, 1 Corinthians, 1 Thessalonians, and Ephesians. See Drummond, "Shepherd of Hermas," in A Committee of the Oxford Society of Historical Theology, *The New Testament in the Apostolic Fathers* (Oxford: Clarendon, 1905), 105–7, 115. Cf. the later analysis of Joseph Verheyden, who is comfortable with the idea that *Hermas* made use both of Matthew and 1 Corinthians specifically: so Verheyden, "The *Shepherd of Hermas* and the Writings That Later Formed the New Testament," in *The New Testament and the Apostolic Fathers*. Vol. 1, *The Reception of the New Testament in the Apostolic Fathers*, ed. Andrew F. Gregory and Christopher M. Tuckett (Oxford: Oxford University Press, 2005), 293–329.

41. Lindemann, "Paul in the Writings," 27. In his earlier work this was not the position he took, arguing instead that *Hermas* reflects an anti-Marcionite perspective, which is the view that I will endorse below. So Lindemann, *Paulus*, 282–90.

Hermas is decidedly anti-Pauline in scope,[42] especially having incorporated parallel phraseology as illustrated in the table above.

But there is certainly cause to envisage that an anti-Marcionite bias may be at work here. This is certainly conceivable, since Rome and its environs were populated with Christian communities that had been influenced by Marcion, his teachings, and his followers.[43] The need to respond with a passive approach to Pauline teachings may have been exactly what was demanded by the author of *Hermas* during those years; the desire to avoid the complications of peripheral authorities (quite specifically, either Marcion or those who taught in his name) may have stood as the issue of the day.[44] The ensuing text surely reflects the very mood of such times.

Martyrdom of Polycarp

The case of the *Martyrdom* is particularly interesting in the light of Polycarp's own interest in Paul and his heritage.[45] There is little question that the bishop of Smyrna, together with such figures as Ignatius of Antioch and Marcion of Sinope, should be included among those who would be defined as a "Pauline school" within early Christian tradition. Each of these personalities made much use of Pauline materials themselves. One wonders why the same cannot be said about those who revered Polycarp to the extent that they recorded his death in the production of the *Martyrdom* as a sign of reverence for his memory and inspiration for those who would be his disciples. Several observations are worth mention in this respect.

42. If one were to argue in this direction, for example, then it would be necessary to argue against all other New Testament writers as sources as well, since *Hermas* seems little dependent upon scripture in the course of building an argument, though not necessarily against the themes of scripture themselves.

43. E.g., cf. the discussions of Walter Bauer, *Orthodoxy and Heresy in Earliest Christianity*, ed. Robert A Kraft and Gerhard Krodel (Philadelphia: Fortress, 1971), 106–7, 113–14, 128, 132. Bauer insists that *Hermas* "has no heresies in view" however (114), though it is clear that, besides Marcion himself, the sympathetic positions of Lucanus (his disciple), Cerdo, and Valentinus were also at work in the region. See also here, W. H. C Frend, *The Rise of Christianity* (Philadelphia: Fortress, 1984), 212–17.

44. One observes that *Hermas* speaks specifically of the authority of "apostles, bishops, teachers, and deacons" (Herm. *Vis.* 3.5.1) and elsewhere of the ministry of "bishops and widows" (Herm. *Sim.* 9.27.2) in these matters, thus to avoid the competitive claims of external teachers.

45. Well known now are the studies of Berding, *Polycarp and Paul*; and Paul Hartog, *Polycarp and the New Testament*, WUNT 2/134 (Tübingen: Mohr Siebeck, 2002), 177–79, 216–35.

Firstly, the *Martyrdom* by its very nature is principally constructed to offer a reflection of Polycarp's last days as an echo of the crucifixion of Jesus of Nazareth known from the New Testament gospels. This is no mystery and is clear from even a hasty reading of the text. Whether this pattern was original to the text or is in fact secondary remains to be settled, yet the design stands at present as an obvious feature of the work. Consequently, there is no particular expectation that Pauline sources should enter into the scenario, and thus the earlier comments of Lindemann with respect to *Barnabas* might likewise be at work here: "he does not himself show any interest in Pauline theology or in Pauline texts, whether he knew them or not...[46]

More to the point is the issue raised previously with the case of *Hermas*, that is, one must question whether the *Martyrdom* is completely devoid of Pauline references and allusions. This would again appear *not* to be the case, as has been suggested by several recent studies.[47] Michael Holmes offers several probable parallels: the blessing "may mercy and peace and love of God the Father and our Lord Jesus Christ be multiplied" (*Mart. Pol.* inscription; cf. 1 Tim 1:2; 2 Tim 1:2); the thought "looking not just to our own interests but to those of our neighbors" (*Mart. Pol.* 1.2; cf. Phil 2:4);[48] the phrase "eyes of the heart" (τοῖς τῆς καρδίας ὀφθαλμοῖς; *Mart. Pol.* 2.3; cf. Eph 1:18); the wording "they looked on good things that neither ear has heard nor eyes seen nor entered the human heart, but the Lord revealed to them" (*Mart. Pol.* 2.3; cf. 1 Cor 2:9);[49] and the concept of paying proper respect "to rulers and authorities appointed by God" (*Mart. Pol.* 10.2; cf. Rom 13:1, 7; Titus 3:1). In the final analysis

---

46. Lindemann, "Paul in the Writings," 27. That any consideration of Paul's own death is missing here might seem curious, except the author of Acts also has not included such a scene at the conclusion of that work. More curious perhaps is that no parallel to Stephen's martyrdom from Acts 7 is brought into play, which itself lacks any association with the passion of Jesus.

47. See Boudewijn Dehandschutter, *Martyrium Polycarpi*, BETL 52 (Leuven: Leuven University Press, 1979), 241–54 (intermingled references); and Michael W. Holmes, "The *Martyrdom of Polycarp* and the New Testament Passion Narratives," in *The New Testament and the Apostolic Fathers*. Vol. 2, *Trajectories through the New Testament and the Apostolic Fathers*, ed. Andrew F. Gregory and Christopher M. Tuckett (Oxford: Oxford University Press, 2005), 427–32.

48. While this is a virtual quotation, Holmes sees it as more of a "conceptual link" with additional parallels at Phil 3:17; Rom 16:17; 1 Cor 10:23, 33; 2 Cor 4:18; and Gal 6:1. See Holmes, "Martyrdom of Polycarp," 428.

49. The question here is the nature of Paul's own source and whether the *Martyrdom* has made use of that source or, instead, of Paul himself.

Holmes concludes with the following observations about possible scriptural parallels in the *Martyrdom*:

> If, for example, one were to ask whether it is probable that the church in Smyrna possessed copies of at least some of the documents now found in the canonical New Testament, the evidence supplied by the letter that the congregation's bishop wrote some years earlier to the church in Philippi suggests that the answer would be an assured 'yes'. It is not possible, however, to confirm that hypothesis on the basis of evidence supplied by the *Martyrdom of Polycarp*.[50]

Nevertheless, two considerations may be worth note at this point. The first of these is that, like *Hermas* before, the language of Pauline rhetoric was certainly in the air and clearly available for use by the authors of the *Martyrdom*. This is evident both in the terminology and in the concepts employed with respect to the account of the bishop's demise. The second element is observed in the virtual quotations of Pauline writing (or Paul's own sources) at *Mart. Pol.* 1.2 and 2.3: the first of these was directed by Paul to the Philippians (so Phil 2.4), with whom Polycarp himself clearly was in touch as known from his own letter; the second of these may have been known regionally by evidence of its use in Corinth (so 1 Cor 2:9).

One might conclude then that, while the *Martyrdom* was composed (or at least edited) with specific gospel passion narratives in mind, the *flavor* of Pauline discourse was well known and available for inclusion when desired.[51] The reality that Paul's witness is not widely employed in this effort is likely more of a comment on its lack of necessity for the argument at hand in the eyes of the authors; the fact that Pauline imagery appears at all is surely a witness to the power and authority that the apostle held for those who preserved the witness of the bishop's death.

Diognetus 11–12

The integrity of *Diognetus* is a matter of much dispute, the specifics of which cannot be rehearsed in the space available here.[52] Suffice it to

---

50. Holmes, "Martyrdom of Polycarp," 432.

51. Thus Hagner, *Use*, 286: "The author of the Martyrdom of Polycarp apparently knew the Pauline corpus. Again the allusions are made with great freedom."

52. Henri Estienne already raised the possibility of disunity in the 1592 publication of his 1586 transcription of the text, and E. H. Blakeney did not include these final chapters in his commentary on the text. See Blakeney, *The Epistle to Diognetus* (London: SPCK; New York: Macmillan, 1943). For a consideration of the issues

say that, for the purposes of argument, I hold chs. 11–12 to derive from completely separate origins than chs. 1–10. In my opinion this is true with respect to authorship, geographical location, and historical setting.

There is no question that chs. 1–10 maintain a rigorous emphasis on Pauline theology and reflect knowledge of numerous letters associated with the heritage of Paul. This has been clearly established and is widely recognized within scholarship, having drawn the careful attention of various researchers over the years.[53] At the same time, most scholars assume that this same emphasis holds true for the concluding chapters (chs. 11–12) as well, largely buttressed by the presence of a direct quotation of 1 Cor 8:1 at *Diog.* 12.5. Indeed, only here does *Diognetus* offer any citation of a source, either scriptural or non-canonical, perhaps suggesting that special emphasis should be given to the passage as an indicator of the author's concern for Pauline tradition.[54]

In point of fact, however, three elements argue against this assumption. In the first instance, nothing else in chs. 11–12 reflects a Pauline orientation. These chapters are instead concerned with Johannine themes and perspectives, incorporating materials from Gen 3 by way of illustration of Johannine theology. Secondly, this singular appearance of a scriptural quotation would actually seem to argue *against* its original place within the document (regardless of whether these chapters are secondary), since this is clearly not the style of the author(s) of the text otherwise. Finally, the appearance of this citation within the author's discussion of the trees of knowledge and life in Gen 2 is wholly unnecessary, providing only a secondary point of emphasis to the basic theme itself. The longer context of the passage is neither oriented around the teachings of Paul nor any theme known to be particularly Pauline.

---

at hand in arguments on this matter, see Clayton N. Jefford, ed., *The Epistle to Diognetus (with the Fragment of Quadratus)*, OAF (Oxford: Oxford University Press, 2013), 43–51.

53. See especially, Andreas Lindemann, "Paulinische Theologie im Brief an Diognet," in *Kerygma and Logos*, ed. A. M. Ritter (Göttingen: Vandenhoeck & Ruprecht, 1979), 337–50; Michael F. Bird, "The Reception of Paul in the *Epistle to Diognetus*," in *Paul and the Second Century*, ed. Michael F. Bird and Joseph R. Dodson, LNTS 412 (London: T&T Clark, 2011), 70–90; and, Jefford, *Epistle to Diognetus*, 80–93.

54. Even here, however, one observes that the citation from 1 Corinthians is attributed to "the apostle" (ὁ ἀπόστολος) and not specifically to Paul by name, thus perhaps to suggest that the author wishes less to appeal to the persona of the man himself and more to the authority of his apostolicity.

As to this concluding observation, the matter is readily demonstrated by a delineation of the text as follows:

> For there is neither life without knowledge nor certain knowledge without true life. Each tree thus was planted near the other… For anyone who claims to know something without knowledge that is true and confirmed by life knows nothing. (12.4, 6a)

Inserted into the midst of these comments is the citation from 1 Corinthians (position indicated by the ellipsis above):

> Having recognized the importance of this, the apostle condemned knowledge used apart from this directive of truth that leads to life, saying, "Knowledge puffs up but love builds up." (12.5)

There is no question that the citation admirably illustrates the author's conclusion with regard to knowledge and life as illustrated by the account of the garden of Eden from Genesis. At the same time, however, Paul's comment about the nature of love and its value to "build up" bears no relevance to the argument, standing as an awkward side comment that carries little weight for the author's point as it stands. It is unexpected; it is unnecessary; it is oblique. One may easily remove 12.5 from the context and, as can be readily observed above, no violence is rendered either to the text or to the author's message concerning knowledge and life.

There is no particular reason, therefore, to think that this verse is original to chs. 11–12. Indeed, there is no assured argument to explain why 12.5 should be attributed to the original form of the text apart from the fact that it existed there in our only known manuscript.

One may wish to argue against this conclusion, of course, since it has not been the traditional view given to the text. But the admission of the possibility itself serves to reinforce the fact that nowhere in chs. 11–12 does the author otherwise make reference to Pauline ideas or theology, and throughout the entire text there is no other direct citation of scripture. The presence of this particular reference thus stands as unique and, probably, as an editorial insertion, perhaps in an effort to make these concluding chapters better suited to the broader Pauline argument of chs. 1–10.[55] We likely shall never know.

---

55. Lindemann follows the argument of C. M. Nielsen here that this quotation was included as a foil against the perspective of Christian Gnosticism, hence the editor's use of the word "apostle" rather than the name of Paul directly. See Lindemann, *Paulus*, 350 (for his review of *Diognetus* generally, see 343–50); also C. M. Nielsen, "The Epistle to Diognetus: Its Date and Relationship to Marcion," *AThR* 52 (1970): 82–83.

What remains is an indication of secondary addition to the original text of *Diognetus* that otherwise stands without evidence of Pauline influence. If one may date the final form of the work to some point late in the second century or even early in the third, as most scholars do, this seems a most unexpected set of circumstances, which leaves several possibilities to consider.

The first option derives from those scholars who have suggested that the author of chs. 11–12 is the same as that of chs. 1–10, perhaps writing at another time under other circumstances. If this is true, then one could argue (together with Lindemann) that the context of chs. 11–12 simply did not call for the inclusion of Pauline materials and tradition. The presence of 12.5 might suggest otherwise if this verse were to be included as original to the materials, but such consideration is only a minor point of emphasis. This option is a possibility then, but seems unlikely based on a number of other factors that argue against the text being by the same hand.[56]

A second possibility is that these chapters are from another (perhaps later) author who, writing at the end of the second century or early in the third, simply was unaware of Pauline traditions. This also is possible, but seems highly unlikely in the light of how such materials were disseminated throughout the second-century church. One might argue (contrary to Lindemann), however, that such traditions were purposefully omitted in this case, either because there was an anti-Marcionite or anti-Gnostic bias at work within the author's perspective or some other hostility toward the Pauline legacy. One thus finds texts such as the *Apocryphon of John* in the Nag Hammadi materials that reflect extensive discussion of human creation and, by default, some concern for the nature of salvation. But any focus on the trees of knowledge and life from Gen 2:15–17 is severely limited here, and the author takes the opposite view from that of *Diognetus*, seeing them as the false promises of the archons who sought to mislead humanity.[57] A text such as this clearly reflects an oppositional perspective that would not have embraced that of the author of *Diog.* 11–12. Therefore, to offer such parallels provides only the weakest comparison with respect to the evolution of traditions and even argues against any shared background of development.

---

56. See a summary of these arguments in Jefford, *Epistle to Diognetus*, 43–56.

57. NHL II,*1* 21.17–22.9 Otherwise, there is an intriguing parallel in II,*1* 23.20–29 in which wisdom (here "Sophia") is identified as "Life" who appears as an eagle on the tree of knowledge in order to teach those who already have tasted perfect knowledge Sophia might be identified with the uncorrupted Eve identified as "the Virgin" in *Diog.* 12.9, but the imagery does not find a ready transition between the author of *Diognetus* and Gnostic exegesis generally.

A third possibility is that chs. 11–12 reflect only a small portion of materials from some author who otherwise is highly disposed to employ Pauline imagery and traditions in other contexts. A good example here might be reflected in the view of those scholars who see Clement of Alexandria as the author of *Diognetus* in general, though I would argue for his possible contribution primarily for these chapters alone.[58] There is no question that Clement was fully steeped in Pauline literature and traditions, thus to offer a possible context for the production of these chapters by someone who otherwise made use of Pauline sources in their writings.[59] A broader Alexandrian context is likewise conducive to the idea that the final arrangement of *Diognetus* may derive from Clement's contributions. Of course, there are other authors and geographical settings in which similar variables existed that were conducive for the addition of chs. 11–12, and so one remains without certainty about the background tradition for the materials. At the same time, Alexandrian Egypt provided a welcomed avenue for such a context, and it is a proximity that many scholars gladly endorse.[60]

---

58. In support of Clement as author, see the arguments of such scholars as Adolf von Harnack, *Die Chronologie der Literatur bis Irenäus nebst einleitenden Untersuchungen* (Leipzig: Hinrichs, 1958), 514; Theofried Baumeister, "Zur Datierung der Schrift an Diognet," *VC* 42 (1988): 105–11; Klaus Wengst, *Schriften des Urchristentums* (Munich: Kösel-Verlag, 1984), 305–9; and Horacio E. Lona, *An Diognet*, KFA 8 (Freiburg: Herder, 2001), 63–69. One observes that this position is largely resident within German scholarship. Curiously, Bird envisions just the opposite situation from what I support here, arguing for the hand of Clement everywhere else within *Diognetus* except for these closing chapters: "The document is more properly a treatise than a letter and as such it closely resembles the *Exhortation* of Clement of Alexandria, while the final two sermonic chapters are analogous to the homiletical style of Melito of Sardis and the writings of Hippolytus of Rome." See Bird, "Reception of Paul," 70.

59. See already the older review by Fritz Buri, *Clemens Alexandrinus und der Paulinische Freiheitsbegriff* (Zurich: Max Niehans, 1939), and more recently the short analysis of Mark W. Elliott, "The Triumph of Paulinism by the Mid-Third Century," in Bird and Dodson, eds., *Paul and the Second Century*, 248–50. Elliott notes specifically that Clement's "Interpretations of Paul are strewn round the *Stromateis*" (248), yet further comments on Paul are certainly not restricted to that writing.

60. Henri I. Marrou argues for the likelihood that Alexandria was the sight of authorship, though he does not prefer Clement himself. See Marrou, *A Diognète*, SC 33, 2nd ed. (Paris: Cerf, 1965), 241–68.

Conclusions

This brief survey brings us to several differing conclusions about those writings within the Apostolic Fathers that appear to have omitted the Pauline legacy from their design. The explanations for this perception vary depending on the situation of each author.

The texts of *Hermas* and the *Martyrdom* may actually have been mislabeled in this process. A review of materials in each instance (taken from a sample in the case of *Hermas*) suggests in fact that the authors were informed of Pauline tradition, having employed its terminology and even quoting from it on occasion, though no direct appeal is made to the authority of the apostle at the time of writing. The rationale for this omission remains undetermined. In the case of *Hermas*, it is suggested here that the author, working within a Roman provenance, may have wished to avoid the influence of Marcion and his followers and thereby chose to avoid direct reference to Paul in the process. In the case of the *Martyrdom*, Lindemann's comment that use of Pauline tradition perhaps was viewed as unnecessary for the context[61] may be correct. There is otherwise no obvious reason not to mention the apostle, especially since Polycarp himself was such an avid proponent of the Pauline legacy.

The case is somewhat different in the situations of the *Didache* and Papias. With respect to the Didachist, one may be left with the reality that the timing was too early in the history of Christian evolution for Paul to have been an obvious choice of reference. But more to be expected, the *Didache* itself likely derives from a shared Matthean context in which the authority of the evangelist superseded that of the apostle. Or possibly, the Didachist may have represented a more traditionally conservative view of the faith that stood in opposition to the teachings of Paul, at least as they were championed by Ignatius of Antioch. As for Papias, the reality is simply that not enough material remains for determination. It is certainly possible that the bishop actually *did* incorporate Pauline traditions into his writings along with those of the gospels, but the evidence is too sparse to make such a claim with certainty.

Finally, the concluding chapters of *Diognetus* suggest a late second-century context in which Paul did not serve as an obvious source of reference, though the probable addition of the quotation of 1 Corinthians in 12:5 suggests that a subsequent editor wished to incorporate the authority of the apostle, a respected source of apostolic authority by this time.

---

61. Lindemann, "Paul in the Writings," 44–45.

One is again left to speculate on the matter, assuming that the otherwise anonymous author of these chapters may even have been predisposed to the teachings of Paul in subsequent writings, though they currently remain unidentified.

In the final analysis, one ultimately is left to agree with Lindemann's own conclusion about Pauline materials in the Apostolic Fathers: "There is certainly no basis for the notion that Paul was forgotten or unimportant in the (wing of the) church in which 'Clement,' Ignatius, and Polycarp did their work."[62] Yet this comment must ultimately extend beyond these three authors. As the above survey suggests, it is entirely plausible that the same conclusion may be drawn about the entirety of the corpus as it is now defined. The evidence simply remains too limited to establish an informed opinion with certainty.

---

62. Lindemann, "Paul in the Writings," 45. He follows the similar conclusion of Dassmann, *Der Stachel*, 108, who asks: "Gibt es daneben im kanonischen Schrifttum der nachapostolischen Zeit Äußerungen, die nicht nur unpaulinisch-neutral sind, sondern antipaulinische Tendenzen bezeugen oder vermuten lassen?"

Chapter 4

THE ABSENCE OF PAUL IN *2 CLEMENT*

Paul Foster

Introduction

The figure of Paul looms large in modern conceptions of the origin and spread of the religious movement now known as Christianity. His role is seen as so fundamental, that books with titles such as *Paul: The Founder of Christianity* claim that Paul was actually the person who established the movement that ostensibly originated with Jesus of Nazareth.[1] In response to these types of perspectives, others have asserted that while Paul was responsible for the spread of the new religious movement, he was essentially a loyal follower of Jesus, and did not fundamentally recast the message of the man from Nazareth.[2] Regardless of which of these two accounts of Paul's role in the early Christian movement is correct, the most significant point of agreement by proponents of both views is that, whether in continuity or discontinuity with the teachings of Jesus, Paul was the driving force behind the new religion and brought about its continuing existence.

Given this account of Christian origins, one would expect Paul to have left an indelible mark on other early Christian leaders and writers. In fact, that is often the case. The second-century bishop, Ignatius of Antioch, not only knew of Paul, but reveals that he knew specific details of Paul's life. In writing to the Ephesians, Ignatius declares, "You are fellow initiates of Paul, who was sanctified, who was approved, who is deservedly blessed – may I be found in his footsteps when I reach

---

1. G. Ludemann, *Paul: The Founder of Christianity* (New York: Prometheus Books, 2002).

2. D. Wenham, *Paul: Follower of Jesus or Founder of Christianity?* (Grand Rapids: Eerdmans, 1995).

God! – who in every letter remembers you in Christ Jesus" (Ign. *Eph.*
12.2). Here Ignatius knows the tradition of Paul's martyrdom.[3] As the
context makes clear, the metaphor to "be found in his footsteps" is a
reference to the shared experience of being put to death by the imperial
authorities in Rome. Ignatius also acknowledges Paul as the author of
various epistles to Christian communities; something else that Ignatius
emulates.[4] Combined with these direct references to the figure of Paul,
Ignatius also makes strong verbal references to some of Paul's letters – in
particular 1 Corinthians.[5]

Various writings among the Apostolic Fathers' texts and other early
Christian writers make similar types of reference to Paul. Polycarp
mentions Paul four times in his letter to the Philippians (Pol. *Phil.* 3.2;
9.1; 11.2, 3). Furthermore, Polycarp "knows that he [Paul] wrote 'letters'
to the Philippian congregation, and commends these documents as a
proper object of study" (3.2).[6] Thus, as Hartog notes, "[t]he letter praises
Paul and uses Pauline literature."[7] Similarly the *Shepherd of Hermas* at
points can demonstrably be seen as having "found inspiration in the letters
of Paul."[8] Examples such as this could be multiplied for other Christian
figures in the second and third centuries.

---

3. For a fuller discussion of this passage, see P. Foster, "Ignatius on Christ and the
Apostles," in *Christian Communities in the Second Century*, ed. M. Grundeken and
J. Verheyden, WUNT 342 (Tübingen: Mohr Siebeck, 2015), 109–26, esp. 111

4. For the suggestion that Ignatius" declaration that Paul makes mention of the
Ephesians in every letter is not exaggeration, but reflects the fact that the writings of
Ignatius only demonstrates knowledge of the four Pauline letters where the apostle
refers to the Ephesians, see P. Foster, "The Epistles of Ignatius of Antioch and the
Writings That Later Formed the New Testament," in *The New Testament and the
Apostolic Fathers*. Vol. 1, *The Reception of the New Testament in the Apostolic
Fathers*, ed. Andrew F. Gregory and Christopher M. Tuckett (Oxford: Oxford University Press, 2005), 159–86.

5. Ibid., 164–67.

6. M. W. Holmes, "Polycarp's *Letter to the Philippians* and the Writings That
Later Formed the New Testament," in Gregory and Tuckett, eds., *The Reception of
the New Testament in the Apostolic Fathers*, 201–2.

7. P. Hartog, ed., *Polycarp's* Epistle to the Philippians *and the* Martyrdom of
Polycarp: *Introduction, Text, and Commentary* (Oxford: Oxford University Press,
2013), 1.

8. J. Verheyden, "The *Shepherd of Hermas* and the Writings That Later Formed
the New Testament," in Gregory and Tuckett, eds., *The Reception of the New Testament in the Apostolic Fathers*, 311.

If the title of the writing contained in the artificially constructed corpus of the Apostolic Fathers, typically known as the *Second Epistle of Clement* or *Clement to the Corinthians B*[9] were meaningful, then commenting on the author's wider knowledge of Paul and his writings would be relatively straightforward. The reason for this being the case is that *1 Clement* knows of Paul by name and clearly cites some of the Pauline epistles. In fact, *1 Clement* not only refers to the name of Paul, but alludes to the background that led to Paul being put on trial in Rome; it describes a number of the physical ordeals he faced, it comments on the scope of his missionary activities, and in metaphorical language depicts his death for the faith:

> Because of jealousy and strife Paul showed the way to the prize for patient endurance. After that he had been seven times in chains, had been driven into exile, had been stoned, had preached in the east and in the west, he won the genuine glory for his faith, having taught righteousness to the whole world and having reached the farthest limits of the west. Finally, when he had given his testimony before the rulers, he thus departed from the world and went to the holy place, having become an outstanding example of patient endurance. (*1 Clem.* 5.5–7).

Furthermore, *1 Clement* makes clear reference to two of Paul's letters – Romans and 1 Corinthians[10] – and alludes to several others.[11] If it were the case that *2 Clement* were genuinely a second writing by the same author as the first letter, then one could draw upon the evident Pauline connection in the epistle known as *1 Clement* not only to assert the author's familiarity with Paul, but to strengthen the case that some of the proposed faint allusions are in fact the result of textual contact with the Pauline epistles. Whatever the genre of *2 Clement* might be,

9. The earliest extant, though incomplete, copy of *2 Clement* is found in the fifth-century Codex Alexandrinus. Although no title occurs with the actual text, in the index to the codex the text is listed as Κλημεντοσ ε[πιστολ]η β'. In eleventh-century (AD 1056) Codex Hierosolymitanus the title is given as κλημεντος προς κορινθθς β', which agrees with the Syriac form (AD 11.69–70).

10. See *1 Clem.* 35.5–6//Rom 1:29–32; *1 Clem.* 32.4–33.1//Rom 5:21–6:2a; *1 Clem.* 32.2//Rom 9:5; *1 Clem.* 47.1–4//1 Cor 1:12; *1 Clem.* 37.5–38//1 Cor 12:12, 14//1 Cor 12:20–28.

11. Gregory states "there is some slight evidence that he may also have used 2 Corinthians, Galatians, Ephesians, Philippians, Colossians, 1 Timothy, and Titus." Andrew F. Gregory, "*1 Clement* and the Writings That Later Formed the New Testament," in Gregory and Tuckett, eds., *The Reception of the New Testament in the Apostolic Fathers*, 143.

and sermon or homily appears to be the most reasonable suggestions,[12] the text certainly does not conform to the epistolary form. Moreover, the text itself does not claim to be anybody named Clement, and in the earliest surviving manuscript there is no title appended that makes that claim – it is only found as part of the index of texts contained in Codex Alexandrinus. Therefore, one cannot infer anything significant about the knowledge and use of Paul and his writings in *2 Clement* on the basis of its alleged connections with the text known as *1 Clement*.

Internal Evidence for Knowledge of Paul in 2 Clement

The relatively short text,[13] labelled as *2 Clement* (or some similar appellation in manuscripts and modern critical editions), does not name Paul or explicitly refer to a figure who might be taken to be Paul. As a result, scholars seeking traces of Pauline influence are forced to consider examples of literary borrowing from the corpus of Pauline writings.[14] The Oxford Committee that published the landmark volume *The New Testament in the Apostolic Fathers* made the general observation that "[a]s regards the N.T. Epistles, the phrase 'The Books and the Apostles' prepares us to find pretty free use of them, even though they are not formally quoted."[15] The phrase occurs in a convoluted argument that mixes Christological, ecclesiological, and soteriological concerns. The author of *2 Clement* states:

> Now I do not suppose that you are ignorant that the living Church is the body
> of Christ, for the scripture says, "God created humankind male and female."
> The male is Christ and the female is the Church. Moreover, the books and

---

12. See P. Parvis, "*2 Clement* and the Meaning of the Christian Homily," in *The Writings of the Apostolic Fathers*, ed. P. Foster (London: T&T Clark, 2007), 34–37.

13. Although divided into twenty chapters these are short units of text. In the recent critical edition of Holmes the Greek text covers fourteen pages. M. W. Holmes, *The Apostolic Fathers: Greek Texts and English Translations*, 3rd ed. (Grand Rapids: Baker, 2007), 138–64, even pages.

14. Here that corpus will be defined widely – not as a collection of seven authentic letters as is frequently described in modern literature (for a questioning of how widespread adherence to such a proposal might actually be see P. Foster, "Who Wrote 2 Thessalonians? A Fresh Look at an Old Problem," *JSNT* 35 [2012]: 150–75) – but rather as the collection was understood in antiquity; that is, as a fourteen-letter collection including the Epistle to the Hebrews. The inclusion of Hebrews is illustrated in the early Pauline P.46, as well as in later Pauline codices such as D 06, F 010, and G 012.

15. A Committee of the Oxford Society of Historical Theology, *The New Testament in the Apostolic Fathers* (Oxford: Clarendon, 1905), 125.

the apostles declare that the Church not only exists now, but has been in existence from the beginning. For she was spiritual, as also was our Jesus, but was revealed in the last days that she might save us. (*2 Clem.* 14.2)

Here there is an appeal to some nebulous and loosely defined authorities. However, the imprecise reference to "the Books" invites examination of the text of *2 Clement* to see if it is possible to identify more specifically these written sources of authority. Tuckett notes that the phraseology of "the books and apostles" is unclear. He notes that "Τὰ βιβλία alone would presumably refer to the Jewish scriptures in toto."[16] In parallel to this expression he likewise notes,

> Οἱ ἀπόστολοι would appear to refer most naturally to the writings of Christian "apostles"; the assumption would be then that the author presupposes the existence, and the authoritative nature (cf. "the apostles" parallel with τὰ βιβλία), of apostolic writings. In one way, the obvious reference would be to some (or all) of the Pauline corpus of letters. However, the reference here is extremely general and unspecific.[17]

Thus it is appropriate to examine the text of *2 Clement* to examine potential parallels with the Pauline epistles.

From the outset it is helpful to note that there are no explicit citations of any of Paul's writings, nor are there passages where significant extended verbatim agreement can be found. Typically these are the types of features one might expect in order to mount the positive case for the dependence of a later literary text on an earlier writing. Instead, in relation to making a case for the dependence of *2 Clement* on the Pauline writings, it needs to be acknowledged that the possible parallels that will be examined here at best have fleeting points of contact. The Oxford Committee came to the conclusion that the case for the use of 1 Corinthians and Ephesians could be assigned to category D, the lowest level of possible literary dependence. The committee defined category D as "books which may possibly be referred to, but in regard to which the evidence appeared too uncertain too allow any reliance to be placed upon it."[18] Furthermore, the potential parallels with Romans and 1 Timothy were unclassified, suggesting that the Committee deemed them inconsequential for establishing a literary relationship with the Pauline corpus.[19] A hundred years

16. C. M. Tuckett, *2 Clement: Introduction, Text, and Commentary*, OAF (Oxford: Oxford University Press, 2013), 253.

17. Ibid.

18. Oxford Society, *The New Testament in the Apostolic Fathers*, iii.

19. Ibid., 137.

later, reflecting on the same question and the intervening scholarly assessments, Gregory and Tuckett offered the following statement. They state, "there is a now a widespread consensus that although 'Clement' employed imagery used also by Paul, nevertheless the evidence suggests that at no point did he make conscious and deliberate reference either to Paul or to his writings, and that no direct citations of, or allusions to, Paul's letters are to be found in *2 Clement*."[20]

Here the evidence will be presented in order of what might be deemed the Pauline writings with strongest potential parallels to material in *2 Clement*. The closest alignment of language occurs with 1 Corinthians. There are three, or perhaps four potential parallels.

1 Cor 9:24–25	2 Clem. 7.1
Οὐκ οἴδατε ὅτι οἱ ἐν σταδίῳ τρέχοντες πάντες μὲν τρέχουσιν, εἷς δὲ λαμβάνει τὸ βραβεῖον; οὕτως τρέχετε ἵνα καταλάβητε. πᾶς δὲ ὁ ἀγωνιζόμενος πάντα ἐγκρατεύεται, ἐκεῖνοι μὲν οὖν ἵνα φθαρτὸν στέφανον λάβωσιν, ἡμεῖς δὲ ἄφθαρτον.	Ὥστε οὖν ἀδελφοί μου ἀγωνισώμεθα εἰδότες ὅτι ἐν χερσὶν ὁ ἀγὼν καὶ ὅτι εἰς τοὺς φθαρτοὺς ἀγῶνας καταπλέουσιν πολλοί ἀλλ' οὐ πάντες στεφανοῦνται εἰ μὴ οἱ πολλὰ κοπιάσαντες καὶ καλῶς ἀγωνισάμενοι.

In this example there are no long sequences of overlapping phrases, just a few scattered words that share corresponding semantic lexemes. For instance *2 Clement* speaks both of the contest ὁ ἀγών and the action of striving ἀγωνισώμεθα, ἀγῶνας, ἀγωνισάμενοι. In 1 Corinthians the text refers to the one who strives ὁ ἀγωνιζόμενος to exercise self-control in all things. The closest point of contact occurs with the two participles ἀγωνιζόμενος/ἀγωνισάμενοι, but the former, from 1 Corinthians, is present tense and singular, whereas the latter from *2 Clement* is aorist and plural. There are two other suggestive examples of parallel vocabulary. In *2 Clem.* 7.1 the action of being crowned is described στεφανοῦνται, whereas in 1 Cor 9:25 the text mentions a στέφανον, which is presumably a laurel wreath because of its non-enduring character. Finally, *2 Clem.* 7.1 speaks of striving after "corruptible things" (τοὺς φθαρτούς), and 1 Cor 9.25 describes athletes competing to receive a corruptible wreath (φθαρτὸν στέφανον). Therefore the case for proposing literary dependence even on the basis of shared terminology is weak. Furthermore, the two contexts differ. In 1 Corinthians Paul depicts athletic games in a stadium, whereas

20. Andrew F. Gregory and Christopher M. Tuckett, "*2 Clement* and the Writings That Later Formed the New Testament," in Gregory and Tuckett, eds., *The Reception of the New Testament in the Apostolic Fathers*, 279.

in *2 Clement* the situation envisaged is generalized as "the contest." So here neither terminology nor the wider context offer strong evidence for proposing a literary relationship. What these texts may illustrate, when set in parallel, is the existence of certain modes of discourse that circulated in early Christian writings that contrasted the value of struggling for the faith to obtain something enduring, in comparison to the human efforts that are devoted to obtaining corruptible rewards. Such a trope is common in religious writings. Consequently, one may see here both authors drawing independently on a wider pool of ideas and common terminology.

1 Cor 3:16	2 Clem. 9.3
Οὐκ οἴδατε ὅτι ναὸς θεοῦ ἐστε καὶ τὸ πνεῦμα τοῦ θεοῦ οἰκεῖ ἐν ὑμῖν. Cf. 1 Cor 6:19 ἢ οὐκ οἴδατε ὅτι τὸ σῶμα ὑμῶν ναὸς τοῦ ἐν ὑμῖν ἁγίου πνεύματός ἐστιν οὗ ἔχετε ἀπὸ θεοῦ, καὶ οὐκ ἐστὲ ἑαυτῶν.	δεῖ οὖν ἡμᾶς ὡς ναὸν θεοῦ φυλάσσειν τὴν σάρκα.

The similarity between 1 Cor 3:16 and *2 Clem.* 9.3 is the use of the two-word phrase ναὸς θεοῦ/ναὸν θεοῦ, "temple of God," with the first word differing in case, and the metaphorical application of temple of God language to believers. However, the internal parallels between the two Pauline passages are far stronger than any connection with *2 Clem.* 9.3. The two passages in 1 Corinthians are framed as questions, and explicitly state that the Spirit dwells within believers. By contrast, *2 Clem.* 9.3 is presented as a statement and there is no reference to the Spirit. Again there may be evidence for the case that the two texts are drawing upon a repository of wider religious metaphors, but the evidence for some level of direct literary dependence is not compelling. There may also be a conceptual correspondence between the use of σάρκα, "flesh," in *2 Clem.* 9.3 and the term σῶμα, "body," in 1 Cor 6:19,[21] but this is not particularly compelling. As Gregory and Tuckett state, "[w]hile a Pauline origin of this idea is not necessarily to be denied, it seems quite likely that it may quickly have become a Christian commonplace."[22]

21. See Andreas Lindemann, *Paulus im ältesten Christentum: Das Bild des Apostels und die Rezeption der paulischen Theologie in der frühchristlichen Literatur bis Marcion*, BHT 58 (Tübingen: Mohr Siebeck, 1979), 269–70.
22. Gregory and Tuckett, "*2 Clement* and the Writings That Later Formed the New Testament", 284.

1 Cor 2:9	2 Clem. 11.7; 14.5
ἀλλὰ καθὼς γέγραπται· ἃ ὀφθαλμὸς οὐκ εἶδεν καὶ οὓς οὐκ ἤκουσεν καὶ ἐπὶ καρδίαν ἀνθρώπου οὐκ ἀνέβη, ἃ ἡτοίμασεν ὁ θεὸς τοῖς ἀγαπῶσιν αὐτόν.	ἃς οὓς οὐκ ἤκουσεν οὐδὲ ὀφθαλμὸς εἶδεν οὐδὲ ἐπὶ καρδίαν ἀνθρώπου ἀνέβη. ἃ ἡτοίμασεν ὁ κύριος τοῖς ἐκλεκτοῖς αὐτοῦ.

The text from 1 Cor 2:9 is introduced with a citation formula ἀλλὰ καθὼς γέγραπται,[23] showing that the material that follows draws from pre-existing tradition. The source of the Pauline citation appears to be LXX Isa 64:3, ἀπὸ τοῦ αἰῶνος οὐκ ἠκούσαμεν οὐδὲ οἱ ὀφθαλμοὶ ἡμῶν εἶδον θεὸν πλὴν σοῦ καὶ τὰ ἔργα σου ἃ ποιήσεις τοῖς ὑπομένουσιν ἔλεον. The deviation of the form in 1 Cor 2:9 from its possible LXX *Vorlage* raises questions concerning the ultimate source of the Pauline form of the citation, and also about which branch of the Greek tradition of Isa 64:3 might stand behind 1 Cor 2:9. Further, Thiselton notes, "*1 Clement* 34.8 repeats almost exactly Paul's words."[24] The form in that context being, λέγει γὰρ Ὀφθαλμὸς οὐκ εἶδεν καὶ οὓς οὐκ ἤκουσεν καὶ ἐπὶ καρδίαν ἀνθρώπου οὐκ ἀνέβη ὅσα ἡτοίμασεν κύριος τοῖς ὑπομένουσιν αὐτόν (*1 Clem.* 34.8). Similarly, the citation in a form close to that in 1 Cor 2:9 occurs elsewhere in the corpus of writings that constitute the Apostolic Fathers: ἃ οὔτε οὓς ἤκουσεν οὔτε ὀφθαλμὸς εἶδεν οὔτε ἐπὶ καρδίαν ἀνθρώπου ἀνέβη (*Mart. Pol.* 2.3).[25] Moreover, the citation, in various forms, also occurs in *Gos. Thom.* 17; *Pr. Paul* I,25–29, and numerous other Christian writings. Given the widespread, if not virtually ubiquitous knowledge of this tradition among early Christian writers (in a form different to that preserved in extant LXX manuscripts) it is impossible to mount a convincing case for *2 Clement* drawing this material directly from 1 Corinthians. Again, it might even be the case that the Pauline citation generated the form utilized by later Christian authors, but even if that were the case it is not possible to give a specific explanation of the source of the citation in *2 Clement*. It should be noted, however, that *1 Clem.* 34.8, *2 Clem.* 11.7 and *Mart. Pol.* 11.7 (as well as LXX Isa 64:3) all preserve the order "ear...eye", whereas 1 Cor 2:9 has the order "eye...ear." This may in fact suggest that *2 Clement*

23. The syntax and force of the introductory word in 1 Cor 2:9 have generated detailed discussion. See B. Frid, "The Enigmatic ΑΛΛΑ in 1 Cor. 2.9," *NTS* 31 (1985): 603–11.
24. A. C. Thiselton, *The First Epistle to the Corinthians*, NICGT (Grand Rapids: Eerdmans; Carlisle: Paternoster, 2000), 250.
25. Hartog, *Polycarp's* Epistle to the Philippians *and the* Martyrdom of Polycarp, 278.

drew on a different branch of early Christian tradition for this citation, and that it did not result from literary knowledge of the Pauline text.

Apart from 1 Corinthians, the Pauline writing that is most likely to have some literary affinity with *2 Clement* is Ephesians. The Oxford Committee listed one passage from *2 Clement* as having a category D parallel with Ephesians, although three passages from Ephesians were set alongside the text drawn from *2 Clement*.[26] Although widely regarded by modern scholars as not stemming from the hand of Paul himself,[27] ancient writers uniformly ascribed Ephesians to Paul,[28] and from the earliest discernible stage of its circulation it was included in the Pauline collection.[29]

Eph 1:22; 5:23; 1:4	*2 Clem.* 14.2
καὶ πάντα ὑπέταξεν ὑπὸ τοὺς πόδας αὐτοῦ καὶ αὐτὸν ἔδωκεν κεφαλὴν ὑπὲρ πάντα τῇ ἐκκλησίᾳ. ὅτι ἀνήρ ἐστιν κεφαλὴ τῆς γυναικὸς ὡς καὶ ὁ Χριστὸς κεφαλὴ τῆς ἐκκλησίας καθὼς ἐξελέξατο ἡμᾶς ἐν αὐτῷ πρὸ καταβολῆς κόσμου	οὐκ οἴομαι δὲ ὑμᾶς ἀγνοεῖν ὅτι ἐκκλησία ζῶσα σῶμά ἐστιν Χριστοῦ λέγει γὰρ ἡ γραφή Ἐποίησεν ὁ θεὸς τὸν ἄνθρωπον ἄρσεν καὶ θῆλυ τὸ ἄρσεν ἐστὶν ὁ Χριστός τὸ θῆλυ ἡ ἐκκλησία καὶ ἔτι τὰ βιβλία καὶ οἱ ἀπόστολοι τὴν ἐκκλησίαν οὐ νῦν εἶναι λέγουσιν ἀλλὰ ἄνωθεν.

Again, the parallels tend to be at the level of individual words, and shared themes and concepts. Since both *2 Clement* and Ephesians are discussing the topic of the church it is unremarkable that they both share the Greek term ἐκκλησία. Also, in both texts conceptions of the church are presented with reference to the male–female pairing, although the way this is formulated in the two texts is significantly different. Ephesians is

26. Oxford Society, *The New Testament in the Apostolic Fathers*, 126–27.

27. Brown states, "A fair estimate might be *at the present moment about 80 percent of critical scholarship holds that Paul did not write Eph.*" R. E. Brown, *An Introduction to the New Testament*, ABRL (New York: Doubleday, 1997), 620. In the survey conducted by the present author, out of 109 respondents, 39 thought Ephesians to be authored by Paul, 42 thought Paul was not the author, and 28 stated they were uncertain. See Foster, "Who Wrote 2 Thessalonians?," 171.

28. One of the earliest writers to cite Ephesians and to mention Paul's special relationship with the Ephesians is Ignatius. Writing to the Ephesians he states, "You are initiated into the mysteries of the Gospel with Paul, …who in all his Epistles makes mention of you in Christ Jesus" (Ign. *Eph.* 12.2).

29. Consider both its place in Marcion's ten-letter collection of Pauline letters – although Ephesians was called Laodiceans in Marcion's corpus – and also the inclusion of Ephesians in the early Pauline manuscript P.46.

more concerned with the idea of "headship," a notion entirely absent in *2 Clement*. Instead, *2 Clement* speaks of Christ as male, and the church as female. In this way the concern appears to be about the closeness of the relationship between Christ and the church in *2 Clement*, rather than the issue of authority as in Ephesians. Notwithstanding the shared use of male and female imagery as a way of understanding Christ's relationship with the church, the different ways in which that imagery is deployed and the different ecclesiologies behind the metaphor strongly tell against direct literary dependence.[30]

In addition to the cases of parallels between 1 Corinthians, or Ephesians with *2 Clement*, there are five potential parallels between Romans and *2 Clement* set out by Gregory and Tuckett.[31] As they acknowledge, two of these cases "may be explained by independent use of a passage in Jewish Scriptures."[32] The two cases are *2 Clem.* 8.2//Rom 9:21//Jer 18:4 and *2 Clem.* 13.2//Rom 2:24//Jer 52:5b (LXX). The remaining three potential parallels are worth setting out in more detail.

Rom 4:17	*2 Clem.* 1.8
καθὼς γέγραπται ὅτι πατέρα πολλῶν ἐθνῶν τέθεικά σε, κατέναντι οὗ ἐπίστευσεν θεοῦ τοῦ ζωοποιοῦντος τοὺς νεκροὺς καὶ καλοῦντος τὰ μὴ ὄντα ὡς ὄντα.	ἐκάλεσεν γὰρ ἡμᾶς οὐκ ὄντας καὶ ἠθέλησεν ἐκ μὴ ὄντος εἶναι ἡμᾶς.

The parallel is based upon the phrase in Paul's letter: καὶ καλοῦντος τὰ μὴ ὄντα ὡς ὄντα (Rom 4:17c). There are some verbal correspondences, such as the use of the verb "to call," καλοῦντος (Rom 4:17c)//ἐκάλεσεν (*2 Clem.* 1.8), as well as the negated participle of εἰμί being used in both contexts. While this similar phraseology μὴ ὄντα ὡς ὄντα (Rom 4:17c)//μὴ ὄντος εἶναι ἡμᾶς (*2 Clem.* 1.8) may appear to present some firmer evidence for literary dependence, the Oxford Committee presented arguments against a direct relationship. Carlyle, the author of that section, noted

30. Contra J. B. Muddiman, "The Church in Ephesians, 2 Clement, and Hermas," in *The New Testament and the Apostolic Fathers*. Vol. 2, *Trajectories Through the New Testament and the Apostolic Fathers*, ed. Andrew F. Gregory and Christopher M. Tuckett (Oxford: Oxford University Press, 2005), 116.

31. Gregory and Tuckett, "*2 Clement* and the Writings That Later Formed the New Testament," 280–83.

32. Ibid., 280–81.

"[t]he correspondence is superficial, and the phrase in some sense is not uncommon."[33] Carlyle directs readers to Lightfoot, who illustrates that this type of phrase is widespread: Philo, *De Creat. Princ.* 7; Herm. *Vis.* 1.1; Herm. *Mand.* 1; and *Ps.-Clem. Hom.* 3.32.[34]

The second example to be considered here also shares a common snippet of phraseology. However, the expression does not contain any particularly unusual terms, nor is it extensive.

Rom 12:16	2 Clem. 17.3
τὸ αὐτὸ εἰς ἀλλήλους φρονοῦντες, μὴ τὰ ὑψηλὰ φρονοῦντες ἀλλὰ τοῖς ταπεινοῖς συναπαγόμενοι. μὴ γίνεσθε φρόνιμοι παρ' ἑαυτοῖς.	ἀλλὰ πυκνότερον προσερχόμενοι πειρώμεθα προκόπτειν ἐν ταῖς ἐντολαῖς τοῦ κυρίου ἵνα πάντες τὸ αὐτὸ φρονοῦντες συνηγμένοι ὦμεν ἐπὶ τὴν ζωήν.

Both passages revolve around the theme of concord between believers, and they express this through a call to like-minded thinking. The harmonious life that is called for by Paul is expressed as "be of the same mind towards one another" (τὸ αὐτὸ εἰς ἀλλήλους φρονοῦντες, Rom 12:16). Much the same idea is put forward in *2 Clement*: "that all being of the same mind" (ἵνα πάντες τὸ αὐτὸ φρονοῦντες, 17.3). This type of exhortation is the basis of common appeals in Christian epistles and homilies. Moreover, the language of concord is prominent in other early Christian writings.[35]

Rom 1:21	2 Clem. 19.2b
διότι γνόντες τὸν θεὸν οὐχ ὡς θεὸν ἐδόξασαν ἢ ηὐχαρίστησαν, ἀλλ' ἐματαιώθησαν ἐν τοῖς διαλογισμοῖς αὐτῶν καὶ ἐσκοτίσθη ἡ ἀσύνετος αὐτῶν καρδία.	ἐνίοτε γὰρ πονηρὰ πράσσοντες οὐ γινώσκομεν διὰ τὴν διψυχίαν καὶ ἀπιστίαν τὴν ἐνοῦσαν ἐν τοῖς στήθεσιν ἡμῶν καὶ ἐσκοτίσμεθα τὴν διάνοιαν ὑπὸ τῶν ἐπιθυμιῶν τῶν ματαίων.

The possible parallel revolves around two shared terms, although the lexical forms are not equivalent, and might also be established on the

---

33. Oxford Society, *The New Testament in the Apostolic Fathers*, 128.

34. J. B. Lightfoot, *The Apostolic Fathers*. Part One, *Clement*, 2 vols. (London: Macmillan, 1889), 2:214.

35. J.-P. Lotz, *Ignatius and Concord: The Background and Use of the Language of Concord in the Letters of Ignatius of Antioch* (New York: Lang, 2007).

basis of related thematic ideas discussing the practice of evil by humans. Paul refers to those who do not know God as one whose heart "was darkened" (ἐσκοτίσθη, Rom 1:21). Clement, while addressing believers cohortatively,[36] speaks of lapses in behaviour when "we are darkened" (ἐσκοτίσμεθα) in understanding (*2 Clem.* 19.2b).[37] The use of the notion of "darkness" to describe ethical deficiencies is hardly a Pauline innovation. In the Septuagint the concept of darkness is used metaphorically to describe sadness, lack of perception, separation from God, and moral stumbling.[38] The second shared term involves the different forms of the verb γινώσκω. The participial form γνόντες is used in Rom 1:21, while the present indicative is used γινώσκομεν in *2 Clem.* 19.2b. Nothing can be based upon the shared use of this extremely common verb.

This example has a further level of complexity since there is also similar phraseology to that in *2 Clem.* 19.2b, "we are darkened in our understanding" (ἐσκοτίσμεθα τὴν διάνοιαν), and that in Eph 4:18 "they are darkened in their understanding" (ἐσκοτωμένοι τῇ διανοίᾳ),[39] as well as *1 Clem.* 36:2, "our understanding having been darkened" (ἐσκοτωμένη διάνοια ἡμῶν).[40] Once again this appears to be an example of widespread early Christian language to describe either the absence of belief, or the condition in which believers found themselves prior to belief, or to refer to ethical lapses when believers obscure the light of God that is seen as now dwelling within them.

Given the ubiquity of the metaphor of darkness as a description of moral deficiency, and also the not uncommon language of one's "understanding being darkened," this language hardly provides a secure basis for seeing a direct literary dependence on the Pauline letters. However, one has to be open to the possibility that Pauline language has been taken up widely in early Christian communities and has begun circulating independently

36. The unity of chs. 19–20 with the rest of the text is debated. However, ch. 19 commences with an address to "brothers and sisters" that strongly suggests that the exhortation is directed towards believers.

37. Tuckett observes that "the writer here does use the first-person plural, including himself (at least on the surface) with those he is directly addressing and implicitly criticizing: the general approach is conciliatory, not directly polemical." Tuckett, *2 Clement*, 295 n. 21.

38. LXX Dan 2:22; Jer 8:21; 14:2; Lam 4:8; 5:17; Ezek 31:15; Mic 6:14; Zeph 1:15.

39. Without further comment Carlyle simply listed this as "unclassified." See Oxford Society, *The New Testament in the Apostolic Fathers*, 127.

40. Tuckett notes these two potential parallels, but sets little store by them. Tuckett, *2 Clement*, 295, n. 22.

of its original context. In that case, it is possible that Pauline phraseology might be the ultimate origin of the expression "we are darkened in our understanding" contained in *2 Clem.* 19.2b. However, even if that is so, then it appears that the author is drawing upon language that has been transmitted through a chain of traditional Christian usage, and perhaps not directly drawn from the epistles of Paul.[41]

Some potential parallels between *2 Clement* and the letters to Timothy have been suggested. Gregory and Tuckett mention three possible parallels with 1 Timothy and one with 2 Timothy.[42] The first is the following.

1 Tim 1:15	2 Clem. 2.5, 7
πιστὸς ὁ λόγος καὶ πάσης ἀποδοχῆς ἄξιος, ὅτι Χριστὸς Ἰησοῦς ἦλθεν εἰς τὸν κόσμον ἁμαρτωλοὺς σῶσαι, ὧν πρῶτός εἰμι ἐγώ.	τοῦτο λέγει ὅτι δεῖ τοὺς ἀπολλυμένους σῴζειν. οὕτως καὶ ὁ Χριστὸς ἠθέλησεν σῶσαι τὰ ἀπολλύμενα καὶ ἔσωσεν πολλούς ἐλθὼν καὶ καλέσας ἡμᾶς ἤδη ἀπολλυμένους.

Perhaps even more so than previous examples, the parallelism is extremely generalized and appears to be based on one of the most central Christian theological affirmations – namely, that Christ's coming had soteriological effect. However, the differences in the two passages are striking. In 1 Tim 1:15 the introductory formulation, "the saying is faithful and worthy of all acceptance," which if paralleled in *2 Clement* would have provided a strong basis for asserting literary dependence, is in fact entirely absent. In the Clementine text, there is no reference to "sinners" or "the world," or even to the apostolic declaration that states Paul's self-identification as a sinner "of whom I am the first." So the most distinctive elements from 1 Tim 1:15 are absent from *2 Clem.* 2.5, 7. Similarly, the most distinctive elements contained in *2 Clem.* 2.5, 7 are in fact absent from 1 Tim 1:15. The language of "perishing" (ἀπολλυμένους) that occurs twice in *2 Clement* is not present in 1 Timothy. Neither is the "calling" (καλέσας) of Christ mentioned. The three slightly parallel items, with the form in 1 Timothy listed first in Greek are:

41. Gregory and Tuckett state that these "parallel references to a darkening of the understanding are examples of a commonplace, so there is no reason to posit literary dependence on either Romans or Ephesians." Gregory and Tuckett, "*2 Clement* and the Writings That Later Formed the New Testament," 283.
42. Ibid., 288–89.

1. A Christological title   Χριστὸς Ἰησοῦς / ὁ Χριστὸς
2. Infinitive forms of the verb "to save"   σῶσαι / σώζειν
3. A form of the verb "to come"   ἦλθεν / ἐλθὼν

Admittedly this leaves aside shared usage of the definite article and the conjunction καί, for those who might see those elements adding any further weight to the case for literary dependence. Furthermore, the "coming" is that of Christ in both cases, and it is that coming that brings about salvation. While the Pauline influence on Christian ideas of salvation must be acknowledged, the similarities between these two passages is only to be found at the most general level of a shared statement, in different forms, related to a central Christian theological affirmation.[43]

The second potential parallel drawn from 1 Timothy displays an equally slender base of shared terminology.

1 Tim 4:16	2 Clem. 15.1 (cf. 2 Clem. 19.1)
ἔπεχε σεαυτῷ καὶ τῇ διδασκαλίᾳ, ἐπίμενε αὐτοῖς· τοῦτο γὰρ ποιῶν καὶ σεαυτὸν σώσεις καὶ τοὺς ἀκούοντάς σου.	Οὐκ οἴομαι δέ ὅτι μικρὰν συμβουλίαν ἐποιησάμην περὶ ἐγκρατείας ἣν ποιήσας τις οὐ μετανοήσει ἀλλὰ καὶ ἑαυτὸν σώσει κἀμὲ τὸν συμβουλεύσαντα μισθὸς γὰρ οὐκ ἔστιν μικρὸς πλανωμένην ψυχὴν καὶ ἀπολλυμένην ἀποστρέψαι εἰς τὸ σωθῆναι.
	Ὥστε ἀδελφοὶ καὶ ἀδελφαί μετὰ τὸν θεὸν τῆς ἀληθείας ἀναγινώσκω ὑμῖν ἔντευξιν εἰς τὸ προσέχειν τοῖς γεγραμμένοις ἵνα καὶ ἑαυτοὺς σώσητε καὶ τὸν ἀναγινώσκοντα ἐν ὑμῖν μισθὸν γὰρ αἰτῶ ὑμᾶς τὸ μετανοῆσαι ἐξ ὅλης καρδίας σωτηρίαν ἑαυτοῖς καὶ ζωὴν διδόντας τοῦτο γὰρ ποιήσαντες σκοπὸν πᾶσιν τοῖς νέοις θήσομεν τοῖς βουλομένοις περὶ τὴν εὐσέβειαν καὶ τὴν χρηστότητα τοῦ θεοῦ φιλοπονεῖν.

Again, any correspondence appears to be at the most general level, with 1 Tim 4:16 and *2 Clem.* 15.1 being related by their common concern that believers work towards the assurance of salvation. For the author of

---

43. Gregory and Tuckett also note possible parallels with Matt 18:11 and Luke 19:10. However, they conclude that these appear "too commonplace for it to be likely that it is a quotation of any of the parallels noted." Ibid., 289.

1 Timothy the certainty of salvation both for Timothy and for those who hear his message is brought about by being watchful both in conduct of life and through adhering to the apostle's teaching. As Towner observes, "[t]hus on the one hand, Paul urges attentiveness to Timothy's own personal conduct and character (i.e. lit. 'yourself'). On the other hand, Timothy is to be equally attentive to his faithfulness in communicating apostolic teaching to the church."[44] Therefore, a full commitment to development of character and intellect is befitting for Timothy, if he is to ensure that "he will bring both his congregation and himself to final salvation."[45] This exhortation in 1 Timothy may be given in response to some pressing situation, real or perceived, that involves deviant teaching from the author's perspective.[46] By contrast, while *2 Clem.* 15.1 (and *2 Clem.* 19.1) is concerned with the salvation of "a wandering and perishing soul," the key issue is ἐγκράτεια, "self-control." Thus the pattern of behaviour of believers is emphasized here, but by using a term of great importance in Greek philosophical virtue lists; "we consider what we call 'moderation' or 'self-control' (ἐγκράτεια) to be a virtue" (Aristotle, *Nic. Eth.* 2.7). So while *2 Clem.* 15.1 shares with 1 Tim 4:16 concern over moral conduct as being related to salvation, it frames the call for appropriate conduct in vastly different terms, perhaps drawing upon prevailing Hellenistic ethical perspectives. The centrality of ethical discussions in philosophical and religious texts tells against seeing any direct literary dependence in this case.

The third example drawn from 1 Timothy and *2 Clement* demonstrates shared verbal expressions in material that might be classified as primitive doxologies. However, Carlyle states, "it seems impossible to lay too much on this, as it is very possible that they are both based on liturgical forms."[47]

1 Tim 1:17	2 Clem. 20.5
Τῷ δὲ βασιλεῖ τῶν αἰώνων, ἀφθάρτῳ ἀοράτῳ μόνῳ θεῷ, τιμὴ καὶ δόξα εἰς τοὺς αἰῶνας τῶν αἰώνων, ἀμήν.	Τῷ μόνῳ θεῷ ἀοράτῳ πατρὶ τῆς ἀληθείας τῷ ἐξαποστείλαντι ἡμῖν τὸν σωτῆρα καὶ ἀρχηγὸν τῆς ἀφθαρσίας δι' οὗ καὶ ἐφανέρωσεν ἡμῖν τὴν ἀλήθειαν καὶ τὴν ἐπουράνιον ζωήν αὐτῷ ἡ δόξα εἰς τοὺς αἰῶνας τῶν αἰώνων ἀμήν.

44. P. H. Towner, *The Letters to Timothy and Titus*, NICNT (Grand Rapids, Michigan: Eerdmans, 2006), 326.

45. I. H. Marshall, *The Pastoral Epistles*, ICC (Edinburgh: T&T Clark, 1999), 571.

46. Mounce describes the perceived false teaching described as the "Ephesian heresy." See W. D. Mounce, *The Pastoral Epistles*, WBC 46 (Nashville: Thomas Nelson, 2000), xlix–lxxvi, 264–65.

47. Oxford Society, *The New Testament in the Apostolic Fathers*, 129.

There are here indeed examples of shared phrases, although it also needs to be acknowledged the doxology is more expansive in nature. The three key points of similarity, with the element from 1 Timothy listed first, are:

1. The address to "only God"   μόνῳ θεῷ / Τῷ μόνῳ θεῷ
2. Use of dative adjective "invisible"   ἀοράτῳ / ἀοράτῳ
3. The closing formula   τιμὴ καὶ δόξα εἰς τοὺς αἰῶνας τῶν
                                      αἰώνων, ἀμήν. / αὐτῷ ἡ δόξα εἰς τοὺς
                                      αἰῶνας τῶν αἰώνων ἀμήν.

While the final element may appear decisive for establishing a literary relationship, having a sequence of seven identical words, this doxological formula, or something very close to it, is widespread. Marshall suggests that the background for such doxologies "is to be found in the Hellenistic synagogue (Tob 13:7, 11)."[48] Such doxologies are frequent in the NT: Rom 16:27; Gal 1:5; Phil 4:20; 2 Tim 4:18; Heb 31:21; 1 Pet 4:11; 5:11; Rev 1:6; 5:13; 7:12. A similar doxology becomes attached to the Matthean version of the Lord's Prayer in later manuscripts: Matt 6:13 perhaps composed on the basis of LXX 1 Chr 29:11–13.[49] It cannot be determined if this addition of the concluding doxology to the Lord's Prayer pre-dates the composition of *2 Clement*. However, even if it is later than the composition of *2 Clement* it does reflect the wider phenomenon whereby fairly standard liturgical or doxological elements are attached to various early Christian traditions or formulations. Therefore, despite the extended sequence of verbatim agreement between 1 Tim 1:17 and *2 Clem.* 20.5, the shared phrase is such a widespread formulation that it is not possible to establish a direct relationship between the Pauline text and *2 Clement*.

Perhaps more intriguing is the combination of the extended verbatim agreement of seven words in combination with the shared use of the term ἀοράτῳ "invisible," and the description of the deity as μόνῳ θεῷ, the "only God." However, the case for literary dependence would certainly be more compelling if any one of these elements were unique to 1 Tim 1:17, or even not in such common circulation among Christian writers.

---

48. Marshall, *The Pastoral Epistles*, 404.
49. Manuscripts that preserve the variant Ὅτι σοῦ ἐστιν ἡ βασιλεία καὶ ἡ δύναμις καὶ ἡ δόξα εἰς τοὺς αἰῶνας. Ἀμήν at the end of Matt 6.13, or a related form of it, include, L W Θ 0233 𝑓[13] 33 𝔐 f g[1] k q sy bo[pt].

2 Tim 4:1	*2 Clem.* 1.1
Διαμαρτύρομαι ἐνώπιον τοῦ θεοῦ καὶ Χριστοῦ Ἰησοῦ τοῦ μέλλοντος κρίνειν ζῶντας καὶ νεκρούς, καὶ τὴν ἐπιφάνειαν αὐτοῦ καὶ τὴν βασιλείαν αὐτοῦ.	Ἀδελφοί οὕτως δεῖ ἡμᾶς φρονεῖν περὶ Ἰησοῦ Χριστοῦ ὡς περὶ θεοῦ ὡς περὶ κριτοῦ ζώντων καὶ νεκρῶν καὶ οὐ δεῖ ἡμᾶς μικρὰ φρονεῖν περὶ τῆς σωτηρίας ἡμῶν.

This final example is less striking. The parallel involves another standard, and ultimately creedal, affirmation[50] concerning Jesus' role as judge of the living and the dead. The two texts express that belief in slightly different forms. In 2 Tim 4:1 the statement focuses on the charge given by Paul to Timothy, which is solemnized by being made in the presence of Christ Jesus "who is about to judge the living and the dead" (τοῦ μέλλοντος κρίνειν ζῶντας καὶ νεκρούς). The eschatological motivation continues with the reference to the coming epiphany of Jesus. By contrast, in *2 Clem.* 1.1, rather than offering a charged depiction of the expectation of the role of "judging" that Christ will exercise in the near future, there is a more measured description of the permanent office Jesus Christ holds as "judge of the living and the dead" (κριτοῦ ζώντων καὶ νεκρῶν). While the expressions in the two texts are somewhat similar, they are far from being identical. Moreover, these two forms express a widespread Christian belief, and hence they probably offer nothing of significance for establishing the case for literary dependence between *2 Clement* and 2 Tim 4:1.

Conclusions

The evidence surveyed does not allow one to make a positive case for the knowledge of Paul and his letters by the author of *2 Clement*. This of course is not the same thing as saying that the author did not know of Paul and his writings. Rather, what is concluded is that in relation to the extant text of *2 Clement* there is no decisive evidence for establishing literary dependence between that text and any of the Pauline letters, or even of the author's knowledge of Paul. Thus the title of the present study speaks neutrally of the "absence" of Paul, in the sense that references to either the apostle or his writings are not demonstrably present in the text of *2 Clement*. This is not necessarily surprising, nor does it say anything

50. Various forms of the Nicene Creed contain affirmation such as καὶ ἐρχόμενον κρῖναι ζῶντας καὶ νεκρούς (text of First Council of Nicaea, 325) or καὶ πάλιν ἐρχόμενον μετὰ δόξης κρῖναι ζῶντας καὶ νεκρούς (text reaffirmed at First Council of Constantinople, 381).

about the status of the Pauline writings or the apostle in the period when *2 Clement* was written. For, as Gregory and Tuckett have noted, "[t]he silence of 'Clement' concerning Paul is not unparalleled in the Apostolic Fathers or in other Christian literature of the second century, and it is not necessary to draw any negative inferences from this."[51] The absence of references to Paul in other second-century writers, such as Justin Martyr, is more striking.[52] In relation to Justin the absence is puzzling given that his writings were composed in Rome, a city that was associated with the martyrdom of Paul already by the second century. Moreover, Justin's contemporary in Rome, Marcion, appears to be familiar with and in fact to be responsible for the circulation of a collection of ten of Paul's letters. This raises the more intriguing possibility that Justin was not simply unaware of Paul and his letters, but that he was "reacting against Marcion and his ultra-Pauline version of Christianity."[53] In relation to Justin, these are fascinating, yet ultimately unprovable theories.

While the case of the absence of references to Paul and his writings in the works of Justin may allow one to explore various possibilities concerning the intentional non-reference to Paul, this is not the case with *2 Clement*. Firstly, nothing specific is known about the location or date of composition of *2 Clement*. So unlike Justin's Roman setting where one might expect some level of knowledge of Paul this cannot be inferred for *2 Clement*. There is also another factor that should be borne in mind. The extant writings of Justin are of significantly greater length than the text of *2 Clement*. Perhaps the author of *2 Clement* simply saw no need to refer to Paul or his writings in his own homiletic text. Authors never deploy all they know in a single text. Given the brevity of *2 Clement*, perhaps drawing upon Pauline material was not seen as being necessary in such a brief literary composition, or perhaps they were not immediately relevant to the way in which the author wished to develop his major themes. While the answer will never be known, perhaps this most mundane explanation is the correct one.

---

51. Gregory and Tuckett, "*2 Clement* and the Writings That Later Formed the New Testament," 279. See also D. Rensberger, "As the Apostle Teaches: The Development of the Use of Paul's Letters in Second-Century Christianity" (PhD diss., Yale University, 1981).

52. P. Foster. "Justin and Paul," in *Paul and the Second Century*, ed. M. F. Bird and J. R. Dodson, LNTS 412 (London: T&T Clark, 2011), 108–25.

53. Ibid., 124.

Chapter 5

PAUL AND THE *EPISTLE OF BARNABAS**

James Carleton Paget

Opening Remarks

In contrast to *1 Clement*,[1] the letters of Ignatius,[2] Polycarp,[3] and the
Epistle to Diognetus,[4] the writer of the *Epistle of Barnabas* never
explicitly mentions Paul or his letters. This might be held to be consistent
with the fact that no character from what one might call early Christian
history is mentioned by Barnabas, save for Jesus and "the apostles,"[5]
and the latter are not mentioned by name. It might also be explained by
reference to the aim of his letter, which, for whatever reason, is bound up
with the exegesis of what Christians came to call the Old Testament, and
so mention of so-called New Testament witnesses, or texts which later
came to be a part of that developing corpus, might seem at cross-purposes
to the writer's purpose.

Lying behind such a set of explanations accounting for the *Epistle
of Barnabas*'s silence about Paul is the niggling feeling that (a) a letter
attributed to Barnabas, the companion of Paul, even if pseudonymous,

* This article repeats a number of observations found in an earlier piece on the
same subject; see J. Carleton Paget, "Paul and the Epistle of Barnabas," *NovT* 38
(1996): 359–81.
1. See *1 Clem.* 5.5 and 47.1.
2. See Ign. *Eph.* 12.2 and Ign. *Rom.* 4.3.
3. See Pol. *Phil.* 3.2 and 9.1.
4. Although Paul is never explicitly mentioned by name in *Diognetus*, at 12.5 the
author quotes 1 Cor 8:1, attributing it to the "apostle."
5. See *Barn.* 5.9, where there is an explicit reference to the "apostles," and 8.3,
where "those who proclaim the Gospel (εὐαγγελισάμενοι)" are clearly the twelve
apostles (note in this context the reference to the fact that there were twelve of them
as there were twelve tribes of Israel).

would surely have some reference to the latter; (b) the author of *Barnabas* probably did have a knowledge of the Pauline corpus, in whatever form; and (c) in many ways his own interests and concerns might have been well served by Paul. The first observation is an intriguing one. While almost all students of the epistle agree that *Barnabas* is pseudonymous,[6] a number argue that the attribution to Barnabas, Paul's erstwhile companion, which is attested relatively early,[7] seems secondary precisely because the letter makes no attempt to exploit the attribution, either by reference to Barnabas, or those who were associated with him.[8] The second observation simply begs the question and it will be part of the aim of the present study to demonstrate whether in fact the epistle shows knowledge of any or some of Paul's epistles. In part the observation is based upon what people, in contradistinction to another period in the history of the discussion, have begun to believe was the widespread knowledge of Paul in the second century (certainly in comparison with most other leading characters associated with the New Testament), though there remain voices who are more skeptical on the subject.[9] Against such a background, it is difficult,

---

6. For a summary of the arguments, see J. Carleton Paget, *The Epistle of Barnabas: Outlook and Background*, WUNT 2/64 (Tubingen: Mohr, 1994), 3–7. These pertain to date (the letter is thought to have been written too late for Paul's companion still to be alive) and content (the letter contains opinions about the law and the Jewish people difficult to attribute to the Barnabas we learn about in Gal 2:1–10). The few who support the authenticity of the attribution, argue for an early date (in the early 70s) and for the possibility that Barnabas was alive then, and for a change of opinion in Barnabas as a result of the Jewish revolt and the apparent persecution Christian Jews suffered at that time. On this see S. Tugwell, *The Apostolic Fathers* (London: Chapman, 1989), 44; and a refutation of his arguments in Carleton Paget, *The Epistle of Barnabas*.

7. The earliest attribution of the letter to Barnabas, the companion of St. Paul, is in Clement of Alexandria, *Strom.* 2.6.31; 2.7.35; 2.20.116; 5.10.63. Apart from G1's *subscriptio* (Ἐπιστόλη Βαρνάβα τοῦ ἀποστόλου συνεκδήμου Παύλου τοῦ ἁγίου ἀποστόλου), none of the other textual witnesses to the epistle ascribe it to Barnabas, Paul's companion (this includes Sinaiticus, Hierosolymitanus and the probably early third-century Latin translation).

8. The first to argue this was H. Windisch, "Der Baranbasbrief," in *Handbuch zum Neuen Testament. Ergänzungsband: Die Apostolischen Väter III* (Tübingen: Mohr, 1920), 413; who claimed that the ascription was made to aid dissemination of the letter, and resulted from the fact that Barnabas was known to be a Levite (Acts 4:36), and so was an appropriate author for a text which took such a strong interest in matters to do with the temple and the law (see *Barn.* 2; 3; 5–7; 9; 10; 15 and 16).

9. See Carleton Paget, "Paul and the Epistle," 359–63, for a brief account of this debate, beginning with Harnack's famous judgment about the minimal influence

so the argument goes, to imagine that Barnabas did not know Paul. The third observation emerges from the fact that in broad terms at least, the concerns of *Barnabas* – the relationship of non-Christian Judaism with Christianity, the law and the covenant (to name but a few) – coincide with some important interests of the Pauline corpus. Here the problem we face is not dissimilar to what scholars encounter when faced with the absence of any direct reference to Paul in the extant writings of Justin Martyr. The failure of the latter to mention Paul seems odd for the same reason that Barnabas's might seem odd. They share many interests in common and it is almost impossible to conceive of the fact that Justin did not know of Paul. Indeed it is Justin's failure to mention Paul, more perhaps than any other early Christian writer, which spawned theories accounting for the absence of interest in Paul on the part of Christian writers.[10]

of Paul on the second century (Adolf von Harnack, *Marcion. Das Evangelium vom fremden Gott*, 2nd ed. [Leipzig: J. C. Hinrichs, 1924], 12) and ending up with a strong assertion of the broadly opposite position in Andreas Lindemann, *Paulus im ältesten Christentum. Das Bild des Apostels und die Rezeption der paulinischen Theologie in der frühchristlichen Literatur bis Marcion*, BHT 58 (Tubingen: Mohr, 1979) (and repeated in many other places including Lindemann, "Paulus in den Schriften der Apostolischen Väter," in *Paulus Apostel und Lehrer der Kirche* [Tübingen: Mohr, 1999], 252–79; and, in the same volume, "Paulus im zweiten Jahrhundert," 294–322). That Lindemann's judgment has by and large won the day is seen in the works of Dassmann 1979 (written independently of Lindemann), and W. Babcock, ed., *Paul and the Legacies of Paul* (Dallas: Southern University Methodist Press, 1990), and most recently in Michael Bird and Joseph R. Dodson, eds., *Paul and the Second Century*, LNTS 412 (London: T&T Clark, 2011), 4, where Dodson in the introduction to the volume writes: "Therefore, when it comes to the role of the apostle in the identity of second-century Christianity, the question is not: 'did Paul have an influence?'" He then goes on to outline a number of questions which are significant, such as the extent of Paul's influence and how it manifested itself. For a recent expression of a view closer to Harnack, but more all-consuming than his, see M. Vinzent, *Christ's Resurrection in Early Christianity and the Making of the New Testament* (Farnham and Burlington: Ashgate, 2012).

10. For recent discussion of the absence of any mention of Paul in Justin, see especially Judith Lieu, "The Battle for Paul in the Second Century," *ITQ* 75 (2010): 12; and Paul Foster, "Justin and Paul," in Bird and Dodson, eds., *Paul and the Second Century*, 108–25. Both of these writers, in particular the second, argue for the lack of evidence of an influence of Paul upon Justin. For Foster, the silence is almost "deathly," though he refuses to commit to any of the three explanations he presents which could account for the silence, some of which build upon observations originally made by Harnack (the absence of a collection of Paul's letters readily available to him; Paul's association with Marcion; the fact that Paul's letters did not share the authority of the Old Testament at this point in Christian history). See Foster, "Justin

The primary aim of this piece, as already stated, will be to see if the *Epistle of Barnabas* does in fact betray knowledge of Paul's letters, at whatever remove. If this is the case, then an attempt will be made to show in what way he has used this material. This subject has become a focus of attention in recent years as interest in the question of reception has become a growing concern of scholars. Most recently, Daniel Marguerat, in a stimulating article in *New Testament Studies*,[11] has suggested that Paul was received in at least three sometimes intersecting ways, described as documentary, biographical and doctoral; and scholars interested in the subject have warmed to such a typology of usage.[12] Insofar as I shall be addressing the question of *Barnabas*'s reception of Paul, it will only be at the so-called doctoral or doctrinal level, for that is, I would contend, the only level of reception which the epistle would appear to betray insofar as it betrays any knowledge of Paul.[13]

Mention of reception leads necessarily to remarks about the problem of determining how we might discern knowledge of Paul's letters in documents which do not formally refer to him (or indeed documents which do this but where questions arise as to which letters the author of the document knew). The matter, of course, is complex and has often been approached with a lack of subtlety, seen in an over-reliance on precise verbal parallels, or the replication of so-called Pauline opinions. As many have noted since the time of the writer of 2 Peter,[14] and probably before that, too, judging from Paul's letters, Paul and his ideas as presented in his letters could be interpreted in a variety of ways, and Paul could become the foundation stone for views which one would find it difficult to associate him with. His letters and his personality were early matters of contention, generating a variety of interpretations.[15] Moreover, Paul could

and Paul," 124. For a strong endorsement of the view that Justin shows knowledge of Paul, see O. Skarsaune, *The Proof from Prophecy: A Study in Justin Martyr's Proof-Text Tradition: Text-Type, Provenance, Theological Profile* (Leiden: Brill, 1987), whose arguments are directly refuted by Foster, "Justin and Paul," 117–23.

11. Daniel Marguerat, "Paul après Paul: une histoire de reception," *NTS* 54 (2008): 317–37. It should be noted that Marguerat builds on similar typologies found in the work of a number of his predecessors, such as Lindemann and Bovon, the later of whom he discusses.

12. For its influence, see especially Bird and Dodson, eds., *Paul and the Second Century*.

13. For possible biographical interest, see my comments on *Barn*. 5.9 below.

14. See 2 Pet 3:16.

15. See especially Lieu, "The Battle," 1–14. Lieu's essay plays up the diversity of usage to which Paul could be put, seeing it as broadly reflecting the complex struggles and diverse identities of the second-century Christian church. An intelligent set of

be the starting point for ideas, which would transform themselves into positions apparently very different from his own. This means that, on the one hand, we need, at least negatively, to be wary of excluding knowledge of Paul on the grounds of the "unpauline" nature of what is being asserted and show ourselves aware of the complex manner in which Paul was understood in the burgeoning church. On the other hand, we need also to be mindful of the fact that even when we are able to point to an apparent similarity of wording between one writer and Paul, that need not imply that the source from which the apparent quotation was taken was in fact a letter of Paul, there being a possibility that it was attained through a mediated form of his letters, possibly an epitome, as one scholar has suggested.[16] Additionally, a similar note of caution needs to be attached to the presence of concepts in individual writers, which we might associate exclusively with Paul. Not only could these have been mediated to the writer through channels other than a reading of Paul's letters, but it is often difficult to know that a particular concept, associated with Paul's letters, was exclusively Pauline.[17]

observations on this point is also found in Dale C. Allison, "James 2:14–26: Polemic against Paul, Apology for James," in *Ancient Perspective on Paul*, ed. T. Nicklas, A. Merkt and J. Verheyden (Göttingen: Vandenhoeck & Ruprecht, 2013), esp. 140–43. Clare Rothschild, *Hebrews as Pseudepigraphon* (Tübingen: Mohr Siebeck, 2009), in supporting her assertion that Hebrews is a Pseudepigraphon, has a number of helpful things to say about adaptation of Paul's ideas.

16. See Marguerat, "Paul après Paul," 335, who, noting Luke's somewhat inadequate summaries of Paul's theology in Acts (cf. Acts 13:38b–39), in which he often uses Pauline-sounding language, suggests that his source for such knowledge was an epitome of the theology of Paul. Such an epitome does not exist, but Marguerat suggests that it more adequately accounts for what we find in Luke than positing Lukan knowledge of Paul's letters. What is especially intriguing about Marguerat's article is his suggestion that we should not give priority to Paul's letters in considering how he was received into the burgeoning church (his importance as an actor in the church's history, the biographic Paul of Acts, should be accorded much more importance than it customarily is in assessments of his reception), and that from his death until the formation of a letter collection, dated by him to 100 CE, the reception of Paul was complex and multifarious, a phenomenon which would continue, and was encouraged, by the image Paul presents of himself in his own letters.

17. Many of these cautionary observations have been applied to those who are interested in discerning knowledge of the Gospels in second-century sources. For an engagement with this matter see especially Andrew F. Gregory and Christopher M. Tuckett, "Reflections on Method: What Constitutes the Use of the Writings That Later Formed the New Testament in the Apostolic Fathers?," in *The New Testament and the Apostolic Fathers*. Vol. 1, *The Reception of the New Testament in the Apostolic*

Barnabas: *Some Introductory Remarks*

The pseudonymous *Epistle of Barnabas*[18] was written between 95 and 135 CE, probably in Alexandria.[19] Agreement upon its purpose has proven elusive, not least because its opening and closing chapters, with their strongly ethical and paranetical character, can appear only tangentially to be connected to its often polemical main section, running from chs. 2 to 16, much of which is taken up with the interpretation of scripture (the Christian Old Testament), which *Barnabas* associates with gnosis, and out of which emerges a singular and striking theology.[20] In this there is one law, the law given by Moses, and that law, if interpreted correctly (that is, non-literally) is in and of itself perfect. For *Barnabas* a view which argues that the original Mosaic law, in particular the so-called second law, or deuterosis,[21] in some accounts given after the worship of the golden

Fathers, ed. Andrew F. Gregory and Christopher M. Tuckett (Oxford: Oxford University Press, 2005), 61–82. We should also note that the question of the reception of Paul's letters has been an especially contentious one on account of debates of a later kind, which sought to argue about the extent to which the church lost sight of what some, especially in the light of the Reformation, took to be the central thrust of Paul's theology (the issue of grace and justification). Here study of reception becomes an evaluative process rather than a strictly historical one. On this see M. Wiles, *The Divine Apostle: The Interpretation of St Paul's Epistles in the Early Church* (Cambridge: Cambridge University Press, 1967), who states that his own study will eschew such evaluative judgments, but ends up, inevitably perhaps, in making them. See especially Wiles, *The Divine Apostle*, 132–39.

18. See n. 6 above.

19. For a summary of these arguments relating to date and provenance, see Carleton Paget, *The Epistle of Barnabas*, 9–42. See also Reidar Hvalvik, *The Struggle for Scripture and Covenant: The Purpose of the Epistle of Barnabas and Jewish-Christian Competition in the Second* Century, WUNT 2/82 (Tübingen: Mohr Siebeck, 1996), 17–42, for a different reading of the evidence. The epistle was definitely written after 70 (see 16.3) but how far after is the question. Some take 16.3–4, which seems to assume a rebuilding of the temple, in whatever form, and to refer either to a mooted expectation of such a thing at the time of Nerva, or an actual building, perhaps of a pagan temple on the site of the destroyed second temple, at the outbreak or the conclusion of the Bar Kokhba revolt.

20. For contrasting views of the purpose of the document, see Hvalvik, *The Struggle for Scripture*, 57–206; and most recently, James N. Rhodes, *The Epistle of Barnabas and the Deuteronomic Tradition*, WUNT 2/188 (Tübingen: Mohr Siebeck, 2004), esp. 201–6.

21. For the idea of a deuterosis, understood as the law given after the Golden Calf incident and including additions to the Ten Commandments, see Justin, *Dial.* 19.5–6; 22.1–5; 46.5 and *passim*; and Irenaeus, *Haer.* 4.15.1.

calf, was somehow flawed or problematic, a concession to Jewish hard-heartedness, and brought to an end by the arrival of Christ. *Barnabas*, in contrast to this position, affirms the Mosaic law in its entirety, even at one point declaring the excellence of Moses' legislation.[22] Consistent with this, *Barnabas* almost never links Christ to the fate of the law, or indicates that he is the bringer of a new law or a law of Christ.[23] True, the law, like the whole of scripture, is correctly interpreted by those who are Christians, who have had the gift of understanding implanted in them (6.10; 9.9; 16.8–10), and this is ultimately linked to the activity of Christ (4.9; 14.4) and his death (see chs. 5–7); but the fate of the law is almost never linked to Christ. An extension of *Barnabas*'s position on the law is found in his conviction that there is just one covenant, given by Moses at Sinai, lost at that point by the Jews and then, through Christ's death, given to the Christians.[24] Linked to this is *Barnabas*'s understanding of typology.[25] Here the sense of historical continuity, found in the fact that an event in the past in its own right has a relationship, albeit a subservient one, to one in the future, seems almost muffled to the point of being mute. Rather what we have is a set of correspondences in which any sense of the historical validity of the type has disappeared, and in which Jewish history and practices have their only meaning in Christian assertion (see 12.2 and 5).[26] For *Barnabas* there is a comprehensiveness to the contents of scripture and those contents are exclusively Christian to such an extent that the history of Israel is not divine history except and insofar as it looks forward to Christian phenomena.[27] In all of this, then, *Barnabas*

22. See *Barn.* 10.12 and the assertion: "See how well Moses legislated!"

23. *Barn.* 2.6 might be regarded as a possible exception to this, on which see our discussion below.

24. See *Barn.* 4.8 and 14.4–6. For an alternative interpretation of these texts which sees them as referring only to a proleptic loss of the covenant and so as an example of hyperbole, see Rhodes, *The Epistle of Barnabas*, 1–16.

25. See 6.11; 7.3, 7, 10, 11; 8.1; 12.2, 5, 6, 10; 13.5; 16.5.

26. Note especially *Barnabas*'s claim that Moses stretches out his hands when the Amalekites are attacking the Israelites in order that he should make a type of the cross and of the one who was about to suffer, that they might realize that if they did not believe in him, they would be attacked forever (*Barn.* 12.5, referring to Num 21). See the comment in Ferdinand R. Prostmeier, "Antijüdische Polemik im Rahmen christlicher Hermeneutik. Zum Streit über christliche Identität in der Alten Kirche. Notizen zum Barnabasbrief," *ZAC* 6 (2002): 48: "In Barn 12 wird nun gezeigt, dass nicht nur das, was Mose geboten hat (see ch. 10), pneumatischen Hintersinn besitzt, sondern ebenso alles, was er tat." The sole referent point of Moses' actions is Christ and all Jewish hopes are absorbed into that event.

27. Ibid., 55.

emerges as radically conservative insofar as he appears to exclude ideas of a developing salvation history through which God's purposes are made manifest and posits a type of unitary unchanging scriptural/Christian truth.

In adopting such a position *Barnabas* pours aspersions on non-Christian Jews – they appear as disinherited from the beginning of their history, as perpetual misinterpreters of their own scriptures in contrast to the Christians,[28] their understanding dimmed by the lust of their flesh and perverted by the devil;[29] and as a consequence of their befuddled under-standing, crucifiers of Jesus.[30]

Evidence of Adaptation of Paul

So to what extent can we see Paul, lingering behind this theology?[31] Some are inclined to argue that *Barnabas* is simply a radicalized form of Paulinism, a point along a mooted Pauline trajectory. Such a case could

28. For contrasts between Jewish and Christian interpretation, often described in terms of "them" and "us," see, *inter alia*, *Barn.* 2.4, 7, 9, 10; 3.1, 3, 6; 4.7, 8, 14; 5.2, 11, 12; 6.7, 8, 12–13; 7.1, 2, 5; 8.7; 9.4; 10.9, 12; 11.1, 11; 13.1; 14.4, 5; 15.8. For the separatist tendencies of the epistle, see M. Kok, "The True Covenant People: Ethnic Reasoning in the Epistle of Barnabas," *Studies in Religion/Science religieuses* 40 (2011): 81–97.

29. See *Barn.* 9.4 and 10.9.

30. See *Barn.* 5.4 and 7.9.

31. The history of the discussion of the subject of the *Epistle of Barnabas*'s rela-tionship to Paul is not an extensive one (indeed since the publication of my article in 1996, no substantive discussion of the matter has been undertaken in spite of an increased interest in the reception of Paul in the early church). The discussion (up to 1996) is summarized in Carleton Paget, "Paul and the Epistle," 367 n. 33. Positions oscillate between those of P. Meinhold, "Geschichte und Exegese im Barnabasbrief," *ZKG* 59 (1940): 255–303, who argued that *Barnabas*'s worldview had its origins in Paul, though it was a radicalized version of Paul's views, an idea partially captured in Pfleiderer's view that *Barnabas* represented a form of gnosticizing deutero-Paulinism, present, in his opinion, in Hebrews, Colossians, Ephesians and the epistles of Ignatius (O. Pfleiderer, *Paulinismus. Ein Beitrag zur Geschichte der urchristlichen Theologie*, 2nd ed. [Leipzig: J. C. Hinrichs, 1890], 393), to the views of P. Vielhauer, *Geschichte der urchristlichen Literatur: Einleitung in das Neue Testament, die Apokryphen und die Apostolischen Väter* (Berlin: de Gruyter, 1975), 606–7; and K. Wengst, *Schriften des Urchristentums. Didache, Barnabasbrief, zweiter Klemensbrief, Schriften an Diognet* (Darmstadt: Wissenschaftliche Buchgesellschaft, 1984), 118, who tenta-tively posit *Barnabas*'s opposition to Paul, to Lindemann's view that *Barnabas* has no knowledge of Paul, or at least his letters (probably held by Ferdinand Prostmeier, *Der Barnabasbrief* [Göttingen: Vandenhoeck & Ruprecht 1999], 129; and definitely by Hvalvik, *The Struggle for Scripture*, 34).

be argued generally, in a comparison of *Barnabas*'s outlook as discussed above, with that of Paul on the same issues, or it could be argued more specifically, by concentrating on passages where Pauline allusions or echoes might be discerned. What I write below shall combine both approaches.

In this context some have wanted to point to the possible influence of 2 Cor 3.[32] Importance here is attached to: (a) the harsh comparison of the ministry associated with Sinai, and that associated with Christ ("For in comparison with its surpassing splendor what was splendid has come to have no splendor at all. For if what faded away [καταργούμενον] came with splendor, how much more splendid what is permanent must be"); (b) the strong claim that even to this day the Jews read the Torah with a veil, their minds hardened (ἐπωρώθη τὰ νοήματα, 2 Cor 3:14), here exploiting the fact that Moses descended from Mount Sinai with a veil around his face; and (c) the reference in the context of a discussion of the giving of the law at Mount Sinai to the Christians as somehow possessing what they need to serve God in their heart and not on tablets, a point made with a possible allusion to Jer 31:33, which *Barnabas* could be seen to pick up at 4.11; 14.5; 16.8–10, the first two references appearing in the context of a discussion of events at Sinai.

Of course, what Paul is saying in 2 Cor 3 is not the same as what *Barnabas* is saying. Paul seems to be implying that the first dispensation was somehow flawed at its inception, and that through Christ a better dispensation has been introduced;[33] but this is a different position to *Barnabas*, for whom there appears to be only one covenant, associated with the one law, which the Christians, through their superior under-standing, and through the actions of Christ, have inherited and understood correctly (at this point possibly reflecting Paul). Such a view excludes what seems implicit even in this passage in Paul, that there was once a legitimate covenant with the Jews, however inevitable its abrogation may have appeared to be.[34] Moreover, there are no verbal echoes of 2 Cor 3 in any passages known to us in *Barnabas*.[35] But the relevant point here may

32. W. Horbury, "Jewish–Christian Relations in Barnabas and Justin Martyr," in *Jews and Christians: In Contact and Controversy* (Edinburgh: T&T Clark, 1998), 142–43.

33. Paul does accord the first dispensation value, but it is a value which pales into insignificance when compared with the dispensation Christ brings. See esp. 2 Cor 3:10–11.

34. On their different uses of καταργέω see below.

35. Even where there is some shared vocabulary, as in the use of καταργέω, the meaning attributed to the word is different.

not be that *Barnabas* has failed to reproduce what Paul has said in 2 Cor 3 but rather that 2 Cor 3 could have acted as an inspiration for what he went on to assert about God's dealings with the Jews.[36] So in this view *Barnabas* has simply radicalized aspects of Paul's writing about the Jews in much the same way as Marcion could be construed to have acted. But this remains no more than a conjecture.

A perhaps better example of a place where *Barnabas* could be seen to be adapting a Pauline position is in *Barn.* 13. The chapter is taken up with arguing which of the people is now the first people, implicitly the Jews or the Christians (though neither word is used). By referring to two separate biblical stories, that of Jacob and Esau (Gen 25) and Manasseh and Ephraim (Gen 48), and by exploiting the notion that in both stories the younger child takes the place of the older, *Barnabas* advances his view that the Christians are rightfully the first people. He then proceeds to another argument, which involves noting that Abraham is the father of the gentiles (and not of the Jews); and it is here that we have the best evidence for knowledge of Paul. At 13.7 *Barnabas* appears to be quoting Gen 15:6 (LXX), here reminding us of Paul in Gal 3:6 and Rom 4:3,[37] although he reads ἐτέθη for Paul's and the LXX's ἐλογίσθη. What seems especially to imply knowledge of Paul at this point, however, is the quotation of Gen 17:4, 5 where *Barnabas* adds the words, τῶν πιστευόντων δι᾽ ἀκροβυστίας, which appear in Rom 4:11, but are not presented as part of an Old Testament citation.[38] This would seem to indicate that the words from Genesis have become conflated with the words from Paul, and that no other suggestion will explain this phenomenon except that knowledge of Romans, at whatever remove, has intruded.[39] Given that *Barnabas* betrays some knowledge of a Pauline passage here,

36. The difficulty here is that *Barnabas* makes a great deal of the smashing of the tablets by Moses, not of the fact that they are tablets of stone, the point which Paul seeks to exploit. For Paul it is a question of καταργούμενον (present), not as in *Barnabas*, κατάργηθεν (past).

37. Citation of this passage is almost exclusively associated with Paul in the New Testament, and where it is not, e.g. James 2:23, it can be argued that Paul is in the background.

38. See J. Carleton Paget, "The *Epistle of Barnabas* and the Writings That Later Formed the New Testament," in Gregory and Tuckett, eds., *The Reception of the New Testament in the Apostolic Fathers*, 240, quoting Bartlett.

39. See Carleton Paget, "*The Epistle* and Writings," 240; also Prostmeier, *Der Barnabasbrief*, 463, esp. n. 40, quoting Windisch with approval. We should also note that *Barnabas*'s use of τί οὖν at 13.7 could be taken as a Paulinism, reflecting Rom 4:1.

what is interesting is that *Barnabas* does not argue the same case as Paul does in Rom 4. For Paul the key to the passage lies in developing the idea that belief, rather than circumcision, is central to the gentiles entering the messianic community, not in excluding the Jews.[40] But in *Barnabas* the passage is concerned to prove that the Christians, not the Jews, are the children of Abraham, that is, there is not just a desire to argue for the inclusion of gentiles without circumcision but also a desire to argue for the exclusion of Jews.[41] This is seen not only from the context of the chapter, which begins with an interpretation of the stories of Jacob and Esau (Gen 25) – found already in Paul, but used in a quite different way[42] – and Manasseh and Ephraim (Gen 48), in which the place of an older child (Judaism) is supplanted by that of a younger one (Christianity), and the deduction is made that the Christians are the children of God, and the Jews excluded (13.6), but also from the observation that *Barnabas* has revised his Pauline source, if that is what it is. For where Paul in Rom 4:11 assumes that Jews, "those of the circumcision," can be justified if they follow Abraham's faith, *Barnabas* only refers to the first half of Paul's statement, namely that

40. See also Gal 3:28.

41. On this see Prostmeier, "Antijüdische," 46; "Dabei ist zu beachten, dass der Scopus der Argumentation nicht die Frage der Beschneidung, sondern der Identifizierung des Gottesvolks ist." On this see also R. Werline, "The Transformation of Pauline Arguments in Justin Martyr's 'Dialogue with Trypho,'" *HTR* 92 (1999): 79–93, esp. 86, who makes a similar point about Justin's use of Paul in broadly the same context in a series of chapters in the *Dialogue*: "Justin's use of the Abraham story in *Dialogue* 11, 23, and 119 and their contexts indicates to what extent he has drifted from Paul's original purposes. For Paul, in Rom 4, the Abraham story proves that both Jew and Gentile share equal standing before God because both have a faith in their common father, Abraham. Justin, however, has employed Paul's argument but has transformed it by coupling it with his ideas of the new covenant, new people, and understanding of the Hebrew prophets as witnesses to Jewish unfaithfulness and rejection."

42. Paul cites Gen 25 and the story of Jacob and Esau, like *Barnabas*, emphasizing the need for the greater to serve the lesser (see Rom 9:11), but the development of the story in Paul has nothing to do with the supplanting of one people by another. Rather it is presented as a justification of God's sovereign will (that is, there is no hint in the passage that Jacob = the Christians and Esau = non-Christian Jews). On this see P. Lanfranchi and J. Verheyden, "Jacob and Esau: Who Are They? The Use of Romans 9:10–13 in Anti-Jewish Literature of the First Centuries," in *Ancient Perspective on Paul*, ed. T. Nicklas, A. Merkt and J. Verheyden (Göttingen: Vandenhoeck & Ruprecht, 2013), 297–316.

"I have made you a father of the nations who believe in God while uncircumcised" (*Barn.* 13.7).[43]

What is striking, then, about the example above is that *Barnabas* shows signs of knowing a Pauline source but reproducing it tendentiously, or at least producing a theology incompatible with it. *Barnabas* has apparently ignored the possible implication both of Paul's arguments in Rom 3–4 and indeed Rom 11 (where Paul appears to be clear about an ongoing relationship with the Jewish people on behalf of God even without belief in Jesus, clearly evidenced in his statement, "All Israel will be saved" at 11:26) to produce his own more antagonistic and exclusivist interpretation.[44] One could, speculatively, argue that *Barnabas* could have arrived at his position through reading Gal 4:23–31, or 1 Thess 2:14–16. Here rejection of those Jews who do not follow Christ seems to be much stronger, in the way it is by implication in the passage we have already looked at, namely 2 Cor 3. This must remain a conjecture and the absence of any verbal allusion to or echo of these Pauline excerpts in *Barnabas* could militate against such a suggestion.[45] It may also be significant that *Barnabas* makes no allusion to any of the scriptural passages referred to in Gal 4:23–31,

43. As I have argued elsewhere, there is evidence in the first part of the chapter of *Barnabas* making use of a source, which argued for an apparently conventional view of the two people, Jews first, and then with the coming of Christ, the gentiles, so as to deny the Jews the status of *ever* being the children of God (see Carleton Paget, *The Epistle of Barnabas*, 163–64). For a similarly tendentious use of Paul, see *Gos. Thom.* 53, where the author seems to betray knowledge of Rom 2–3 on circumcision, but appears to ignore Paul's claim that there is an advantage to circumcision, and rather to contradict that view. On this see S. Gathercole, *The Composition of the Gospel of Thomas: Original Languages and Influences* (Cambridge: Cambridge University Press, 2012), 229–33. Michael Bird, "The Reception of Paul in the *Epistle to Diognetus*," in Bird and Dodson, eds., *Paul and the Second Century*, 87–88, sees Paul as lying behind the attack in *Diognetus* upon Jewish practices and Jewish ideas of election, at 3.1–4.6, but is clear that the author's exclusion of any idea of Jewish election is an obvious misrepresentation of Paul's theology.

44. This point is made in Lanfranchi and Verheyden, "Jacob and Esau," 301–3.

45. There is possibly an allusion to 1 Thess 2:16 at *Barn.* 5.11, where both relate sinful Jewish activity (in *Barnabas*'s case relating to the persecuting of Christ, in Paul's case to attempts to hinder the work of Christian missionaries) to the filling out of sins. We should, however, note that *Barnabas* uses a different verb for "fill out" from Paul (ἀνακεφαλαίω in *Barnabas*; ἀναπληρόω in Paul), and more importantly, he relates the filling out to Christ's incarnation, that is, for *Barnabas* Christ came in the flesh in order that the sins of the Jews would be filled out (by killing him, in the same way as they had persecuted the prophets). In Paul such filling out appears to be related more generally to Jewish attempts to prevent Christians from proselytizing

including Isa 54:1 and Gen 21. But what remains the case is that in a passage with strong evidence of allusions to Paul, we see a somewhat different theology emerging.

Similar evidence, though less compelling, of *Barnabas* bending a Pauline idea to suit his own purposes may be found in *Barn*. 2.6. Here the writer, in the midst of a passage in which he attacks Jewish understanding of the sacrificial laws, refers to the abolition of "a new law of our Lord Jesus Christ without yoke of necessity" (ὁ καινὸς νόμος τοῦ κυρίου ἡμῶν Ἰησοῦ Χριστοῦ ἄνευ ζυγοῦ ἀνάγκης). The reference to a law associated with Christ has its parallel in Rom 6:2 and 1 Cor 9:21; the verb καταργέω appears in a number of places in Paul referring to the abolition of Jewish prescriptions (see Rom 3:31; 7:6; 2 Cor 3:7, 11, 13; Eph 2:15) and could be taken as a feature of Pauline vocabulary;[46] and Paul also mentions the yoke of the law, or as he puts it, the yoke of slavery (Gal 5.1: ζυγῷ δουλείας). The problem with this parallel is that the phrase does not accord precisely with anything found in Paul, who never uses the term "the new law of Christ."[47] But that may be to adopt too literalist and clumsy an approach to the question of dependency.[48] What is interesting is that if we do assume a Pauline allusion, however muffled, *Barnabas*'s understanding of the new law seems different from that of Paul,[49] for *Barnabas*'s new law does not imply a diminishing of the Mosaic law's importance as the result of the arrival of Christ, or a possible critique of its contents, or even its partial

gentiles. The fact that *Barnabas* relates their filling out of sins with the persecution of the prophets does, however, broadly echo Paul's sentiments in 1 Thess 2:15, though the sentiment is found in Matthew, who refers to filling out sins (see Matt 23:31–32).

46. Apart from an occurrence in Luke 13:7 and Heb 2:14, the verb appears only in letters of Paul.

47. Καινός is never associated with νόμος in Paul, though it is associated with "covenant," an important concept for *Barnabas* (see 1 Cor 11:25; 2 Cor 3:6), but one he never associates with the word 'new'.

48. For further evidence of literary dependence, see Carleton Paget, *"The Epistle and the Writings,"* 242–44.

49. We should note that the reference to a yoke of necessity (ζυγοῦ ἀνάγκης) could have a non-Pauline provenance, implying that there were two laws, the first being the Ten Commandments, and the second being the laws which were presented after the worshipping of the Golden Calf. These laws, some Christians argued, were given to curb the idolatrous tendencies of the Jews, shown in their worship of the calf (that is, they were given out of necessity, or in some cases, as a punishment). In such a view the authority of the second law, or *deuterosis*, is considerably diminished and necessarily falls away when Christ comes. For this see Carleton Paget, *The Epistle of Barnabas*, 106–7, and references to Irenaeus, *Haer.* 4.15.1, the *Didascalia*, and Cyprian, *Test.* 1.13.

replacement,[50] all possible, though by no means uncontested, interpretations of Paul's usage.[51] Rather it refers to the excellence of the law he is espousing, which is the only law (Moses' law) interpreted correctly (hence "new" law) with the aid of Christ. Again *Barnabas* does not develop this idea in explicit conversation with an alternative understanding of the new law – what in fact we may be privy to here is an appropriation of a term which in its new context takes on a meaning different from the one it originally had.[52]

Such apparent adaptation of Pauline language, possibly seen both in the passage just discussed but with greater probability in the passage in *Barn.* 13 about the identity of God's people, could be seen by some as coming close to confrontation with a Pauline position, and I want to spend the next section looking at a number of places where such opposition has been espied. I shall follow this with some comments on a few other pieces of evidence which have been taken to betray a Pauline influence; and then finish with some tentative conclusions.

Evidence of Opposition to Paul?

The view that the *Epistle of Barnabas* is opposing Paul, which, of course, implies the influence of Paul on *Barnabas* but from a negative perspective, can be advanced at a general level. In such a view *Barnabas*, appropriately perhaps, given the implication of the so-called incident at Antioch, recorded at Gal 2:11–15, where *Barnabas* appears to find himself at odds with Paul,[53] is seen as a harsh critic of what some take to be the standard

---

50. See Gal 3:19; Rom 10:4, and the passages already mentioned where καταργέω appears to refer to the law's abolition.

51. As well as subsequent uses, though here with a clear association of newness with the law.

52. So *Barnabas* would appear to have changed the meaning of καταργέω from "abrogate" to "reject." Interestingly, the latter meaning is not listed as a possibility in Liddell and Scott (see LSJ, 908). G. W. H. Lampe, ed., *A Patristic Greek Lexicon* (Oxford: Clarendon, 1961), 716, follows Liddell and Scott, citing 'render unnecessary' as a meaning appropriate to *Barnabas*, but allowing for a translation of κατάργησις as refutation. For a fascinating discussion of *Barnabas*'s use of the verb, see D. R. Schwartz, *Studies in the Jewish Background of Christianity*, WUNT 1/60 (Tübingen: Mohr Siebeck, 1992), 147–53; here arguing for the meaning of abrogate and one which has as its primary reference events associated with the Bar Kokhba revolt. For an attempt to refute Schwartz's ideas, see Carleton Paget, *The Epistle of Barnabas*, 29.

53. It has been pointed out that 1 Cor 9:6, and to a lesser extent, Col 4:10, imply that the two men rekindled their friendship after the incident at Antioch.

Christian idea of a two-covenant understanding of salvation history.[54] An allusion to this idea is seen in 4.6b, where, in a textually contested section of the epistle, *Barnabas* attributes the following words to what appear to be opponents: "The covenant is both theirs and ours."[55] These words, which are taken from a slightly emended version of the Latin text of *Barnabas*, are interpreted by those who would see *Barnabas* as an opponent of a two-covenant view, and by extension of Paul, as meaning that the covenant was once theirs but is now ours, *Barnabas*'s citation in some sense being a caricature of their opinion. The problem here is that such an interpretation of the words attributed to a mooted opponent seems unduly forced. The natural meaning of the words could either imply the need to obey the law of Moses as the Jews do (here understanding

54. Sebastian Moll, *The Arch-Heretic Marcion* (Tübingen: Mohr, 2010), 142, questions the extent to which *Barnabas*'s one covenant/unitary view would have been "unusual" (here quoting Hvalvik, *The Struggle for Scripture*, 92). He argues that there is little evidence for a two-covenant position before *Barnabas*, dismissing Pauline evidence (2 Cor 3:6–18) and that from Hebrews as too early to be important, and that from Justin and Irenaeus, the other witnesses to a two covenant theology cited by Hvalvik, as too late. Moll goes on to note that neither Ignatius nor the writer of *1 Clement* have "a reflective distinction between two different covenants/testaments," pointing out that both writers take for granted the idea that the Old Testament is a Christian book, adding that there is little sign of the two-covenant theology in *Hermas* either. "Therefore," he concludes, "Barnabas is by no means the isolated instance we occasionally see him as, but may on the contrary and with good reason be called a man of his times" (Moll, *Marcion*, 143). Moll's argument has some strong points – I agree, for instance, that it is difficult to discern an explicit two-covenant theology in *1 Clement* or Ignatius. But should Moll be allowed to dismiss evidence from the New Testament, especially evidence from Hebrews, which seems to come from a similar theological milieu to *Barnabas* (see Carleton Paget, *The Epistle of Barnabas*, 214–25) as too early, or that from Justin and Irenaeus as too late, especially when we consider the fact that both authors could have been using sources? Also we could add Melito, *Peri Pascha*, to the witnesses to a two-covenant schema, at least by implication. Moreover, as I have attempted to show, there are signs in *Barnabas* of knowledge of a two-covenant schema; and conversely, very little evidence, outside *Barnabas*, of an explicitly one-covenant schema.

55. For the various readings and arguments in favor of L's reading (*testamentum illorum et nostrum est*) see Prostmeier, *Der Barnabasbrief*, 191–92. For another reading, which gives the passage a quite different sense, see James Rhodes, "*Barnabas* 4.6B: The Exegetical Implications of a Textual Problem," *VC* 58 (2004): 365–92; and for an attempted refutation of his emendation, see J. Carleton Paget, "Barnabas and the Outsiders: Jews and Their World in the *Epistle of Barnabas*," in *Communities in the Second Century: Between Ideal and Reality*, ed. M. Grundeken and J. Verheyden (Tübingen: Mohr Siebeck, 2015), 182–83.

covenant as essentially another way of talking about the law), or be an attempt to show that Jews and Christians share the same heritage, and so are in some senses the same thing.[56]

The next place where some have espied an anti-Pauline position occurs in *Barn.* 9, which concerns itself with the subject of circumcision. After a series of attempts to argue against the literal implementation of circumcision, at one point attributing literal understanding of the commandment to the work of an evil angel (9.4),[57] *Barnabas* writes, "But you will say, 'Surely the people has received circumcision as a seal (σφραγίδα)?' Yes, but every Syrian, and Arab, and all the priests of the idols have been circumcised. Are all of these within their covenant?" (*Barn.* 9.6). Such a statement could be taken as refuting Paul's claim at Rom 4:11 that circumcision is in fact a seal. "In this interpretation of the verse the interlocutor's question ('But surely the people have received circumcision as a seal?') does not imply the need for Christians to be circumcised, but rather is an assertion that circumcision did once have a valid role in salvation history."[58] The strength of the case just made might be said to lie in (a) the fact that *Barnabas* may already have betrayed knowledge of Rom 4 in 13.7 (see above); and (b) that σφράγις is a term Paul uses in connection with circumcision and yet is not found in the Old Testament.[59] But the view that *Barnabas* is opposing a Pauline interpretation of circumcision here seems unlikely. First, *Barnabas* is principally taken up in this passage with attacking the literal implementation of circumcision, not with arguing against a particular inner-Christian view of its previous function in Jewish history. Secondly, the term σφράγις, though not biblical, was probably a Jewish term for circumcision, and so would be perfectly understandable in the mouth of a Jewish or Jewish Christian interlocutor.[60]

56. For a position close to this one see *Ps.-Clem. Hom.* 8.6, where the author appears to accept the legitimacy of both an ongoing covenant with Moses (implicitly for the Jews) and one with Jesus (implicitly for the Christians). For a discussion of the passage, see J. Carleton Paget, "*Pseudo-Clementine Homilies* 4–6: Rare Evidence of a Jewish Literary Source from the Second Century CE," in *Jews, Christians, and Jewish Christians in Antiquity* (Tübingen: Mohr Siebeck, 2010), 445.

57. See J. Carleton Paget, "Barnabas 9.4: A Peculiar Verse on Circumcision," in *Jews, Christians, and Jewish Christians in Antiquity*, 77–89.

58. Carleton Paget, "Paul," 372.

59. See Gen 17:11b, where circumcision is referred to as σημεῖον διαθήκης, an assertion not so far from what *Barnabas* assumes in this passage where circumcision is implicitly seen as a seal of the covenant.

60. See a number of rabbinic passages in this context, e.g., *Ber.* 9.3; *Exod. R.* 19; *Tg. Cant.* 3.8. All of these are sources later than *Barnabas*, and so the possibility remains that the use of the term in the rabbinic sources is a response to Christian

Two more passages need to be brought forward as possibly implying opposition to Paul. Both are related to the question of Paul's influence on *Barnabas*'s theological position, understood as his interpretation of the biblical heritage.

In *Barn.* 4.9b–13, in the midst of a passage exhorting his readers to behave in a way which will prevent what he terms the entry of the wicked one, he writes: "Let us flee from all vanity, let us utterly hate the deeds of wickedness. Do not by retiring apart live alone as if you were already made righteous (ὡς ἤδη δεδικαιωμένοι), but come together and seek out the common good" (4.10). *Barnabas* seems here to be in the presence of over-enthusiastic Christians, who think that they are already saved, and it is precisely the use of a form of the verb δικαιόω (δεδικαιωμένοι) which has led some to think that Paul lies in the background.[61] Of course, even if we accept that such people are influenced by Paul, it is another step to assert that *Barnabas*'s opposition to them reflects opposition to Paul himself. Interestingly, *Barnabas*'s response to these individuals is to appeal to their status as temples of God (γενώμεθα ναὸς τέλειος). This argument could be said to reflect a similar position to Paul in 1 Cor 3 and 4 where the apostle refers to people as temples of God (3:16–17), admittedly in a different context and with different language, and goes on, in the next chapter of his epistle, to rebuke those who think themselves already satisfied (ἤδη κεκορεσμένοι) and believe that they have become rich (ἤδη ἐπλουτήσατε, 4:8), although Paul does not connect the two assertions. Indeed, it might be the case that *Barnabas*, far from opposing Paul in this instance, is attacking individuals who misread elements of his theology, though proving this would be very difficult. However, such an interpretation is not certain and some might think that in my own comments I assume too easily that *Barnabas* was an accurate reader of Paul.[62]

claims – but this would seem unlikely. In Exod 28:11, 21, the seal is associated with priestly gems representing the twelve tribes of Israel and this usage may hint at why it was a word associated with the covenant in *Barnabas*. For further associations of the word both in Jewish and Christian literature, see Prostmeier, *Der Barnabasbrief*, 363–64 n. 50.

61. Prostmeier (ibid., 220–21) fails to discuss δεδικαιωμένοι at all (and certainly not its Pauline resonances), though he hints at the fact that he thinks the individuals concerned showed signs of a "blasphemische Selbstgerechtigkeit."

62. Discussion of this passage's relationship to Paul immediately suggests the same kinds of issues which arise when discussing the relationship of the writer of the Epistle of James and Paul as this relates to James 2:14–26. Some have understood the passage as a direct assault upon Paul's theology, others as a correction of false interpretations of his theology, and others as a simple endorsement of what Paul in fact taught. Allison, who sets out a helpful and nuanced typology of these various

At 5.9 *Barnabas* states that Jesus chose as his disciples those who had
sinned beyond all others (ὄντας ὑπὲρ πᾶσαν ἁμαρτίανἀνομωτέρους). Some
years ago Lindemann suggested that such a harsh reference could not be
made of the disciples but thought it more likely to refer to passages in
Paul where he referred to his sinful past (1 Cor 15:8–11; Eph 3:8; 1 Tim
1:15).[63] Lindemann is clear that this need not refer negatively to Paul or
his theology, but it might be a warning not to accord him too high a status.
The reference seems, however, to fit the disciples of Jesus much better, not
least because *Barnabas* is referring at this point in his letter to the incarnation, and indeed it is not so unlikely that a tradition about the sinfulness
of the disciples had in fact grown up, not least because the disciples
had been sinners.[64] Origen, interestingly, repeats this tradition about the
disciples found in *Barnabas*, but nowhere disputes the obvious reading
(that Jesus' disciples were sinners).[65] It is not impossible that *Barnabas*
has Paul somewhere in the back of his mind, just as Origen proceeds to
discuss Paul in the same passage from *Contra Celsum*, but he is not to
the forefront (or directly linked with the citation from *Barnabas*), and it
is very difficult to see the reference as negative in any oppositional sense.

Miscellaneous Indications of Knowledge of Paul

Some years ago Klaus Wengst argued for the view that the theology of
Barnabas, at least in terms of the atmospherics of its piety and morality,
reflected the Pastorals.[66] So both *Barnabas* and the Pastorals show a

positions (see Allison, "Polemic," 123–25), presents a fascinating case for the old
view that the author is refuting what he understands to be a Pauline position. He
supports this by noting the considerable evidence we have in Acts, in Paul's letters,
and in the work of other early readers of Paul of what we might term antinomian
misinterpretations of Paul. Why should we assume that James was an apparently more
careful reader of Paul than these individuals? Allison goes on to argue that James is,
as he suggests at the beginning of his letter, addressing Jews, both within and outside
the church, and he is attempting to distance himself from positions associated with
the likes of Paul in 2:14–26. See esp. Allison, "Polemic," 141–43. Allison's reasoning
could equally be applied to the *Barnabas* case we have discussed, not least because
we know that some members of Paul's communities did engage in an over-realized
view of his eschatology (cf. 1 Cor 4:8). See now Dale C. Allison, *James*, ICC (New
York, London etc.: Bloomsbury T&T Clark, 2014), 444–57.
    63. Lindemann, *Paulus im ältesten Christentum*, 276.
    64. E.g. see Mark's representation of the disciples, though this hardly fits the
hyperbolic language of *Barnabas*.
    65. See *Cels.* 1.63.
    66. Wengst, *Schriften*, 117–18.

knowledge of the relationship between faith and justification (*Barn*. 13.7; 2 Tim 4:7) but nowhere exploit the matter theologically; they both use the word for righteousness in terms of moral righteousness (*Barn*. 1.4, 6; 4.12; 5.1; 1 Tim 6:11; 2 Tim 2:22; 3:16); they define faith in terms of "Gläubigkeit" (*Barn*. 1.4, 5; 1 Tim 1:5, 19; 5:8); they both speak of baptism in terms of renewal (*Barn*. 6:11, 14; Titus 3:5); and see Christ's work as bound up with atonement (*Barn*. 5.1; 7.2; 14.6; 1 Tim 2:6; Titus 2:14); and they emphasize hope (*Barn*. 1.4, 6; 4.8; 11.11; 1 Tim 1:16; Titus 1:2), and judgment (*Barn*. 4.12; 5.2; 7.2; 15.5; 21.6; 1 Tim 5:24; 2 Tim 4:1). But little of what Wengst refers to here has a compelling specificity about it (could we not find numbers of sources which reflect a similar religious and moral atmosphere?), and the Pastorals seem a long way from *Barnabas*'s exegetical traditions or his altogether looser view of hierarchy.

Finally, some have wanted to argue that *Barnabas*'s reference to the second goat in his Christocentric development of the ritual of the Day of Atonement as ἐπικατάρατος recalls language found in Gal 3:10 and 13, which is not repeated anywhere else either in the New Testament or the other writings normally designated "The Apostolic Fathers." But too much cannot be built upon this:[67] after all, the term ἐπικατάρατος in its original context in Paul comes from Deut 27:26, and it is equally possible that *Barnabas* could have taken the word from there; in a similar development of the two goats ritual, Tertullian (at *Marc*. 3.7.7), uses the word *maledictus* to describe the goat, a Latin equivalent of ἐπικατάρατος; and *Barnabas* nowhere betrays any knowledge of the original context of Paul's usage in Galatians.

Final Reflections

Some might argue that there is little in what I have written above which requires that *Barnabas* knew Paul's letters, and in the strictest sense that is true. And yet I still believe that there are some grounds for thinking that *Barnabas* did know at the very least traditions associated with Paul. So, for instance, it is difficult to conceive of how *Barnabas* could have written the final section of ch. 13 of his epistle if he was not in contact with a Pauline tradition; or that those who refer to themselves as already justified do not in such a claim reveal muffled connections with a Pauline idea; or that *Barnabas*'s reference to a new law of Christ at 2.6 betrays a Pauline origin. It is important also to note that the claim that *Barnabas* did know Paul would seem *prima facie* likely, given the general popularity of Paul,

---

67. On this see Carleton Paget, "*The Epistle* and the Writings," 242.

in whatever guise, in the second century moving forward, and that his failure explicitly to mention him is explained on the grounds that *Barnabas* is primarily taken up with arguing about the scriptures, understood as the Christian New Testament. But none of this proves that he was working with Paul's letters, that he gleaned what he did from a reading of a Pauline letter, rather than a tradition influenced by Paul.[68] If we assume some sort of knowledge of Paul in *Barnabas*, discerning the level of influence of the former upon the latter is more difficult. Insofar as there were some influences, I am clear that these were not negative, that is that *Barnabas* forged his own position in opposition to Paul. Insofar as anything is likely, it is that *Barnabas* has adapted Pauline positions to accommodate his own view in circumstances which, in terms of the relationship to non-Christian Jews, were different from anything Paul faced.[69] But even this is a precarious position. If it were true, one might perhaps have expected more evidence of engagement with passages in Paul whose polemical aspect appeared to the fore, especially passages from Galatians and possibly Philippians; and one might also have expected more references than we

68. Foster, "Justin and Paul," 118, in a discussion of Justin's reference to circumcision and uncircumcision in *Dial.* 92.21–22, accepts that it "does resonate with material from Rom 2:25–27," but refuses to accept that it betrays any reading on the part of Justin of Paul's epistles. For him Paul's thinking on circumcision had a considerable impact on developing Christian thought and had been widely disseminated. Justin simply reflects this wide dissemination. This could explain *Barn.* 13.7, though here the betrayal of knowledge of Paul seems greater than in the Justin passage, though this does not exclude the possibility that it comes from a tradition influenced by Paul. Prostmeier, *Der Barnabasbrief*, 127, would appear to imply such an idea in his reference to "Wendungen und Theologoumena aus dem Corpus Paulinum."

69. Determining the circumstances which caused the writing of *Barnabas* is problematic. A number of scholars assume a situation in which Jews and Christians were separate entities, but in which some of the latter may have been emphasizing their proximity to Jews culturally and in other ways. Such activity may have been influenced by a growing sense of nationalist excitement, possibly encouraged by rumors that the temple would be rebuilt (see *Barn.* 16.3–4). But all elements of this thesis can be questioned, as they have been. See especially Hvalvik, *The Struggle for Scripture*, for a much more generalized purpose, though still involving Jews; and Rhodes, *Deuteronomic Tradition*, for a very different purpose in which Jews as a reality in *Barnabas*'s environment barely play any role. The latter position in particular is discussed in Carleton Paget, "Barnabas and the Outsiders," 189–90. For a similarly contextually based attempt to explain a mooted transformation of Paul's thought about the Jewish people in Justin, see Werline, "Transformation."

have to pertinent passages from scripture used by Paul in these contexts. Moreover, *Barnabas*'s arguments against Jewish interpretation of the law barely carry the imprint of the christocentrism of Paul, as manifested in Gal 2:21; 3:11, 19; or Rom 10:4, to mention but a few passages (with the possible exception of *Barn.* 2.6). None of this need exclude Paul as a part of the material out of which *Barnabas* created his own position, for, as we have noted, Paul could be understood in a variety of ways from an early stage in his reception; but it makes it more difficult to understand him as centrally important to *Barnabas*, that *Barnabas* is somehow a point along a Pauline trajectory.[70] In fact, to some it may be more compelling to see *Barnabas* as emerging from a different setting. So, for instance, the work could have emerged from a Jewish-Hellenistic milieu, which, through those Luke calls "the Hellenists," took on a particular profile within Christianity,[71] possibly finding its most sophisticated early expression in the Epistle to the Hebrews.[72] Or it could have emerged from a background not dissimilar to that from which Justin came, a possibility suggested not just by some evidence of knowledge of the same traditions, but also by the fact that the two authors share so much scriptural material in common.[73] What is more likely than any of these suggestions, however, is that *Barnabas* came to his own singular conclusions as the result of the intermingling of a variety of sources and traditions.

What is clear from all of this is that we cannot demonstrate a multi-layered interaction with Paul on the part of *Barnabas* as this has been presented in recent times by Marguerat, and might be seen in a similarly

70. For a recent critique of the trajectories approach to Christian origins, see Larry Hurtado, "Interactive Diversity: A Proposed Model of Christian Origins," *JTS* 64 (2013): 445–62. Hurtado's preference for what he terms a model of "interactive diversity" accords much more closely with my conception of how *Barnabas*'s theology came into being. See the concluding part of my *Final Reflections*.

71. For this argument, see Carleton Paget, "Paul," 377–80. This builds upon observations in Carleton Paget, *The Epistle of Barnabas*, 200–207, where parallels between *Barnabas* and Stephen's speech in Acts 7:2–53 are discussed, though no definite conclusion about the nature of the relationship between the epistle and the speech arrived at.

72. On this see Carleton Paget, *The Epistle of Barnabas*, 214–25.

73. On this see Skarsaune, *The Proof from Prophecy*, 110–13. It should be noted that the Hellenists and the author of the Epistle to the Hebrews have been thought to have had a relationship with Paul. For the idea that the Hellenists influenced Paul, see H. Räisänen, "'The Hellenists': A Bridge Between Jesus and Paul?," in *Jesus, Paul and Torah: Collected Essays* (Sheffield: JSOT, 1992), 149–202. Rothschild, *Hebrews*, has presented the most robust defense of a Pauline origin for Hebrews.

early Christian writer like Ignatius.[74] Insofar as Paul appears as a feature of this peculiar epistle, it is not as a writer or as a figure whose biography is of significance, but rather as a "doctoral" influence, and even in this context, he is at best a shadowy presence whose precise significance for the author who may have named himself after a former companion of St. Paul, is difficult to grasp.

---

74. For a recent engagement with Ignatius' use of Paul, see C. B. Smith, "Ministry, Martyrdom, and Other Mysteries: Pauline Influence on Ignatius of Antioch," in Bird and Dodson, eds., *Paul and the Second Century*, 37–56; and also Lindemann, "Schriften," 294–322.

Chapter 6

THE RECEPTION OF PAUL IN *1 CLEMENT*

Clare K. Rothschild

Introduction

Generically speaking, *1 Clement* is correctly classified as a deliberative (συμβουλευτικός, *1 Clem.* 58.2) letter.[1] As such, it exemplifies the specific qualities of an epistolary plea (ἔντευξις in *1 Clem.* 63.2; δέησις in 22.6 and 59.2; ἱκετεύω in 2.3, 7.7, and 48.1) for *peace* and *concord* or περὶ ὁμονοίας, as Van Unnik once demonstrated.[2] Toward this goal of concord,

---

1. Cf. *2 Clem.* 19.1

2. W. C. van Unnik, *Studies over de zogenaamde eerste brief van Clemens I Het littéraire genre* (Amsterdam: N. V. Noord-Hollandsche Uitgevers Maatschappij, 1970). L. L. Welborn writes: "From his wide reading, van Unnik recognized how close Clement's 'plea for peace and concord' was to the writings of contemporary philosophers and rhetoricians who sought, through their speeches and pamphlets, to calm the occasional outbreaks of faction in the cities of the Roman Empire. Such works, customarily entitled *peri homonoias*, constituted a sub-category of the *symbouleutikon genos*, regularly discussed by writers on rhetoric after Aristotle. Several excellent examples have come down to us from Dio of Prusa and Aelius Aristides, in which, as in *1 Clement*, the authors can be seen to dissuade from *stasis* and promote *homonoia*, employing various *paradeigmata* and urging consideration of what is 'beneficial' (*sympheron*)." Laurence L. Welborn, "On the Date of *1 Clement*," *BR* 29 (1984): 45. Important primary literature includes Aristotle, *Rhet.* 1.1422a-b, 2.1424b; Dio Chrysostom, *Or.* 38–41; Aelius Aristides, *Or.* 23 and 24. On *homonoia* in general, see H. Kramer, "Quid valeat homonoia in littens graecis" (PhD diss., Göttingen University, 1915). See the discussion of the speeches on concord in C. P. Jones, *The Roman World of Dio Chrysostom* (Cambridge, MA: Harvard University Press, 1978), 83–94, and, on the genre in general, J. Klek, *Symbuleu-tui qui dicitur sermoms historia critica* (Kirchhain: Schmersow, 1919). In addition, *1 Clement* supports the *imperium Romanum*. It is, therefore, more than just a model for his argument. It is a reality the author backs.

it relies on 1 Corinthians as both substructure and warrant.[3] That is, *1 Clement* maps a new epistolary scenario on an older authoritative one because the older model shares a similar purpose[4] and was regarded as genuine and authoritative, particularly on the topic of στάσις. As Margaret M. Mitchell unassailably demonstrates, Paul's attack on factionalism explains virtually every aspect of his letter. 1 Corinthians, therefore, provides any later divisive Christian community with a rich, authoritative source for encouraging reconciliation. Clement never descends to slavish copying; the two letters certainly possess important differences. Rather, the way in which *1 Clement* depends upon 1 Corinthians is two-fold. First, it relies on *structural elements* of 1 Corinthians, including its epistolary form and rhetorical species, its prescript and postscript, and its occasion, the outbreak of a faction. Second, it echoes seminal *content* of Paul's first letter to Corinth, citing or alluding to it, including one allusion to the letter *qua* letter.[5] This essay discusses both types of agreement for what they reveal about the overall project and purpose of Clement's letter.

3. Whereas Holt H. Graham emphasizes similarities with Paul's letter, Lightfoot's otherwise capacious treatment of all aspects of the text avoids this topic. Preliminarily, both works have the same primary topic: division within a community based on allegiance to different leaders. They each deal with bodily resurrection and love. They emphasize Moses over Abraham. They insist on a lineage of revelation that validates present leaders. On 1 Corinthians, see Margaret M. Mitchell, *Paul and the Rhetoric of Reconciliation: An Exegetical Investigation of the Language and Composition of 1 Corinthians* (Louisville: Westminster John Knox, 1992), esp. 138–40 and 250–56.

4. Donald A. Hagner observes, "It is not surprising that the NT writing best attested in Clement's epistle is Paul's First Epistle to the Corinthians. Not only did both epistles have the same destination, but both were written for the same purpose: to restore order and unity to a strife-torn church. It is therefore easily understandable that Clement often alludes to, and indeed makes explicit reference to the Apostle's letter which the Corinthian Church had received probably a mere forty years earlier." Donald A. Hagner, *The Use of the Old and New Testaments in Clement of Rome*, NovTSup 34 (Leiden: Brill, 1973), 195. Contra L. Welborn, "Clement, Epistle of," *ABD* 1:1057.

5. Clement assumes 1 Corinthians is available in both Corinth and Rome. Older but still influential works concerning the influence of Paul on *1 Clement* include A. E. Barnett, *Paul Becomes a Literary Influence* (Chicago: University of Chicago Press, 1941); H. Köester, *Synoptische Überlieferung bei den Apostolischen Vätern*, TU 65 (Berlin: Akademie Verlag, 1957); Andreas Lindemann, *Paulus im ältesten Christentum. Das Bild des Apostels und die Rezeption der paulinishchen Theologie in der frühchristlichen Literatur bis Marcion*, BHT 58 (Tübingen: Mohr Siebeck, 1979); and Hagner, *Use of the Old and New Testaments in Clement of Rome*.

Structural Elements

Structurally speaking, *1 Clement* corresponds to 1 Corinthians in both formal aspects and occasion. Each is discussed in turn.

Generic Comparison

1 Clement is a Pauline epistle.[6] It does not, however, claim to be written by Paul (or even Clement), but by the church of God *sojourning* or *dwelling temporarily* in Rome (ἡ ἐκκλησία τοῦ θεοῦ ἡ παροικοῦσα Ῥώμην).[7] Some time later, tradition – evidently unsatisfied with this attribution – appended to this letter a second attribution, to Clement, a (presumably) famous Christian personage[8] to whom a substantial amount of pseudepigraphic

Relatively recent and important articles on the topic include Andrew Gregory, "*1 Clement* and the Writings That Later Formed the New Testament," in *The New Testament and the Apostolic Fathers*. Vol. 1, *The Reception of the New Testament in the Apostolic Fathers*, ed. Andrew F. Gregory and Christopher M. Tuckett (Oxford: Oxford University Press, 2005), 129–57; Andreas Lindemann, "Paul's Influence on 'Clement' and Ignatius," in *The New Testament and the Apostolic Fathers*. Vol. 2, *Trajectories through the New Testament and the Apostolic Fathers*, ed. Andrew F. Gregory and Christopher M. Tuckett (Oxford: Oxford University Press, 2005), 9–24. See also sections of commentaries Andreas Lindemann, *Die Clemensbriefe*, HNT 17 (Tübingen: Mohr Siebeck, 1992), 18–20; and H. E. Lona, *Der erste Clemensbriefe*, KAV 2 (Göttingen: Vandenhoeck & Ruprecht, 1998), 48–58.

6. Contrast the view of Clayton N. Jefford: "Like those New Testament letters that are clearly 'letter-like' in format, but not so closely patterned according to Pauline guidelines, the author of *1 Clement* has written to the Corinthian church in an acceptable style of ancient epistolography, but has not chosen to use any particular Pauline features beyond the required greeting and concluding blessing." Clayton N. Jefford, *The Apostolic Fathers and the New Testament* (Peabody, MA: Hendrickson, 2006), 43.

7. All manuscript evidence for *2 Clement* connects it to *1 Clement*, viewing both as letters of Clement of Rome to a church in Corinth. See, e.g., C. Tuckett, *2 Clement: Introduction, Text, and Commentary*, OAF (Oxford: Oxford University Press, 2012), 14, 59–60.

8. *1 Clement* is not *specifically* attributed to Clement, *bishop of Rome*, until Irenaeus (for whom it is the lynchpin in an argument for apostolic succession). On the identity of *Clement*, see J. B. Lightfoot, *Apostolic Fathers, Part 1: Clement* (Peabody, MA: Hendrickson, 1889), 1:14–103; and Welborn, "On the Date of *1 Clement*," 35–36. *1 Clement* makes no pretensions to Pauline authorship. Rather, it reports the death of Paul (5.5) and refers to 1 Corinthians by name as "the epistle of the blessed Paul, the Apostle" (47.1). The author of *1 Clement* exhorts its audience to pick up 1 Corinthians and read it (47.1–3). See the discussion below.

literature from the second to fourth centuries is ascribed.[9] The *Martyrdom of Polycarp* (150–160 CE),[10] Polycarp's *Epistle to the Philippians*,[11] and the *Letter from Vienna and Lyons*[12] (178 CE) are likewise second-century texts attributed to "churches sojourning"; none of these texts, however, attracted a second attribution.[13] *1 Clement* may be the only text with an internal attribution that attracted a second attribution. Perhaps canonization (e.g., Codex Alexandrinus) demanded a title distinguishable from Paul's letter.[14]

Furthermore, the epithet given to the addressee (and to the sender) "sojourning" or "temporarily dwelling" (παροικοῦσα) may have carried with it a non-literal, figurative intention. Elsewhere Christians use the verb παροικεῖν metaphorically to imply temporary residence on earth but permanent residence with the Lord in heaven.[15] For example, 1 Pet 1:17

9. Some surmise that the appeal of Clementine attribution was based on the presumed authenticity of *1 Clement*. Works attributed to Clement (perhaps on the basis of the "high esteem" of *1 Clement*) include *2 Clement*, *De virginitate*, the *Apostolic Constitutions*; cf. Pseudo-Clementine, *Homilies* and *Recognitions* (third century); cf. also posthumous martyrdom: *Martyrium Clementis* (fourth century). See Welborn, "Clement, First Epistle of," 1:1056.

10. *Mart. Pol.* 1, "The Church of God which sojourns in Smyrna, to the Church of God which sojourns in Philomelium, and to all the sojournings of the Holy Catholic Church in every place." K. Lake, *Apostolic Fathers*, vol. 1, LCL (Cambridge, MA: Harvard University Press, 1912).

11. Polycarp, *Phil.* 1a, "Polycarp and the Elders with him to the Church of God sojourning in Philippi" (Lake, LCL). On the dating of the *Martyrdom of Polycarp*, see C. Moss, "On the Dating of Polycarp: Rethinking the Place of the Martyrdom of Polycarp in the History of Christianity," *EC* 1, no. 4 (2010): 539–74.

12. "The servants sojourning in Vienne and Lyons in Gaul to the brethren in Asia and Phrygia, who have the same faith and hope of redemption as you," *apud* Eusebius, *Hist. eccl.* 5.1.1–2 (Lake, LCL).

13. Polycarp's *Letter to the Philippians* is ascribed to Polycarp; the *Martyrdom of Polycarp*, to Socrates (22.2).

14. The *Martyrdom of Polycarp* has a similar prescript, but includes, in ch. 22, a complicated string of attributions to named individuals, beginning with Socrates.

15. *1 Clem.* 47.2–3: Κατανοήσωμεν τοὺς στρατευομένους τοῖς ἡγουμένοις ἡμῶν, πῶς εὐτάκτως, πῶς εἰκτικῶς, πῶς ὑποτεταγμένως ἐπιτελοῦσιν τὰ διατασσόμενα. Οὐ πάντες εἰσὶν ἔπαρχοι οὐδὲ χιλίαρχοι οὐδὲ ἑκατόνταρχοι οὐδὲ πεντηκόνταρχοι οὐδὲ τὸ καθεξῆς, ἀλλ᾽ ἕκαστος ἐν τῷ ἰδίῳ τάγματι τὰ ἐπιτασσόμενα ὑπὸ τοῦ βασιλέως καὶ τῶν ἡγουμένων ἐπιτελεῖ. In the case of *1 Clement*, however, the reconciliation sought is not between the actual cities of Rome and Corinth but – because Christianity is one big city and its citizens viewed as exiles in their respective geographical locations (prescript) – between rival leaders therein. See the reference in 1.1 to those in both churches as sojourning in their respective cities. In his *Orations*, Dio writes to one

states, "If you invoke as Father the one who judges all people impartially according to their deeds, live in reverent fear during the time of your exile (τὸν τῆς παροικίας ὑμῶν χρόνον)" (cf. 1 Pet 2:11).[16] Associating temporary residence or *exile* with a specific city (i.e., Corinth) may suggest a literal community in residence, but may alternatively have a symbolic meaning, such as "those who define their existence according to their interpretation of Paul's first epistle to the Corinthians," thinking, for example, of *gnostic* self-identification as πνευματικοί (e.g., 1 Cor 2:13, 15; 3:1; 14:37).[17] Correspondingly, the superscription (sender) might imply: "those identifying themselves with proto-orthodoxy [in Rome]."[18] The only other place *1 Clement* mentions Rome is ch. 5, where the reference is elliptical, denoting Paul's final *dwelling place* (τὸ τέρμα τῆς δύσεως). *Sojourners in Rome* may, thus, suggest Paul's authority in the city following his death as a martyr,[19] or, perhaps, Peter's authority in that city. That is, Peter's

city regarding strife with another city. In *1 Clement*, a church (Rome) writes to another church (Corinth) regarding strife within that latter group specifying certain individuals as the root cause. In Paul's letters to the Corinthians, Paul writes to the church regarding strife within that body also specifying certain individuals as root causes. The similarities–together with the high estimation in which Paul is held in this letter – all but guarantee that the anonymous author of *1 Clement* deliberately assumes Paul's authority, albeit for circumstances following Paul's death. Stoic resonances are also likely: *cosmopolis* or notion of the universe as the über-State of sorts. H. C. Baldry, *The Unity of Mankind in Greek Thought* (Cambridge: Cambridge University Press, 1965); Eric Brown, "Hellenistic Cosmopolitanism," in *A Companion to Ancient Philosophy*, ed. Mary Louise Gill and Pierre Pellegrin (Oxford: Blackwell, 2006), 549–58; Gerd van den Heuvel, "Cosmopolite, Cosmopolitisme," in *Handbuch politisch-sozialer Grundbegriffe in Frankreich 1680–1820*, ed. Rolf Reichardt and Eberhard Schmidt (Munich: Oldenbourg, 1986), 41–55; J. L. Moles, "Cynic Cosmopolitanism," in *The Cynics: The Cynic Movement in Antiquity and Its Legacy*, ed. R. Bracht Branham and Marie-Odile Goulet-Cazé (Berkeley and Los Angeles: University of California Press, 1996), 105–20; Malcolm Schofield, *The Stoic Idea of the City* (Cambridge: Cambridge University Press, 1991); cf. the very important Stoic concept παντοκράτωρ in *1 Clem.* 2.3; 32.4; 56.6; 60.4; 62.2; παντοκρατορικός in 8.5.

16. Καὶ εἰ πατέρα ἐπικαλεῖσθε τὸν ἀπροσωπολήμπτως κρίνοντα κατὰ τὸ ἑκάστου ἔργον, ἐν φόβῳ τὸν τῆς παροικίας ὑμῶν χρόνον ἀναστράφητε. Cf. Philodemus, *Mort.* 38.

17. Regarding Valentinian *gnostics*, see E. Pagels, *The Gnostic Paul: Gnostic Exegesis of the Pauline Letters* (London: Continuum, 1975), 13–46.

18. Cf. 1 Pet 1:1, Πέτρος ἀπόστολος Ἰησοῦ Χριστοῦ ἐκλεκτοῖς παρεπιδήμοις διασπορᾶς Πόντου, Γαλατίας, Καππαδοκίας, Ἀσίας, καὶ Βιθυνίας.

19. Some interpreters infer Spain from the expression, "limits of the West" (ἐπὶ τὸ τέρμα τῆς δύσεως ἐλθὼν [*1 Clem.* 5.7]); however, the qualifying phrase (καὶ μαρτυρήσας ἐπὶ τῶν ἡγουμένων) suggests that the author implies Rome.

followers must now reiterate what Peter's friend Paul once said in his first letter to the Corinthians. Since, for the first half of the second century, no evidence other than *1 Clement* exists that (1) an actual church in Rome perceived itself with the authority to offer other churches advice,[20] and (2) an actual church in Corinth persisted in the schism of Paul's day and was dogged by a challenger to its "bishopric," involving individuals Paul knew (*1 Clem.* 65.1),[21] a metaphorical reading (non-literal albeit not fictitious) is as, or more, plausible than a historical one. With the sole exception of Eusebius's testimony of Dionysius of Corinth (date of 171 CE fixed by Soter), *1 Clement* is our only evidence of a thriving church in Corinth *after* 2 Corinthians and *before* the second half of the second century when Hegesippus (*apud* Eusebius, during the time of Pope Anicetus, ca. 155–66 CE) evidently visited that city.

Together these observations suggest a rare phenomenon among early Christian texts, namely, that *1 Clement* is a letter to Corinth only formally.[22] Functionally, it is neither written from a church in Rome nor delivered to (or even intended for) a church in Corinth.[23] Rather, it should be classified as an allegorical letter – an epistolary type Ps.-Demetrius describes as a letter

---

20. Although the *Shepherd of Hermas* mentions a Christian named Clement with an administrative role in the city of Rome (Herm. *Vis.* 8.3: "Therefore, you will write two little books, and you will send one to Clement and one to Grapte. Then Clement will send it to the cities abroad, because that is his job"), it does not specifically associate this Clement with *1 Clement*. In fact, the Shepherd never cites *1 Clement*, which is odd if (as commonly supposed) both were written there.

21. Cf. Acts 18.

22. It becomes necessary, therefore, to distinguish fictional from real exigencies of the letter. Cf. Robert Matthew Calhoun, "The Resurrection of the Flesh in *3 Corinthians*," in *Christian Body, Christian Self: Concepts of Early Christian Personhood*, ed. C. K. Rothschild and T. W. Thompson (Tübingen: Mohr Siebeck, 2011), 235–57.

23. Contra David G. Horrell, whose erudite study assumes the historical veracity of *1 Clement*'s address to a church in Corinth; see his *The Social Ethos of the Corinthian Correspondence: Interest and Ideology from 1 Corinthians to 1 Clement*, SNTIW (Edinburgh: T&T Clark, 1996). See also reviews by Barbara E. Bowe: *CBQ* 60 (1998): 566–68; and John Hurd: *JBL* 118 (1999): 768–69. Trevor Thompson, citing Margaret M. Mitchell, refers to such a literary phenomenon as "double pseude-pigraphon," neither *from* its purported author, nor *to* its purported addressee. Trevor W. Thompson, "Writing in Character: Claudius Lysias to Felix as a Double-Pseude-pigraphon," in *The Interface of Orality and Writing: Seeing, Speaking, Writing in the Shaping of New Genres*, ed. A. Weissenrieder and R. B. Coote, WUNT 260 (Tübingen: Mohr Siebeck, 2010), 393–407. This designation may apply to a broad cross-section of all early Christian pseudepigrapha.

in which the addressee is the only person who understands what is truly meant and in which the sender intimates one thing by means of another.[24] Taking advantage of some degree of inherent instability regarding text and canon in the second century, *1 Clement* convincingly maps a new epistolary scenario on an older authoritative one,[25] using verisimilitude to create a *world* its intended readers can translate but a majority of other, especially later readers are inclined to accept as actual.[26] The text relies on argument *and* authority, yet its argument preserves the Pauline custom of exhorting over mandating, even as the concept of episcopal authority had moved to the forefront among the proto-orthodox. And, its authority is not a product of Pauline *attribution*, but of a Pauline situation, that is, a letter to Corinth against factionalizing. *1 Clement* is, thus, a kind of pseudepigraphon.[27] Floating in ancient space and time, elements of its *new* epistolary scenario are our only foothold into the problems of actual authorship, addressee, and occasion.[28] As a pseudepigraphon, *1 Clement*

24. This definition comes from Ps.-Demetrius, *Epistolary Types* 15; text and translation in A. J. Malherbe, *Ancient Epistolary Theorists*, SBL 19 (Atlanta: Scholars Press, 1988), 38–39. For comparison, *3 Corinthians* is also a third letter to the Corinthian church (albeit in Paul's name) written during the last third of second century against *gnostics*. N.B. *3 Corinthians* circulated with the letter from the church in Corinth evidently prompting it! For these insights I wish to thank Trevor W. Thompson.

25. On the pseudepigraphic strategy involved, see Trevor W. Thompson, "As if Genuine: Interpreting the Pseudepigraphic Second Thessalonians," in *Pseudepigraphie und Verfasserfiktion in frühchristlichen Briefen*, ed. J. Frey et al., WUNT 246 (Tübingen: Mohr Siebeck, 2009), 471–88. Also Clare K. Rothschild, *Hebrews as Pseudepigraphon: The History and Significance of the Pauline Attribution of Hebrews*, WUNT 1/235 (Tübingen: Mohr Siebeck, 2009), Chapter 5.

26. Ps.-Demetrius, *Epistolary Types* 15, "allegorical" (Malherbe).

27. Both Hebrews and *1 Clement* emphasize Paul's identity in the postscript. Contrast the view of C. N. Jefford: "There is no doubt that the text [*1 Clement*] was written from the church in Rome and intentionally directed toward the church in Corinth" (*Apostolic Fathers and the New Testament*, 163). Jefford refers to both *1 Clement* and Polycarp's *Letter to the Philippians* as "true letters" (43).

28. As discussed below, if *1 Clement*'s opponents were "gnostics" in any sense, then "the church sojourning in Rome" could be an allegorical reference to theological ideas accepted by the Roman bishopric and those (formally and/or informally) adhering to its doctrinal decisions. Bentley Layton discusses the proximity of pseudonymity and allegory among gnostic texts as follows: "it [allegory] permitted thinkers to assert that their own philosophical views (the "allegorical meaning") had been recognized long before by an even more authoritative person, such as Homer, Moses,

is directed at the question of Pauline legacy, in particular, its implications for church leadership, a point upon which the actual author and addressee evidently do not agree. This is the actual *stasis* addressed in the letter. Given their mutual affinity for Paul, the author appeals to Paul's letters to manage the disagreement. Solutions offered include: (1) submission to present authority, (2) recognition of differences in love, (3) expulsion/ self-exile when necessary, and most importantly (4) capitulation to what Paul himself had to say. The implied point of inquiry to be adjudicated in this letter is: as Paulinists, will the addressee(s) heed their apostle or not?

Other similarities with the prescript and similarities with the postscript of 1 Corinthians further suggest that *1 Clement* maps its argument on Paul's letter. For example, *1 Clement* agrees with the *adscriptio* of 1 Corinthians: "To the church of God" and "in Corinth," as well as with the epithets Paul uses for the church members, κλητοί ("those called") and ἡγιασμένοι ("made holy") by "our Lord Jesus Christ." Whereas Paul separates "those called" ("saints") in Corinth from "those called" living elsewhere,[29] *1 Clement* collapses these two phrases, adding, as noted, that those in Corinth only dwell there temporarily or as non-citizens (i.e., παροικοῦσα).

The postscript exhibits at least four similarities with 1 Corinthians. First, Clement expresses greetings to a person named Fortunatus (*1 Clem.* 65.1), a person Paul greets by name in 1 Cor 16:17. In addition to Fortunatus, Clement also greets two others: Claudius Ephebus and Valerius Vito. If these individuals are, as is suggested by J.B. Lightfoot, slaves manumitted by Claudius and his wife Valeria, then they are people known to have lived in Paul's day (people Paul *might* have known). These references may be coincidental. Alternatively, they may develop a *Corinthian* fiction, building upon the authority of 1 Corinthians by acknowledging individuals Paul knew in Corinth in order to suggest a setting not long after Paul died in Rome. Twice, *1 Clem.* 5.1 internally dates the text to precisely this period:

Jesus, or St. Paul. This function is analogous to the pseudepigraphy of classic gnostic scripture, in which a modern thinker's views are passed off as an ancient document left by an authoritative figure of the past." Bentley Layton, *Gnostic Scriptures*, ABRL (New York: Doubleday, 1987), 273.

29. τῇ ἐκκλησίᾳ τοῦ θεοῦ, ἡγιασμένοις ἐν Χριστῷ Ἰησοῦ, τῇ οὔσῃ ἐν Κορίνθῳ, κλητοῖς ἁγίοις, σὺν πᾶσιν τοῖς ἐπικαλουμένοις τὸ ὄνομα τοῦ κυρίου ἡμῶν Ἰησοῦ Χριστοῦ ἐν παντὶ τόπῳ αὐτῶν καὶ ἡμῶν· ("To the church of God that is in Corinth, to those who are sanctified in Christ Jesus, called to be saints, together with all those who in every place call on the name of our Lord Jesus Christ, both their Lord and ours," 1 Cor 1:2).

But to stop giving ancient examples, let us come to those who became athletic contenders [Peter, Paul] *in quite recent times* (ἔγγιστα). We should consider the noble examples of *our own generation* (τῆς γενεᾶς ἡμῶν).[30]

Second, the imperative in *1 Clem.* 65.1 to "send back" the three envoys, "in peace" (Τοὺς δὲ ἀπεσταλμένους ἀφ' ἡμῶν)[31] echoes Paul's comment about Timothy in 1 Cor 16:11: "send him on his way in peace" (προπέμψατε δὲ αὐτὸν ἐν εἰρήνῃ).[32] Third, the extension of grace in *1 Clem.* 65.2 resembles 1 Cor 16:23.[33] And, fourth, the phrase, "and with all those everywhere who are called by God through him" (*1 Clem.* 65.2b)[34] echoes 1 Cor 1:2, "with all those who in every place call on the name of our Lord Jesus Christ, both their Lord and ours."[35]

In sum, similarities in the prescript and postscript (sections of a letter most often exploited to establish a pseudepigraphical setting) suggest that the author of *1 Clement* imitates Paul's first *letter* to the Corinthians without assuming Paul's *identity*. The historical interpretation of this imitation, inferred by those accepting authorship by Clement, bishop of Rome ca. 96–97 CE, is that forty or so years after Paul's death, the situation of the church in Corinth had returned to the identical circumstances Paul faced

---

30. Ἀλλ' ἵνα τῶν ἀρχαίων ὑποδειγμάτων παυσώμεθα, ἔλθωμεν ἐπὶ τοὺς ἔγγιστα γενομένους ἀθλητάς· λάβωμεν τῆς γενεᾶς ἡμῶν τὰ γενναῖα ὑποδείγματα. Through verisimilitude, the Latin names the author greets in the postscript perpetuate the fictive epistolary situation. Good forgeries anticipate attacks on *their authenticity*. The greater the number of verisimilitudinous devices a pseudonymous text has, the more likely the author anticipated this charge. *1 Clement*'s selective use of Paul's letters, emphasizing 1 Corinthians, is another aspect of its pseudepigraphal strategy. Like *stasis* of precisely the type Paul faced in Corinth (only conceivably recurring immediately after Paul died) and friends, such as Fortunatus (only conceivably alive for a decade or two after Paul died), limited citation of the *corpus Paulinum* indicated the time period right after Paul was martyred. All three elements contributed to the letter's eventual attribution to Clement. I am grateful to Trevor W. Thompson for a discussion of these ideas. See Lightfoot, *Apostolic Fathers*, 1:27.

31. Τοὺς δὲ ἀπεσταλμένους ἀφ' ἡμῶν Κλαύδιον Ἔφηβον καὶ Οὐαλέριον Βίτωνα σὺν καὶ Φορτουνάτῳ ἐν εἰρήνῃ μετὰ χαρᾶς ἐν τάχει ἀναπέμψατε πρὸς ἡμᾶς (*1 Clem.* 65.1).

32. προπέμψατε δὲ αὐτὸν ἐν εἰρήνῃ, ἵνα ἔλθῃ πρός με, ἐκδέχομαι γὰρ αὐτὸν μετὰ τῶν ἀδελφῶν (1 Cor 16:1).

33. Cf. Ἡ χάρις τοῦ κυρίου ἡμῶν Ἰησοῦ Χριστοῦ μεθ' ὑμῶν (*1 Clem.* 65.2) with ἡ χάρις τοῦ κυρίου Ἰησοῦ μεθ' ὑμῶν (1 Cor 16:23).

34. καὶ μετὰ πάντων πανταχῇ τῶν κεκλημένων ὑπὸ τοῦ θεοῦ δι' αὐτοῦ (*1 Clem.* 65.2b).

35. σὺν πᾶσιν τοῖς ἐπικαλουμένοις τὸ ὄνομα τοῦ κυρίου ἡμῶν Ἰησοῦ Χριστοῦ ἐν παντὶ τόπῳ αὐτῶν καὶ ἡμῶν (1 Cor 1:2).

there, including many of the people Paul knew. In contrast, the allegorical interpretation put forward in this essay is that the imitation creates a fictitious scenario in which the historical circumstances of 1 Corinthians act as a template in which the author represents Paul and the author's opponents represent the factionalizing church in Corinth to whom Paul wrote.

Occasion

1 Clement also mimics 1 Corinthians in its argument that στάσις has overtaken the community.[36] Στάσις is not to be translated generally as *strife* or *discord*, but specifically (as set forth in *1 Clem.* 1.1–2 and repeated in 51.1) as *faction* or *schism*, that is, as a reference to a separate party of believers *within one church*, threatening that church's peace and concord.[37] *1 Clement*'s factionalizing has always, like its *superscriptio* and *adscriptio*, been viewed literally, that is, as referring to a literal factionalizing party at the end of the first century in the city of Corinth. If, however, like certain elements of the prescript, *1 Clement* adopts this theme from 1 Corinthians (ἔρις, "rivalry," 1 Cor 3:3[38]) in order to apply it to a new epistolary circumstance, then the *faction* within the church in Corinth may be less actual than metaphorical. In such a case, it may imply the mid-second-century separation of one group of Pauline interpreters from another, irrespective of their location within the empire.[39]

---

36. Contra Welborn, "Clement, Epistle of," 1:1057.

37. See BDAG s.v. στάσις 2: "But it is difficult to differentiate in *1 Cl* betw. this sense and the foll. one, with focus on the component of discord" (p. 940).

38. 1 Cor 3:1–4: Κἀγώ, ἀδελφοί, οὐκ ἠδυνήθην λαλῆσαι ὑμῖν ὡς πνευματικοῖς ἀλλ' ὡς σαρκίνοις, ὡς νηπίοις ἐν Χριστῷ. γάλα ὑμᾶς ἐπότισα, οὐ βρῶμα, οὔπω γὰρ ἐδύνασθε. ἀλλ' οὐδὲ ἔτι νῦν δύνασθε, ἔτι γὰρ σαρκικοί ἐστε. ὅπου γὰρ ἐν ὑμῖν ζῆλος καὶ ἔρις, οὐχὶ σαρκικοί ἐστε καὶ κατὰ ἄνθρωπον περιπατεῖτε; ὅταν γὰρ λέγῃ τις· Ἐγὼ μέν εἰμι Παύλου, ἕτερος δέ· Ἐγὼ Ἀπολλῶ, οὐκ ἄνθρωποί ἐστε.

39. Discussion of the expulsion of church leaders is, perhaps, on that basis. Gnostic evidence of this exists; on the Valentinians, see Pagels, *Gnostic Paul*. Cf. *1 Clem.* 2.6; 3.2 (ἔρις); 14.2; 46.9 (σχίσμα); 54.2 (Εἰπάτω· Εἰ δι' ἐμὲ στάσις καὶ ἔρις καὶ σχίσματα, ἐκχωρῶ, ἄπειμι, οὗ ἐὰν βούλησθε, καὶ ποιῶ τὰ προστασσόμενα ὑπὸ τοῦ πλήθους· μόνον τὸ ποίμνιον τοῦ Χριστοῦ εἰρηνευέτω μετὰ τῶν καθεσταμένων πρεσβυτέρων); 57.1 (Ὑμεῖς οὖν οἱ τὴν καταβολὴν τῆς στάσεως ποιήσαντες ὑποτάγητε τοῖς πρεσβυτέροις καὶ παιδεύθητε εἰς μετάνοιαν κάμψαντες τὰ γόνατα τῆς καρδίας ὑμῶν; 63.1, Θεμιτὸν οὖν ἐστιν τοῖς τοιούτοις καὶ τοσούτοις ὑποδείγμασιν προσελθόντας ὑποθεῖναι τὸν τράχηλον καὶ τὸν τῆς ὑπακοῆς τόπον ἀναπληρῶσαι, ὅπως ἡσυχάσαντες τῆς ματαίας στάσεως ἐπὶ τὸν προκείμενον ἡμῖν ἐν ἀληθείᾳ σκοπὸν δίχα παντὸς μώμου καταντήσωμεν).

On this reading, "your *name* has been blasphemed"[40] would imply not that the Corinthians *themselves*, but *that their subsequent reputation* is being appropriated in a way that the author of *1 Clement* does not endorse, as in the case of Valentinus in the opinion of Clement of Alexandria.

A final structural aspect that *1 Clement* and 1 Corinthians hold in common is necessity of the removal of a corrupt individual for the restoration of community concord (1 Cor 5:5; *1 Clem.* 54.2).[41] As Margaret M. Mitchell points out, Paul links the man sleeping with his father's wife in 1 Cor 5:1[42] to the problem of *stasis* in the community by means of the broader allegation of boasting.[43] In 1 Cor 5:2, Paul writes: "And you are arrogant! Should you not rather have mourned, so that he who has done this would have been removed from among you?"[44] The Corinthian congregation continues to boast, Mitchell argues, despite the fact that the pure social *mixture* of their community *on which harmony relies* (Paul uses the analogy of yeast in a lump of dough) has been tainted, resulting in *stasis*. Mitchell draws an analogy to disease in a body:[45] when only one member is infected, the entire body is affected.[46]

1 Clement too alleges that a single member (or perhaps two, see 47.6) of the community must be ejected to restore peace: "It is shameful, loved ones, exceedingly shameful and unworthy of your conduct in Christ, that the most secure and ancient church of the Corinthians is reported to have created a faction against its presbyters, at the instigation of one or two persons." Boasting is again at issue. *1 Clement* 13.1 exhorts, "Let us therefore be lowly minded, brothers, laying aside all arrogance and conceit and folly and anger, and let us do what is written. For the Holy Spirit says, 'Let not the wise man boast in his wisdom, nor the strong in his strength, neither the rich in his riches; but he that boasts let him boast in the Lord, that he may seek Him out, and do judgment and righteousness.'" *1 Clement* 37.4 specifies that "the greater ones" need "the lowly ones" and *vice versa* to maintain the particular mixture or balance

---

40. ὥστε τὸ σεμνὸν καὶ περιβόητον καὶ πᾶσιν ἀνθρώποις ἀξιαγάπητον ὄνομα ὑμῶν μεγάλως βλασφημηθῆναι (*1 Clem.* 1.1).

41. See n. 36.

42. Ὅλως ἀκούεται ἐν ὑμῖν πορνεία, καὶ τοιαύτη πορνεία ἥτις οὐδὲ ἐν τοῖς ἔθνεσιν, ὥστε γυναῖκά τινα τοῦ πατρὸς ἔχειν.

43. Mitchell, *Paul and the Rhetoric of Reconciliation*, 228–29.

44. καὶ ὑμεῖς πεφυσιωμένοι ἐστέ, καὶ οὐχὶ μᾶλλον ἐπενθήσατε, ἵνα ἀρθῇ ἐκ μέσου ὑμῶν ὁ τὸ ἔργον τοῦτο ποιήσας (1 Cor 5:2).

45. Mitchell, *Paul and the Rhetoric of Reconciliation*, 229.

46. *1 Clement* also utilizes the language of "boasting" (13.1; cf. self-praise, 30.6).

necessary for survival. "Those who are great cannot survive without the lowly, nor the lowly without the great. There is a certain co-mixture in all things, and this proves to be useful for them."[47] As Mitchell's interpretation of 1 Corinthians suggests, the analogy in *1 Clement* also derives from medical literature[48] in which, like the human body, social *bodies* require a balanced mixture to maintain harmony and peace.[49]

To summarize the similarities between the letter's occasions, both letters to the Corinthians, Paul's and Clement's, insist on the removal of factionalizing individuals as a means of achieving the community imperative of harmony analogized as homeostasis.

Allusions to 1 Corinthians in 1 Clement

1 Clement incorporates a number of allusions[50] to early Christian literature. The largest proportion of verbal parallels alludes to letters attributed to Paul.[51] However, the letter also includes an allusion to the 1 Corinthians *qua* letter.

---

47. Οἱ μεγάλοι δίχα τῶν μικρῶν οὐ δύνανται εἶναι, οὔτε οἱ μικροὶ δίχα τῶν μεγάλων· σύγκρασίς τίς ἐστιν ἐν πᾶσιν, καὶ ἐν τούτοις χρῆσις (*1 Clem.* 37.4).

48. See Mitchell, *Paul and the Rhetoric of Reconciliation*, 228–30; cf. 112–16.

49. N.B. Στάσις, among ancient texts, frequently refers to disease in the body. See Mitchell, *Paul and the Rhetoric of Reconciliation*, 158 and n. 564.

50. This essay will not delineate parameters of citation, allusion, echo, and whisper. Careful work in this area remains a desideratum of scholarship, notwithstanding Richard B. Hays's study: *Echoes of Scripture in the Letters of Paul* (New Haven: Yale University Press, 1989). Annette Merz and Nicole Franck speak about Paul's letters used as "reference works." Elsewhere, I describe Hebrews as a "reading guide" to Romans. The present essay addresses a wide range of points of interaction between *1 Clement* and 1 Corinthians, from structural elements to verbal imitation. Verbal imitation, in turn, covers a range, from verbatim citation with implied referentiality (i.e., intentionally invoking the prior text in order that readers consider the citation *qua* citation) to ephemeral echoes. Until further work is done on the theory and practice of intertextuality, I will not delineate lines of specificity between the various types of verbal imitation, rather referring to them all as "allusions." Since Hays's study, the classification "allusion" may have narrowed in semantic domain. I will, however, use it in its prior, broader sense, incorporating varying amounts of verbatim agreement. A. J. Carlyle asserts that *1 Clement*'s New Testament references are "made from memory." See A Committee of the Oxford Society of Historical Theology, *The New Testament in the Apostolic Fathers* (Oxford: Clarendon, 1905), 42.

51. Hagner, *Use of the Old and New Testaments in Clement of Rome*; Andreas Lindemann, "Paul in the Writings of the Apostolic Fathers," in *Paul and the Legacies*

1 Corinthians as Rhetorical Artifact

1 Clement 47.1 exhorts readers to take up "the letter of the blessed Paul, the apostle," inquiring (rhetorically) as to what it says: "Take up the epistle of that blessed apostle, Paul. What did he write to you at first, at the beginning of his proclamation of the gospel?"[52] *1 Clement* 47.3, then, echoes the details of the circumstances in Corinth from 1 Cor 1:12:[53] "To be sure, he sent you a letter in the Spirit concerning himself and Cephas and Apollos, since you were even then engaged in partisanship."[54] These references to the letter and occasion of 1 Corinthians have at least two strategic effects on the overall argument of *1 Clement*. First, they recognize Paul, and specifically 1 Corinthians, as authoritative, explicitly drawing *1 Clement* into association with both. Second, the references usher 1 Corinthians into the foreground such that readers have it "at hand" as they read and reflect on *1 Clement*. Verses 4–7 even spell out a comparison between the two letters, arguing that the present situation is even graver than the one Paul addressed. Although *1 Clement*'s opponents have assumed positions of *leadership* (without warrant according to Clement), this passage compares them not to leaders of the Corinthian congregation but to the Corinthian congregation itself, that is, to those permitting factions to develop and, thus, creating rifts within the community. In fact, *1 Clement*'s opponents are worse than Paul's Corinthian congregation because they factionalize based on a few *unapproved* rather than other *approved* leaders.[55]

of Paul, ed. W. S. Babcock (Dallas: Southern Methodist University Press, 1990), 25–45; idem, "Paul's Influence on 'Clement' and Ignatius"; idem, *Paulus im ältesten Christentum*; idem, "Der Apostel Paulus im 2. Jahrhundert," in *The New Testament in Early Chritianity*, ed. J.-M. Sevrin, BETL 86 (Leuven: Leuven University Press, 1989), 39–67; D. K. Rensberger, "As the Apostle Teaches: The Development of the Use of Paul's Letters in Second-Century Christianity" (PhD diss., Yale University, 1981); Cf. Oxford Society, *The New Testament in the Apostolic Fathers*.

52. Ἀναλάβετε τὴν ἐπιστολὴν τοῦ μακαρίου Παύλου τοῦ ἀποστόλου. Τί πρῶτον ὑμῖν ἐν ἀρχῇ τοῦ εὐαγγελίου ἔγραψεν (*1 Clem.* 47.1).

53. Paul writes: "What I mean is that each of you says, 'I belong to Paul,' or 'I belong to Apollos,' or 'I belong to Cephas,' or 'I belong to Christ'" (λέγω δὲ τοῦτο ὅτι ἕκαστος ὑμῶν λέγει· Ἐγὼ μέν εἰμι Παύλου, Ἐγὼ δὲ Ἀπολλῶ, Ἐγὼ δὲ Κηφᾶ, Ἐγὼ δὲ Χριστοῦ, 1 Cor 1:12).

54. Ἐπ᾿ ἀληθείας πνευματικῶς ἐπέστειλεν ὑμῖν περὶ ἑαυτοῦ τε καὶ Κηφᾶ τε καὶ Ἀπολλώ, διὰ τὸ καὶ τότε προσκλίσεις ὑμᾶς πεποιῆσθαι (*1 Clem.* 47.3).

55. See *1 Clem.* 1.6, δοκιμάζω in *1 Clem.* 1.2; 42.4; 1 Cor 3:13; 16:3. προσεκλίθητε γὰρ ἀποστόλοις μεμαρτυρημένοις καὶ ἀνδρὶ δεδοκιμασμένῳ παρ᾿ αὐτοῖς.

This comparison, at a minimum, implies that the actual opponents of *1 Clement* were responsive to Paul. To be sure, the rhetorical force of this section relies on their high estimation of him and his letter to Corinth. *1 Clement* turns their affection back on them. By factionalizing, it argues, they emulate not Paul, a leader who sought to remedy factionalizing, but the Corinthian congregation who factionalized. Insofar as the opponent views himself in the tradition of Paul, Clement recommends that he should now emulate Paul by opposing factions. In this way, *1 Clement's* interpretation of 1 Corinthians is tailored to a new circumstance. Paul's letter plays the role of rhetorical artifact, providing proof of Paul's stance as a faction fighter and exhibiting an ironic foil for the opponents who tout themselves as his imitators.

Verbal Parallels

1 Clement also incorporates numerous verbal allusions to early Christian literature. Of these allusions, 1 Corinthians ranks first in rate of occurrence.[56] The following list shares most passages in common with those of the Oxford Society and Holt Graham:[57]

Chart 1. *Allusions to 1 Corinthians*

1 Corinthians	*1 Clement*
1:1–3	Sal.
1:11–13	47.1[A58]
1:31	13.1
2:9	34.8[C]
2:10	*40.1*[C (depths of God)]
4:10	3.3

56. Romans, Philippians, First Timothy, Ephesians, Titus, Galatians, Colossians, 1 Thessalonians, and 2 Timothy are also cited. Allusions to Hebrews are also clear; Hebrews may be perceived as Pauline by the author of *1 Clement*. Whereas Lindemann, Lona, and Carlyle prefer to assert Clement's secure knowledge of only Romans and 1 Corinthians, Hagner believes that the author of *1 Clement* knows "the greater part, if not the whole, of the Pauline corpus." Hagner, *Use of the Old and New Testaments in Clement of Rome*, 237. According to Welborn, in *1 Clement*, "1 Corinthians is cited repeatedly (24:1; 35:5–6; 37:5–38:2; 47; 49:5–6)." Welborn, "Clement, Epistle of," *ABD* 1:1056.

57. Robert M. Grant and Holt H. Graham, *The Apostolic Fathers*. Vol. 2, *First and Second Clement* (New York: Thomas Nelson, 1965), 103–4.

58. Superscript letters indicate the class of probability awarded the passage by the committee of the Oxford Society of Historical Theology who prepared *The New Testament in the Apostolic Fathers*. See Appendix 2 below for their list of parallel passages.

4:14	7.1
5:27	*30.1 (standard imperative/indicative exhortation)*
9:24	*5.1, 5^D (athletes + prize)*
12:4	38.1^A
12:8–9	48.5
12:20–28	37.5^A
13:3	55.2
13:4–7	49.5^C
15:20	24.1^B
15:23	37.3^C
15:35–38	24.5^B [59]
16:15	42.4^B [60]
16:17	38.2^C
16:23	*65.2 (Closing extension of grace)*

This essay will not delineate parameters of citation, allusion, echo, and whisper.[61]

Allusions to 1 Corinthians in 1 Clement

We observe two kinds of verbal parallels between *1 Clement* and 1 Corinthians: (1) what I will refer to as single allusions and (2) what I will refer to as clusters of allusions to a single chapter of Paul's letter.[62] Each is examined in turn.

About the parallels, A. Gregory concludes (see Appendix 3), "None of these possible references is compelling in itself, and each may be explained on grounds other than of direct literary dependence, but the fact that Clement clearly used 1 Corinthians means that the possibility that each parallel arises from direct literary dependence (or at least an intimate acquaintance with the letter, such that Clement draws on his language and content quite unconsciously) should not be underestimated" (Gregory, "*1 Clement* and the Writings That Later Formed the New Testament," 144–48).

59. Oxford Society of Historical Theology's Committee includes *1 Clem.* 24.4 here (*The New Testament in the Apostolic Fathers*, 41). N.B. The text used most frequently by Gnostics is not cited (1 Cor 15:50); those around it, however, are. Cf. *3 Corinthians*.

60. Of the additional group of citations (i.e., *1 Clem.* 24.1; 35.5–6; 37.5–38.2; 47; 49.5–6) Welborn lists in "Clement, First Epistle of" (*ABD* 1:1056), I can only corroborate the allusion to 1 Cor 1:12 in *1 Clem.* 47.3. Ehrman (LCL, 119) also includes this reference.

61. Notwithstanding Hays, *Echoes of Scripture in the Letters of Paul*; see n. 51 above

62. Chapters were not added until the Middle Ages, nevertheless may be relied upon (frequently, not always) to indicate section breaks.

(1) *Single Allusions. 1 Clement* exhibits three single allusions to 1 Corinthians: (a) 1 Cor 1:31 in *1 Clem.* 13.1; (b) 1 Cor 2:9 in *1 Clem.* 34.8;
and, (c) 1 Cor 16:15 in *1 Clem.* 42.4. The function of each allusion in
1 Clement is now examined in relationship to Paul's letter.

(a) *1 Clement* 13.1. *1 Clement* 13.1 alludes to 1 Cor 1:31 (cf. 1 Cor
15:31; 2 Cor 10:17).[63] In 1 Corinthians, the passage, in turn, alludes to
Jer 9:23–24.[64] In 1 Corinthians, the passage constitutes another form
of rebuttal to the notional problem of factionalism in the community.
Boasting (or praising oneself) is, Paul argues, characteristic of factionalizing. Whereas being praised by others typifies unity.[65] Appropriate
behavior, Paul writes in 1 Cor 3:21, is represented by the slogan: "Let no
one boast in men."[66] In 1 Cor 1:31, Paul puts the same slogan positively:
"Let the one who boasts, boast in the Lord (ὁ καυχώμενος ἐν κυρίῳ
καυχάσθω)."

1 Clement 13.1 offers the same saying for precisely the same purpose:

> And so we should be humble-minded, brothers, laying aside all arrogance,
> conceit, foolishness, and forms of anger; and we should act in accordance
> with what is written. For the Holy Spirit says, "The one who is wise should
> not boast about his wisdom, nor the one who is strong about his strength, nor

---

63. Cf. 2 Cor 10:17 (ὁ δὲ καυχώμενος ἐν κυρίῳ καυχάσθω). G. Bornkamm argued
that Clement did not know 2 Corinthians (*Die Vorgeschichte des sogenannten Zweiten
Korintherbriefes*, SHAW 2 [Heidelberg: Winter, 1961], 33; repr. with Addendum in
Gesammelte Aufsätze. IV. Geschichte und Glaube, BevT 53 [Munich: Chr. Kaiser,
1971], 162–94; cf. "The History of the Origin of the So-called Second Letter to the
Corinthians," *NTS* 8 [1961–62]: 258–64). Whether Clement knew it or not does not
affect the argument here; the citation in 1 Corinthians makes the point.

64. Jer 9:23–24 (LXX) states: "Thus says the Lord, Let not the wise man boast
in his wisdom, and let not the strong man boast in his strength, and let not the rich
man boast in this wealth; but let him that boasts boast in this, the understanding and
knowing that I am the Lord that exercises mercy, and judgment, and righteousness,
upon the earth; for in these things is my pleasure, says the Lord" (Τάδε λέγει Κύριος·
μὴ καυχάσθω ὁ σοφὸς ἐν τῇ σοφίᾳ αὐτοῦ, καὶ μὴ καυχάσθω ὁ ἰσχυρὸς ἐν τῇ ἰσχύϊ
αὐτοῦ, καὶ μὴ καυχάσθω ὁ πλούσιος ἐν τῷ πλούτῳ αὐτοῦ, ἀλλ᾽ ἢ ἐν τούτῳ καυχάσθω
ὁ καυχώμενος, συνίειν καὶ γινώσκειν ὅτι ἐγώ εἰμι Κύριος ὁ ποιῶν ἔλεος καὶ κρίμα καὶ
δικαιοσύνην ἐπὶ τῆς γῆς, ὅτι ἐν τούτοις τὸ θέλημά μου, λέγει Κύριος).

65. Mitchell, *Paul and the Rhetoric of Reconciliation*, 91.

66. 1 Cor 3:21–23: ὥστε μηδεὶς καυχάσθω ἐν ἀνθρώποις· πάντα γὰρ ὑμῶν ἐστιν,
εἴτε Παῦλος εἴτε Ἀπολῶς εἴτε Κηφᾶς εἴτε κόσμος εἴτε ζωὴ εἴτε θάνατος εἴτε ἐνεστῶτα
εἴτε μέλοντα, πάντα ὑμῶν, ὑμεῖς δὲ Χριστοῦ, Χριστὸς δὲ θεοῦ. Cf. 1:12; 3:4. See
Mitchell, *Paul and the Rhetoric of Reconciliation*, 91, 93.

the one who is wealthy about his wealth; instead, the one who boasts should boast about the Lord (ὁ καυχώμενος ἐν κυρίῳ καυχάσθω), seeking after him and doing what is just and right."[67]

1 Clement introduces this allusion with a quotation formula attributing the saying to the Holy Spirit – λέγει γὰρ τὸ πνεῦμα τὸ ἅγιον – perhaps because the author recognizes the dual authorities behind the saying, that is, both Jeremiah and Paul. The underlying appeal of the assertion in all three (Jeremiah, Paul, and Clement) is to humility. For Paul and the author of *1 Clement*, humility is a strategy for compelling the addressee(s) to act on the exhortation to peace and concord.

(b) *1 Clement* 34.8. *1 Clement* 34.8 alludes to 1 Cor 2:9. Both Paul and *1 Clement* present the saying as a quotation.

But, as it is written, "[What] no eye has seen, nor ear heard, nor the human heart conceived, what God has prepared for those who love him (τοῖς ἀγαπῶσιν αὐτόν)." (1 Cor 2:9)[68]

For he says, "No eye has seen nor ear heard, nor has it entered into the human heart, what the Lord has prepared for those who await him (τοῖς ὑπομένουσιν αὐτόν)." (*1 Clem.* 34.8)[69]

Both passages share language and ideas in common with Isa 64:3–5 (LXX):[70]

Whenever you will perform glorious deeds; the mountains will be seized with quaking because of you. From ages past we have not heard, neither have our eyes seen a God besides you, and the deeds that you do for those awaiting your mercy (τοῖς ὑπομένουσιν ἔλεον).[71]

---

67. Ταπεινοφρονήσωμεν οὖν, ἀδελφοί, ἀποθέμενοι πᾶσαν ἀλαζονείαν καὶ τῦφος καὶ ἀφροσύνην καὶ ὀργάς, καὶ ποιήσωμεν τὸ γεγραμμένον· λέγει γὰρ τὸ πνεῦμα τὸ ἅγιον· Μὴ καυχάσθω ὁ σοφὸς ἐν τῇ σοφίᾳ αὐτοῦ μηδὲ ὁ ἰσχυρὸς ἐν τῇ ἰσχύϊ αὐτοῦ μηδὲ ὁ πλούσιος ἐν τῷ πλούτῳ αὐτοῦ, ἀλλ' ὁ καυχώμενος ἐν κυρίῳ καυχάσθω, τοῦ ἐκζητεῖν αὐτὸν καὶ ποιεῖν κρίμα καὶ δικαιοσύνην.

68. ἀλλὰ καθὼς γέγραπται· Ἃ ὀφθαλμὸς οὐκ εἶδεν καὶ οὖς οὐκ ἤκουσεν καὶ ἐπὶ καρδίαν ἀνθρώπου οὐκ ἀνέβη, ὅσα ἡτοίμασεν ὁ θεὸς τοῖς ἀγαπῶσιν αὐτόν.

69. Λέγει γάρ· Ὀφθαλμὸς οὐκ εἶδεν καὶ οὖς οὐκ ἤκουσεν καὶ ἐπὶ καρδίαν ἀνθρώπου οὐκ ἀνέβη, ὅσα ἡτοίμασεν κύριος τοῖς ὑπομένουσιν αὐτόν.

70. Cf. Isa 52:15.

71. ὅταν ποιῇς τὰ ἔνδοξα, τρόμος λήψεται ἀπὸ σοῦ ὄρη. ἀπὸ τοῦ αἰῶνος οὐκ ἠκούσαμεν, οὐδὲ οἱ ὀφθαλμοὶ ἡμῶν εἶδον Θεὸν πλὴν σοῦ καὶ τὰ ἔργα σου, ἃ ποιήσεις τοῖς ὑπομένουσιν ἔλεον.

1 Clement's application of this passage shares similarities and differences with Paul's. First, *1 Clement* appears to conform its conclusion to Isaiah. Second, whereas Paul concludes the saying, "what ὁ θεὸς has prepared for those who *love* him," *1 Clement* records, "what the κύριος has prepared for those who *await* him." Although *1 Clement* excludes the concept of mercy present in Isaiah (LXX),[72] it reflects the Isaianic claim that those who *wait*, rather than the Pauline claim that those who *love* will be rewarded. This same idea is also subsequently repeated in the rhetorical question in the next chapter: "What therefore has been prepared for those who wait?" (*1 Clem.* 35.3).[73] As such, this passage in *1 Clement* constitutes a modification of Paul's letter in the direction of eschatological endurance.[74] In modifying Paul's letter, *1 Clement* reflects a new epistolary scenario in which harmony (ὁμόνοια, *1 Clem.* 33.7) appears to be prioritized over love (ἀγάπη).[75] If, however, the goal of *1 Clement* here is simply to conform the saying to Isaiah, then too much should not be made of the shift from ἀγάπη to endurance. In such a case, however, the elimination of "mercy" takes on additional significance, denoting an emphasis on obedience over forgiveness. In both letters, the purpose of the passage is essentially the same: to hold out a promise of eschatological reward. Those Paul addresses in 1 Corinthians must demonstrate proper love; those Clement addresses in *1 Clement* must *persist* to the end (*1 Clem.* 34.7).

(c) *1 Clement* **42.4.** *1 Clement* 42.4 adopts Paul's reference to *first fruit* from 1 Cor 16:15 (cf. 1 Cor 15:20, 23; Rom 8:23, 11:16; 16:5; *1 Clem.* 24.1; 29.3). In 1 Cor 16:15–16 Paul refers to initial converts in the province of Achaia as "first fruit," urging the church in Corinth to recognize and serve them on account of this status:

> Now brothers and sisters, you know that members of the household of Stephanas were the first fruit (ἀπαρχή) in Achaia and they have devoted themselves to the service of the saints; I urge you to put yourselves at the service of such people, and of everyone who works and toils with them.[76]

---

72. Absent from the MT: ומעולם לא־שמעו לא האזינו עין לא־ראתה אלהים זולתך יעשה למחכה־לו (Isa 64:3–5). If, as I argue elsewhere, *1 Clement* attacks Marcionism, so the exclusion of *mercy* makes sense on these terms.

73. Τίνα οὖν ἄρα ἐστὶν τὰ ἑτοιμαζόμενα τοῖς ὑπομένουσιν.

74. Cf. Isa 64:5 (LXX).

75. Ἔχοντες οὖν τοῦτον τὸν ὑπογραμμὸν ἀόκνως προσέλθωμεν τῷ θελήματι αὐτοῦ· ἐξ ὅλης τῆς ἰσχύος ἡμῶν ἐργασώμεθα ἔργον δικαιοσύνης (*1 Clem.* 33.8).

76. Παρακαλῶ δὲ ὑμᾶς, ἀδελφοί· οἴδατε τὴν οἰκίαν Στεφανᾶ, ὅτι ἐστὶν ἀπαρχὴ τῆς Ἀχαΐας καὶ εἰς διακονίαν τοῖς ἁγίοις ἔταξαν ἑαυτούς· ἵνα καὶ ὑμεῖς ὑποτάσσησθε τοῖς τοιούτοις καὶ παντὶ τῷ συνεργοῦντι καὶ κοπιῶντι.

Similarly, the expression refers to apostolic succession in *1 Clem.* 42.4:

> And as they preached throughout the countryside and in the cities, they appointed the first fruits of their ministries as bishops and deacons of those who were about to believe,[77] testing them by the Spirit.[78]

This allusion to Paul's letter is critical to the overarching argument of *1 Clement*.[79] Paul refers to leaders he appointed and endorses as *first fruit* in a region. *1 Clement* adopts the expression to map contemporary bishops and deacons on to Paul's prior scheme as a form of legitimation, check, and control.[80] *1 Clement* 44.2 spells out this inference as follows:

> For this cause therefore, having received complete foreknowledge, they ["the apostles"][81] appointed the aforesaid persons, *and afterwards they provided a continuance*, that if these should fall asleep, other approved men should succeed to their ministration.[82]

The immediate passage in 42.5 is capped off by a version of Isa 60:17 (LXX)[83] in which leadership roles similar to those espoused by Paul are traced back to ancient Israel. Isaiah now backs the author's argument for the indelibility of Pauline lineage, an argument from antiquity (*post hoc ergo propter hoc*):

> And this was no recent development. For indeed, bishops and deacons had been mentioned in writings long before: For thus the Scripture says in one place, "I will appoint their bishops in righteousness and their deacons in faith."[84]

---

77. As Graham (*Apostolic Fathers*, 2:71) observes, *1 Clement*'s reference to "bishops and deacons" (*1 Clem.* 42.4) may be an inference from 1 Cor 16:16.

78. κατὰ χώρας οὖν καὶ πόλεις κηρύσσοντες καθίστανον τὰς ἀπαρχὰς αὐτῶν, δοκιμάσαντες τῷ πνεύματι, εἰς ἐπισκόπους καὶ διακόνους τῶν μελλόντων πιστεύειν.

79. This particular section of the argument began in *1 Clem.* 42.

80. Graham (*Apostolic Fathers*, 2:71 n. "42:1–5") sums up the passage in *1 Clement* as follows: "The orderliness of apostolic order serves to prove its divine origin."

81. "Apostles" seems mainly to imply Paul, since the author notes it is those apostles who traveled in the countryside and in cities appointing the first fruits of their ministries (*1 Clem.* 42.4).

82. Διὰ ταύτην οὖν τὴν αἰτίαν πρόγνωσιν εἰληφότες τελείαν κατέστησαν τοὺς προειρημένους καὶ μεταξὺ ἐπινομὴν ἔδωκαν, ὅπως, ἐὰν κοιμηθῶσιν, διαδέξωνται ἕτεροι δεδοκιμασμένοι ἄνδρες τὴν λειτουργίαν αὐτῶν.

83. καὶ δώσω τοὺς ἄρχοντάς σου ἐν εἰρήνῃ καὶ τοὺς ἐπισκόπους σου ἐν δικαιοσύνῃ.

84. καὶ τοῦτο οὐ καινῶς· ἐκ γὰρ δὴ πολλῶν χρόνων ἐγέγραπτο περὶ ἐπισκόπων καὶ διακόνων· οὕτως γάρ που λέγει ἡ γραφή· Καταστήσω τοὺς ἐπισκόπους αὐτῶν ἐν δικαιοσύνῃ καὶ τοὺς διακόνους αὐτῶν ἐν πίστει.

For *1 Clement*, "first fruit" is, thus, Pauline and *apostolic* language for leaders God endorses.[85] Describing initial leaders in Corinth as "first fruit" and subsequent leaders as their successors attempts to convey Paul's endorsement of certain contemporaneous bishops but not others.[86] The motif plays into the changed situation of the second century when submission to authority becomes the standard solution to factionalizing. "First fruit" allows Clement to recommend demotion and even excommunication to any faction leader unable to trace episcopal lineage back to election by Paul. In contrast, Fortunatus, greeted as *envoy* in *1 Clem.* 65.1, exemplifies "first fruit" in 1 Cor 16:17. *1 Clement*'s point is hardly subtle: Christians shall be subject to leaders in direct succession to Paul's appointments alone. The seemingly innocuous expression, "first fruits," now constitutes crucial proof in *1 Clement*'s argument against purported usurpers to the καθέδρα. The letter's opponent cannot serve in the role of bishop, Clement argues, because the opponent is not in the direct lineage of Paul.

(2) *Clusters of Allusions.* We have only one example of allusions to different chapters of 1 Corinthians occurring together in *1 Clement*. *1 Clement* 37.3 contains an allusion to 1 Cor 15:23 and *1 Clem.* 37.5 contains an allusion to 1 Cor 12:21–22. Conversely, there are four examples of allusions to a single chapter of 1 Corinthians distributed throughout *1 Clement*: two allusions to 1 Cor 4 (*1 Clem.* 3.3 and 7.1); three allusions to 1 Cor 12 (*1 Clem.* 38.1; 48.5, and 37.5); two allusions to 1 Cor 13 (*1 Clem.* 55.2 and 49.5); and three allusions to 1 Cor 15 (*1 Clem.* 24.1, 5; 37.3). These five examples are examined next.

(a) *1 Clement 37.3, 5. 1 Clement* 37 features two allusions to 1 Corinthians: *1 Clem.* 37.3 alludes to 1 Cor 15:23a and *1 Clem.* 37.5 alludes to 1 Cor 12:21–22. Although the theme of orderliness and divinely ordained sequence is the same in each, the purpose of the allusions in their individual contexts is different. We take Paul's context first. In 1 Cor 15:23a, writing about resurrection from the dead, Paul describes Jesus as *first fruit* of those risen. Jesus rose first, Paul writes, according to divine order: Adam introduced death; Jesus introduced life after death. At his return, those belonging to Jesus will also rise. Paul summarizes with a principle: "But each in his own order" (ἕκαστος δὲ ἐν τῷ ἰδίῳ τάγματι). *1 Clement* 37

85. To what extent these leaders are Paul's chosen successors in a region is unclear.
86. N.B. The expression "first fruit" has an eschatological overtone in 1 Cor 15:23, suggesting that those Paul appoints, he appoints to an eschatological destiny, namely resurrection from the dead. Interestingly, 1 Cor 16:17–18 suggest that together with Stephanas and Achaicus, Fortunatus was one of the first fruits of Achaia.

opens with the analogy of an army: "not all are commanders-in-chief or commanders over a thousand troops, or a hundred, or fifty, and so on." Rather, the text states, kings and other leaders issue commands while subjects perform them. The principle governing such behavior is, as in 1 Cor 15:23a: "each according to his own rank" (ἀλλ' ἕκαστος ἐν τῷ ἰδίῳ τάγματι, *1 Clem.* 37.3).

Subsequently, an army is favorably compared to the human body, borrowing from 1 Cor 12. In 1 Cor 12:20, Paul uses the body as a metaphor to emphasize unity. In the following passage, Paul draws special attention to the indispensability and honor of weaker members:

> The eye cannot say to the hand, "I have no need of you," nor again the head to the feet, "I have no need of you." On the contrary, the members of the body that seem to be weaker are indispensable, and those members of the body that we think less honorable we clothe with greater honor, and our less respectable members are treated with greater respect; whereas our more respectable members do not need this. (1 Cor 12:21–24a)[87]

In contrast, the body metaphor as applied to the army in *1 Clem.* 37 emphasizes subjection of *all parts* to a single ὑποταγή, noting the necessity and *utility*, rather than the necessity and *honor* of the lesser parts:

> Take our own body. The head is nothing without the feet, just as the feet are nothing without the head. And our body's most insignificant parts are necessary and useful for the whole. But all parts work together in subjection to a single order, to keep the whole body healthy. (*1 Clem.* 37.5)[88]

The two allusions to 1 Corinthians in *1 Clem.* 37 (i.e., order and body), thus, express Clement's primary exhortation to his addressee: relinquish authority and accept voluntary exile (esp. *1 Clem.* 54.2).[89] Paul sets forth the principle of orderliness (albeit in an unrelated argument about

---

87. οὐ δύναται δὲ ὁ ὀφθαλμὸς εἰπεῖν τῇ χειρί· Χρείαν σου οὐκ ἔχω, ἢ πάλιν ἡ κεφαλὴ τοῖς ποσίν· Χρείαν ὑμῶν οὐκ ἔχω· ἀλλὰ πολλῷ μᾶλλον τὰ δοκοῦντα μέλη τοῦ σώματος ἀσθενέστερα ὑπάρχειν ἀναγκαῖά ἐστιν καὶ ἃ δοκοῦμεν ἀτιμότερα εἶναι τοῦ σώματος, τούτοις τιμὴν περισσοτέραν περιτίθεμεν, καὶ τὰ ἀσχήμονα ἡμῶν εὐσχημοσύνην περισσοτέραν ἔχει.

88. Λάβωμεν τὸ σῶμα ἡμῶν· ἡ κεφαλὴ δίχα τῶν ποδῶν οὐδέν ἐστιν, οὕτως οὐδὲ οἱ πόδες δίχα τῆς κεφαλῆς· τὰ δὲ ἐλάχιστα μέλη τοῦ σώματος ἡμῶν ἀναγκαῖα καὶ εὔχρηστά εἰσιν ὅλῳ τῷ σώματι· ἀλλὰ πάντα συνπνεῖ καὶ ὑποταγῇ μιᾷ χρῆται εἰς τὸ σώζεσθαι ὅλον τὸ σῶμα.

89. Εἰπάτω· Εἰ δι' ἐμὲ στάσις καὶ ἔρις καὶ σχίσματα, ἐκχωρῶ, ἄπειμι, οὗ ἐὰν βούλησθε, καὶ ποιῶ τὰ προστασσόμενα ὑπὸ τοῦ πλήθους· μόνον τὸ ποίμνιον τοῦ Χριστοῦ εἰρηνευέτω μετὰ τῶν καθεσταμένων πρεσβυτέρων (*1 Clem.* 54.2).

Jesus as first fruit), a principle ably demonstrated by the human body. That Paul's celebrated σῶμα metaphor for church unity is adapted to a contrary purpose, that is, for subjugating certain church members to others, suggests Clement may be groping for a way to maintain full continuity with Pauline tradition, while tacitly acknowledging its insufficiency for the church's political needs in the second century. Alternatively, it suggests the author's assertiveness as an interpreter of the Pauline tradition, adapting Paul's letter to a radically new epistolary end.

(b) *Two Allusions to 1 Corinthians 4.* *1 Clement* possesses two allusions to 1 Cor 4: (i) *1 Clem.* 3.3 alludes to 1 Cor 4:10; and, (ii) *1 Clem.* 7.1 alludes to 1 Cor 4:14.[90]

(i) *1 Clement* **3:3.** 1 Corinthians 4:10 offers another example of the view that boasting plays a deleterious role in promoting schism (noted above).[91] In a prime example of sarcasm, Paul writes: "We are fools for the sake of Christ, but you are wise in Christ. We are weak, but you are strong. You are held in honor, but we in disrepute."[92] *1 Clement* 3.3 mixes its allusion to this passage with the language of Isa 3:5, perhaps because Isaiah is its presumed origin:

> And so the dishonorable rose up against the honorable, the disreputable against the reputable, the senseless against the sensible, the young [or *the new*] against the old [or *the presbyters*]. (*1 Clem.* 3.3)[93]

Isaiah 3:5 (LXX) records:

> And the people shall fall, man upon man, and every man upon his neighbor; the child shall insult the elder man, and the base the honorable (προσκόψει τὸ παιδίον πρὸς τὸν πρεσβύτην, ὁ ἄτιμος πρὸς τὸν ἔντιμον).

Juxtaposition of ἄτιμος with ἔντιμος, in addition to the concepts of young *versus* old, together suggest that *1 Clement* adapted its text from Isaiah. The question then arises as to where Paul derived his version of the saying.

90. Bart Ehrman does not acknowledge either of these allusions (Ehrman, LCL, 41, 47).

91. Mitchell, *Paul and the Rhetoric of Reconciliation*, 91.

92. ἡμεῖς μωροὶ διὰ Χριστόν, ὑμεῖς δὲ φρόνιμοι ἐν Χριστῷ· ἡμεῖς ἀσθενεῖς, ὑμεῖς δὲ ἰσχυροί· ὑμεῖς ἔνδοξοι, ἡμεῖς δὲ ἄτιμοι (1 Cor 4:10).

93. Οὕτως ἐπηγέρθησαν οἱ ἄτιμοι ἐπὶ τοὺς ἐντίμους, οἱ ἄδοξοι ἐπὶ τοὺς ἐνδόξους, οἱ ἄφρονες ἐπὶ τοὺς φρονίμους, οἱ <u>νέοι</u> ἐπὶ τοὺς <u>πρεσβυτέρους</u>.

It is unclear why Paul selected ἔνδοξος ("held in esteem," "approved," "glorious") over ἔντιμος ("honored") as contrastive to ἄτιμος ("dishonored"). At least the following four explanations are possible: (1) Paul's version of the passage in Isaiah (LXX) had ἔνδοξος; (2) Paul accidentally forgot the precise wording of the passage supplying instead a synonym; (3) Paul deliberately changed the wording of the passage; or (4) Paul is not citing Isaiah. Given uses of the δοξ- stem elsewhere in 1 Corinthians (esp. 1 Cor 15:35–49),[94] if Paul deliberately changed the wording, his motivation may have been eschatological. That is, his opponents attempt to seize their heavenly reward (or *glory*) too soon and/or wrest from Paul and his coworkers their rightful reward. If Paul implied, or if *1 Clement* infers, this usage, then *1 Clement*'s restoration of the LXX version suggests a de-emphasis of eschatological condemnation, favoring rather a focus on the earthly church. *1 Clement* also seems to import a version of Isaiah's phrase, τὸ παιδίον πρὸς τὸν πρεσβύτην in the form of οἱ νέοι ἐπὶ τοὺς πρεσβυτέρους. This supplementation bolsters the claim against the presbyters with an additional prooftext (e.g., *1 Clem.* 3.3; 21.6). Thus, the adoption in *1 Clement* of Isaiah's version of the prooftext is two-fold: it deemphasizes eschatology in favor of more pressing concerns and emphasizes the overarching concern to denounce and expel controversial claimants to the bishopric (*1 Clem.* 54.2; cf. *1 Clem.* 1.3; 3.3 [or "elder"]; 21.6 [or "elder"]; 44.5; 47.6; 55.4; 57.1).[95]

(ii) *1 Clement* 7.1. In 1 Cor 4:14, Paul states that admonition is the purpose of his letter: "I am not writing this to make you ashamed, but to admonish you as my beloved children."[96] *1 Clement* 7.1 states this same purpose,

---

94. A passage Clement cites at *1 Clem.* 24.5.

95. ἐπισκοπή in *1 Clem.* 50.3 may constitute a play-on-words involving the "episcopate." Cf. ἐπισκοπή in *1 Clem.* 44.1, 4; and 50.3 (for the prepositional phrase, ἐν τῇ ἐπισκοπῇ, Lake translates: "at the visitation"; Ehrman translates with the finite verb, "appears"). Cf. ἐπίσκοπος in *1 Clem.* 42.4, 5 (×2); and 59.3 (Lake: "watcher"; Ehrman: "overseer"). If the noun, ἐπισκοπή ("visit," "episcopate") ultimately derives from the noun, ἐπισκοπή ("overseer," "bishop"), then the "visit" made by an "overseer" may imply some kind of reckoning. Of seven occurrences of the ἐπισκοπ- stem in *1 Clement*, all but two refer to the church episcopate. Of the two other occurrences, 1 *Clem.* 50.3 refers to the "kingdom of God" and *1 Clem.* 59.3 refers to God himself as both creator and "overseer" – that great "bishop" in the sky. Since *1 Clem.* 50.4 discusses hiding from judgment as God passes by (i.e., a form of visitation), then, together with its eschatological overtones, the "visitation" of the "kingdom of God" in 50.3 seems to offer a play on the visits that second-century bishops made as an aspect of their work for the "episcopate."

96. οὐκ ἐντρέπων ὑμᾶς γράφω ταῦτα, ἀλλ᾽ ὡς τέκνα μου ἀγαπητὰ νουθετῶν.

appending, however, that it serves also as a reminder to the author: "We are writing these things, loved ones, not only to admonish you but also to remind ourselves. For we are in the same arena and the same contest is set before us."⁹⁷ *1 Clement*'s adoption of this passage is significant insofar as it explicitly characterizes its message as Paul characterizes 1 Corinthians.

(c) *Three Allusions to 1 Corinthians 12 – Body Metaphor.* 1 Clement alludes to 1 Cor 12 three times: (i) *1 Clem.* 38.1 alludes to 1 Cor 12:4; (ii) *1 Clem.* 48.5 alludes to 1 Cor 12:8–9; and (iii) *1 Clem.* 37.5 alludes to 1 Cor 12:21–22. The allusions in 1 Clem. 38:1 (i) and 37:5 (iii) are addressed together in the next section, in the order in which they arise in 1 Clement.

(i) *1 Clement* 38.1. In 1 Cor 12:4, Paul writes: "Now there are varieties of gifts, but the same Spirit."⁹⁸ In this passage, Paul argues against στάσις by arguing *for* unity in the face of diversity, based on the Spirit's mutual distribution of all gifts. Paul maintains that each person in the community has an individual gift. These individual gifts contribute to unity because a single spirit (cf. 1 Cor 8:6; 12:11) is their source and governs them.⁹⁹ About this passage, Margaret M. Mitchell sums it up well: "How can there be discord in the church when there is unity in these strongest of forces?"¹⁰⁰ In 1 Cor 12:12–31, Paul adds that the way in which diverse gifts contribute to unity might be compared to the human body (12:12–31); the human body, in fact, *requires* diverse members in order to maintain health. Although in 1 Cor 12:21–22 Paul's body metaphor *proceeds from* his pronouncement of the Spirit's governance of individual gifts, *1 Clement* neglects mention of the spirit and reverses the order. The argument begins in *1 Clem.* 37 with the metaphor of the army for the community (including citation of 1 Cor 15:23, discussed below). Although the author notes that army generals ("the great") cannot survive without the rank and file ("the lowly") and vice versa, the section emphasizes subjection of soldiers to commanders. Even when acknowledging a kind of mutual necessity of all parts, the idea is summarized as submission to "a single order" (*1 Clem.* 37.5). In this regard, Paul's body metaphor is appropriated as a prooftext and second metaphor.

97. Ταῦτα, ἀγαπητοί, οὐ μόνον ὑμᾶς νουθετοῦντες ἐπιστέλλομεν, ἀλλὰ καὶ ἑαυτοὺς ὑπομιμνήσκοντες· ἐν γὰρ τῷ αὐτῷ ἐσμὲν σκάμματι, καὶ ὁ αὐτὸς ἡμῖν ἀγὼν ἐπίκειται (*1 Clem.* 7.1).
98. διαιρέσεις δὲ χαρισμάτων εἰσίν, τὸ δὲ αὐτὸ πνεῦμα (1 Cor 12:4).
99. Mitchell, *Paul and the Rhetoric of Reconciliation*, 268.
100. Ibid., 268.

1 Clement 38 then summarizes the body metaphor, reiterating the importance not of equality (or with Paul: *deference* to weaker members as crucial to the avoidance of dissension, 1 Cor 12:22–25) but submission:

> And so let our whole body be healthy [or *saved*] in Christ Jesus, and let each person be subject to his neighbor, in accordance with the gracious gift he has received. (*1 Clem.* 38.1)[101]

The introductory statement of this passage, "Let the body be healthy (or *saved*)," echoes Paul's idea that communities function like bodies. Different from Paul, however, *1 Clement* inserts that each person must also be subject to his neighbor. The parallelism of the two exhortations of the body (to be healthy) and of the individual (to his neighbor) suggests that the *health* of a social body demands the subjection.[102] The author of *1 Clement*, thus, appropriates Paul's body metaphor, not in its original, Pauline sense as a symbol of unity, but in a new and contradictory sense as a symbol of subjugation. It seems, again, that Clementine interpretation of 1 Corinthians is carefully guided by its own agenda, namely, the prompt expulsion of opponents.[103]

(ii) *1 Clement* 48.5. In 1 Cor 12:8–9, 11, Paul writes:

> To one is given through the Spirit the utterance of wisdom, and to another the utterance of knowledge according to the same Spirit, to another faith by the same Spirit, to another gifts of healing by the one Spirit... All these are activated by one and the same Spirit who allots to each one individually just as the Spirit chooses.[104]

---

101. Σωζέσθω οὖν ἡμῶν ὅλον τὸ σῶμα ἐν Χριστῷ Ἰησοῦ, καὶ ὑποτασσέσθω ἕκαστος τῷ πλησίον αὐτοῦ, καθὼς ἐτέθη ἐν τῷ χαρίσματι αὐτοῦ.

102. A desideratum of this argument is whether the verb σώζω here insinuates special interest – perhaps even a double entendre – in the physical body. As such it might constitute an argument against Marcion who held a decidedly negative position on the matter of Jesus' corporeal existence.

103. Cf. ἱνατί διέλκομεν καὶ διασπῶμεν τὰ μέλη τοῦ Χριστοῦ καὶ στασιάζομεν πρὸς τὸ σῶμα τὸ ἴδιον (*1 Clem.* 46.7). Graham includes it as a parallel (Graham, *Apostolic Fathers*, 2:66, 104); Ehrman does not (Ehrman, LCL, 103).

104. ᾧ μὲν γὰρ διὰ τοῦ πνεύματος δίδοται λόγος σοφίας, ἄλλῳ δὲ λόγος γνώσεως κατὰ τὸ αὐτὸ πνεῦμα, ἑτέρῳ πίστις ἐν τῷ αὐτῷ πνεύματι, ἄλλῳ χαρίσματα ἰαμάτων ἐν τῷ ἑνὶ πνεύματι...πάντα δὲ ταῦτα ἐνεργεῖ τὸ ἓν καὶ τὸ αὐτὸ πνεῦμα, διαιροῦν ἰδίᾳ ἑκάστῳ καθὼς βούλεται.

1 Clement 48.5 delineates a closely related list of possible gifts (i.e., faith, knowledge, wisdom, deeds) a Christian might possess.[105] Different from Paul, however, *1 Clement* recommends that individuals exercise their gifts in humility, striving not for personal gain but for the good of the group. The most gifted, according to *1 Clem.* 48.5, should exercise the most humility:

> Let a person be faithful, let him be able to speak forth knowledge, let him be wise in his discernment of words, let him be pure in deeds. For the more he appears to be great, the more he should be humble, striving for the good of all, not just himself.[106]

1 Clement 48.5 presumes the same unifying effect of the exercise of different gifts that Paul names. However, whereas Paul implies that the pure exercise of a gift contributes to unity, Clement specifies that gifts must be exercised in humility and "for the good of all" in order to achieve this effect. Thus, all three passages emphasizing unity in 1 Cor 12 are reappropriated to emphasize subjugation in *1 Clement*.

(d) *Two Allusions to 1 Corinthians 13 – Love.* *1 Clement* alludes to 1 Cor 13 twice (i.e., *1 Clem.* 55.2 and 49.5). These allusions are significant because they incorporate five full verses of Paul's letter. Concerning Clement's allusion to 1 Cor 13:4–7, Carlyle writes, "It can hardly be doubted that many of the phrases in Clement were suggested by the recollection of the passage in Corinthians."[107]

(i) *1 Clement* 55.2. *1 Clement* 55.2, alludes to 1 Cor 13:3, a passage Holt Graham once called "*oddly reminiscent* of 1 Cor 13:3."[108] Donald Hagner, too, comments, "The words παραδεδωκότας and ἐψώμισαν in Cl. 55.2 may recall the similarly used ψωμίσω and παραδῶ of 1 Cor. 13.3."[109] In 1 Cor 13:3, Paul addresses factions by focusing on the impor-

---

105. Πιστός–πίστις, γνῶσις–λογός γνώσεως, σοφὸς ἐν διακρίσει λόγων–λόγος σοφίας. This list suggests to Carlyle "probable" reminiscence of 1 Corinthians (Oxford Society, *The New Testament in the Apostolic Fathers*, 42).

106. Ἤτω τις πιστός, ἤτω δυνατὸς γνῶσιν ἐξειπεῖν, ἤτω σοφὸς ἐν διακρίσει λόγων, ἤτω ἁγνὸς ἐν ἔργοις. τοσούτῳ γὰρ μᾶλλον ταπεινοφρονεῖν ὀφείλει, ὅσῳ δοκεῖ μᾶλλον μείζων εἶναι, καὶ ζητεῖν τὸ κοινωφελὲς πᾶσιν, καὶ μὴ τὸ ἑαυτοῦ.

107. Oxford Society, *The New Testament in the Apostolic Fathers*, 41.

108. Graham, *Apostolic Fathers*, 2.87 n. "55:2–6," emphasis added.

109. Hagner, *Use of the Old and New Testaments in Clement of Rome*, 208.

tance of internal motivation.[110] For sacrifice to be effective, Paul writes, even including *self-sacrifice*, it must be motivated by love. In circumstances of faction, however, where boasting (not love) is a hallmark characteristic, self-sacrifice is stripped of its intrinsic, and particularly its στάσις-dissolving, value:

> If I give away all my possessions, and if I hand over my body so that I may boast, but do not have love, I gain nothing. (1 Cor 13:3)[111]

According to Paul, the social harmony gained from giving over possessions and even one's own body in 1 Cor 13 is lost when the sacrificial act lacks an internal motivation of love.

1 Clement 55:2 imports 1 Cor 13:3 to make a related, yet distinctive, point. Self-sacrifice, according to *1 Clement*, also dissolves στάσις, yet for Clement the act is sufficient, *irrespective* of the individual's internal motivation:[112]

> Among ourselves, we know many who put themselves in prison in order to ransom others; many placed themselves in slavery and fed others with the purchase price they received. (*1 Clem.* 55.2)[113]

The contrast with Paul's statement is stark. For Clement, sacrifices such as imprisonment and slavery are effective without qualification. For Paul, however, such acts are void and *ineffective* apart from love. Clement's position on self-sacrifice makes sense in terms of the letter's primary exhortation to its addressee(s) to accept voluntary exile (*1 Clem.* 54.2). If the opponent's internal disposition were favorable toward self-imposed exile, the letter would not need to recommend (i.e., εἰπάτω) it. The logic of *1 Clement* requires freedom of internal motivation in self-sacrificial acts.[114]

---

110. In this regard, 1 Cor 13 is similar to the Sermon on the Mount, although I do not wish to suggest that this makes the theme of internal motivation unique to these two texts or to Christian texts in general.

111. καὶ ἐὰν ψωμίσω πάντα τὰ ὑπάρχοντά μου, καὶ ἐὰν παραδῶ τὸ σῶμά μου, ἵνα καυθήσομαι, ἀγάπην δὲ μὴ ἔχω, οὐδὲν ὠφελοῦμαι.

112. N.B. *1 Clem.* 55 explicitly claims to offer the exempla for *1 Clem.* 54.1–4.

113. Ἐπιστάμεθα πολλοὺς ἐν ἡμῖν παραδεδωκότας ἑαυτοὺς εἰς δεσμά, ὅπως ἑτέρους λυτρώσονται· πολλοὶ ἑαυτοὺς παρέδωκαν εἰς δουλείαν καὶ λαβόντες τὰς τιμὰς αὐτῶν ἑτέρους ἐψώμισαν.

114. Allusions to the Corinthian correspondence in this passage in *1 Clement* are not limited to 1 Cor 13. Also incorporated are 1 Cor 9:19 (Ἐλεύθερος γὰρ ὢν ἐκ πάντων πᾶσιν ἐμαυτὸν ἐδούλωσα, ἵνα τοὺς πλείονας κερδήσω) and 2 Cor 12:9–10 (καὶ εἴρηκέν μοι· Ἀρκεῖ σοι ἡ χάρις μου· ἡ γὰρ δύναμις ἐν ἀσθενείᾳ τελεῖται. ἥδιστα

Thus, in a passage regarded as very close to 1 Corinthians, the underlying message is fundamentally opposed.

(ii) *1 Clement* 49.5. *1 Clement* 49.5 alludes to 1 Cor 13:4–7,[115] the passage in which Paul writes:

> Love is patient; love is kind; love is not envious or boastful or arrogant or rude. It does not insist on it own way; it is not irritable or resentful; it does not rejoice in wrongdoing, but rejoices in the truth. It bears all things, believes all things, hopes all things, endures all things.[116]

As Margaret Mitchell demonstrates, this passage in Paul's letter corresponds exactly to Paul's description of Corinthian factionalists elsewhere

---

οὖν μᾶλλον καυχήσομαι ἐν ταῖς ἀσθενείαις μου, ἵνα ἐπισκηνώσῃ ἐπ’ ἐμὲ ἡ δύναμις τοῦ Χριστοῦ). In 1 Cor 9:19, Paul uses himself as an exemplar of self-sacrifice on behalf of the gospel, characterizing himself paradoxically as "free" despite his status as "slave to all" (Ἐλεύθερος γὰρ ὢν ἐκ πάντων πᾶσιν ἐμαυτὸν ἐδούλωσα, ἵνα τοὺς πλείονας κερδήσω). Likewise, in 2 Cor 12:9, Paul narrates a revelation in which the Lord tells him – again exploiting paradox – that "weakness," that is, self-sacrifice, "perfects" or "completes" his power in Paul and is, thus, an acceptable (i.e., concord-promoting) boast (καὶ εἴρηκέν μοι· Ἀρκεῖ σοι ἡ χάρις μου· ἡ γὰρ δύναμις ἐν ἀσθενείᾳ τελεῖται. ἥδιστα οὖν μᾶλον καυχήσομαι ἐν ταῖς ἀσθενείαις μου, ἵνα ἐπισκηνώσῃ ἐπ’ ἐμὲ ἡ δύναμις τοῦ Χριστοῦ). As we will see, both of these additional Pauline allusions direct *1 Clement*'s purpose for borrowing from 1 Cor 13:3.

115. Conzelmann argued that 1 Cor 13:1–3 and 1 Cor 13:8–13 should be understood as distinct sections. Hagner offers the following helpful table:

1 Clem. 49.5	1 Cor 13
ἀγάπη πάντα ἀνέχεται	7. πάντα στέγει ... πάντα ὑπομένει
πάντα μακροθυμεῖ	4. ἡ ἀγάπη μακροθυμεῖ
οὐδὲν βάναυσον ἐν ἀγάπῃ,	6. οὐ χαίρει ἐπὶ τῇ ἀδικίᾳ
οὐδὲν ὑπερήφανον	4. οὐ περπερεύεται, οὐ φυσιοῦται
ἀγάπη σχίσμα οὐκ ἔχει,	5. οὐ ζητεῖ τὰ ἑαυτῆς,
ἀγάπη οὐ στασιάζει,	οὐ παροξύνεται,
ἀγάπη πάντα ποιεῖ ἐν ὁμονοίᾳ	οὐ λογίζεται τὸ κακόν
ἐν τῇ ἀγάπῃ ἐτελειώθησαν	? [10, ὅταν δὲ ἔλθῃ τὸ τέλειον]
πάντες οἱ ἐκλεκτοὶ τοῦ θεοῦ	cf. 1 John 4:18
δίχα ἀγάπης οὐδὲν εὐάρεστόν	? (= Heb 11:6)
ἐστιν τῷ θεῷ.	

(*Use of the Old and New Testaments in Clement of Rome*, 200).

116. Ἡ ἀγάπη μακροθυμεῖ, χρηστεύεται ἡ ἀγάπη, οὐ ζηλοῖ ἡ ἀγάπη, οὐ περπερεύεται, οὐ φυσιοῦται, οὐκ ἀσχημονεῖ, οὐ ζητεῖ τὰ ἑαυτῆς, οὐ παροξύνεται, οὐ λογίζεται τὸ κακόν, οὐ χαίρει ἐπὶ τῇ ἀδικίᾳ, συγχαίρει δὲ τῇ ἀληθείᾳ· πάντα στέγει, πάντα πιστεύει, πάντα ἐλπίζει, πάντα ὑπομένει.

in 1 Corinthians.[117] Thus, as a clear counter to factionalism, the passage finds an obvious home in *1 Clement*.[118] Different from Paul, however, who here defines love *qua* love *presuming* its deleterious effect on schisms, *Clement*'s echo of the passage specifies love's anti-schismatic effect:

> Love binds us to God; love hides a multitude of sins; love bears all things and endures all things. There is nothing vulgar in love, nothing haughty. Love has no schism. Love creates no faction, love does all things in harmony. Everyone chosen by God has been perfected in love; apart from love nothing is pleasing to God. (*1 Clem.* 49.5)[119]

Both allusions to 1 Cor 13 in *1 Clement*, thus, emphasize any form of self-sacrifice over schism.

(e) *Three Allusions to 1 Corinthians 15 – Resurrection.* Finally, *1 Clement* alludes to 1 Cor 15 three times: 1 Cor 15:20 in *1 Clem.* 24.1; 1 Cor 15:35–38 in *1 Clem.* 24.5; and 1 Cor 15:23 in *1 Clem.* 37.3. The final allusion was treated above. The next section, therefore, treats *1 Clem.* 24.1 and 24.5, with a concluding remark about the collective intention of all three.

1 Clement 24 alludes to 1 Cor 15 twice: 15:20 and 15:35–38. In their original context in 1 Corinthians, both passages defend resurrection. In 1 Cor 15:20, Paul presents his concept of ἀπαρχή ("first fruit"). Rather than the conversion of new believers in Achaia (second occurrence of this expression in 1 Cor 16:15), in this instance ἀπαρχή refers to Jesus' resurrection:[120]

---

117. Mitchell, *Paul and the Rhetoric of Reconciliation*, 168–71.

118. Hagner, *Use of the Old and New Testaments in Clement of Rome*, 200. Hagner notes that after Clement of Alexandria paraphrases this passage in *1 Clement* (*Strom.* 4.111.3), he cites 1 Cor 13:3, 1 (200 n. 1).

119. Ἀγάπη κολλᾷ ἡμᾶς τῷ θεῷ, ἀγάπη καλύπτει πλῆθος ἁμαρτιῶν, ἀγάπη πάντα ἀνέχεται, πάντα μακροθυμεῖ· οὐδὲν βάναυσον ἐν ἀγάπῃ, οὐδὲν ὑπερήφανον· ἀγάπη σχίσμα οὐκ ἔχει, ἀγάπη οὐ στασιάζει, ἀγάπη πάντα ποιεῖ ἐν ὁμονοίᾳ· ἐν τῇ ἀγάπῃ ἐτελειώθησαν πάντες οἱ ἐκλεκτοὶ τοῦ θεοῦ· δίχα ἀγάπης οὐδὲν εὐάρεστόν ἐστιν τῷ θεῷ. Love's role in "perfecting" or "completing" (ἐν τῇ ἀγάπῃ ἐτελειώθησαν) God's chosen ones may echo 2 Cor 12:9: "But he said, 'My grace is sufficient for you, for power is made perfect in weakness." So I will boast all the more gladly of my weaknesses, so that the power of Christ may dwell in me.'" *1 Clement*'s reliance on 2 Corinthians is disputed. See Hagner, *Use of the Old and New Testaments in Clement of Rome*, 209.

120. Carlyle comments about this allusion: "This would appear to be almost certainly a reminiscence. The word ἀπαρχή, used in this sense of our Lord, in reference

But in fact Christ has been raised from the dead, the first fruits of those who
have died. (1 Cor 15:20)[121]

Adopting this expression from Paul, *1 Clem.* 24.1 too refers to Jesus'
resurrection as ἀπαρχή:

> We should consider, loved ones, how the Master continuously shows us the
> future resurrection that is about to occur, of which he made the Lord Jesus
> Christ the first fruit by raising him from the dead.[122]

Following its initial presentation and defense, *1 Clement* bolsters its
argument for bodily resurrection with two proofs. The first proof is the
succession of days and nights: each new day represents a *resurrection* of
the previous day's death (i.e., night):

> Day and night reveal to us a resurrection: the night sleeps and the day arises;
> the day departs and the night arrives. (*1 Clem.* 24.3)[123]

The second proof is the seasonal rotation of crops (*1 Clem.* 24.5):

> We should consider the crops: how, and in what way, does the sowing
> occur? The sower goes out and casts each of the seeds onto the soil. Because
> they are dry and barren they decay when they fall onto the soil. But then the
> Master raises them up out of their decay, and from the one seed grow more,
> and so bring forth the crop.[124]

The crop analogy relies on 1 Cor 15, where Paul describes resurrection
as life stemming from perceptibly "dead" (ἐκ τῆς διαλύσεως, "decayed" in
1 Clem. 24.5) seeds:

to the resurrection, seems to make this plain" (Oxford Society, *The New Testament
in the Apostolic Fathers*, 41). So also Gregory, "Clement and the Writings That Later
Formed the New Testament," 147. Lindemann argues for literary reliance; see his
Paulus im ältesten Christentum, 183; idem, *Clemensbriefe*, 86.

121. Νυνὶ δὲ Χριστὸς ἐγήγερται ἐκ νεκρῶν, ἀπαρχὴ τῶν κεκοιμημένων.

122. Κατανοήσωμεν, ἀγαπητοί, πῶς ὁ δεσπότης ἐπιδείκνυται διηνεκῶς ἡμῖν τὴν
μέλλουσαν ἀνάστασιν ἔσεσθαι, ἧς τὴν ἀπαρχὴν ἐποιήσατο τὸν κύριον Ἰησοῦν Χριστὸν ἐκ
νεκρῶν ἀναστήσας (*1 Clem.* 24.1).

123. Ἡμέρα καὶ νὺξ ἀνάστασιν ἡμῖν δηλοῦσιν· κοιμᾶται ἡ νύξ, ἀνίσταται ἡ ἡμέρα·
ἡ ἡμέρα ἄπεισιν, νὺξ ἐπέρχεται.

124. Ἐξῆλθεν ὁ σπείρων καὶ ἔβαλεν εἰς τὴν γῆν ἕκαστον τῶν σπερμάτων· ἅτινα
πεσόντα εἰς τὴν γῆν ξηρὰ καὶ γυμνὰ διαλύεται· εἶτ' ἐκ τῆς διαλύσεως ἡ μεγαλειότης
τῆς προνοίας τοῦ δεσπότου ἀνίστησιν αὐτά, καὶ ἐκ τοῦ ἑνὸς πλείονα αὔξει καὶ ἐκφέρει
καρπόν.

But someone will ask, "How are the dead raised? With what kind of body do they come?" Fool! What you sow does not come to life unless it dies. And as for what you sow, you do not sow the body that is to be, but a bare seed, perhaps of wheat or of some other grain. But God gives it a body as he has chosen, and to each kind of seed its own body. (1 Cor 15:35–38)[125]

The importation of these two agricultural analogies from 1 Corinthians – (1) Christ as the ἀπαρχή of those who have died ("fallen asleep") and (2) the example of the seed – cohere with *1 Clement*'s reliance on 1 Corinthians, as well as with its affinity for concrete exempla. The following chapter, *1 Clem.* 25, strengthens this argument with a third example, the phoenix. As an aggregate, however, these three allusions have special force – namely, they mount an attack on the same type of opponents Paul addresses in his letter: those refusing, at some level, the possibility of resurrection.[126] In Paul's argument, 1 Cor 15:20 specifies Christ as risen, 1 Cor 15:23 emphasizes the resurrection of believers ("each in his own order"),[127] and 1 Cor 15:35–38 offer an illustration of where else in the physical world this phenomenon can be observed. *1 Clement*'s argument is essentially the same, only amplified by a few additional examples.

As in 1 Corinthians, moreover, the two allusions in *1 Clem.* 24 constitute pieces of an eschatological section of warnings beginning in *1 Clem.* 23.5 and intended to compound the urgency of the letter's central mandate of concord. Like Paul, *1 Clement* addresses resurrection because it is an issue broadening the community's schism. Like Paul, it attempts to reverse the issue's divisive effect by defending the phenomenon with concrete examples and emphasizing its unifying potential. According to both texts, resurrection unifies communities by stipulating one goal, one

125. Ἀλλὰ ἐρεῖ τις· Πῶς ἐγείρονται οἱ νεκροί, ποίῳ δὲ σώματι ἔρχονται; ἄφρων, σὺ ὃ σπείρεις, οὐ ζωοποιεῖται ἐὰν μὴ ἀποθάνῃ· καὶ ὃ σπείρεις, οὐ τὸ σῶμα τὸ γενησόμενον σπείρεις ἀλλὰ γυμνὸν κόκκον εἰ τύχοι σίτου ἤ τινος τῶν λοιπῶν· ὁ δὲ θεὸς δίδωσιν αὐτῷ σῶμα καθὼς ἠθέλησεν, καὶ ἑκάστῳ τῶν σπερμάτων ἴδιον σῶμα.

126. At this point it may be of some benefit to assess the plausibility of a historical interpretation of the letter. *1 Clem.* 1.2 claims that after a history of factionalizing and skepticism concerning the resurrection from the dead, the Corinthian church had acquired a reputation of a "highly virtuous and stable faith," putting away all of the problems with which Paul confronted them in his first letter. Now, however, Clement claims that the Corinthian church has withdrawn into precisely those same problems such that a "church sojourning in Rome" is compelled to write a missive (reliant on both the understanding and authority of Paul's prior letter) featuring the same solutions.

127. The order is: Christ as first fruit, believers as subsequent fruit.

hope (*1 Clem.* 27.1), and one victory over one enemy, death.[128] What is more, the magnitude of the truth of resurrection dwarfs other quarrels, nullifying them by lending perspective. Margaret M. Mitchell explains this effect as follows, "In the case of the resurrection [i.e., 1 Cor 15:1–57] Paul transforms a subject of dispute into the very τέλος or goal which should govern all Christian decision making and against which all feeble and insignificant struggles are to be compared and belittled."[129] *1 Clement*'s argument takes the form of a rhetorical question in *1 Clem.* 26.1, following the example of the phoenix (*1 Clem.* 25):

> Do we then think that it is so great and marvelous that the Creator of all things will raise everyone who has served him in a holy way with the confidence of good faith when he shows us the magnificence of his promise even through a bird? (*1 Clem.* 26.1)[130]

According to *1 Clement*, Christians can and should observe proofs of the resurrection in nature because such proofs destroy factions by serving as reminders of a shared and ultimate goal. Observing such proofs, Christians will, according to Clement, effortlessly accept that a compassionate God (*1 Clem.* 23.1) plans to reward them (*1 Clem.* 23.2) and will, therefore, await (*1 Clem.* 23.5) this promise in peace (*1 Clem.* 22.5) and without faction.

Conclusion

1 Clement's structural elements and allusions to Corinthians map this letter on Paul's prior, authoritative letter to address a new, non-literal, epistolary situation.[131] One such situation is anti-gnostic – precisely the way *1 Clement* is appropriated by its first readers Irenaeus, Clement of Alexandria, Tertullian, and Origen. That said, its opponent is sufficiently vague and its message, sufficiently universal, for applications in Corinth already by the time of Dionysius of Corinth (170 CE) and elsewhere among Christians, into (at least) the sixth and seventh centuries.[132]

128. Mitchell, *Paul and the Rhetoric of Reconciliation*, 283–84.

129. Ibid., 283.

130. Μέγα καὶ θαυμαστὸν οὖν νομίζομεν εἶναι, εἰ ὁ δημιουργὸς τῶν ἁπάντων ἀνάστασιν ποιήσεται τῶν ὁσίως αὐτῷ δουλευσάντων ἐν πεποιθήσει πίστεως ἀγαθῆς, ὅπου καὶ δι' ὀρνέου δείκνυσιν ἡμῖν τὸ μεγαλεῖον τῆς ἐπαγγελίας αὐτοῦ; cf. Matt 6:25–33.

131. Cf. *1 Clem.* 63.2 (cf. *1 Clem.* 23.2) where the text may refer to itself as "scripture."

132. According to Soter, bishop of Rome (ca. 170, *apud* Eusebius, *Hist. eccl.* 4.23.11), the church in Corinth (Dionysius of Corinth in a letter-response to a letter

Appendix 1

Allusions to other undisputed Pauline letters:

	1 Clement
Rom 1:29–32	35.5–6
Gal 3:1	2.1
Phil 1:1	42.4
Phil 4:15	47.2

Allusions to disputed Pauline letters and Hebrews:

	1 Clement
Eph 4:4–6	46.6
Eph 4:32–5:1	14.3
Eph 5:21	38.1
1 Tim 1:17	61.2
1 Tim 2:7	60.4
Titus 3:1	2.7; 33.1; 34.4
Heb 1:3–5, 7, 13	36.2–5
Heb 2:17; 3:1	36.1

and gift from Soter) had a copy of *1 Clement*. How it arrived (and was owned) by the church in Corinth by the time of Dionysius of Corinth is hardly an issue since the letter achieved rapid and broad dissemination as witnessed by citations and reference in the works of Irenaeus (*Haer.* 3.3.3.), Clement of Alexandria (*Strom.* 1.7.38; 4.6.32, 33; 4.17–19, 105–21; 4.17.112; 4.18.113; 5.12.81; 6.8.64, 65); Tertullian (*Praescr.* 32), Origen (*Princ.* 2.3.6 et al.). If, as I argue, it was not really intended for the church in Corinth, however, the question arises as to whether someone in Corinth would not have recognized it as a forgery. This question involves levels of skepticism about the authenticity of texts in the late second-century church. In fact, the letter's authenticity would probably never have risen at the church in Corinth since it added to this church's prestige (two letters is good, three, is better; cf. *3 Corinthians*). A spirit of skepticism is, after all, rarely evenly applied; something usually happens to trigger it. Moreover, if *1 Clement* broadly supported an anti-gnostic or even anti-Marcionite agenda (as it was used by various proto-orthodox Christians and as I argue elsewhere), not only would there be no reason to doubt its authenticity, there would be a reason to suppress such doubts in Corinth and elsewhere. Of course, I would expect that gnostics questioned its authenticity and marshaled weapons of fraud detection against it. It is not surprising, however, that such rebuttals would be lost. On my reading, gnostics would have immediately recognized *1 Clement* as an allegorical letter, that is, a letter in which the addressee is the only person who understands what is truly meant and in which the sender intimates one thing by means of another. This definition comes from Ps.-Demetrius, *Epistolary Types* 15; text and translation in Malherbe, *Ancient Epistolary Theorists*, 38–39.

Heb 3:2, 5	43.1
Heb 3:7; 10:15	13.1; 16.2 (cf. 8.1; 22.1; 45.2)
Heb 4:12	21.9
Heb 4:15	36.1
Heb 6:18	27.2
Heb 11	9–11
Heb 11:37	17.1
Heb 12:9	64
1 Pet 4:8	49.5

Appendix 2

		1 Clement	1 Corinthians
A			
	1.	37.5	12:12ff.
	2.	38.1	12:12ff. (cf. *1 Clem.* 46.7 and 1 Cor 6:15)
	3.	47.1	1:11–13
	4.	49.5	13:4–7
B			
	5.	24.1	15:20, 23
	6.	24.4, 5	15:36, 37
C			
	7.	5.1, 5	9:24
	8.	34.8	2:9 (Isa 64:4)
	9.	37.3	15:2
	10.	38.2	16:17 (Phil 2:30; cf. 2 Cor 9:12; 11:9)
	11.	40.1	2:10 (cf. Rom 11:33)
	12.	48.6	10:34, 33 (cf. Phil 2:4)

The Oxford Committee describes their four classes of probability as follows: "It was decided to arrange the books of the New Testament in four classes, distinguished by the letters A, B, C, and D, according to the degree of probability of their use by the several authors. Class A includes those books about which there can be no reasonable doubt, either because they are expressly mentioned, or because there are other certain indications of their use. Class B comprises those books the use of which, in the judgment of the editors, reaches a high degree of probability. With class C we come to lower degree of probability. In class D are placed those books which may possibly be referred to, but in regard to which the evidence appeared too uncertain to allow any reliance to be placed upon it" (Oxford Society, *The New Testament in the Apostolic Fathers*, iii).

Appendix 3

1 Clement	1 Corinthians
Sal.	1:1–3 (epistolary convention)
47.1–4	1:12
37.5–38.2	12:12, 14 20–28
49.5	13:4–7
24.1	15:20, 23
24.4–5	15:36–37
48.5	12:8–9
5.1–5	9:24
34.8	2:9
65.2	16:23
30.1	5:27

(Gregory, "*1 Clement* and the Writings That Later Formed the New Testament,"
144–48.)

Chapter 7

IGNATIUS AND PAUL ON SUFFERING AND DEATH:
A SHORT, COMPARATIVE STUDY

Todd D. Still

In *"Mori Lucrum*: Paul and Ancient Theories of Suicide," an essay
published in *Novum Testamentum* in 1988, Arthur J. Droge examines Phil
1:21–26 in light of the ancient Greek and Roman discussion concerning
suicide. Droge begins his study by considering salient passages on the
subject of suicide in Plato's *Phaedo* and Aristotle's *Nicomachean Ethics*.
Thereafter, he takes up Cynic, Epicurean, and Stoic views on the topic,
devoting particular special attention to the Stoic Seneca, who "extolled
[suicide] as the greatest triumph of an individual over fate."[1] It is against
this literary backdrop that Droge interprets Phil 1:21–26. In so doing, he
posits that Paul is pondering the possibility, indeed desirability, of suicide
"for himself and presumably Christians."[2]

Albeit a novel and provocative proposal, it is not the aim of this brief
chapter to enter into dialog with Droge regarding his reading of Phil
1:21–26.[3] Rather, in what follows I would like to examine a comparison
that Droge makes in his article between Paul on the one hand and Ignatius
on the other. It is to this supposed parallel that we now turn.

Near the outset of his essay, Droge suggests that Paul had "a general
fascination with death."[4] Later in his paper, while surveying Christian
literature on the subject of suicide beyond the NT and prior to Augustine,
Droge depicts Ignatius as having a "pathological craving for martyrdom."[5]
Thereafter, in treating Phil 1:21–26, Droge describes Paul as one who

1. Arthur J. Droge, *"Mori Lucrum*: Paul and Ancient Theories of Suicide," *NovT*
30 (1988): 263–86, here 264.
2. Ibid., 264.
3. I have done so elsewhere. See Todd D. Still, *Philippians & Philemon*, Smyth &
Helwys Bible Commentary 22 (Macon: Smyth & Helwys, 2011), 40–41.
4. Droge, *"Mori Lucrum,"* 264.
5. Ibid., 277.

"lusts after death"[6] and aligns the apostle "with a tradition on suicide which can be traced back to Socrates."[7] Then, as he draws to a close his comparison of Paul with other ancient authors on the subject of suicide, Droge writes, "Like Ignatius after him, Paul seems almost pathologically fascinated with his sufferings and possible death, and he devotes considerable space to their theological implications."[8]

Droge's comparison of these two figures on this matter arrested my attention and spawned this investigation. The complex, multifaceted nature of this inquiry conspires against my ability to offer a thoroughgoing analysis of this matter here. Be that as it may, it is possible to consider a number of the relevant Ignatian and Pauline passages, many of which are cited by Droge, in an attempt to ascertain how apposite such a comparison is. In doing so, we will be able to see more clearly whether, or to what extent, Ignatius of Antioch and Paul of Tarsus were "pathological peas in a pod."

Although Ignatius's desire to suffer (e.g., Ign. *Trall.* 4.2) and to fight with wild beasts (note Ign. *Eph.* 1.2; Ign. *Trall.* 10.1) are recurring themes within his letters, "it is in his epistle to the Romans that Ignatius provides his fullest reflection upon martyrdom."[9] "[A]s he turns his face to Rome in writing, he has space to consider the significance of the events that await him."[10] In his letter to the Roman church, Ignatius pleads with them not to impede his entombment in the stomachs of wild beasts. Indeed, he implores believers in Rome to allow him "to be eaten by the beasts, through whom [he] can attain to God." Referring to himself as "God's wheat," he pictures himself being "ground by the teeth of wild beasts so that [he might] be found to be the pure bride of Christ" (Ign. *Rom.* 4.1).

Even as Ignatius is fighting with wild beasts – ten "leopards" in the form of a company of soldiers to be precise – while he journeys from Syria to Rome, he "long[s] for the beasts that are prepared for [him]." Moreover, he "pray[s] that they might be found prompt for [him]." Lest the beasts be lethargic, however, Ignatius signals his willingness to "entice them," even "force them," "to devour [him] promptly" (Ign. *Rom.* 5.2). He perceives the beasts as sacrificial "instruments" and hopes that they will "leave no trace of [his] body" (Ign. *Rom.* 4.2).

---

6. Ibid., 282.

7. Ibid., 284.

8. Ibid., 285.

9. Paul Foster, "The Epistles of Ignatius of Antioch (Part 2)," *ExpTim* 118 (2006): 2–11 (on 7).

10. Ibid., 7.

Then, in a rhetorical flourish, which is not a little disconcerting, Ignatius exclaims, "Let there come on me fire, and cross, and struggles with wild beasts, cutting, and tearing asunder, rackings of bones, mangling of limbs, crushing of my whole body, cruel tortures of the devil, may I but attain to Jesus Christ" (Ign. *Rom.* 5.3). In light of such a troubling text, there is little wonder why any number of scholars suggest that Ignatius viewed "his impending death with a vivid, almost macabre, eagerness."[11] Neither does it come as a surprise to read interpreters who contend that Ignatius's "letters display a state of exultation bordering on mania."[12]

Given such scholarly assessments, it is both fair and fitting to consider Ignatius's attitude toward his greatly anticipated martyrdom before shifting our focus to Paul. On the one hand, it seems both foolhardy and unnecessary to deny that Ignatius displays a certain, if not considerable, degree of morbidity regarding his hoped-for death. On the other hand, Michael W. Holmes has identified three factors that preclude any overly simplistic view of the matter, namely: Ignatius's "sincere desire to imitate the suffering of Jesus and thereby become a true disciple";[13] Ignatius's employment of hyperbolic rhetoric in "an effort to bolster his courage so as not to fail in the course to which he had publicly committed himself";[14] and, Ignatius's anxiety regarding a fractured Antiochene church and his concomitant hope that his imminent martyrdom might be a "means by which to reclaim the deteriorating situation in Antioch or to redeem his reputation as a bishop and a Christian."[15]

Three other influences that might have further shaped Ignatius's view of death include: a fascination with, if not fixation upon, martyrdom in his culture writ large;[16] a counter-cultural attitude in some strains of early

11. Michael W. Holmes, "Ignatius of Antioch," *DLNT* (1997): 530–33.

12. W. H. C. Frend, *Martyrdom and Persecution in the Early Church: A Study of a Conflict from the Maccabees to the Donatists* (Garden City: Anchor Books, 1965), 197.

13. Holmes, "Ignatius," 532. See further Willard M. Swartley, "The *Imitatio Christi* in the Ignatian Letters," *VC* 27 (1973): 81–103; and Michael J. Wilkins, "The Interplay of Ministry, Martyrdom, and Discipleship in Ignatius of Antioch," in *Worship, Theology and Ministry in the Early Church: Essays in Honor of Ralph P. Martin*, JSNTSup 87 (Sheffield: Sheffield Academic, 1992), 294–315.

14. Albert O. Mellink, "Ignatius' Road to Rome: From Failure to Success or in the Footsteps of Paul?," in *Recycling Biblical Figures*, ed. by Athalya Brenner and Jan Willem van Henten (Leiden: Deo, 1999), 127–65.

15. Michael W. Holmes, *The Apostolic Fathers: Greek Texts and English Translations*, 3rd ed. (Grand Rapids: Baker Academic, 2007), 169–70.

16. Cf. Judith Perkins, "The 'Self' as Sufferer," *HTR* 85 (1992): 245–72; see also Droge, "*Mori Lucrum*," 264.

Christianity "whereby acts of martyrdom became world negating events that served to rob the empire and the dominion of Satan of their power, and in an uncompromising way [demonstrate] the victory of Christ over the world";[17] and Ignatius's desire to be found in the footsteps of his apostolic hero Paul (Ign. *Eph.* 12.2).[18]

As David M. Reis has noted, "The parallel circumstances surrounding the lives of Ignatius and Paul seem to have left a deep impression on the bishop... In a broad sense...it may be said that Ignatius 'imitated' Paul through the fulfillment of [his] journey [to Rome]."[19] To press his point further, Reis contends that Ignatius "encourages his readers to think of him as a Paul *redivivus*."[20] It does in fact appear that for Ignatius *imitatio Pauli* was not too far removed from *imitatio Christi*. It is to Ignatius's model, the apostle Paul, that we now turn.

In painting a picture of Paul, who akin to Ignatius "seems almost pathologically fascinated with his sufferings and possible death,"[21] Droge appeals to a number of Pauline passages. As noted above, he gives pride of place to Phil 1:21–26. In particular, Droge focuses upon v. 21 (Ἐμοὶ γὰρ τὸ ζῆν Χριστὸς καὶ τὸ ἀποθανεῖν κέρδος) and v. 23 (συνέχομαι δὲ ἐκ τῶν δύο, τὴν ἐπιθυμίαν ἔχων εἰς τὸ ἀναλῦσαι καὶ σὺν Χριστῷ εἶναι, πολλῷ [γὰρ] μᾶλλον κρεῖσσον). Drawing upon the earlier work of D. W. Palmer,[22] as well as certain passages in Philippians (esp. 1:7, 13, 14, 17, 30; 2:17, 27; 3:10; 4:11–12, 14) and 2 Corinthians (1:8–9; 5:18; 6:4–5; 11:24–29; cf. 4:8–11), Droge contends that Paul "lust[ed] after death" "not only because it entail[ed] union with Christ, but also because it [brought] deliverance from life's miseries."[23] These facts notwithstanding, Droge contends that Paul opted for life over suicide because of the obligation he felt toward the Philippians.[24] "[I]n so doing," Droge posits, Paul "aligns himself with a tradition on suicide which can be traced back to Socrates."[25]

---

17. Foster, "Ignatius," 8.

18. Cf. Robert Stoops Jr., "If I Suffer...Epistolary Authority in Ignatius of Antioch," *HTR* 80 (1987): 161–78; also Mellink, "Road to Rome," 127–65.

19. David M. Reis, "Following in Paul's Footsteps: *Mimēsis* and Power in Ignatius of Antioch," in *The New Testament and the Apostolic Fathers*. Vol. 2, *Trajectories through the New Testament and the Apostolic Fathers*, ed. Andrew F. Gregory and Christopher M. Tuckett (Oxford: Oxford University Press, 2005), 287–305 (on 295).

20. Ibid., 297.

21. Droge, "*Mori Lucrum*," 285.

22. See Palmer, "To Die is Gain (Philippians 1:21)," *NovT* 17 (1975): 203–18.

23. Ibid., 282.

24. Ibid., 283.

25. Ibid., 284.

To borrow a line from Paul, "What shall we say then to these things?" (Rom 8:31). To begin, one might note that in the verse prior to the text Droge treats in his essay, that is Phil 1:20, Paul indicates his confidence that he will "with full courage now as always" honor Christ in his body "whether through life or through death." The apostle conveys a similar conviction in Rom 8:38–39. There he exclaims that neither death nor life nor anything else in all creation will sever believers from God's love in Christ. Later in that letter, Paul writes, "We do not live to ourselves, and we do not die to ourselves. If we live, we live to the Lord, and if we die, we die to the Lord; so then, whether we live or whether we die, we are the Lord's. For to this end Christ died and rose again so that he might be Lord of both the dead and the living" (Rom 14:7–9).

Additionally, although Droge quotes 2 Cor 5:1–8 to support his view that Paul preferred death to life, he neglects to note 2 Cor 5:9, which states, "So whether we are at home or away, we make it our aim to please him."[26] Similarly, Paul writes in 2 Cor 5:14–15, "For the love of Christ urges us on, because we are convinced that one died for all; therefore all have died. And he died for all, so that those who live might no longer live for themselves, but for him who died and was raised for them." One might also note 2 Cor 4:11, where Paul propounds, "For while we live, we are always being given up to death for Jesus' sake, so that the life of Jesus may be made visible in our mortal flesh." Galatians 2:19–20 strikes a similar chord.

While Paul indicates a preference for death over life in passages like 2 Cor 5:8 and Phil 1:23, one can detect elsewhere in Paul a certain indifference regarding life or death. For example, he assures the Thessalonians that "God has not destined us for wrath but for obtaining salvation through our Lord Jesus Christ, who died for us, so that whether we are awake or asleep we may live with him" (1 Thess 5:9–10). Arguably, this relative indifference arises in no small part from Paul's confidence in the coming of the resurrected Christ and in the resurrection and union of Christians with Christ. Such hope is not, as sometimes suggested, a vestige of a so-called early Paul, for even in Philippians, seemingly one of his later letters, he maintains, "For our citizenship is in heaven, and from it we await a Savior, the Lord Jesus Christ, who will transform the body of our humiliation that it may be conformed to the body of his glory, by the power that enables him to make all things subject to himself" (Phil 3:19–20).

26. Ibid., 282.

One will search in vain for similar theological reflection upon "last things" in Ignatius. Consequently, I must confess that Albert O. Mellink's suggestion that one finds in Ignatius the same dialectical tension between the "already" and "not yet" and between the theological indicative and the ethical imperative as one finds in Paul leaves me left wondering if we are reading the same literary *corpi*![27] More adroit and accurate, it seems to me, are the remarks of Richard A. Bower. He notes, "[T]he eschatological tension between present and future is negligible in Ignatius. Final salvation is not linked to a future, historical unfolding; rather it can be realized in an immediate way [namely, in his martyrdom]."[28]

To be fair to the disposed bishop of Antioch, he wrote his letters en route to martyrdom. As a result, his preoccupation with, if not fixation upon, death (and the instruments thereof) is understandable. J. B. Lightfoot offers this salutary reminder: "It is a cheap wisdom which at the study table or over the pulpit desk declaims against the extravagance of the feelings and language of Ignatius, as the vision of martyrdom rose up before him. After all it is only by an enthusiasm which [people] call extravagance that the greatest moral and spiritual triumphs have been won."[29]

Such a sympathetic perspective, however, does not alter my view that there is precious little truly comparable material between Ignatius and Paul regarding suffering and death, even if the apostle does symbolically suggest that he "fought with wild beasts in Ephesus" (1 Cor 15:32). Whereas Ignatius seems to have viewed his sufferings soteriologically, allowing "for [in] his martyrdom all the blessings and perfections of salvation which are the lot of those who know perfect union with God,"[30] "Paul," as Victor Paul Furnish rightly concludes in his essay "Paul the MARTUS," "interpreted his sufferings kerygmatically: he believed in what he suffered no less than in what he said, 'Jesus Christ was portrayed as crucified'" (Gal 3:1 RSV).[31]

27. Mellink, "Ignatius' Road to Rome," 164–65.

28. Richard A. Bower, "The Meaning of EPITUCHEIN in the Epistles of St. Ignatius of Antioch," *VC* 28 (1974): 1–14 (on 14).

29. J. B. Lightfoot, *The Apostolic Fathers: Clement, Ignatius, and Polycarp.* Part 2, vol. 1: *Ignatius and Polycarp*, 2 parts in 5 vols., 2nd ed., repr. (Grand Rapids: Baker, 1981 [1889]), 38.

30. Bower, "Meaning," 13–14.

31. Victor Paul Furnish, "Paul the MARTUS," in *Witness and Existence: Essays in Honor of Schubert M. Ogden*, ed. Philip E. Devenish and George L. Goodwin (Chicago: University of Chicago Press, 1989), 73–88.

Ignatius regarded Paul as a model and viewed himself as something of a "new" or "second" Paul.[32] In writing to the Romans, Ignatius even applies 1 Cor 15:8–9 to himself, claiming to be least among the Antiochene Christians as well as an ἔκτρωμα (Ign. *Rom.* 9.2; cf. 4.3). Reis may be right in arguing that both Ignatius and Paul leveraged the suffering and trials they experienced to their own rhetorical and ecclesial advantage.[33] Be that as it may and despite Droge's claim to the contrary, I am hard pressed to find as comparable the bishop's and the apostle's remarks regarding suffering and death in their extant letters. Perhaps Ignatius and Paul were both pathological peas. They were not, however, two peas in a pod, at least not in the mess of peas picked for and examined in this study. While both Ignatius and Paul regarded *mors* as *lucrum*, they had decidedly different ways of conceptualizing and articulating their hoped-for futures.

32. So, Reis, "Paul's Footsteps," in Gregory and Tuckett, eds., *Trajectories through the New Testament and the Apostolic Fathers*, 287–305.
33. Ibid.

Chapter 8

THE PAULINE CONCEPT OF UNION WITH CHRIST
IN IGNATIUS OF ANTIOCH

David J. Downs

Introduction

There is no doubt that Ignatius of Antioch was influenced by the memory and writings of the apostle Paul.[1] Less clear, however, is the nature and extent of this Pauline influence. Frequently discussed are those passages in Ignatius's letters in which the bishop cites or alludes to material from the Pauline epistles, including texts from 1 Corinthians and Ephesians.[2]

---

1. I assume the modern consensus, established by the work of J.B. Lightfoot (*The Apostolic Fathers, Part 2: S. Ignatius; S. Polycarp*, 3 vols. [London: Macmillan, 1885]) and Theodor Zahn (*Ignatius von Antiochien* [Gotha: Perthes, 1873]), that the seven letters of the so-called middle recension are authentic. Given recent discussions that have questioned the assumption that Ignatius's letters should be dated to the reign of Trajan (98–117 CE; cf. Eusebius, *His. Eccl.* 3.36), I would posit a broad timeframe for the letters sometime in the first half of the second century, although the arguments in this essay do not depend on a precise dating within that time period. See Timothy D. Barnes, "The Date of Ignatius," *ExpTim* 120 (2008): 119–30; Paul Foster, "The Epistles of Ignatius of Antioch," in *The Writings of the Apostolic Fathers*, ed. Paul Foster (London: T&T Clark, 2007), 81–107; Thomas Lechner, *Ignatius Adversus Valentinianos? Chronologische und theologischichtliche Studien zu den Briefen des Ignatius von Antiochien*, VCSup 47 (Leiden: Brill, 1999); and the articles by Reinhard M. Hübner, Andreas Lindemann, Georg Schöllgen, and M. J. Edwards in vols. 1 and 2 of *ZAC* (1997–98).

2. For a careful discussion of Ignatius's use of the Pauline epistles, see Paul Foster, "The Epistles of Ignatius of Antioch and the Writings That Later Formed the New Testament," in *The New Testament and the Apostolic Fathers*. Vol. 2, *Trajectories through the New Testament and the Apostolic Fathers*, ed. Andrew F. Gregory and Christopher M. Tuckett (Oxford: Oxford University Press, 2005), 160–86. The strongest textual parallels are *Eph.* 16.1//1 Cor 6:9–10; *Eph.* 18.1//1 Cor 1:18, 20;

Certainly the memory of Paul as a faithful martyr shaped the "last words" penned by Ignatius as the bishop was transported in chains from Antioch to face his death in Rome.[3] Twice among his seven letters Ignatius mentions Paul by name (*Eph.* 12.2; *Rom.* 4.3), in both instances holding out the apostle as a model of one who has ascended to God through death.[4]

But to what extent did the memory of Paul or the Pauline epistles influence "the structure of Ignatian theological thinking"?[5] It is well-known, for example, that Ignatius never speaks explicitly about justification by faith, the doctrine considered by many to be at the center of Paul's gospel.[6] On the other hand, in spite of some significant differences between the first-century apostle and the Antiochian bishop, Rudolf Bultmann considered Ignatius to be the only early Christian writer, with the exception of John, to have joined Paul in understanding "the Christian faith as an

Magn. 10.2//1 Cor 5:7–8; *Rom.* 5.1//1 Cor 4:4; *Rom.* 9.2//1 Cor 15:8–10; cf. *Eph.* Inscr.//Eph 1:3–4; *Pol.* 5.1//Eph 5:25. I find quite plausible Foster's suggestion that Ignatius possessed a collection of Paul's letters that included only 1 Corinthians, Ephesians, 1 Timothy, and 2 Timothy, all of which mention or allude to the Christ-believing community in Ephesus (cf. *Eph.* 12.2); cf. Heinrich Rathke, *Ignatius von Antiochien und die Paulusbriefe*, TU 99 (Berlin: Akadamie, 1967).

3. See Andreas Lindemann, "Paul's Influence on 'Clement' and Ignatius," in Gregory and Tuckett, eds., *Trajectories through the New Testament and the Apostolic Fathers*, 11–24, and James W. Aageson, *Paul, the Pastoral Epistles, and the Early Church*, LPS (Peabody, MA: Hendrickson, 2008), 123–40.

4. My understanding of these texts is shaped by Alexander N. Kirk's excellent dissertation, "Paul's Approach to Death in His Letters and in Early Pauline Effective History" (PhD diss., Oxford University, 2013), 83–98.

5. The phrase in quotation marks comes from Lindemann, "Paul's Influence," 21. One might equally speak of Ignatius's "theologizing."

6. This observation stands behind Thomas F. Torrance characteristically polemical and dismissive discussion of Ignatius's doctrine of justification (*The Doctrine of Grace in the Apostolic Fathers* [Edinburgh: Oliver & Boyd, 1948], 67–70). Ignatius employs the verb δικαιόω twice, and in both instances he frames justification as a future reality (*Rom.* 5.1; *Phld.* 8.2; cf. the adjective δίκαιος in *Magn.* 12.1 [though in a citation of LXX Prov 18:17] and the adverb δικαίως in *Eph.* 15.3 and *Magn.* 9.2). The closest Ignatius comes to a Pauline-like formulation of justification by faith is his statement in *Eph.* 1.1 that believers in Ephesus possess their much-loved name because of their "righteous nature (φύσει δικαίᾳ), according to faith and love in Christ Jesus our Savior" (but cf. *Phld.* 8.2). Ignatius's one use of the noun δικαιοσύνη (*Smyrn.* 1.1) reflects an intriguing and much-discussed parallel to Matt 3:15. Although it is not possible definitively to demonstrate Ignatius's dependence upon Matthew, the phrase ἵνα πληρωθῇ πᾶσα δικαιοσύνη ὑπ᾽ αὐτου is certainly more Matthean than Pauline (see Foster, "The Epistles of Ignatius of Antioch and the Writings," 173–76).

existentiell attitude."[7] The possibility of a Pauline shaping of Ignatius's christology, his understanding of the relationship between Judaism and Christianity, his concept of martyrdom, and his ecclesiology has been considered in multiple studies.[8] In this essay, I would like to explore a relatively neglected topic, namely, the connection between Paul and Ignatius on the theme of union with Christ.[9] Given that the landscape of Pauline theology itself has shifted significantly in the past two decades, the time is ripe for a reconsideration of the reception of Paul's theology in the second century and beyond. Albert Schweitzer's famous declaration that the doctrine of justification by faith is for Paul a "subsidiary crater, which has formed within the rim of the main crater – the mystical doctrine of redemption through the being-in-Christ" may have been an overstatement, but Schweitzer's observation points to the fact that heirs of Paul in the first several centuries who do not highlight the Pauline concept of justification by faith, or who contextualize this motif in different ways, may still be considered careful and engaged interpreters of the Pauline writings and legacy, particularly if these later interpreters appropriate and develop other Pauline motifs, such as the central role of participation in Christ in Paul's theology.[10]

In this essay I am interested in two distinct yet related questions. First, how does the concept of union with Christ in Ignatius's letters compare with that found in the Pauline epistles? And second, can the motif of union with Christ in Ignatius plausibly be traced to Pauline influence? The first

7. Rudolf Bultmann, "Ignatius and Paul," in *Existence and Faith: Shorter Writings of Rudolf Bultmann*, ed. and trans. Schubert M. Ogden (London: Hodder & Stoughton, 1961), 267.

8. These four topics are the focus of Carl B. Smith's recent contribution, "Ministry, Martyrdom, and Other Mysteries: Pauline Influence on Ignatius of Antioch," in *Paul and the Second Century*, ed. Michael F. Bird and Joseph R. Dodson, LNTS 412 (London: T&T Clark, 2011), 37–56. Smith's otherwise insightful essay does not consider the theme of union with Christ.

9. To the best of my knowledge, the only study specifically devoted to this topic is Ferdinando Bergamelli, "L'unione a Cristo in Ignazio di Antiochia," in *Cristologia e catechesi patristica: Convegno di studio e aggiornamento, Pontificium Institutum Altioris Latinitatis (Facoltà di lettere cristiane e classiche), Roma, 17–19 febbraio 1979*, ed. S. Felici, BibScRel 31, 2 vols. (Rome: Libreria Ateneo Salesiano, 1980), 1:73–109.

10. Albert Schweitzer, *The Mysticism of Paul the Apostle*, trans. William Montgomery (Baltimore: The Johns Hopkins University Press, 1998), 225. For a study that examines the re-contextualization of the soteriology and cosmology of Romans in *1 Clement*, see David J. Downs, "Justification, Good Works, and Creation in Clement of Rome's Appropriation of Romans 5–6," *NTS* 59 (2013): 415–32.

question is comparative, and can be investigated without recourse to any particular view of the literary relationship between Paul and Ignatius.[11] The second question, which is more difficult to answer, is genealogical in that it inquires about the nature and extent of Paul's influence upon a specific and central element of Ignatius's theology.[12]

Union with Christ in the Pauline Epistles

Christ mysticism. Spiritual union. Participationist eschatology. Covenantal participation. Christosis. All these terms – and many others – have been invoked to describe the peculiar reality that serves as the subject for this investigation, namely, believers' sharing with, or participation in, the crucified and risen Christ.[13] Studies of this theme in the Pauline epistles often point, for example, to the ubiquity of the prepositional phrase ἐν Χριστῷ, a construction that occurs seventy-three times in Paul's thirteen letters.[14] The precise locutions ἐν Χριστῷ Ἰησοῦ and ἐν Ἰησοῦ Χριστῷ occur

11. This is Bultmann's approach in "Ignatius and Paul."

12. To be clear, in this essay the terms "Paul" and "Pauline" refer to the thirteen letters ascribed to Paul in the canon of the New Testament. The conclusions of modern critical scholars regarding the possible presence of pseudepigraphical compositions in the Pauline corpus are immaterial to the question of Pauline influence upon Ignatius, since Ignatius would not have recognized such distinctions (so also Smith, "Ministry," 38 n. 8). Moreover, that the relationship between Ignatius and "Paul" is built upon evidence of Ignatius's interaction with canonical epistles – and not, say, *3 Corinthians* – is an indication that Ignatius's Paul is the canonical Paul. See the discussion in Kirk, "Paul's Approach to Death," 27–33.

13. This sampling of terms comes from, in order, Schweitzer, *Mysticism*; John Murray, *Redemption – Accomplished and Applied* (Grand Rapids: Eerdmans, 1955); E. P. Sanders, *Paul and Palestinian Judaism: A Comparison of Patterns of Religion* (Minneapolis: Fortress, 1977); Michael S. Horton, *Covenant and Salvation: Union with Christ* (Louisville: Westminster John Knox, 2007); Ben C. Blackwell, *Christosis: Pauline Soteriology in Light of Deification in Irenaeus and Cyril of Alexandria*, WUNT 2/314 (Tübingen: Mohr Siebeck, 2011).

14. The number seventy-three does not include instances in which the preposition ἐν is followed immediately by the article or the postpositive conjunction γάρ before the noun Χριστός (1 Cor 4:15; 15:22; 2 Cor 2:14; Gal 5:6; Eph 1:10, 12, 20; 3:11) or instances in which the object of the preposition is a synonymous designation for Christ such as κύριος (Rom 14:14; 16:2, 8, 11, 12, 13, 22; 1 Cor 1:31; 4:17; 7:22, 39; 9:1, 2; 11:11; 15:58; 16:19; 2 Cor 2:12; 10:17; Gal 5:10; Eph 1:15; 2:21; 4:1, 17; 5:8; 6:1, 10, 21; Phil 1:14; 2:19; 3:1; 4:1, 2, 4, 10; Col 3:18, 20; 4:7, 17; 1 Thess 3:8; 4:1; 5:12; 2 Thess 3:4, 12; Phlm 16; 20) or a pronoun (1 Cor 1:5; 2 Cor 1:19–20; 5:21; 13:4; Eph 1:4, 6–7, 9–11, 13; 2:15, 21–22; 3:12; 4:21; 6:20; Phil 3:9; Col 1:14, 16–17, 19; 2:3, 6–7, 9, 11–12, 15; 2:10; 2 Thess 1:12).

twenty-three times in the seven letters of Ignatius.[15] In addition, Christ (Jesus) is the antecedent of a pronoun that follows ἐν in *Eph.* 11.2; *Magn.* Inscr.; 1.2; 10.2; *Trall.* 2.2; 13.3; *Rom.* 4.3; 8.2; *Phld.* 5.1, 2; 7.2.[16] The story of union with Christ in Ignatius's theology certainly cannot be told on the basis of a numerical listing of one prepositional phrase. But even an initial glance at the frequency with which Ignatius employs the language of being "in Christ Jesus" suggests that a careful consideration of this theme in the letters of Ignatius may bear fruitful comparison to the motif in the Pauline epistles.

Yet before we can compare the concept of union with Christ in the Pauline and Ignatian letters, we need to be clear about what precisely is meant by this idea in the antecedent corpus. This definitional task is itself fraught with difficulty, for the topic of union with Christ is as complicated as it is ubiquitous in Paul's letters. Fortunately, however, an excellent recent monograph by Constantine Campbell, *Paul and Union with Christ*, offers a definition that can serve as a helpful heuristic guide for the present investigation. Having compiled and discussed a wealth of exegetical and theological data, at the conclusion of his study Campbell offers the following fourfold definition of "union with Christ" in the Pauline epistles, a definition centered on the terms *union, participation, identification,* and *incorporation*:

> *Union* gathers up faith union with Christ, mutual indwelling, trinitarian, and nuptial notions. *Participation* conveys partaking in the events of Christ's narrative. *Identification* refers to believers' location in the realm of Christ and their allegiance to his lordship. *Incorporation* encapsulates the corporate dimensions of membership in Christ's body. Together these four terms function as 'umbrella' concepts, covering the full spectrum of Pauline language, ideas, and themes that are bound up in the metatheme of

15. Ἐν Χριστῷ Ἰησοῦ: *Eph.* 1.1; 11.1; 12.2; *Magn.* Inscr.; *Trall.* 1.1; 9.2; *Rom.* 1.1; 2.2; *Phld.* 10.1; 11.2; ἐν Ἰησοῦ Χριστῷ: *Eph.* Inscr.; 3.1, 2; 8.2; 10.3; 20.2; 21.2; *Magn.* Inscr.; 6.2; *Trall.* 13.2, 3; *Rom.* Inscr.; *Phld.* 10.2 (although the order is reversed in some manuscripts of *Phld.* 10.2). The reading ἐν Ἰησοῦ Χριστῷ in *Eph.* 20.2a, which is preserved in Codex Mediceo-Laurentianus and in Latin and Syrian translations, is rightly amended to ἐνὶ Ἰησοῦ Χριστῷ by Lightfoot and Holmes. Interestingly, Ignatius always uses the form ἐν Χριστῷ Ἰησοῦ or ἐν Ἰησοῦ Χριστῷ. This, of course, reflects a larger pattern in Ignatius's writings, since Ignatius rarely uses the name Ἰησοῦς apart from the honorific Χριστός, and vice versa. For the use of Ἰησοῦς alone, see *Eph.* 15.2; *Magn.* 1.2; and *Phld.* 5.1; for the use of Χριστός alone, see *Eph.* 14.2; *Magn.* 13.2; *Smyr.* 1.1; 6.1; and some manuscripts of *Rom.* 4.1–2. The ordering ἐν Ἰησοῦ (Χριστῷ) is not found in the Pauline epistles.

16. To this list we might add the phrase ἐν υἱῷ in *Magn.* 13.1.

'union with Christ.' Furthermore, all four terms entail ethical expectations, as Paul draws upon the implications of union, participation, identification, and incorporation to inform the Christian life.[17]

Although slightly unwieldy, this definition has the advantage of capturing as well as any the comprehensive, multidimensional reality that many have attempted to describe in the Pauline epistles. Using Campbell's definition as a guide, I shall seek to explore, where present, these aspects of union with Christ in the letters of Ignatius, noting both thematic connections with this Pauline definition and points at which Ignatius's presentation of the theme of union with Christ does not fit neatly within this Pauline framework.[18]

Union

Among the four terms featured in Campbell's definition, the first is perhaps the most difficult to describe. Of the term "union" itself Campbell writes, "Believers are described as being 'in' Christ and he being in them such that there is a mutual indwelling by the Spirit. Likened to a nuptial union, this mutual indwelling appears to be derivative of the nature of relationships within the inner life of the Godhead, in which Father, Son, and Spirit co-inhere one another."[19] This Pauline concept of mutual indwelling, according to Campbell, is rooted in and effected by "faith union with Christ," in the sense that "believers are united to Christ by *faith*."[20]

Ignatius's letters contain numerous references or allusions to union and mutual indwelling between Christ and those "in Christ." Some of these texts will be covered below, but here it is perhaps sufficient to point out that, according to Ignatius, Christ dwells in believers (*Eph.* 15.3;

---

17. Constantine R. Campbell, *Paul and Union with Christ: An Exegetical and Theological Study* (Grand Rapids: Zondervan, 2012), 413.

18. Citing this definition alone does not do justice to the rich and detailed exegetical and theological work that prepares Campbell to proffer this definition at the end of his study. As Campbell points out, his ordering of these four terms might be construed as indicative of a logical (and not temporal) sequence: "A believer is united to Christ at the moment of coming to faith; their union is established by the indwelling of the Spirit. The person united to Christ therefore enters into participation with Christ in his death, resurrection, ascension, and glorification. As a participant in Christ's death and resurrection, the believer dies to the world and is identified with the realm of Christ. As a member of the realm of Christ, the believer is incorporated into his body, since union with Christ entails union with his members" (414).

19. Campbell, *Paul and Union*, 410.

20. Ibid., 385 (emphasis original).

Magn. 12.1; *Rom.* 6.3) just as they abide in him (*Eph.* 8.2; 10.3; 11.1; 20.2). Actions of believers such as mutual love (*Magn.* 6.2) and singing to the Father (*Rom.* 2.2) take place "in Christ." Importantly, for Ignatius union with Christ serves as a warrant for unity among believers. In the context of exhorting the Ephesians to "run together in harmony in the purpose of God" (συντρέχητε τῇ γνώμῃ τοῦ θεοῦ), for example, Ignatius provides a theological and ecclesiological rationale for this instruction: "For Jesus Christ, our unwavering life, is the purpose of the Father, just as also the bishops appointed in every quarter are in the purpose of Jesus Christ (ἐν Ἰησοῦ Χριστοῦ γνώμῃ)" (*Eph.* 3.2).[21] Jesus Christ is the purpose of the Father in the sense that the events of his incarnation, death, and resurrection fulfill the divine will, and the rightly appointed bishops are in the purpose of Jesus Christ in that their actions correspond to Christ's and reflect his ruling power.[22] Thus, one significant ecclesiological and ethical implication for Ignatius's concept of union with Christ is that the unity that believers and Christian leaders share with Christ is the warrant for solidarity within Christian communities (cf. *Magn.* 7.2; 13.2).[23]

There are at least two points at which Campbell's definition of "union" does not neatly fit the Ignatian letters, however. First, unlike Paul, Ignatius never presents the relationship between Christ and the church in bridal metaphors (e.g., 2 Cor 11:2–3; Eph 5:21–32; cf. 1 Cor 6:15–17). Second, the motif of "union with Christ" in the Pauline letters has often been called "spiritual union" because of the extent to which this notion is rooted in Paul's understanding of the presence of the Spirit among those joined with Christ.[24] Campbell's suggestion that union with Christ in Paul's theology "appears to be derivative of the nature of relationships within the inner life of the Godhead, in which Father, Son, and Spirit co-inhere one another" invites consideration of whether union with Christ is developed in connection with Trinitarian theology in Ignatius.

A strong case can be made that Ignatius's exalted Christology coheres with the apostolic tradition and paves the way for the Christological perspective developed later at the Council of Chalcedon: Christ is truly

---

21. Unless otherwise noted, all translations in this essay are my own; cf. 1 Cor 2:16, where believers *have* the mind of Christ.

22. On the importance of the threefold office in Ignatius, see, e.g., Allen Brent, "History and Eschatological Mysticism in Ignatius of Antioch," *ETL* 65 (1989): 309–29; William R. Schoedel, *Ignatius of Antioch*, Hermeneia (Philadelphia: Fortress, 1985), 22–23.

23. So also Bergamelli, "L'unione a Cristo," 98–103.

24. Campbell, 360–63; cf. Murray, *Redemption*, 201–12.

divine (*Eph.* Inscr.; 15.3; 18.2; 19.3; *Rom.* Inscr.; 3.3; 6.3; *Smyrn.* 1.1; *Pol.* 8.3) and truly human (*Eph.* 19.3; *Trall.* 9–10; *Phld.* 5.1; *Smyrn.* 5.2).[25] Moreover, although the language is more precisely binitarian than Trinitarian, in *Magn.* 7.2 and 13.2 union between Christ and the Father also serves as the basis for unity among believers.[26]

Ignatius does not speak of the Spirit with the same regularity with which he discusses the activity and identity of the Son, however. The bishop of Antioch sometimes draws together the work of the Father, the Son, and the Spirit, as in *Eph.* 9.1, where readers are imaged as "stones of a temple, prepared for the building of God the Father, lifted up to the heights by the crane of Jesus Christ, which is the cross, using as a rope the Holy Spirit." And the Spirit is involved in Jesus' birth (*Eph.* 18.2), in teaching the prophets (*Magn.* 9.2), in establishing the bishop, presbyters, and deacons (*Phld.* Inscr.), in exposing things hidden (*Phld.* 7.1), and in empowering Ignatius's prophetic speech (*Phld.* 7.2). Perhaps only in *Magn.* 13.1 is there a hint that believers participate in Christ along with the Father and the Spirit, for the actions of the Magnesians, established as they are in the decrees of the Lord and the apostles, prosper them in whatever they do, "in flesh and in spirit, in faith and in love, in the Son and the Father and in the Spirit, in the beginning and in the end, together with your most worthy bishop and the worthily woven spiritual crown that is your presbytery and the godly deacons." As Schoedel comments on this text, "[U]nity in the church (whose fullness is indicated by the polarities of flesh and spirit and of faith and love) is grounded 'in' the divine unity (Son, Father, Spirit) and marked as total even more forcefully by the concluding reference to 'beginning' and 'end.'"[27]

---

25. As Larry W. Hurtado writes, "We should beware of crediting Ignatius with philosophical developments that came later. But it is fairly clear that he represents the profound commitment to Jesus' divinity and real human existence that demanded those efforts toward the distinctive Christian idea of God, and especially toward the idea of Jesus' 'two natures,' doctrinal efforts that heavily occupied the developing orthodox/catholic tradition well through the fourth century" (*Lord Jesus Christ: Devotion to Jesus in Earliest Christianity* [Grand Rapids: Eerdmans, 2003], 640); see also Thomas G. Weinandy, "The Apostolic Christology of Ignatius of Antioch: The Road to Chalcedon," in Gregory and Tuckett, eds., *Trajectories through the New Testament and the Apostolic Fathers*, 71–84; Smith, "Ministry," 41–4; Bergamelli, "L'unione a Cristo," 81–86.

26. Some manuscripts (G and L) do add καὶ τῷ πνεθματι in *Magn.* 13.2.

27. Schoedel, *Ignatius*, 130. Although *Magn.* 1.2; 15.1, and *Rom.* Inscr. also feature the rhetoric of unity and the language of "spirit," I would not interpret πνεῦμα in those contexts as a references to the Holy Spirit.

A related question is raised by Campbell's use of the term "faith union," a phrase that indicates Campbell's conviction that union with Christ for Paul is established by faith. Although this topic would be worthy of a full study in its own right, several texts in the Ignatian corpus appear at least to connect union with Christ and belief in him, even if this connection is not a regular feature of Ignatius's language of πίστις/πιστεύω. In *Trall.* 9.2, for example, Ignatius declares that, in the same way that God raised Jesus from the dead, "his Father will also raise us in Christ Jesus, we who believe in him (ἡμᾶς τοὺς πιστεύοντας αὐτῷ), without whom we do not have true life." Here sharing in the resurrection life of Christ Jesus is a blessing granted to those who have faith in him. Another key text is *Phld.* 5.2, where Ignatius says of the prophets, "because they also believed in him [i.e., Jesus], they were saved *in unity with Christ Jesus*, as saints worthy of love and worthy of admiration, approved by Jesus Christ and counted together in the gospel of the shared hope." Although ἑνότης in Ignatius typically refers to unity within the Christian community (so *Eph.* 4.2 [×2]; 5.1; *Phld.* 2.2; 3.2; 8.1; *Pol.* 8.3), it is difficult to see how the phrase ἐν ἑνότητι Ἰησοῦ Χριστοῦ could refer, as Schoedel opines, "most naturally to the unity conferred on the church by God," not least because Ignatius is speaking about the prophets who anticipated the gospel and not his contemporary (Christian) readers.[28] I would prefer to take the prepositional phrase ἐν ἑνότητι Ἰησοῦ Χριστοῦ with the preceding prepositional phrase ἐν ᾧ καὶ πιστεύσαντες ἐσώθησαν, rather than with the following clause.[29]

28. Schoedel, *Ignatius*, 202. In *Eph* 14.1 ἑνότης denotes the unity of faith and love. With Schoedel, I would interpret the phrase ἑνότητα θεοῦ in *Phld.* 8.1 and 9.1 as a genitive of source: "unity from God" (not "with God"). On the other hand, the phrase ἐν ἑνότητι θεοῦ καὶ ὑμῶν in *Smyrn.* 12.2 seems to me to refer to the unity that Jesus Christ shares with God and with the Smyrnaeans. Schoedel's suggestion that the genitives do not have "the same force," and that therefore it is "better to conform to Ignatius' usage elsewhere (cf. *Phld.* 8.1; 9.1; *Pol.* 8.3) and to take the expression to mean 'unity from God and among you'" (*Ignatius*, 252) ignores the fact that that the string of datives – ἐν ὀνόματι Ἰησοῦ Χριστοῦ καὶ τῇ σαρκὶ αὐτοῦ καὶ τῷ αἵματι, πάθει τε καὶ ἀναστάσει σαρκικῇ τε καὶ πνευματικῇ, ἐν ἑνότητι θεοῦ καὶ ὑμῶν – are all governed by the verb ἀσπάζομαι at the beginning of the sentence and all refer to Jesus Christ. Ignatius sends greetings "in the name of Jesus Christ and in his flesh and blood, in his suffering and resurrection – a resurrection both physical and spiritual – in his unity with God and with you."

29. Several English translations seem to suggest that the prophets were saved because of their "belonging to the unity centered in Jesus Christ" (so Holmes), rather than that this unity comes as a result of their faith union with Christ.

In conclusion, while there is little doubt that, broadly defined, "union" between Christ and believers is important in Ignatius's theology, there are only hints in Ignatius's letters that the Spirit is involved in inaugurating and maintaining union with Christ. Moreover, while texts like *Trall.* 9.2 and *Phld.* 5.2 highlight the role of faith in establishing union with Christ, this is not a major theme in Ignatius's writings, and nuptial imagery is not a metaphorical field that Ignatius employs in speaking of the relationship between Christ and his people.

Participation

The second aspect of Campbell's definition of union with Christ in Paul is "participation," a dynamic category that captures "the participation of believers in the events of Christ's narrative, including his death and burial, resurrection, ascension, and glorification."[30] According to some recent interpreters of Paul, the notion that believers participate in the story of Christ is key not only to Paul's concept of union with Christ but also to the entire construct known as "Pauline theology." Thus, Michael Gorman can describe "the core of Paul's theology" as "a narrative soteriology of Spirit-enabled full identification with and participation in the God revealed in Christ crucified, such that the gospel of God reconciling the world in Christ becomes also the story of God's justified, holy, Spirit-led people in the world."[31]

Identifying "the story of Christ" in the letters of Ignatius is relatively clear, particularly in passages in which Ignatius appears to be drawing upon early Christian creedal traditions (*Eph.* 7.2; *Trall.* 9.1–2; cf. *Eph.* 16.2).[32] The central characters, settings, and events in this narrative trajectory

---

30. Campbell, *Paul and Union*, 408.

31. Michael J. Gorman, *Inhabiting the Cruciform God: Kenosis, Justification, and Theosis in Paul's Narrative Soteriology* (Grand Rapids: Eerdmans, 2009), 8; cf. Richard Hays's suggestion that, among four complementary ways of understanding "real participation in Christ" in Paul's letters, which Hays lists as familial belonging, political or military solidarity with Christ, participation in the ἐκκλησία, and living within the Christ story, ecclesial and narrative participation "are epistemologically primary: they provide the symbolic and experiential framework within which the first and second models become intelligible" ("What Is 'Real Participation in Christ': A Dialogue with E. P. Sanders on Pauline Soteriology," in *Redefining First-Century Jewish and Christian Identities: Essays in Honor of Ed Sanders*, ed. Fabian E. Udoh et al. [Notre Dame: University of Notre Dame Press, 2008], 347).

32. For the concept of "story" that undergirds this brief summary, see Edward Adams, "Paul's Story of God and Creation: The Story of How God Fulfils His Purposes in Creation," in *Narrative Dynamics in Paul: A Critical Assessment*, ed. Bruce W.

might be summarized as follows: the incarnate Christ (*Magn.* 6.1), a descendent of David (*Eph.* 18.2; 20.2; *Trall.* 9.1; *Rom.* 7.3; *Smyr.* 1.1), was born of Mary and was baptized (*Eph.* 18.2–19.1, 3; *Trall.* 9.1); Christ suffered and was crucified (*Eph.* 16.2; 19.2; *Trall.* 2.1); Christ was raised from the dead by God the Father (*Eph.* 20.1; *Phld.* Inscr.), is presently with the Father in unity (*Eph.* 5.2), and will return to exercise judgment (*Eph.* 15.3; *Smryn.* 10.2; *Pol.* 3.1).[33]

But to what extent may it be said that Christians, according to Ignatius, participate in this narrative? One obvious way of answering this query would be to highlight Ignatius's sense of his own participation in the Christ story, particularly as the bishop imitates and shares in the martyrdom of his Lord.[34] The issue of Ignatius's imitation of, or participation in, the death of Christ has occasioned no small debate in the history of scholarship on Ignatius, much of it centered on questions related to the *Religionsgeschichte* context of Ignatius's ideas or Ignatius's alleged understanding of his own death as an atoning sacrifice, perhaps reenacted through the Eucharistic mysteries.[35]

It seems to me that Ignatius does understand his own suffering as a sharing in the suffering of Christ. Ignatius pleads with his audience in Rome, for example, "Permit me to be an imitator of the suffering of my God" (ἐπιτρέψατέ μοι μιμητὴν εἶναι τοῦ πάθους τοῦ θεοῦ μου, *Rom.* 6.3).

Longenecker (Louisville: Westminster John Knox, 2002), 19–43 (esp. 19–24). The question of an underlying narrative core to Ignatius's theology is one that would benefit more sustained attention than can be given here.

33. The question of Ignatius's eschatology, and especially the importance or even existence of the expectation of Christ's *parousia* in Ignatius's thought, is disputed. For a thoughtful defense of the view that Ignatius holds to a traditional hope for Christ's return, see A. O. Mellink, "Death as Eschaton: A Study of Ignatius of Antioch's Desire for Death" (PhD diss., University of Amsterdam, 2000), 321–27.

34. This is not to ignore the point that Ignatius's characteristic humility and admiration for the apostles sometimes leads him to frame his own anticipated martyrdom as an imitation of Paul (*Eph.* 12.2; *Rom.* 4.2–3); see the discussion of Ignatius's μίμησις of Paul in David M. Reis, "Following in Paul's Footsteps: *Mimēsis* and Power in Ignatius of Antioch," in Gregory and Tuckett, eds., *Trajectories through the New Testament and the Apostolic Fathers*, 287–305; cf. Alexander N. Kirk, "Ignatius' Statements of Self-Sacrifice: Intimations of an Atoning Death or Expressions of Exemplary Suffering?," *JTS* 64 (2013): 66–88.

35. See, e.g., Theo Preiss, "La mystique de l'imitation de Christ et de l'unité chez Ignace d'Antioch," *RHPR* 18 (1938): 197–241; Hans W. Bartsch, *Gnostisches Gut und Gemindetradition bei Ignatius von Antiochien* (Gütersloh: Bertelsmann, 1940); Willard M. Swartley, "The *Imitatio Christi* in the Ignatian Letters," *VC* 27 (1973): 81–103.

It is often observed that *Rom.* 6.3 is the only instance in Ignatius's letters in which the bishop uses the word μιμητής in connection with Christ's death (cf. *Eph.* 1.1; 10.3; *Trall.* 1.2; *Phld.* 7.2), whereas elsewhere Ignatius typically features the language of "imitation" to encourage readers "to imitate Christ and God in their divine love, mildness, endurance, and obedience, so that all may live in perfect harmony and unity."[36] Yet Ignatius depicts his suffering not merely as an *imitatio Christi* but also as a *participatio Christi.* When the bishop writes of his impending death to the Smyrnaeans, he claims that his experience of the sword and of beasts will bring him near to God, but "only as [this suffering] is in the name of Jesus Christ, so that I might suffer together with him (εἰς τὸ συμπαθεῖν αὐτῷ). I endure all things because he, the perfect human being, empowers me" (*Smyrn.* 4.2).[37] Thus, Ignatius shares the Pauline concept of co-suffering with Christ, even if Ignatius does not speak explicitly, as Paul does, of co-crucifixion (Gal 2:19; Rom 6:6). Moreover, Ignatius also hopes for his own resurrection in Christ (*Rom.* 2.2; 4.3; cf. *Pol.* 7.1, if the reading αναστασει in G and L is preferred).

At the same time, the notion of participation in the narrative of the crucified and risen Christ is not limited to the soon-to-be-martyred bishop, for Ignatius both assumes that his readers also join in this story and exhorts them to do so. Ignatius calls his readers in Ephesus and Philadelphia to imitate Christ (*Eph.* 10.3; *Phld.* 7.2; cf. the imitation of God in *Eph.* 1.1 and *Trall.* 1.2). With reference to the cross, Ignatius writes to the Magnesians of two possible futures, death and life:

> For just as there are two kinds of coin, the one of God and the other of the world, and each of them has its own stamp impressed upon it: the faithless have the stamp of this world, but the faithful in love have the stamp of God the Father through Jesus Christ, through whom, unless we voluntarily choose to die into his suffering, we do not have God's life in us. (*Magn.* 5.2)

36. Mellink, "Death as Eschaton," 66; cf. Candida Moss, *The Other Christs: Imitating Jesus in Ancient Christian Ideologies of Martyrdom* (Oxford: Oxford University Press, 2010), 41–44.

37. Given that the verb συμπαθέω in *Smyrn.* 4.2 clearly denotes co-suffering with Christ, I am also inclined to interpret the statement εἴ τις αὐτὸν ἐν ἑαυτῷ ἔχει νοησάτω ὃ θέλω καὶ συμπαθείτω μοι εἰδὼς τὰ συνέχοντά με in *Rom.* 6.3 (which features the only other instance of συμπαθέω in the Ignatian corpus) as a call to mutual suffering together with Christ (and not, as in most English translations, an appeal for readers merely to "sympathize" with Ignatius): "If anyone has Christ in himself, let that person understand what I wish *and let that person suffer together with me*, knowing the things that constrain me."

Here Ignatius frames the attainment of God's life-giving imprint as available, on the basis of God's love, through his and his readers' participation in the death and resurrection of Christ.[38]

This note of partaking in the narrative trajectory that culminates in Christ's resurrection is sounded even more clearly twice in Ignatius's letter to the Trallians. First, in the salutation Ignatius calls Christ "our hope in the resurrection into him" (τῆς ἐλπίδος ἡμῶν ἐν τῇ εἰς αὐτὸν ἀναστάσει). Second, in 9.2 Ignatius punctuates a protocreedal declaration by linking the resurrection of Christ with the resurrection of believers who are "in Christ." Jesus, Ignatius affirms, "truly was raised from the dead when his Father raised him," a statement followed by the phrase ὃς καὶ κατὰ τὸ ὁμοίωμα, which connects the Father's action in raising Jesus from the dead with the future resurrection of believers: "in the same way his Father will also raise us in Christ Jesus, we who believe in him, without whom we do not have true life."[39] Other references to the hope of future life through participation in the narrative of Christ Jesus could also be cited (*Eph.* 11.1; 20.2; *Magn.* 1.2).

An integral aspect of Ignatius's theology, therefore, is the notion that he and other followers of Jesus participate in the story of Christ's death and resurrection. While Ignatius may not root this participationist soteriology in the event of baptism, as Paul does in Rom 6:1–14, there is a significant level of continuity between Paul and Ignatius in terms of the narrative structure of believers' sharing in the Christ narrative.[40]

Identification

The third characteristic of Campbell's definition of union with Christ is "identification," which Campbell describes as involving both location and belonging: "Situated within the realm of his rule, believers' identity is shaped by their belonging to Christ, the Second Adam."[41]

---

38. So Schoedel, *Ignatius*, 110. Ignatius's assertion in *Trall.* 11.2 that those who are of the Father's planting appear as "branches of the cross" may also draw on this narrative of participation in Christ's suffering.

39. Following both Holmes and Ehrman, who adopt the reading in L as opposed to κατα το ομοιωμα ος και in G.

40. Ignatius is aware of Jesus' baptism by John (*Eph.* 18.2; *Smyrn.* 1.1), and he alludes to the Christian ritual of baptism (*Smyrn.* 8.2; *Pol.* 6.2), but he does not link baptism with union with Christ.

41. Campbell, *Paul and Union*, 408. Ignatius does not present Adam and Christ as anti-types as Paul does in Rom 5 and 1 Cor 15. An argument could be made, however, that, like Paul, Ignatius views Jesus Christ as the one true human being.

With regard to the location of Christians, Ignatius uses a variety of expressions to suggest the position of believers "in Christ." Of chief importance here are instances in which the phrase ἐν Χριστῷ appears to denote a spatial relationship. Believers "abide in Christ, physically and spiritually" (*Eph.* 10.3); they hope to be "found in Christ" (*Eph.* 11.1; cf. *Trall.* 2.2; 13.3) and "to live forever in Jesus Christ" (*Eph.* 20.2). Ignatius himself carries around his chains in Christ (*Eph.* 11.2; *Trall.* 1.1; *Phld.* 5.1). Ignatius's reminder to his readers in *Eph.* 8.2 that they do "everything in Jesus Christ" (ἐν Ἰησοῦ γὰρ Χριστῷ πάντα πράσσετε), especially as this statement comes in the context of a reflection on "the coinherence of the spheres of flesh and spirit," functions as a helpful summary statement: the Ephesians do all things in the realm of Christ (cf. *Magn.* 13.1).[42]

Interestingly, like Paul, who primarily writes of believers being "in Christ" but who also occasionally states that Christ is "in" him and/or his readers (Gal 1:16; 2:20; Rom 8:10; 2 Cor 13:5; Col 1:27), Ignatius also speaks of Christ dwelling within believers. For example, in *Eph.* 15.3, Ignatius writes:

> Nothing escapes the Lord's notice, but even our secrets are near to him. Therefore, let us do everything with the knowledge that he dwells in us, in order that we may be his temples and he may be our God in us – as indeed he is, and he shall appear before our face by the love that we rightly have for him.

For the purposes of this essay, an important question concerns the identity of ὁ κύριος: Is it God or Christ? Several factors suggest that "the Lord" in this text is Christ. First, Ignatius employs the term κύριος as a title thirty-three times in his letters. In nineteen of those instances κύριος clearly or likely designates Christ (*Eph.* 7.2; 10.3; 17.1; 19.1; *Magn.* 7.1; *Trall.* 8.1; 10.1; *Phld.* Inscr. [×2, if the variant in Gg(A)is counted]; 1.1; 4.1; 9.2; 11.2; *Smyrn.* 1.1 [×2]; 4.2; 5.2; *Pol.* Inscr.; 5.2). Thirteen references are at least potentially ambiguous in that they could refer to Christ or to the Father (*Eph.* 6.1; 20.2; 21.1; *Magn.* 13.1; *Phld.* 8.1; 11.1; *Smyrn.* 10.1; *Pol.* 1.2; 4.1; 5.1 [×2], 2; 8.3), and only once does the term κύριος likely denote God the Father, although even that text is debatable (*Eph.* 17.2). This pattern of usage suggests that κύριος in the Ignatian letters *generally* refers to Christ, although this preference is not universal, and therefore contextual considerations play an important role in determining any specific referent of κύριος.

---

42. Schoedel, *Ignatius*, 64.

Second, and more importantly, the immediate context of *Eph.* 15.3 suggests that κύριος denotes Christ. Having encouraged frequent and harmonious meetings in 13.1–2, Ignatius promotes faith and love in 14.1–2. This leads to a discussion of silence and the value of supporting one's speech or silence with deeds, just as was true of the "one teacher, who spoke and it happened" (15.1).[43] If the one "who spoke and it happened" seems initially to be God, with an allusion to God's creative speech in Gen 1, the following clause makes it clear that the teacher is Christ: "indeed, even the things that he has done in silence are worthy of the Father." It is possession of the "word of Jesus" that allows one to understand Christ's silence (15.2). Thus, the "Lord" from whom nothing escapes notice is the Lord Jesus Christ, a point made even clearer at the end of 15.3, where the statement "he shall appear before our face by the love that we rightly have for him" both anticipates the *parousia* of Christ and parallels the call to have "perfect faith and love for Christ" in the beginning of this section (14.1).

Thus, if ὁ κύριος in *Eph.* 15.3 is a reference to Christ, then we have an important statement from Ignatius that Christ "dwells in us" and that "he may be our God in us." Similarly, Ignatius reminds the Magnesians that they have Jesus Christ within them (Ἰησοῦν γὰρ Χριστὸν ἔχετε ἐν ἑαυτοῖς, *Magn.* 12.1). And in *Rom.* 6.3, immediately after expressing his desire to be an "imitator of the suffering of my God," Ignatius writes in the protasis of a conditional sentence: εἴ τις αὐτὸν ἐν ἑαυτῷ ἔχει, with Christ as the antecedent of the pronoun αὐτόν.

In addition to being located in Christ, union with Christ in Ignatius's letters involves assertions that Ignatius and his readers belong to Christ. The role played by Ignatius in the construction of a distinctly "Christian" identity is debated, as is the extent to which the image of "Christian" identity projected in Ignatius's letters, including the antinomy between "Judaism" and "Christianism," reflects the realities of his own social context.[44] What is relatively clear, however, is that Ignatius assumes that his identity and that of his readers is "Christian." This can be seen, of course, in Ignatius's repeated use of the terms Χριστιανός (*Eph.* 11.2; *Magn.* 4.1; *Trall.* 6.1; *Rom.* 3.2; *Pol.* 7.3) and Χριστιανισμός (*Magn.* 10.1, 3 [×2]; *Rom.* 3.3; *Phld.* 6.1), the latter term both representing the earliest use of the proper noun "Christianity" in ancient literature and

43. Presumably this discussion returns to the issue of the silent bishop in *Eph.* 6.1.

44. See, e.g., the different perspectives in Thomas Robinson, *Ignatius of Antioch and the Parting of the Ways: Early Jewish–Christian Relations* (Peabody, MA: Hendrickson, 2009); and Judith Lieu, *Image and Reality: The Jews in the World of the Christians in the Second Century* (Edinburgh: T&T Clark, 1996).

serving Ignatius's construction of an antithesis between Χριστιανισμός and Ἰουδαϊσμός (cf. *Magn*. 8.1; 10.3; *Phld*. 6.1).[45] The point here is not to unpack the loaded theological and historical issues involved in Ignatius's use of this terminology, but to illustrate that Ignatius defines both his own identity and that of his readers and his understanding of *the* valid way to follow Jesus (i.e., what we might call "religion") in terms of belonging to Christ. Indeed, as Ignatius says in *Magn*. 10.1: "Therefore, having become his [i.e., Jesus Christ's] disciples, let us learn to live according to Christianism. For whoever is called by a name other than this one does not belong to God."[46]

Incorporation

Incorporation designates the "corporate dimensions of membership in Christ's body," symbolized prominently in the Pauline epistles in the image of the church as the σῶμα of Christ (cf. Rom 12:4–5; 1 Cor 6:15–16; 10:16–17; 11:29–31; 12:12–27; Eph 4:4, 11–16; 5:23–30; Col 1:18, 24; 2:19; 3:15).[47]

Ignatius, too, regularly images the church as the corporate embodiment of Christ. The one instance in which Ignatius employs the term σῶμα to denote this corporate solidarity is found in *Smyrn*. 1.2, where, at the

---

45. Lieu, *Image and Reality*, 23–56; see also Anders Runesson, "Inventing Christian Identity: Paul, Ignatius, and Theodosius I," in *Exploring Early Christian Identity*, ed. Bengt Holmberg, WUNT 226 (Tübingen: Mohr Siebeck, 2008), 59–92 (esp. 84–88).

46. In addition to his use of the terms Χριστιανός and Χριστιανισμός, Ignatius establishes and solidifies believers' identity in Christ by, for example, sending greetings and farewells in Christ or in the name of Christ (*Eph*. Inscr.; *Magn*. Inscr. [2×]; *Trall*. 13.2; *Rom*. Inscr. [×2]; *Phld*. Inscr.: "in the blood of Jesus Christ"; 11.2; *Smyrn*. 12.2; *Pol*. 8.3: "in our God Jesus Christ"; cf. *Magn*. 15.1; *Smyrn*. 4.2; *Pol*. 5.1). Unlike Paul, Ignatius does not regularly use the term ἐν Χριστῷ as a periphrasis for believers (see Rom 16:3, 7, 9; 1 Cor 3:1; 4:15; 16:24; 2 Cor 12:2; Gal 1:22; Phil 1:1; 4:21; Col 1:2; 1 Thess 2:14; see Campbell, *Union with Christ*, 120–27), perhaps because Ignatius has available to him the term Χριστιανός.

47. See, e.g., Sang-Won Son, *Corporate Elements in Pauline Anthropology: A Study of Selected Terms, Idioms, and Concepts in the Light of Paul's Usage and Background*, AnBib 148 (Rome: Pontifical Biblical Institute, 2001). Campbell also includes in his study the metaphor of the church as a temple or building (i.e., 1 Cor 3:9, 16–17; 6:19–20; 2 Cor 6:16; Eph 2:21–22). Given that this cultic/architectural imagery is consistently theocentric in the Pauline letters (with the possible exception of Eph 2:21–22, if κύριος in v. 21 denotes Christ), it seems to me confusing to include Pauline metaphors of the church as a temple or building in a study of union with Christ.

conclusion of what may be a citation of a protocreedal unit of early Christian tradition, Ignatius affirms that the purpose of Christ's passion was that God "might raise a sign for the ages through his [i.e., Christ's] resurrection for his saints and faithful ones, whether among Jews or among Gentiles, in the one body of his church (ἐν ἑνὶ σώματι τῆς ἐκκλησίας αὐτοῦ)." But Ignatius depicts the church as the body of Christ even in texts in which he does not use the word σῶμα. In the musical metaphor of *Eph.* 4.2, for example, Ignatius writes, "And may each of you be a chorus, so that by being harmonious in concord, receiving the key from God, you may sing with one voice through Jesus Christ to the Father, in order that he may both hear you and recognize you, through the things you do well, as members of his son." The purpose of this exhortation to sing with one voice "through Jesus Christ to the Father" (cf. *Rom.* 2.2) is to encourage unanimity and harmony among believers and with the bishop (so *Eph.* 4.1). Christ is not the active agent of this song; rather, he is the instrument through which the tune is vocalized. Importantly, the purpose of this corporately embodied hymn is that God will hear and, through the actions of the Ephesians, recognize the chorus as "members of his son" (μέλη ὄντας τοῦ υἱοῦ αὐτοῦ).[48] Moreover, as Ignatius makes clear at the end of this line of thought, the goal of perfect unity among believers – a unity symbolized by the harmonious tune of their lives – is that "you may always have a share in God" (ἵνα καὶ θεοῦ πάντοτε μετέχητε, *Eph.* 4.2).

48. Schoedel dismisses the importance of this figuration of the Ephesians as parts of Christ's body. Suggesting that μέλη represents a continuation of the musical imagery, with the term denoting service as "melodies" of God's son, Schoedel writes, "Ignatius makes little use of the body imagery; and even though he may know a form of it that has moved in a Gnostic direction (see on *Tr.* 11.2; *Sm.* 1.2) the (apparent) play on words here suggests that it does not weigh heavily on him" (*Ignatius*, 53). The claim that Ignatius's use of the term μέλη continues the musical metaphor is difficult to support, however, not least because of a lack of evidence for the noun μέλη functioning within the conceptual field of musical imagery. Indeed, Schoedel's claim that μέλη continues a play on musical imagery is confusing: the Ephesians join a chorus so that in harmonious concord they can sing with one voice, with the result that God hears their singular, melodious song and recognizes them...as melodies? More naturally, God recognizes in the song that he hears the voices of the members of the body of Christ, and so *Eph.* 4.2 is one of several instances in Ignatius's letters in which the church is imaged as the body of the risen Lord (*Trall.* 11.2; *Smyrn.* 1.2). Schoedel appears to set aside the importance of the body metaphor in *Eph.* 4.2 because of his claim that this imagery does not figure prominently elsewhere in Ignatius's correspondence. This may be a difference of degree, but I find the occurrences in *Trall.* 11.2 and *Smyrn.* 1.2 to be quite significant and not particularly rare when compared with instances of the body of Christ image in the Pauline letters.

The other key text in which Ignatius employs the concept of the church as the body of Christ also features the term "members" (μέλη; cf. *Eph.* 4.2 discussed above). In *Trall.* 11.1–2, as part of an encouragement to flee false teachers, Ignatius utilizes a constellation of images. The opponents are described, using horticultural language, as "evil offshoots who bear deadly fruit"; that the fruit of these offshoots kills is an indication that they are not the Father's planting (11.1). In contrast, Ignatius suggests, those who bear imperishable fruit appear as "branches of the cross," an instrument of death "through which he [i.e., Christ; cf. 9.1], in his suffering, calls you who are his members" (ὑμᾶς ὄντας μέλη αὐτοῦ). The image concludes with the implicit affirmation that Christ is the "head" (κεφαλή) of the "members" of his body: "A head, therefore, cannot be born without members, because God promises unity, which he himself is" (11.2).[49] As in the Pauline letters, for Ignatius belonging to the body of Christ means also belonging together with others in Christ.

Conclusion

The preceding analysis suggests a fairly high level of conceptual correspondence between Paul and Ignatius on the theme of union with Christ. Using Campbell's fourfold definition of "union with Christ" in the Pauline epistles as a heuristic guide, we have identified significant similarities and small differences in terms of the motifs of union, participation, identification, and incorporation. In spite of the very different circumstances and contexts of their letters, Ignatius seems to have articulated a theology of union with Christ that coheres quite closely with that found in the Pauline epistles.

But can Ignatius's concept of union with Christ be attributed to the influence of Paul? Ignatius certainly knew of the apostle Paul, and almost certainly had access to at least some of Paul's writings, perhaps a collection that included 1 Corinthians, Ephesians, 1 Timothy, and 2 Timothy. It seems to me, however, that caution should be exercised when investigating the possibility of a genealogical line of influence from Paul to Ignatius on any specific theological motif. Where Ignatius specifically mentions Paul and the apostle's legacy – specifically "the departed and *ascended* Paul" – lines

---

49. Other images for the corporate union of believers in Ignatius, though not necessarily related to union with Christ, include the claims that believers are temple stones in God's building (*Eph.* 9.1), temples of the Lord (*Eph.* 15.3), or "one temple of God" (*Magn.* 7.2).

of influence are traceable.[50] But it is not possible to attribute with certainty Ignatius's concept of union with Christ to the influence of the Pauline tradition. Partly this is because the apostle Paul was not the only early Christian writer to advocate something like a theology of participatory union with Christ. Several of the salient features of Paul's concept of union with Christ, for example, are also paralleled in the Gospel of John, such as mutual indwelling between Christ and his followers (John 6:56; 15:4–7; 17:21, 23, 26) and participation within and belonging to an organic body/vine of Christ (John 15:1–5).[51] Considering at least the possibility that Ignatius knew and used the Gospel of John, Ignatius could have developed his concept of union with Christ in conversation with the Johannine tradition.[52] At the same time, in light of Ignatius's familiarity with and respect for the apostle Paul, and given the general coherence between Paul and Ignatius on the theme of union with Christ, Paul's influence on Ignatius on this point seems not only plausible but likely, even if an exact line of dependence cannot be drawn.

50. Kirk, "Paul's Approach to Death," 98. Kirk's chapter on Ignatius is a model of this kind of careful investigation.

51. See Campbell, *Paul and Union*, 417–20.

52. On the possibility of Ignatius's use of John, see Foster, "The Epistles of Ignatius of Antioch and the Writings," 183–84.

Chapter 9

PAUL, IGNATIUS AND THIRDSPACE:
A SOCIO-GEOGRAPHIC EXPLORATION

Harry O. Maier

Introduction

"People are not put into place, they put place into being."[1] Johnathan Z. Smith furnishes the departure point for this spatial analysis of the letters of Paul and of Ignatius of Antioch. As such it extends the "spatial turn" to post-canonical literature and contributes to the social-geographical study of emergent Christianity, an application that is still in its nascent stages and, at the time of writing, has not been directed to the letters of Ignatius.[2] With the help of socio-geographical studies by Edward Soja, Michel Foucault, and Robert Sacks the following discussion seeks to analyze and compare the representation of meeting places in Paul and Ignatius as products of social imagination.[3] Both Paul and Ignatius borrow heavily from political terms and concepts at home in their civic contexts and in their respective applications to the church reveal a social imagination wedded with the physical spaces of religious gatherings. With the help of a civic imaginary, Paul and Ignatius bring place into being and populate it with figures who play ideal or less than ideal roles, live out narratives that invite particular practices of place, and encourage behaviors that conform to imaginative configurations of social space.

1. Johnathan Z. Smith, *To Take Place: Toward a Theory in Ritual* (Chicago: University of Chicago Press, 1992), 30.
2. Eric Steward, "New Testament Space/Spatiality," *Biblical Theology Bulletin* 42 (2012): 139–50.
3. Edward W. Soja, *Thirdspace: Journeys to Los Angeles and Other Real-and-Imagined Places* (Oxford: Blackwell, 1996); Michel Foucault, "Of Other Spaces," *Diacritics* 16 (1986): 22–7; Robert David Sack, *Human Territoriality: Its Theory and History*, Cambridge Studies in Historical Geography (Cambridge: Cambridge University Press, 1986).

Soja, Foucault and Spatial Imagination

The quotation from Smith cited above implicitly contests the Kantian notion of space as a priori. Kant conceives of space as subjective and ideal; it is a transcendent and necessary condition for any experiential reality. As such it furnishes an antecedent form or structure for the ordering of sensations and is thus the precondition for anything to appear in place.[4] The social geographers I take up here challenge this view: they rather argue that there is no space without action; people put place into being. Place is not a receptacle filled with content; place rather comes about through action, imagination, and interaction of humans with their lived and socially constructed environment. Robert David Sack has coined the phrase "homo geographicus" to describe this process of the creation of place. "We humans" he writes, "are geographical beings transforming the earth and making it into a home, and that transformed world affects who we are."[5] Henri Lefebvre and Edward Soja, who has extended Lefebvre's analysis, give more theoretical precision to this observation in their theorization of social geography. Lefebvre distinguishes between perceived, conceived, and lived space.[6] Perceived space denotes the empirical world and material spatial practices humans undertake that go along with it, such as forms of work, play, the living out of family roles, and so on. Conceived space describes the way the practice relating to perceived space is represented, organized, directed, and given normative meanings in human culture by governing elites. For Lefebvre one of the roles of culture, politics, and ideology is to make the perceived and conceived "natural" – that is, to conceive the social construction of space and its organization of humans for the tasks of social life as self-evident or normative. "Lived space" takes up the ways representation of perceived and conceived space arise in new and unique ways in society, usually from a non-elite point of view that transgresses and questions normalizing practices and interpretation indicated in perceived and conceived space.

Edward Soja has developed Lefebvre further by discussing perceived, conceived, and lived space as First, Second and Thirdspace, respectively. Soja gives particular attention to Thirdspace as an imaginative break

4. For discussion, Gary Hatfield, "Kant on the Perception of Space (and Time)," in *The Cambridge Companion to Kant and Modern Philosophy*, ed. Paul Guyer (Cambridge: Cambridge University Press, 2006), 77–82.

5. Robert David Sack, *Homo Geographicus: A Framework for Action, Awareness, and Moral Concern* (Baltimore: The John Hopkins University Press, 1997), 1.

6. Henri Lefebvre, *The Production of Space*, trans. Donald Nicholson Smith (Oxford: Blackwell, 1991), 39–41.

or transgression with First- and Secondspace that is known in practices that do not fit into First- and Secondspace formulations. Thirdspace is a dynamic, unfolding, creative appropriation of pre-existing structures and meanings. Soja's emphasis on Thirdspace is the space of rupture, of creating the unanticipated and unpredictable from the elements of first and Secondspace. Thirdspace, he explains, "can be described as a creative recombination and extension, one that builds on Firstspace perspective that is focused on the 'real' material world and a Secondspace perspective that interprets this reality through 'imagined' representations of spatiality." Thus Thirdspace is "*real-and-imagined*" space.[7]

Soja relates his understanding of Thirdspace to Michel Foucault's notion of "heterotopia," a conception Foucault nowhere developed systematically, but which Soja nevertheless uses to describe his own conceptualization. For Foucault heterotopia consists of "places…outside of all places"; heterotopias are real, physical, or imagined spaces that co-exist with visible spaces and derive their meaning and practices from the world around them, but are places in which "other" practices are made possible or are contained. Foucault describes heterotopia as "something like counter-sites, a kind of effectively enacted utopia in which the real sites, all the other real sites, that can be found in culture, are simultaneously represented, contested, and inverted."[8]

Soja's appropriation of Lefebvre and Foucault furnishes the theoretical backdrop for what follows and represents important insights for the socio-historical study of emergent Christianity in general and its application to the Ignatian corpus in particular. Whereas excellent insights have been furnished in the study of both Paul and Ignatius through archaeological and anthropological study, socio-geographical analysis offers important nuance to such investigation. If we think of space not as given, or as a stage or neutral backdrop for behavior to unfold – as putting people into place – and rather conceive of it as a dynamic product of geography, imagination, and practice we will be able to recognize the creative ways in which Paul and Ignatius conceive the real-and-imagined space of the communal gathering, and how their writings represent, contest, and invert their social world.

Paul, Thirdspace, and Heterotopia

Imagination, specifically its ability to juxtapose and make simultaneous meanings that are kept separate in normative social practices of place, puts place into being. In the case of Paul, both in the undisputed and disputed

7. Soja, *Thirdspace*, 6.
8. Foucault, "Spaces," 24.

corpus, imaginative juxtapositions can be seen in the way he unites the death of Jesus with civic vocabulary and imperial social goods.[9] The recent turn to "Empire" in Pauline studies has given special attention to the imperial language embedded in the Pauline corpus, in both the earlier and later letters. Usually this has been interpreted as evidence of a resistance to the Roman Empire: Paul and his followers adopted the vocabulary of the Empire as a counter to hegemonic imperial claims, and as means to promote a belief system in direct and conscious opposition to the emperor and his political order.[10] This account rehearses a point of view developed in the first half of the twentieth century, when archaeological discovery of imperial inscriptions and temples dedicated to emperor worship revealed the degree to which the New Testament contains vocabulary and metaphors that were commonplace in imperial political discourse.[11] It is indeed remarkable that Paul's letters so regularly turn to imperial language to describe and champion the beliefs and ideals of Christ followers. But it is not so clear that its presence reflects a desire to resist the imperial order, however much monotheistic allegiance to the God of Israel through Christ would have represented a challenge to pre-existing religious practices, including those on which the imperial system depended for its ideological legitimation. From a socio-geographical perspective, a function of this civic language, metaphor, and imagination could as much reflect forms of integration with the imperial world as confrontation. Given Paul's eschatological belief that "the form of this world is passing away," such integration is of course wholly unintended and reflects the hybridity of Pauline religious thinking with respect to imperial realities in that it both borrows from and marks itself as separate from the political order.

The value of social geographic investigation is that it investigates the simultaneous juxtaposition of spatial imagination without resolving tensions into one side of a binary or another. The work of Soja, Foucault, and Sack furnishes valuable tools for advancing a more nuanced account of Pauline identity in its civic context and offers, as we will see, important insights for understanding Ignatius of Antioch's appropriation of civic

9. The following focuses on the undisputed letters and specifically the Corinthian correspondence; for discussion of the disputed letters and their uses of civic vocabulary and imagery see Harry O. Maier, *Picturing Paul in Empire: Imperial Image, Text and Persuasion in Colossians, Ephesians and the Pastoral Epistles* (London: T&T Clark, 2013), 63–196.

10. For a review with bibliography, see David J. Lull, "Paul and Empire," *RelSRev* 36 (2010): 252–62.

11. For review see Peter Oakes, *Philippians: From People to Letter*, SNTSMS 110 (Cambridge: Cambridge University Press, 2001), 129–38.

language and its role in constructing social geography. Recent social study of Paul from the perspective of patterns of patronage, the organization of household spaces, and the roles of actors in the urban honorific culture of the Roman Empire proves useful here.

Paul's Urban Geography

Whereas an earlier generation of New Testament scholars urged attention to civic practices and urban identity in the interpretation of Paul, social geography weds practice and identity to space and time. Peter Oakes in particular, building on the work of Andrew Wallace-Hadrill, locates Paul's correspondence with the Corinthians and the churches in Rome amidst the housing and patronage culture of the Roman city.[12] Wallace-Hadrill has shown that, unlike modern North American cities where those of similar socio-economic identity cluster in neighborhoods, in Pompeii, Herculaneum, Ostia, and Rome neighborhoods developed around patron and client networks so that workshops, tabernae, popinae, temples, baths, market places, buildings of associations, and so on joined together by clientship clustered around the living quarters of patrons or others with sufficient means to draw on the goods on offer in a given urban area. He describes ways that urban housefuls of groups of varying socio-economic identity radiated out alongside of wealthier households and thus formed a kind of urban social unit.[13] The social organization preserved and physically inscribed vertical social distinctions through size and quality of habitations. Rich and poor not only lived alongside each other, they lived above and below one another.[14]

Oakes expands Wallace-Hadrill's account to issues of patronage, wealth, and poverty in 1 Corinthians where, he argues, disputes over the consumption of idol meat and the presence in temples by Christ followers, outlined

---

12. Peter Oakes, "Urban Structure and Patronage: Christ Followers in Corinth," in *Understanding the Social World of the New Testament*, ed. Dietmar Neufeld and Richard E. DeMaris (London: Routledge, 2010), 187–93; idem, *Reading Romans in Pompeii* (London: SPCK; Minneapolis: Fortress, 2009); Andrew Wallace-Hadrill, "*Domus* and *Insulae* in Rome: Families and Housefuls," in *Early Christian Families in Context: An Interdisciplinary Dialogue*, ed. Carolyn Osiek and David L. Balch (Ann Arbor, MI: Eerdmans, 2003), 3–18.

13. Wallace-Hadrill, "*Domus*," 13.

14. For discussion of disparities of wealth in the urban context and the realities of poverty in imperial cities, see Justin Meggitt, *Paul, Poverty and Survival*, Studies in the New Testament and its World (Edinburgh: T&T Clark, 1998).

in 1 Cor 8–10, should be interpreted not only according to socio-demographic realities of the sort identified by Gerd Theissen and others, but also with a view to urban spatial realities and the social networks of first-century Corinth.[15] Eating at a temple (1 Cor 8:10), being hosted at a meal (1 Cor 10:27–29), or hosting one (1 Cor 11:18–22) have patronage networks as their social backdrop. Such actions rendered these networks visible and in the case of the Corinthians, with respect to temple banqueting and mishandling of the common meal described in 1 Cor 11, reinscribed them in ways Paul rejected. To eat in a temple, Oakes argues, was to reveal divine patronage (1 Cor 10:14–22), even as to banquet in someone's home as an invited guest was to enjoy and thus reinforce a relation of either patron–client or friendship, and thus practice social demarcation.

Two points about Oakes' model should be made – one more critical, the other to bring out more fully a key insight of his analysis for our purposes here. Pompeii, Rome, and environs evince an urban topography that is not easily transferred to Roman Corinth, at least in the light of archaeological evidence that has been unearthed to date. Nevertheless, as Oakes rightly argues, one must resist the tendency of contemporary scholars to locate the wealthier of Pauline Christ followers and their meetings in the dining rooms of urban villas.[16] Archaeological evidence from Corinth presents another possibility as the setting for Christ worship and ritual, namely the tabernae, popinae, and workshops of Corinthian small business owners, with some means, who probably owned slaves, and sufficient space to invite believers into living quarters above their shops.[17] Even in these more modest conditions patterns of patronage and vertical lines of social relationship organized Corinthian social realities as clients of higher up patrons themselves functioned as patrons to those below them, to whom they were thus beholden. Oakes' model is especially useful because it draws attention to these social realities at lower strata of Paul's social world.

15. Gerd Theissen, "Soziale Integration und sakramentales Handeln: Eine Analyse von 1 Cor. 11:17–34," *NovT* 16 (1974): 145–74; for discussion with further literature, see David Horrell, *The Social Ethos of the Corinthian Correspondence: Interests and Ideology from 1 Corinthians to* 1 Clement (Edinburgh: T&T Clark, 1996), 126–98.

16. For example, Jerome Murphy O'Connor, *St Paul's Corinth: Texts and Archaeology*, 3rd ed. (Collegeville, MN: Liturgical Press, 2002), 178–85, presumes the triclinium of the Anaploga Villa as the physical setting of the Last supper outlined in 1 Cor 11:17–33. For the prevalence of this model in modern scholarship, see David Horrell, "Domestic Space and Christian Meetings at Corinth: Imagining New Contexts and the Buildings East of the Theatre," *NTS* 50 (2004): 349–69, at 349–53.

17. Horrell, "Space," 360–68.

Attention to social geography extends and develops Oakes' model in three ways. First, it reveals that Paul's Corinthian correspondence challenges the perceived–conceived/Firstspace–Secondspace practice that rendered first-century social relations natural and the societal construction of them all but invisible. Second, it sets the stage for understanding Paul's rejoinders to this situation as Thirdspace practice. Third, it helps to recognize Paul's uses of civic and imperial language as a tactic for outlining a different model of social geography and practice of space. Paul contests how people have followed typical spatial practices to the detriment of the community and then through the construction of heterotopia urges them toward bringing a new space into being that expresses their locational identity in Christ.

It is clear Paul is fighting an uphill battle with the Corinthians. Not only in his correspondence with them in 1 Corinthians, but also in his response to those he brands as "super apostles" in 2 Cor 12:11, Paul contests a social order that patronage renders natural and irrefutable, an order inscribed not just through patterns of patronage of the sort outlined above, but by the urban practices and display represented in public benefactions, local processions, religious ritual, monuments, inscriptions, imperial favors, numismatic imagery, portraiture, and indeed the very organization of neighborhoods.

Paul's response is to overwrite this "natural" social geography with an alternative one. Here is where Foucault's notion of heterotopia proves fruitful, as "counter-site" and as a "utopia" where social geographical sites in culture "are simultaneously represented, contested, and inverted." Critical to both Foucault's and Soja's conceptualization is that heterotopia/Thirdspace takes place within and in relation to normative space practices. It is remarkable from this perspective that Paul uses the motif of the body to describe the believers in Corinth (1 Cor 11:27–32; 12:12–31). The image of the body was not only a longstanding metaphor for outlining the righty functioning state, in Paul's urban culture sculpture, reliefs, frescoes, and numismatic imagery idealized the beautiful body and associated it with the properly governed and hierarchically organized state.[18] A visual ideology of imperial harmony created through Augustan and Julio-Claudian achievement, which reinforced already existing public portraiture and its political messages, filled cities with full-size statues of the emperor and his family, or of local ruling elites. Temples housed statues similarly represented as perfectly formed bodies.

18. For the use of the metaphor and physiognomics in politics, see Dale B. Martin, *The Corinthian Body* (New Haven: Yale University Press, 1995), 35–37; for its use in civic visual culture in the Roman imperial cities, Maier, *Paul*, 57–59.

It is remarkable, then, that when Paul represents the church as body in 1 Cor 12:22–23 he draws attention to the priority of the "weaker" (ἀσθενέστερα) and "less honorable" (ἀτιμότερα) and "unpresentable" (ἀσχήμονα) parts as receiving greater honor. In the visual culture that has shaped the imagination and expectations of the Corinthians this creates a jarring picture. Paul contests and inverts the reigning ideology and challenges the natural order as unnatural. The same logic unfolds in his admonitions of misbehavior at the Lord's supper. Here the typical status-oriented eating rituals, where those with more honor receive more food as a means of reinforcing social hierarchies, Paul challenges as a failure to discern the body of Christ.

Pauline Imperial Tactics

Paul in the words of Soja takes a "'real' material world and a Secondspace perspective" and "interprets this reality through 'imagined' representations of spatiality." In this "imagined" spatiality a whole new set of relations and practices are enacted. These are most dramatically outlined in Paul's advice concerning marriage and celibacy (1 Cor 7:25–40), where he portrays the dissolution of the prevailing structure of the world. Wives are to live as though they were not married; those who mourn as though not mourning; those who rejoice as though not rejoicing; those who buy as though they had no goods, those who deal with the world as though they had no dealings with it (7:29–31). Here Paul exhorts with a view to a partially realized eschatology. However, his instructions also have spatial dimensions in that they have as their setting the household, the market place, and the practices of daily life. Paul uses eschatology to make a new configuration take place, literally, in the imagined social spaces of Corinthian gathering and relationships. In this heterotopic space cultural sites "are simultaneously represented, contested and inverted."

I have shown elsewhere, building on the studies of Margaret Mitchell, Peter Marshall, and L. L. Welborn, the prevalence in 1 Corinthians of civic vocabulary dedicated to social ideals associated with political concord as well as faction and discord.[19] 1 and 2 Corinthians are suffused with civic

---

19. Maier, "The Politics of Discord and Concord in Paul and Ignatius of Antioch," in *The New Testament and the Apostolic Fathers*. Vol. 2, *Trajectories through the New Testament and the Apostolic Fathers*, ed. Andrew F. Gregory and Christopher M. Tuckett (Oxford: Oxford University Press, 2005), 307–24; Margaret M. Mitchell, *Paul and the Rhetoric of Reconciliation: An Exegetical Investigation of the Language and Composition of 1 Corinthians* (Louisville: Westminster John Knox, 1991); Peter Marshall, *Enmity in Corinth: Social Conventions in Paul's*

language, as is the Pauline corpus as whole. What we find in the Corinthian correspondence is present in the other undisputed letters as well. For example, in Phil 3:20 Paul describes the Philippian Christ followers as having a "citizenship in heaven" (πολίτευμα ἐν οὐρανοῖς) and in 1 Thess 4:17 he represents the coming of Jesus as an imperial *adventus* when the Thessalonians will "go out to meet the Lord" (ἀπάντησιν τοῦ κυρίου). And I have now extended this analysis to the study of the contested letters. Ephesians 2:19, for example, represents a densely formulated Pauline description of the integration of social goods members in the church have achieved.[20] Civic language and use of political metaphor has been explored for its possible anti-imperial sentiments. However, the language also expresses a socio-geography: whatever civic goods attain in the Roman Empire through the government and political rituals, the body of believers created by Paul's Gospel inserts itself invisibly within the larger political discourse and poaches upon its language and ideals in the creation of a "place outside of place." The attempt to wrest from Paul a counter-imperial political sentiment neglects the constructive imaginary representations of space inserted within the domestic meeting places of Paul's communities. Michel de Certeau uses the word "tactics" to describe the ways in which the daily practices of life insert themselves within over-arching blueprints for social interactions – what he names "strategies."[21] Like Thirdspaces and heterotopias, tactics represent new spatial practices that both depend upon and contest and invert norms. The paradox that emerges in Paul's letters is the paradox of Thirdspace more generally – the apostle transforms the civic and domestic sites for normative spatial practices but transposes them into a new register. The result is a series of spatial practices that resemble Firstspace/Secondspace formulations, but contest them by rehearsing them in unpredictable and highly imaginative ways. Paul reminds his readers of their new location in Christ and in doing so he brings space into being.

Relations with the Corinthians, WUNT 2/23 (Tübingen: Mohr Siebeck, 1987); L. L. Welborn, "On the Discord in Corinth: 1 Corinthians 1–4 and Ancient Politics," *JBL* 106 (1987): 85–111.

20. Maier, *Paul*, 107–18; see also Carmen Bernabé Ubieta, "'Neither *Xenoi* nor *paroikoi*, *sympolitai* and *oikeioi tou theou*' (Eph 2.19): Pauline Christian Communities, Defining a New Territoriality," in *Social Scientific Models for Interpreting the Bible: Essays by the Context Group in Honor of Bruce J. Malina*, ed. John J. Pilch (Leiden: Brill, 2001), 260–80, who independently makes similar observations with the help of the social geographical theorization of Sacks.

21. Michel de Certeau, *The Practice of Everyday Life*, trans. Steven Rendall (Berkeley: University of California Press, 1984), 34–39.

Putting Ignatius of Antioch in Place

Possibly as many as three generations after Paul wrote his letters to the Corinthians, Ignatius of Antioch passed through cities of Asia Minor on his way to execution in Rome.[22] Along the way Ignatius met with leaders whom he identified as local bishops and interpreted as also representing the elders and deacons, which together formed the legitimate leadership of local churches. Ignatius urged the audiences of his letters to submit to the authority of these leaders and he judged as legitimate only those rituals conducted by them or their appointees.[23] He disqualified those gatherings consisting of those with Christological teachings he pilloried as heretical or worse, and ruled out any meetings gathered around those not approved by the bishop.

Too often scholarly accounts consider Ignatius's letters from a strictly theological point of view, or with a view to literary influences on his thought by New Testament authors.[24] What insights might socio-geography bring to the social situation Ignatius presumes in his letters? How does the Ignatian correspondence reflect a social geography that differs from what we have discovered in our Thirdspace analysis of the urban social world of Paul's first-century Christ followers? I hope to show that Ignatius's polemic against those he opposes reflects an application of Thirdspace imagination. Two social geographies emerge in Ignatius's letters, one associated with

22. For a summary of issues and arguments relating to dating, Paul Foster, "The Epistles of Ignatius of Antioch," in *The Writings of the Apostolic Fathers*, ed. Paul Foster (London: T&T Clark, 2007), 84–89.

23. Here I emphasize the collective authority of bishops, elders, and deacons as Ignatius considers them a unit, while at the same time singling out a figure he identifies as the singular bishop. In my view, Ignatius is constructing rather than mirroring this social reality as a means of social control; for discussion with literature see, Harry O. Maier, *The Social Setting of the Ministry as Reflected in the Writings of Hermas, Clement, and Ignatius*, Studies in Christianity and Judaism/Études sur le christianisme et le judaisme 12 (Waterloo, ON: Wilfred Laurier University Press, 2002), 170–82.

24. Representative accounts are Hans von Campenhausen, *Ecclesiastical Authority and Spiritual Power in the Churches of the First Three Centuries*, trans. J. A. Baker (London: A. & C. Black, 1969), 97–123; Peter Meinhold, *Studien zu Ignatius von Antiochien*, Veröffentlichungen des Instituts für europäische Geschichte Mainz 97 (Wiesbaden: Franz Steiner, 1979), 57–66; F. A. Sullivan, *From Apostles to Bishops: The Development of the Episcopacy in the Early Church* (Mahwah, NJ: Newman Press, 2001), 103–25; Carl B. Smith, "Ministry, Martyrdom, and Other Mysteries: Pauline Influence on Ignatius of Antioch," in *Paul and the Second Century*, ed. Michael F. Bird and Joseph R. Dodson, LNTS 412 (London: T&T Clark, 2011), 57–69.

those whom he promotes and another with those he opposes. Attention to Thirdspace allows us to recognize a critical aspect of Ignatius's rhetorical strategy of promoting a particular vision of ecclesial leadership. Like the earlier Pauline corpus a civic imagination dominates. While Ignatius draws on a Pauline legacy, especially as found in 1 Corinthians which he most certainly knew, he develops the thinking found there in new ways that represent a kind of naturalization of Paul's thinking and the creation of normative ecclesiastical practice over against others practices.[25]

It is not possible to gain a comprehensive picture of the urban geography of the cities associated with Ignatius's journey through Asia Minor. To date, archaeological investigation of urban centers of western Asia Minor has focused, almost exclusively, as elsewhere, on monuments and elite residences. Further, there is nothing like Pompeii, Herculaneum, or Ostia with which to compare eastern cities. Nevertheless, there is good evidence to furnish a general picture helpful in assessing the social geographical world Ignatius's letters presume and construct around themselves. For example, excavations have revealed that first-century CE Roman Pergamon contained tenements made up of housing ranging from more luxurious peristyle houses, modest courtyard houses, shops with living quarters, and one-bedroom rentals.[26] Similarly, in Ephesus the workshops and living quarters lining the "Kuretes" street were directly alongside the luxury apartments of elites.[27]

---

25. For discussion of Ignatius's knowledge of 1 Corinthians as well as other New Testament writings, see W. R. Inge "Ignatius," in A Committee of the Oxford Society of Historical Theology, *The New Testament in the Apostolic Fathers* (Oxford: Clarendon, 1905), 61–83; Paul Foster, "The Use of the Writings That Later Formed the New Testament in the Epistles of Ignatius of Antioch," in *The New Testament and the Apostolic Fathers*. Vol. 1, *The Reception of the New Testament in the Apostolic Fathers*, ed. Andrew F. Gregory and Christopher M. Tuckett (Oxford: Oxford University Press, 2005), 159–86; Harry O. Maier, "The Politics and Rhetoric of Discord and Concord in Ignatius and Paul," in *The New Testament and the Apostolic Fathers*. Vol. 2, *Trajectories through the New Testament and the Apostolic Fathers*, ed. Andrew F. Gregory and Christopher M. Tuckett (Oxford: Oxford University Press, 2005), 307–24.

26. Monika Trümper, "Material and Social Environment of Greco-Roman Households in the East: The Case of Hellenistic Delos," in *Early Christian Families in Context: An Interdisciplinary Dialogue*, ed. Carolyn Osiek and David L. Balch (Ann Arbor, MI: Eerdmans, 2003), 36–37.

27. For discussion, see Bradly S. Billings, "From House Church to Tenement Church: Domestic Space and the Development of Early Urban Christianity: The Example of Ephesus," *JTS* 62 (2011): 541–69.

One important difference in the layout of peristyle houses from their analogues in Italy is the absence of an atrium with impluvium, surrounded by symmetrically closed and open rooms. The chief difference from a social perspective is that whereas the Roman atrium house distinguished between a space for formal reception and less but still potentially public spaces for "private" living, peristyle and courtyard houses outside of Italy offered no distinction for fields of accessible space and provided a separate area shut-off entirely from public view for the life of the leading members of the household. Passersby on the street could see into the courtyard but no further, unless the door leading from the courtyard to the living quarters were opened, in which case they could have seen right through to the end of the house. Monika Trümper suggests that in such a social situation, access to both courtyard and living quarters were dependent upon porters and household owners – the first who could give access to the more public courtyard and the second who alone could give access to spaces associated with the more intimate aspects of family life: eating, sleeping, and so on.

Association spaces, where identifiable, could distinguish themselves as halls for larger assembly by the presence of long dining halls either with permanent klinae or with space to furnish them for the common meals typical of guilds. Again, evidence from first-century CE Pergamon is instructive: a hall of an association of cowheards was comprised of a long narrow space (24 × 10 metres) with an altar for sacrifice at the centre of the room, and klinae and benches along the walls, where up to 70 people could recline and place their food.[28]

I have focused on these two kinds of gathering places – the sequestered and invisible space of dining in the Pergamene courtyard house and the rented space of the association dining hall – to set the spatial backdrop for the picture of the ideal community Ignatius of Antioch places before his audience. First, Ignatius seeks to regulate a situation where he knows of more than one eucharistic assembly taking place in the urban churches his letters address. This is why he condemns any eucharist as not being a real eucharist that does not occur in the presence of the person he can single out as a bishop. Thus he condemns those who do not join "the common assembly" (*Eph.* 5.2–3), but separate themselves, or who "do not meet in accordance with the commandment" (*Magn.* 4.1). He similarly implies the existence of separate meetings where he commands churches to do

28. For discussion with literature, see Philip Harland, *Associations, Synagogues, and Congregations: Claiming a Place in Ancient Mediterranean Society* (Minneapolis: Fortress, 2003), 78–79.

nothing without the presence or the permission of the bishop (*Magn.* 7.1–2; *Trall.* 2.2; 7.2; *Smyrn.* 9.1). Although Ignatius does not describe this situation in more detail, it is very possible that he is opposing those who, like him, have found a means of access to the churches he addresses, through networks of patronage. Ignatius uses such networks to his benefit. At the same time his letters presuppose the presence of people hosted in households and who represent teachings Ignatius rejects. A clear strategy of his letters is to de-legitimate these meetings. He expects that one person alone will receive visitors, the bishop, and that he will determine whether they ought to be welcomed or not, and whether ritual meals may be conducted by or in his or her presence. In a situation like this, the courtyard household with porter and householder controlling access offers a way of conceiving such access as well as surveillance of others. This is not to say that the churches enjoyed access to this kind of space or patronage, only that from a social-geographical perspective, regulated access to space was already a feature of daily urban experience. Further, the model of people living in close tenement quarters allows for the kind of visibility required for supervision of relatively private events such as common meals.

Concord, Urban Imagination, and Thirdspace in Ignatius

Less speculative is the way Ignatius idealizes worship gatherings in harmony with bishops, elders, and deacons with the help of the civic language of concord and the imperial language of sacrifice. Here it is not so much the space of Greek associations that is informative so much its epigraphy that celebrates the virtues of leaders and outlines the duties of members, as well as punishment by exclusion of those who transgress association rules.[29] These epigraphic data are apiece with the larger civic ideals of urban associations, where an identical set of social ideals is regularly set forth. The rhetorical topoi associated with civic concord, and its opposite, faction, are recurring motifs in Ignatius's letters.

John-Paul Lotz and Allen Brent have dedicated excellent discussions to the prevalence of themes of concord in the Ignatian correspondence. Further, they have shown how the high frequency of terms and concepts associated with *homonoia* must be read against a larger urban and

---

29. For virtues, expectations, and rules and further literature see Alicia Batten, "The Moral World of Greco-Roman Associations." *Studies in Religion* 36 (2007): 135–51; and Harland, *Associations*, 76; for association virtues and leadership in 1, 2 Timothy, and Titus, probably contemporary with Ignatius' letters, see Maier, *Paul*, 168–69, 173.

imperial backdrop that acclaimed the achievement of civic concord as a chief social good.[30] For example, the same cities Ignatius names in his letters issued coins with *homonoia* imagery to celebrate the treaties that marked the end of rivalries. Further, rhetors like Dio of Prusa, who was sometimes delegated as an ambassador to urge the end of inter-urban conflict, dedicated speeches to the ideals of concord and peace. Ignatius's own *homonoia* language should be interpreted against this setting, even as he takes that language and develops it in new directions as a means of ecclesial control.

Ignatius uses the term ὁμόνοια seven times in his letters to describe communal ideals (*Eph.* 4.1, 2; 13.1; *Magn.* 6.1; 15.1; *Trall.* 12.2; *Phld.* 11.2). The pictures of the church living peaceably and obediently with its bishop, elders, and deacons (whom Ignatius significantly always assumes function as a unity) draw from commonplaces found in the rhetorical presentations of concord or *homonoia* found in Dio of Prusa, Plutarch, and, later, Aristides: the ship (*Smyrn.* 11.3; *Pol.* 2.3), the choir or music (*Eph.* 4.1; *Rom.* 2.2; *Phld.* 1.2), the army (*Pol.* 6.2), the body (*Eph.* 4.2; *Trall.* 4.2; 11.2; *Smyrn.* 1.2), the building/temple (*Eph.* 5.2; 6.1; 9.1; 15.3; 16.1; *Magn.* 7.2; *Trall.* 7.2; *Phld.* 4.1).[31] He draws indefatigably on cognates related to oneness (ἕνωσις; ἑνότης; ἑνόειν – for example, *Eph.* 4.2; *Magn.* 1.2; 6.2; 7.1, 2; 13.2; *Trall.* 11.2; *Phld.* 2.2; 4.1; *Smyrn.* 3.3; 12.2; *Pol.* 1.2; 5.2; 8.1), and consistently deploys words with the prefix "sun" (see especially, *Pol.* 6.1; also *Eph.* 13.1; 20.2; *Magn.* 4.1; 7.1–2).

On the other side, he employs commonplace language in the representation of civic faction – ἔρις; μερισμός; αἵρεσις; σχίζειν – *Eph.* 6.2; 8.1; *Magn.* 6.2; *Trall.* 6.1; *Phld.* 2.1; 3.1, 3; 7.2; 8.2; *Smyrn.* 7.2). Ignatius's enemies are always arrogant, argumentative, boastful, and divisive. Unlike the bishop who brings harmony through his controlled and studied orthodox speech, those Ignatius opposes bring rancor through their heretical babble. The bishops display all the virtues outlined in the civic honorific culture of his day to celebrate the ideal leader: moderation, piety, gentleness, self-control, generosity, and hospitality. The result is a portrait

---

30. John-Paul Lotz, *Ignatius and Concord: The Background and Use of the Language of Concord in the Letters of Ignatius of Antioch*, Patristic Studies 8 (New York: Lang, 2007); Allen Brent, *Ignatius of Antioch and the Second Sophistic: A Study of an Early Christian Transformation of Pagan Culture*, Studien und Texte zu Antike und Christentum 36 (Tübingen: Mohr Siebeck, 2006), 254–311, which builds on Lotz.

31. For parallels in Dio, Plutarch, and Aristides see Maier, "Politics," 307–24.

of an ideal community that achieves all the goods of a shared civic urban order, but realized in the meeting that harmoniously gathers around its bishop for a common meal and instruction.

Allen Brent has related the presence of the language of *homonoia* and *eris* to Ignatius's larger imperial culture which was at home in speeches and epigraphy dedicated to ending inter-city rivalries as well as a means of expressing both independence from and integration with the Roman *pax*.[32] In addition to this inter-urban and imperial backdrop, concord language also appears in association inscriptions and honorific monuments and thus reflects its importance in promoting social integration amongst the densely populated and ethnically diverse urban populations of first-century imperial cities like Pergamon.[33] In the case of associations, dislocated people of the same ethnic origins found in such language a means to express with a common set of metaphors and terms integration into a larger urban order. Or, on the other hand, they discovered a shared social life in associations that overcame obstacles of differing ethnicity, social origins, and economic position.[34] Its presence in Christian literature, association epigraphy, and civic oratory alike expresses well what Philip Harland describes as the vitality of early imperial civic life.[35] Its appearance in Ignatius's letters urges us to recognize the paradoxical aspects of a prisoner about to be executed in Rome who uses language at home in his civic world to promote ecclesial ideals. The ideal vision of Christian community here does not speak of a religious phenomenon over against the urban life of the first century, but rather, if paradoxically, fully participant in it. The question then is not one of replacement, but of imagination of the civic ideals on other terms.

Ignatius offers a Thirdspace articulation of his urban ecclesiastical spaces where he links them with eucharistic assemblies gathered around confession of the physically crucified Jesus. Indeed, for Ignatius, union with the bishops, elders, and deacons with the right Christological confession is the place where one finds all the desired goods of civic life. Ritual, following Jonathan Z. Smith, creates place and space.[36] In Ignatius's case, it creates the place of harmonious community and cooperation idealized in political treatment of concord. Ritual must be combined with proper

---

32. *Ignatius of Antioch*, 254–311.

33. For inscriptions and discussion, see Batten, "The Moral World," 142; for monuments, Maier, *Paul*, 170–71.

34. For integration of ethnic groups via associations, see Philip Harland, *Dynamics of Identity in the World of the Early Christians* (London: T&T Clark, 2009), 123–42.

35. Harland, *Associations*, 89–114.

36. Smith, *Place*, 1–23.

leadership, so that the church can only be where the bishop, the presbyters, and deacons are. Ignatius regularly links the bishop's presence in union with the presbyters and/or deacons with a metaphysical sacred space associated with God, Jesus, and sometimes the apostles joined together in harmony (*Eph.* 4.1–2; *Magn.* 2.1; 6.1–2; 7.1; 13.2; *Trall.* 2.1–3; 3.1; 12.2; *Phld.* 3.2; *Smyrn.* 8.1–2). It has been argued that this reflects a platonic view of the earthly ecclesial order reflecting a heavenly one.[37] Considered from a social-geographical perspective of Thirdspace, however, the use of such correspondences has the effect of creating an imaginary utopian space out of the unlikely place of house or tenement social geography. Further, this becomes a form of subversive space in as much as Ignatius regularly returns the correspondence of earthly church and heavenly hierarchy back to the physical death of Jesus (*Phld.* 4.1; *Smyrn.* 7.1; see *Eph.* 5.2). The place where ritual is centred in the confession of the physical crucifixion, suffering, and death of Jesus becomes for Ignatius the space of realizing political ideals of civic harmony and concord. Ignatius reinforces this conception by linking his own death with that of Jesus and his own suffering as a means for promoting concord amongst the Asia Minor churches (*Eph.* 3.2; 11.2; *Magn.* 1.2; *Trall.* 12.2; *Smyrn.* 12.2) and ultimately for restoring peace in the church in Antioch (*Eph.* 1.2; *Rom.* 9.1; *Phld.* 10.1–2; *Smyrn.* 9.1–3). Thus crucifixion, imprisonment, and martyrdom are the places where concord is realized. This represents a dramatic reappropriation of civic ideas and the reconfiguration of an urban imagination with its most cherished ideas and goals.

Territoriality and Imagination

"He who is within the sanctuary is pure; but he who is without the sanctuary is not pure: that is to say whoever does anything apart from the bishop and the presbytery and the deacons is not pure in his conscience" (*Trall.* 7.2). Ignatius draws sharp distinctions between the harmonious life within the space of the church and the discordant life outside it. Whereas all the social goods of harmony, peace, and divine blessing belong to the inside world of the churches joined with leaders in right confession, outside is a mythic space of disorder. In his letter to the Ephesians, for example, Ignatius populates this space with "ravening dogs" (7.1), "the powers of Satan" (13.1), war (13.2), carnality and infidelity (8.2), the devil's plant (10.3), corrupters of families (16.2), and the Prince of this

---

37. Henry Chadwick, "The Silence of Bishops in Ignatius," *HTR* 43 (1950): 169–72.

world (19.1). Robert Sack develops the term "territoriality" to describe
the creation and delimitation of social space and practice. "Territoriality
for humans is a powerful geographic strategy to control people and things
by controlling area."[38] As "a primary geographical expression of social
power" it marks off spaces, time, and practices as a means of organizing
social life. Sack focuses his study of territorialism on the shifting conceptions of society, time, and space in history as a means of comparison,
contrast, and analysis. He describes in passing the letters of Ignatius as
evidence of the creation of ecclesial territory through association with
bishops, elders, and deacons.[39] This is only half of the story, however. For
in Ignatius's letters, legitimating space by associating it with civic virtue
and rendering space illegitimate by associating it with vice represents
a use of territorial imagination as a means of competition. Thirdspace
imagination territorializes gathering places; what Ignatius deems true
confession and false belief creates space by gathering around itself legitimate and illegitimate meetings, and by associating each with civic virtue
conducive to harmonious social life and the vices that undermine urban
ideals. Ignatius creates competing places outside of place and populates
them with differing actors who conform and fail to conform to well-
rehearsed social goods. This represents a creative appropriation of both
rhetorical commonplace and civic norms: the church rather than the city
is the place where civic ideals are most fully realized.

   Like the Corinthian correspondence, Ignatius overwrites the urban
spaces of household assemblies with civic language and metaphor.
Traditional networks of patronage that inscribe social spaces are redrawn
and reimagined in his letters to realize and promote communal goals, and
to rule out behaviors that undermine intended outcomes. Whereas with
Paul, however, where we encounter a destabilization of the social imagination by linking the harmonious functioning body of believers with the
honoring of the weakest members, Ignatius tends toward more traditional
formulations. In the uncontested Pauline corpus Thirdspace represents
the insertion of ecclesiological imagination in a larger civic imaginary
but with the result that the latter is revised. With Ignatius, since the main
preoccupation is polemical, the civic imaginary constitutes the church
along much more predictable lines. Still, however, since it is the future
martyr who writes his letters while passing through Asia Minor, and since
ecclesiology is linked both to Ignatius's fate and Jesus' physical suffering,
the civic notions Ignatius appropriates as means of persuasion represent
also heterotopia.

   38. Sack, *Territoriality*, 5.
   39. Ibid., 103.

Civics by Other Means

In the letters of Paul and Ignatius social geography and its conceptualization via civic language result in Thirdspaces that are linked but have
different functions. Both use political language and metaphor to place
before their audiences' eyes pictures of ideally functioning community.
Both uniquely link civic ideals with the death of Jesus to form a unique
religious imagination and communal self-understanding. Both overwrite
urban social geography, with its networks of patronage, its practices of
hospitality, and practices of civic life with a new configuration of urban
relations centred in unique confession and ritual. In both instances the
remembered death of Jesus puts place into being and places people in
new sets of relations, modes of self-fashioning, and ways of practicing
community. If we can relate these spaces to households, or tabernae, or
even association spaces, physical settings form the stage for idiosyncratic
practices of civic life. High-minded ideals that usually describe the urban
conduct and aspirations of elite culture find a new place in the much more
humble settings of non-elite city dwellers. Paradoxically both, uninten-
tionally, encourage integration into an overarching civic identity even as
they urge a break with imperial religious realities.

For Paul in the uncontested corpus, Jesus' death for others and God's
exaltation of him in resurrection marks out a pattern for community
practice. Paul represents God's universal achievement through the Christ
event with a universal grammar of imperial and civic politics. The
churches are *ekklesiai*, "civic assemblies," Paul's message is a "gospel,"
Paul is an ambassador; he is even a captive in Christ's triumphal
procession. Paul uses civic and imperial language to flesh out his gospel
and its universal reach. The churches he founds are but the beginning of a
process that is underway, the first blush of a spring whose life enjoyed in
the assemblies is but a promise of the deeper green to come. How Christ
assemblies practice their life together, use their urban networks to express
their religious commitments, reconfigure hierarchies, are telling of the
future that is now. There is a boundless openness about the undisputed
Paul's posture to the future. Paul's religious genius lies in his capacity to
reconfigure the urban elements around him to express this openness. The
church as Thirdspace is a civic assembly whose citizenship is in heaven
and whose earthly practices make present a new politics that is about to
sweep the world.

Ignatius too invites listeners into Thirdspace configuration of civic
politics and social geography. As Allen Brent, following the lead of
William Schoedel, has shown, much of Ignatius's sacrificial language has
direct connection with the imperial cult; the one "chained to ten leopards"

on his way to martyrdom is in a religious procession and deploys the language of civic sacrifice and the imperial cult to celebrate his journey to make of his own life an offering.[40] On this account, Ignatius's ideals of the civic harmonious community, regulated by its gate-keeping bishops, finds a means toward peace, harmony, and urban identity through the victim of imperial violence rather than the celebration of imperial rule as represented in the imperial cult that was flourishing in Asia Minor during the reigns of Trajan and Hadrian. Properly regulated liturgical spaces united by correct confession become for Ignatius a rightly operating citizenship by other means. This has the paradoxical result, again, of creating a space that is outside all space. It is the representation of a material world of urban living that at the same time calls into question the traditional basis of the Empire and becomes the avenue of its renewal.

For Ignatius, Christianity is marked by greatness when it is hated by the world (*Rom.* 3.1). Whereas for Paul there is an openness to the future that the Christ-confessing assemblies embody, for Ignatius, the church centres around a confession whose limits are guaranteed by rightly believing leaders who regulate gatherings. In this aspect, Ignatius's letters are closest to the Pastoral Epistles where Paul's faith in Christ has become a confession of belief handed down by delegates to rightly appointed presbyters/bishops (1 Tim 1:18–19; 2 Tim 3:14–15; see also 1 Tim 3:16; 6:2–5; Titus 2:1; 3:1–8). Here civic imagination is not in the service of creating a space outside of space for a yet to be seen future, but serves the urban world in which it inserts itself and expresses itself with proper Christological confession. Inside the sanctuary is purity; outside is impurity; inside is concord and outside is social strife and division. Ignatius's Thirdspace social imagination has a Pauline imprint, but under the pressure to assert institutional control and regulation of Christological confession it no longer imagines the church as a sign of things to come but as a place for securing right belief, proper control of social networks, and access to ecclesial space. As place outside of place it is a shadow polis. Unlike Paul's suffering for the gospel which points away from the church to what God is doing with creation, Ignatius's suffering, notwithstanding its obviously personal salvific impulse, is in the service of the church, for the sake of unity with the bishop and his co-leaders.

40. Allen Brent, *The Imperial Cult and the Development of Church Order: Concepts and Images of Authority in Paganism and Early Christianity before the Age of Cyprian* (Leiden: Brill, 1999), 229–30; Schoedel, *Ignatius of Antioch*, Hermeneia (Minneapolis: Fortress, 1985), 11–12, 213.

Chapter 10

NEITHER "PURE EVANGELIC MANNA" NOR "TAINTED SCRAPS": REFLECTIONS ON THE STUDY OF PSEUDO-IGNATIUS*

L. Stephanie Cobb

Introduction

Ignatius of Antioch, that second-century staunch defender of proto-orthodoxy, zealous supporter of the monarchial episcopacy, and possible masochistic martyr (who confesses "I love to suffer"[1]), wrote twelve letters as he traveled from Syria to Rome to face death: nine to churches – *Ephesians, Magnesians, Trallians, Romans, Philadelphians, Smyrnaeans, Tarsians, Philippians, Antiochians* – and three to individuals – *Polycarp, Mary of Cassobola, Hero*. Or, at least, such was the thought for the better part of 1200 years. Indeed, these twelve letters, plus a letter from Mary of Cassobola to Ignatius, circulated as the Ignatian epistolary corpus from the late fourth century until 1644.[2]

---

* The quoted phrases in the title of this study are John Milton's. See J. B. Lightfoot, *The Apostolic Fathers: Clement, Ignatius, and Polycarp* (Peabody, MA: Hendrickson, 1989), 2.1:242.

1. Ign. *Trall.* 4.1: ἀγαπῶ μὲν γὰρ τὸ παθεῖν. All translations are the author's unless otherwise noted.

2. Another three letters – one to the apostle John, one to Jesus' mother Mary, and a reply from Mary to Ignatius – were added to the collection sometime during the medieval period. See J. B. Lightfoot, *Apostolic Fathers* (London: Macmillan, 1889), 2.1:235; Bart D. Ehrman, *Forgery and Counterforgery: The Use of Literary Deceit in Early Christian Polemics* (New York: Oxford University Press, 2013), 460.

James Ussher's investigations of the Ignatian corpus are worth
recounting, both as testimony to the results of historical inquiry and as
background for understanding – and reclaiming – the study of Pseudo-
Ignatius. Thus, I begin with Ussher's story, before inquiring into ways
that scholarly emphasis on historical authenticity has led us to devalue
important literary evidence for Christianity in Antioch, literature that
sheds light not merely on the Arian controversy but also on the complicated use of apostolic authority to undermine the claims of a massive
social/sexual movement: asceticism. In what follows, I will argue that
Pseudo-Ignatius should reenter the canon of late antiquity – not merely as
a foil for Ignatius but, rather, as an author in his own right whose literary
output is both sizable and important. Specifically, I am interested in the
ways in which Pseudo-Ignatius remembers (or reconstructs) the apostle
Paul as a proponent of marriage, a particular reconstruction of history
that serves him well in countering arguments for a rigorous asceticism in
fourth-century Antioch.[3]

In Search of Ignatius

From perhaps as early as the fifth century to the middle of the seventeenth
century, the Ignatian corpus circulated primarily as the thirteen letters
listed above.[4] Medieval references to Ignatius's writings are almost all to
the "Long Recension," that is, the thirteen-letter corpus.[5] But our earliest
references to Ignatius's writings – Eusebius (*Hist. eccl.* 3.36), Jerome (*Vir.
ill.* 16), and Theodoret (*Dial. immutab.* 1.4.33a) – demonstrate knowledge
of only seven letters. The make-up of the collection, therefore, was open

---

3. On ascetic impulses in early Syrian Christianity, see Susan Ashbrook Harvey,
Asceticism and Society in Crisis: John of Ephesus and the Lives of the Eastern Saints,
The Transformation of the Classical Heritage (Berkeley: University of California
Press, 1990), 4–21.

4. This is not to say that the thirteen-letter corpus went unquestioned. As Helmut
Köester notes, the authenticity of the collection was disputed even in the Renaissance
period (*Introduction to the New Testament* [Berlin: de Gruyter, 2000], 58).

5. Scholars typically date Ignatius's undisputed letters to the early second century,
sometime during the reign of Trajan, ca. 98–117 CE. See William R. Schoedel,
Ignatius of Antioch: A Commentary on the Letters of Ignatius of Antioch, Herme-
neia (Philadelphia: Fortress, 1985), 5 n. 30. The additional letters that comprise the
Long Recension are typically dated to the fourth century. See discussion in C. P. H.
Bammel, "Ignatian Problems," *JTS* 33 (1982): 62–63; Elizabeth A. Clark, *Founding
the Fathers: Early Church History and Protestant Professors in Nineteenth-Century
America* (Philadelphia: University of Pennsylvania Press, 2011), 63.

to debate since the manuscript tradition included more epistles than are mentioned by the early church fathers.

Disputes regarding the authenticity of the Ignatian corpus became heated at various times of ecclesiastical crisis. During the Reformation, for instance, Catholic scholars defended the authenticity of the letters while Protestants rejected varying aspects of them.[6] Calvin, uniquely, rejected all of the letters: "Nothing can be more nauseating than the absurdities which have been published under the name of Ignatius" (*Institutes* 1.13.29).[7] Utilizing Ignatius to bolster a particular position during a time of ecclesiastical strife was not unique to the period of the Reformation.

Between 1639 and 1641, a number of tracts were published concerning apostolic teachings on the episcopacy, based in part on the letters of Ignatius. John Milton, participating in these debates, complained about scholars – including Ussher – who appealed to Ignatius in arguments for the episcopacy "when they cannot know what is authentic of him." We should not, Milton argued, season the "pure evangelic manna" of the authentic letters with "tainted scraps and fragments from an unknown table."[8] Unfortunately for and unbeknownst to Milton, Ussher had already found the manuscript evidence he needed to separate the genuine Ignatian epistles from the spurious letters and interpolations.

At least as early as 1631, Ussher noted that quotations of Ignatius in the English writers Robert of Lincoln (ca. 1250), John Tyssington (ca. 1381), and William Wodeford (ca. 1396) differed from the known Ignatian corpus but agreed with Patristic quotations. He rightly surmised that there might be manuscripts in English libraries that would solve the vexing problem of authenticity: Ussher found two Latin manuscripts containing only the seven letters known to Eusebius, and these in shorter form than what had been previously accepted as authentic. With the publication of Ussher's uninterpolated seven-letter collection in 1644, genuine Ignatius

---

6. See Arthur Middleton, *Fathers and Anglicans: The Limits of Orthodoxy* (Hertfordshire: Gracewing, 2001), 230; Henry Scott Holland, *The Apostolic Fathers* (London: SPCK, 1897), 129. The German theologian Abraham Scultetus, furthermore, argued that the letters were Ignatius's but contained interpolations. See the discussion in Irena Backus, *Historical Method and Confessional Identity in the Era of the Reformation (1378–1615)*, Studies in Medieval and Reformation Thought (Leiden: Brill, 2003); J. B. Lightfoot, *Apostolic Fathers* (London: Macmillan, 1889), 2.1:238–42.

7. John Calvin, *Institutes of the Christian Religion* (trans. Henry Beveridge; Edinburgh: Edinburgh Printing, 1845), 1:186.

8. Lightfoot, *Apostolic Fathers*, 2.1:242.

had been resurrected, in spirit if not *ipsissima verba*: Ussher found Latin but not Greek manuscripts.[9]

The Greek epistles, however, were soon discovered in Florence and published by Isaac Voss in 1646. Voss's edition included only six of the now-accepted seven letters; it did not contain the *Epistle to the Romans*. Finally though, in 1689, all seven of Ignatius's Greek letters were published together – *Romans* having been discovered in *Parisinus Graec. 1451* – by Thierry Ruinart in his *Acta Martyrum Sincera*.[10] Thus the years 1644–1689 mark a watershed moment for the rediscovery, if not the final reestablishment, of the genuine Ignatian corpus, referred to by most scholars now as the "Middle Recension."

One remaining theory deserves mention: in 1845 William Cureton published his findings of two Syriac manuscripts, which contained three Ignatian letters: *Polycarp*, *Ephesians*, and *Romans*. He argued that only these letters were genuine – and in the shorter form found in Syriac. Cureton's collection has become known as the "Short Recension," which is generally understood today to be an epitome of a Syriac translation of the Greek Middle Recension.[11] There have been other challenges to the Middle Recension, but none has attracted a strong following.[12] Indeed, it seems as if the work of Ussher – with help from Zahn and Lightfoot – has convinced most scholars that the Middle Recension is authentic.[13]

---

9. Ussher, following Jerome, maintained that only six letters were, in fact, authentic since he rejected the Epistle to Polycarp, conflating it with the Epistle to the Smyrnaeans.

10. Thierry Ruinart, *Acta primorum martyrum sincera et selecta* (Paris: Muguet, 1689).

11. William Cureton, *The Ancient Syriac Version of Saint Ignatius* (London: Rivington, 1845). See the discussion in C. P. H. Bammel, "Ignatian Problems," *JTS* 33 (1982): 62–63; Clark, *Founding the Fathers*, 415 n. 110 and n. 111; Horton Harris, *Tübingen School* (Oxford: Clarendon, 1975), 215–16.

12. The two most significant arguments against the Middle Recension are typically understood to be: Robert Joly, *Le dossier d'Ignace d'Antioche*, Université libre de Bruxelles, Faculté de Philosophie et Lettres 69 (Brussels: Éditions de l'Université de Bruxelles, 1979); and J. Rius-Camps, *The Four Authentic Letters of Ignatius, the Martyr*, Christianismos 2 (Rome: Pontificium Institutum Orientalium Studiorum, 1979). For a refutation of both, see Schoedel, *Ignatius*, 5–7; Bammel, "Ignatian Problems."

13. Theodor Zahn, *Ignatius von Antiochien* (Gotha: Perthes, 1873); Lightfoot, *Apostolic Fathers*. On the textual witness for the Middle Recension, see Schoedel, *Ignatius*, 3–4.

Recensions of Ignatian Corpus		
Long Recension	**Middle Recension**	**Short Recension**
Ephesians	*Ephesians*	*Ephesians*
Romans	*Romans*	*Romans*
Polycarp	Polycarp	Polycarp
Magnesians	Magnesians	
Philadelphians	Philadelphians	
Smyrnaeans	Smyrnaeans	
Trallians	Trallians	
Hero		
Philippians		
Tarsians		
Antiochians		
Mary		

Consequences of the Quest for Authenticity

The statement with which I ended the previous section – "the Middle Recension is authentic" – raises an important question: authentic to what? Of course, on the one hand, the answer is obvious: these seven letters represent correspondence of the historical Ignatius as he traveled to Rome to face martyrdom.[14] The scholarly debates I have rehearsed above focus on privileging a subapostolic witness in the service of particular ecclesiastical conflicts; they make claims for or against a construction of church polity promoted by an author who subsequently came to be included in the canon of Apostolic Fathers. Determining what Ignatius *really* said has import not only for understanding the growth and structure of the second-century church, but also – as debates in the Reformation and later periods demonstrate – for how the church should subsequently be structured.[15]

14. Although it is important to note that we do not, in fact, have historically verifiable evidence of Ignatius's death. His letter to the *Romans* presupposes his martyrdom in Rome, but the accounts of his death itself are late and legendary.

15. Elizabeth A. Clark has shown that debates over the authenticity of the Ignatian letters were also heated among Reformed Protestant American professors in the nineteenth century, arguing against high church Episcopal and Roman Catholic polity (*Founding Fathers*, 205–37, esp. 223–28). For one example of this strand of argumentation, see Roswell D. Hitchcock, "Origin and Growth of Episcopacy," *The American Presbyterian and Theological Review* 5, no. 17 (1867): 133–59, esp. 137–46.

On the other hand, while the work that has been done to differentiate the second-century collection from later accretions is undeniably important for the historian of early Christianity, one might argue that the accretions are *also* authentic. Pseudonymity aside, the additional letters and interpolations are authentic representations of the concerns of a particular community located in a particular social setting. From this perspective, the categories "authentic" and "inauthentic" are subordinated to inquiry into the historical and social context of the author and his community. Bart Ehrman expresses the distinction this way: "knowing *that* a book is forged is crucial, but only as the beginning, not the end, of the investigation. Other – arguably even more important and interesting – questions involve such matters as the motivations and functions of the forgery."[16] Unfortunately, this aspect of historical inquiry into the Pseudo-Ignatian epistles has not received the attention it deserves.[17]

To date, scholarship has, by-and-large, privileged concerns about author-ship over concerns about social function. When scholars have investigated the social milieu of the Pseudo-Ignatian letters, they have typically focused on their relationship to the Arian controversy. Lightfoot associated the author with the "diluted" Arianism of the *Apostolic Constitutions*. More recently, scholars have gone one step further than Lightfoot by asserting that Pseudo-Ignatius and the author of the *Apostolic Constitutions* were one and the same person.[18] The position of the author vis-à-vis the Arian controversy has been hotly debated, however, including associating him

16. Ehrman, *Forgery*, 4.

17. Indeed, Ehrman rightly notes that "a full critical commentary on the Pseudo-Ignatians (including the interpolations) is a major desideratum in the field" (ibid., 469). To make a comparison to Gospel studies, it is as if scholars had not inves-tigated the social communities that produced the Gospels of Matthew and Luke, simply because they were dependent upon Mark. Just as Mark is considered by many scholars to be a source for Matthew and Luke, so Ignatius is a source for Pseudo-Ig-natius. But also, I argue, just as scholars have examined the ways in which Mark is changed to meet later Christian needs within specific communities, so Pseudo-Igna-tius should be given more scholarly attention for its witness to the way Ignatius was changed to meet specific needs for its particular community.

18. C. E. Hammond, *Liturgies Eastern and Western: Being the Texts Original or Translated of the Principal Liturgies of the Church* (Oxford: Clarendon, 1965), xxvii, xxix; Adolf von Harnack, *Die Lehre der zwölf Apostel nebst Untersuchungen zur Geschichte der Kirchenverfassung und des Kirchenrechts* (Leipzig: J. C. Hinrichs, 1844), 244–65. The same author also wrote the *Commentary on Job*. See Ehrman, *Forgery*, 394; Dieter Hagedorn, *Der Hiobkommentar des Arianers Julian* (Berlin: de Gruyter, 1973), esp. liii. Ehrman argues that the *Commentary on Job* may be more

with strong Arianism,[19] Apollinarianism,[20] and with a neo-Arian position.[21] Ehrman is surely correct in his explanation of this scholarly disagreement: it has proven difficult to associate the text with a specific position because "the author – probably Julian – did not have a distinctively theological agenda to promote in this particular writing."[22] Thus, studies of the Trinitarian leanings of this author may not have a significant payoff. We might do better to recall that the Arian controversy was not the only crisis in town, and it very well may not have been the conflict that was of most importance – or at least not the only one of importance – to our author. I suggest, then, that our understanding of the situation that motivated the creation of new Ignatian letters will deepen if we approach the texts with a different set of questions, ones that concern lived Christian social ethics more than intellectual Christian theology.

Socio-Political Setting Reflected in Pseudo-Ignatius

Setting Pseudo-Ignatius in late fourth-century Antioch places our author not only in the midst of raging Trinitarian arguments but also in the midst of a social and ethical crisis. Indeed, it is precisely in this period that we see the rise of an extreme form of asceticism developing in Syria. Peter Brown's justly famous essay "The Rise and Function of the Holy Man" outlines the development of a distinctive form of asceticism in Syria and the ways it impinged on society – in contrast to the monasticism that developed in Egypt.[23] A detailed history of Syrian asceticism is beyond the scope of my argument here, but it is relevant to note that it was not happily embraced by all. Indeed, as Robert Wilken observes, "to grow up

helpful than *Apostolic Constitutions* for the Pseudo-Ignatian corpus in ascertaining the theological position of the author because in the commentary he is not restricted by concerns about verisimilitude. See Ehrman, *Forgery*, 394, 464.

19. See, for instance, Hagedorn, *Der Hiobkommentar*. For a discussion of the debates regarding the Trinitarian tendencies of Pseudo-Ignatius, see ibid., 393–94.

20. For example, Franz X. Funk, *Die apostolischen Konstitutionen: eine litterar-historische Untersuchung* (Rottenburg: W. Bader, 1891), 105–7, 367.

21. For example, Georg Wagner, "Zur Herkunft der Apostolischen Konstitu-tionen," in *Mélanges liturgiques offerts au R. P. dom Bernard Botte à l'occasion du cinquantième anniversaire de son ordination sacerdotale (4 juin 1472)* (Louvain: Abbaye du Mont César, 1972).

22. Ehrman, *Forgery*, 394. Here Ehrman discusses *Apostolic Constitutions*, but the point is equally applicable to the Long Recension.

23. Peter Brown, "The Rise and Function of the Holy Man in Late Antiquity," *JRS* 61 (1971): 80–101.

in the Christian Church in Antioch during the late fourth century was to know a divided community."[24] We know that there was resistance to the movement within the aristocratic ranks of Syria, and the resistance was strong enough to prompt John Chrysostom to pen a treatise in defense of asceticism, *Against the Detractors of the Monastic Life*.[25]

Literature from proponents of asceticism has been, perhaps, best preserved, but the voices of the other side of this social and ecclesiastical issue were not wholly silenced. The *Apostolic Constitutions* – also written by the author of the pseudepigraphic Ignatian letters – displays a concern to temper a rigorous ascetic impulse.[26] A similar interest is found as well in the Long Recension. Indeed, over half a century ago, K.J. Woollcombe observed, "Two topics to which the forger gives unusual prominence are marriage and asceticism."[27] Given the time and place of forgery, the author's interest in these topics is hardly surprising. It is to an examination of aspects of the Long Recension reflecting this concern that I now turn.

Moderating Asceticism in Pseudo-Ignatius

One way our author counters a strenuous ascetic agenda is by limiting – though not condemning – rigorous devotional acts. In the *Letter to Hero*, for instance, Pseudo-Ignatius argues for moderation as a religious rule. He writes,

> Devote yourself to fasting and prayer, but not beyond measure (ἀλλὰ μὴ ἀμέτρως), lest you strike yourself down. Do not altogether abstain from wine and flesh, for these things are not abominable (βδελυκτά), since [the Scripture] says, "You shall eat the good things of the earth.' And again,

24. Robert Wilken, *John Chrysostom and the Jews: Rhetoric and Reality in the Late 4th Century* (Berkeley: University of California Press, 1983), 13.

25. See the discussion in S. P. Brock, "Early Syrian Asceticism," *Numen* 20 (1973): 1–19; and Elizabeth A. Clark, "Antifamilial Tendencies in Ancient Christianity," *Journal of the History of Sexuality* 5, no. 3 (1995): 356–80.

26. See, for instance, the concerns with rejection of marriage in *Const. ap.* 4.2.14. See also the discussion below.

27. K. J. Woollcombe, "The Doctrinal Connexions of the Pseudo-Ignatian Letters," *StPatr* 6 (1962): 272. Woollcombe goes on to state that the author shows no indication of knowing about the rise of monasticism, but he dates Pseudo-Ignatius several decades earlier (ca. 365 CE) than most scholars do now: it is more common to date Pseudo-Ignatius, with Lightfoot, in the latter part of the fourth century (Lightfoot, *Apostolic Fathers*, 2.1:273). The concern for asceticism in the passages Woollcombe cites above must be related to the social situation of the author in the latter part of the fourth century.

'You shall eat flesh even as herbs." And again, "Wine maketh glad the heart of man, and oil exhilarates, and bread strengthens him." But be measured and orderly, as supplied by God (ἀλλὰ μεμετρημένως καὶ εὐτάκτως, ὡς Θεοῦ χορηγοῦντος). (*Hero* 1)

Pseudo-Ignatius does not altogether dismiss religious disciplinary practices such as fasting and prayer. He does not argue, in other words, that one should *never* fast or that one should *never* abstain from wine and meat. Rather, he argues that acts of piety are good, but they must be measured (μετρέω); they must, it seems, end.[28] His argument is one of moderation on both sides: the repetition of μετρέω guards against both rigorous abstinence and undisciplined eating and drinking. The emphasis on moderation suggests that the author may be mediating a polarized discourse within his community. It is impossible to know with certainty whether the two positions were held by different factions or whether the ascetic party constructed a licentious foil, an association with which Pseudo-Ignatius is careful to avoid. But notably, the danger described in *Hero* 1 is with excessive *askesis* not with gluttony, implying that the primary aim of Pseudo-Ignatius's warning is at strict asceticism.[29] It is possible that the ascetic party argued that the community was in danger of destruction if it did not follow rigorous acts of piety. In such a case, our author may be using the term καταβάλλω in conscious rejection of these opposing teachings. There would be no occasion to suggest that one might destroy oneself (καταβάλης) by excessive acts of piety if the community had not been confronted with the teachings of an ascetic agenda. In *Hero* 1, therefore, the author not only urges a restrained and carefully measured approach to the discipline of fasting, but he also rejects the notion that wine and meat are "abominable" (βδελυκτός). This, as we shall see, is a key term in Pseudo-Ignatius's writings on asceticism.

28. Lightfoot notes that *Const. ap.* 1.9 also employs the sequence μεμετρημένως καὶ εὐτάκτως. In that instance, the author uses the phrase in relation to women's bathing. There, too, the author insists that abstinence and over-indulgence are equally inappropriate. The phrase, in other words, appears to be used by this author to articulate activities that are inherently neither good nor bad but which must be pursued thoughtfully, with the understanding of appropriate time, place, and frequency.

29. The author characteristically, but notably different from his exemplar, Ignatius, strings together scriptural quotations – from Genesis, Isaiah, and Psalms – to underscore his position. Our author, therefore, is clearly adept at bringing together various strains of biblical tradition to apply to the problem at hand. Milton Brown writes, "It is safe to estimate that about one-half of the interpolated matter in the seven letters consists of scriptural quotation alone." Milton P. Brown, Jr., "Notes on the Language and Style of Pseudo-Ignatius," *JBL* 83 (1964): 147.

Aspects of Pseudo-Ignatius's argument on moderation are reminiscent of passages in the Pauline epistles.[30] First, the specific interest in arguing against avoidance of wine recalls the pastor's advice in 1 Tim 5:23, "No longer drink only water, but take a little wine for the sake of your stomach and your frequent ailments." 1 Timothy, like *Hero*, is concerned with a variety of behaviors that are, in the opinion of their authors, extreme; in both cases, the authors argue for moderating ethical positions. A second way in which *Hero* is reminiscent of Pauline epistles is in the structure of the argument. In this case, we note particular similarities with Paul's discussion of sex in 1 Cor 7, in which Paul addresses his church's concern about sexual continence. His answer is more complex than it would seem according to some later interpreters (e.g., *Acts of Paul and Thecla* and 1 Timothy). Although chastity is an ideal for Paul (1 Cor 7:7), he teaches that "it is better to marry than to burn" (1 Cor 7:9), and he demands moderation between sex and continence within marriage: spouses may agree to devote themselves to prayer "for a set time" but then they must "come together again, so that Satan may not tempt" them (1 Cor 7:5). There is ample evidence that Pseudo-Ignatius utilized 1 Corinthians, so it is not beyond the realm of possibility that Pseudo-Ignatius has 1 Corinthians in mind as he writes on moderation.

Seeing *Hero* 1 as reflecting the structure of argument in 1 Corinthians may be more persuasive when we consider another portion of this Pseudo-Ignatian letter, one which takes up similar content interests as 1 Cor 7. This passage introduces a second manner by which Pseudo-Ignatius combats a rigorous ascetic agenda: by countering arguments that degrade sex and family. In *Hero* 4, Pseudo-Ignatius describes Jesus' birth. The author concedes the virginal conception, but he offers a carefully constructed argument for why God chose this manner of generation:

---

30. Although I agree with scholars who differentiate between genuine and pseudepigraphic Pauline epistles in the New Testament, since the author of Pseudo-Ignatius would have accepted the Pastoral and Deutero-Pauline Epistles as genuine Pauline epistles, I will not make a distinction here. For my present purposes, all of the canonical attributions will be treated as Pauline. For discussions of which New Testament books Pseudo-Ignatius was clearly aware of, see James W. Aageson, *Paul, the Pastoral Epistles, and the Early Church* (Peabody, MA: Hendrickson, 2008), 126; Andreas Lindemann, "Paul in the Writings of the Apostolic Fathers," in *Paul and the Legacies of Paul*, ed. William S. Babcock (Dallas: Southern Methodist University Press, 1990), 32; and Paul Foster, "The Epistles of Ignatius of Antioch and the Writings That Later Formed the New Testament," in *The New Testament and the Apostolic Fathers*. Vol. 1, *The Reception of the New Testament in the Apostolic Fathers*, ed. Andrew F. Gregory and Christopher M. Tuckett (Oxford: Oxford University Press, 2005), 159–86.

And, indeed, the incredible birth of the Lord from a virgin alone was not because lawful intercourse (νομίμου μίξεως) is abominable (βδελυκτῆς), but because this birth was fitting for a god. For it was seemly for the Creator not to make use of the customary method of generation, but of one that was incredible and foreign, as the Creator.

It seems likely that behind his argument lies a concern with asceticism: he strenuously rejects the notion that God chose this manner of conception because marital intercourse is "abominable." As with the concern about fasting in *Hero* 1, this is a case that only needs to be made when an opponent has argued precisely that point.[31]

Pseudo-Ignatius introduces this christological explanation with a broader warning to his male listeners: "Do not hold women in abomination [βδελύττου], for they have given you birth and brought you up. It is fitting, therefore, to love those who were the authors of our birth (but only in the Lord), inasmuch as a man can produce no children without women. It is right, therefore, that we should honor those who have had a part in giving us birth" (*Hero* 4). In making this argument about honoring women as mothers, Pseudo-Ignatius draws directly on Paul's argument in 1 Cor 11:11 that "neither is the man without the woman nor the woman without the man." Procreation, the author argues, is not an abomination. Jesus, like Adam and Eve, represents not a prototype of ideal behavior, but, rather, an exception.[32] These two passages – about Mary in particular and women in general – work together to form a forceful argument against continence as the only acceptable choice for Christians. Whereas μετρέω was a key term in *Hero* 1, we note here the repetition of forms of βδελύσσομαι: Pseudo-Ignatius wishes to dismantle arguments that equate marital intercourse with abomination. From the movement of his argument in *Hero* 4, we can surmise that his opponents claimed that Mary's virginity provided a model for Christian life: as she was (and remained[33]) a virgin, so also

31. Such an argument places Pseudo-Ignatius's opponents far beyond the ascetic interests of writers such as Chrysostom, Clement of Alexandria, and Augustine. On the sanctity of marriage in ascetic authors – albeit a sanctity inferior to virginity – see the discussion in Clark, "Antifamilial Tendencies," 375–76. Jerome's *Against Jovinian* was perceived by his peers as an attack on marriage. David Hunter sets Jerome's comments in the context of fourth-century discourses of asceticism. Hunter, *Augustine: Marriage and Virginity*, WSA I/9 (Hyde Park, NY: New City, 1999), 29–32.

32. Indeed, the author's emphasis on the fittingness and incredibleness of Jesus' conception may suggest that imitating it is impious: to imitate Mary's virginity compromises the singularity of God's act.

33. I assume the author holds to a doctrine of perpetual virginity since he – in the voice of Mary of Cassobola – refers to Mary as "the Virgin Mary" (*Mary* 1).

Christians should choose a life of continence. Here, as elsewhere, the author offers a counter argument that posits the – well-ordered – family as God-ordained, and he argues forcefully against its rejection.

In the following chapter, Pseudo-Ignatius aims his ire directly at the false teachers who teach "beyond what is commanded." Even though these teachers may "fast," "live in continence," "work miracles," and have the "gift of prophecy," they are, in reality, merely wolves "in sheep's clothing laboring for the destruction of the sheep" (*Hero* 2). It is, notably, these teachers, along with those who hold christological heresies, who are "abominable" (βδελυκτός). Here again, Pseudo-Ignatius employs a key term, "abomination," but now he turns it back on his ascetic opponents. Those who, according to Pseudo-Ignatius, teach beyond what is commanded regarding continence and fasting are akin to those who hold false christologies and it is they, not those who hold to moderate Christian ethics, who are abominations.

That Pseudo-Ignatius affirms a mediating position between polarized stances regarding sex and marriage is also evident in *Philadelphians* 6. In this chapter, Pseudo-Ignatius warns against a variety of heresies, mostly relating to Jewish-Christianity (a theme he adopts from Ignatius's chapter). Embedded in this heresiologically focused chapter are warnings against two extremes: rigorous asceticism and licentiousness. On the one hand, he writes, "If anyone confesses these things, but calls lawful inter-course (τὴν νόμιμον μίξιν) and the procreation of children 'destruction' and 'pollution' (φθορὰν δὲ καὶ μολυσμὸν), or certain foods 'abominable' (βδελυκτὰ), that one has the serpent of apostasy inhabiting him." The concern here is with an extreme form of asceticism that rejects out of hand "lawful intercourse" – whose aim is procreation – and that labels certain foods as abominations. Milton P. Brown observes, "There are hints in both spurious and interpolated letters that a monastic tendency has made itself felt, fostering the idea of celibacy, and perhaps leading some Christians to despise marriage. Such an attitude is probably the background for the context of the word μίξις, used in both places for the marriage relationship, and defended against its detractors."[34] Brown is certainly correct to see a concern for rigorous asceticism, but the author argues equally against licentiousness: "If anyone confesses these things… but declares unlawful intercourse (τὰς παρανόμους μίξεις) to be a good and sets abundant pleasure as the goal (τέλος εὐδαιμονίας ἡδονὴν τίθεται)…that

---

34. Brown, "Language and Style," 151. Brown notes this – though he does not develop the argument – in a discussion of ecclesiastical office in Pseudo-Ignatius, as compared with Ignatius's second-century context.

one is not able to be a lover of God nor a lover of Christ but is a corrupter (φθορεὺς) of his own flesh and because of this is bereft of the Holy Spirit and an enemy of Christ." The repetition of the word μῖξις throughout the passage must reflect the author's interest in defining Christian sexual ethics over against polarized positions, whether historical or discursive.

A third way Pseudo-Ignatius counters rigorous ascetic interests is by the proliferation of *Haustafeln*.[35] Ignatius's *Letter to Polycarp* 5 may have given Pseudo-Ignatius inspiration for including in his letters discussions on household relationships, but he extends his purview significantly by relying on Pauline writings, particularly Ephesians. The importance of these household codes for our author may be measured by the fact that Pseudo-Ignatius includes them in each of his fabricated letters, with the exception of the epistle to *Mary*; he adds the *Haustafel* into Ignatius's letter to the *Philadelphians*; and he retains the pre-existing household code in Ignatius's letter to *Polycarp*.[36] In each case, we see an author who is careful to avoid extremes: he does not disparage those who choose virginity, but he warns against the denigration of marriage and family.

In his letter to *Polycarp*, Ignatius gives the bishop of Smyrna advice concerning a number of issues, including marriage relationships.[37] It is noteworthy that Pseudo-Ignatius follows his exemplar so closely since the other Pseudo-Ignatian letters tend to expand the original text significantly. In the *Haustafel* in ch. 5, both Ignatius and Pseudo-Ignatius call for wives

35. Scholars have disagreed on the origins and purpose of the New Testament *Haustafeln*. That I see the *Haustafeln* of Pseudo-Ignatius as, at least in part, employed against teachings of continence, will be demonstrated below. This attribution does not, of course, rule out other social concerns. Literature on *Haustafeln* is vast; see, for instance, John Fitzgerald, "Haustafeln," *ABD* 3:80–81; J. E. Crouch, *The Origin and Intention of the Colossian Haustafel*, FRLANT 109 (Göttingen: Vandenhoeck & Ruprecht, 1972); John H. Elliott, *A Home for the Homeless: A Social-Scientific Criticism of 1 Peter, Its Situation and Strategy* (Minneapolis: Fortress, 1981); David L. Balch, *Let Wives Be Submissive: The Domestic Code in 1 Peter*, SBLMS 26 (Chico: Scholars Press, 1981).

36. See *Hero* 5; *Philippians* 13; *Tarsians* 9; and *Antiochians* 9; and *Philadelphians* 4 (discussed above). The author also composes *Haustafeln* in the *Const. ap.* 4.2; 7.1.

37. Of note in this letter is the repeated use of athletic imagery: Ignatius imagines Polycarp as "contending" in a wide variety of contests for which he needs endurance. The language of "athlete" and "contest," as Lake notes in his LCL translation, would also resonate with a community in conversation with asceticism, as these terms were adopted by the ascetic movement after the age of persecution had ended (Kirsopp Lake, *Apostolic Fathers*, LCL [Boston: Harvard University Press, 1985], 1:269 n. 1. On this, see also Brock, "Early Syrian Asceticism," 2–3.

to be "content in flesh and spirit" (ἀρκεῖσθαι σαρκὶ καὶ πνεύματι) with their husbands – a far cry from celibacy – but both authors continue with an exhortation to those who are virgins: "If anyone is able to remain in purity to the honor of the flesh of the Lord, let him remain so without boasting. If he boasts, he is destroyed. And if it comes to be known by anyone other than the bishop, he is ruined."[38] Ignatius and Pseudo-Ignatius respect those who remain virgins, but they both issue concerns about the evangelizing of that vocation: one's virginity is a personal – not a public – way of honoring the Lord. Both authors continue with a discussion of marriage, thereby implying the equality of the vocations. "And it is proper for men and women who marry to make the union with the consent of the bishop in order that the marriage be according to the Lord and not according to lust (ἐπιθυμίαν)." Marriage, like virginity, falls under the purview and power of the bishop: in both cases, the bishop's knowledge or consent makes the vocation one that honors the Lord. We see in Ignatius a moderating position that suits Pseudo-Ignatius's needs perfectly: virginity may lead to piety, but it is not the only way of honoring the Lord. Marriage, equally, can be a Christian calling.

Of particular interest to our understanding of the author's articulation of a moderating Christian sexual ethic is the household code in *Philadelphians* 4. In Ignatius's letter, this very brief chapter – consisting of only one (very complex) Greek sentence – is concerned with unity in regards to the Eucharist. In Pseudo-Ignatius's much-expanded chapter – consisting of fourteen (equally complex) sentences[39] – unity of the Eucharist is not the main point. Rather, it is merely an illustration of a larger claim for unity in the divine plan. The author expounds the oneness of the elements of faith to make a point about harmony: "it is necessary for you, as a special people and a holy nation, to accomplish all things with harmony in Christ." This teaching on harmony leads into a *Haustafel*, inspired by a wide variety of scriptural texts, prominent among them the Pauline epistles.[40] In the section pertaining to husbands, wives, and children, Pseudo-Ignatius writes:

38. See also Pseudo-Ignatius, *Philippians* 13. In *Const. ap.* 8.5.47.51, the apostles state that any clergy who "abstains from marriage, flesh, and wine, not for his own exercise but because he abominates these things" should be cast out from the church. The same punishment is set for laity.

39. I recognize the difficulty in comparing ancient texts based on number of sentences, but for my very simple present purposes – i.e., demonstrating the extraordinary amount of interpolation into the chapter – the difficulties do not pose a problem.

40. It seems probable that Pseudo-Ignatius draws inspiration from the following Pauline letters: Ephesians, Titus, 1 Corinthians, Galatians, Colossians, and Philippians.

Wives be subordinate (ὑποποτάγητε) to your husbands in the fear (ἐν φόβῳ) of God; virgins to Christ in incorruption, do not abhor (βδελυσσόμεναι) marriage but aim at what is better (χρείσσονος), not with the goal of slandering unions (συναφείας) but for the sake studying the law. Children, obey your parents, and love them as co-workers with God in your birth... Husbands, love your wives, as fellow-slaves to God, as inhabiting your body, as partners in life and co-workers in childbearing.

The first injunction recalls Paul's teaching in Eph 5:21: "Be subordinate (ὑποτασσόμενοι) to one another in the fear (ἐν φόβῳ) of Christ." Similarly, the opening invocation to husbands recalls Eph 5:25.[41] Pseudo-Ignatius draws on Pauline authority to establish his own *Haustafel*. Rather than simply copying from Ephesians, he focuses on his community's specific concerns, which are not merely household order but, more particularly, the divinely ordained goodness of marriage and family. This is not – as we have already seen in Pseudo-Ignatius – an argument that necessarily negates the blessings of the life of virginity. The author is careful, though, to emphasize the mutuality – between husband and wife as well as between parents and God – that exists in marriage, an emphasis that underscores its importance.

Virgins are exhorted not to abhor – βδελύσσομαι again – unions, and they are not to seek a life of virginity for the purpose of slandering marriage.[42] The author places restrictions around the reasons one might enter into a life of virginity: it is only to pursue the study of the law. Indeed, the emphasis on the negative – οὐ/οὐκ – in the sentence devoted to virginity is notable; it is the only negative command given in this household code. This author defines virginity more in terms of what it is not than in terms of what it is: virginity is not a means of disparaging marriage and procreation. Pseudo-Ignatius's rhetoric again implies the existence of an opponent who has promoted a Christian social ethic focused exclusively on virginity.

In the exhortations to both children and husbands, it is interesting that women's roles as *co*-workers are highlighted: women are depicted here as equal partners in giving birth and in raising children. Women are made partners both with their husbands and, importantly, with God.[43] Marriage as an institution that leads to procreation is characterized by a fundamental

---

41. The exhortation that husbands should love their wives "as their own bodies" is similar, though the language used to express it differs.

42. A similar exhortation is made in *Const. ap.* 4.2.14; 8.3.24.

43. The mutuality is implicit in the terms συνεργοὺς (twice) and ὁμοδούλους.

mutuality between the sexes, and its inherent goodness is manifest in the fact that this short *Haustafel* devotes significantly more time to praising the role of parents than it does the virtue of the virgin.

Why might Pseudo-Ignatius add a long interpolation regarding social relationships to a chapter that originally dealt with the unity of the Eucharist under the bishop? One possibility is that Pseudo-Ignatius sees his community on the brink of division – divided over views of asceticism, over views of the Trinity, over ecclesiastical authority, and perhaps other issues as well – and he finds Ignatius's brief comments on Eucharistic unity a fitting occasion for discussing larger issues of communal harmony. This author repeatedly attempts to bridge polarizing positions relating to Christian ethics. In the case of the *Haustafel* in *Philadelphians*, we see him accepting virginity as a worthy form of Christian piety but this position does not compromise his views of the holiness of marriage and procreation within marriage. This is not an author who appears interested in condemning the ascetic movement altogether, but neither is he willing to accept it on terms that denigrate what he views as an equally valid form of Christian life. His appeal to apostolic authority – notably Pseudo-Pauline epistles – bolsters his case, and it is to an examination of the role of apostolic authority that I now turn.

Apostolic Authority in Pseudo-Ignatius

In his recent monograph on ancient forgery, Ehrman notes that a significant amount of early Christian pseudepigraphical literature may be identified as participating in "internecine disputes" among opposing Christian groups.[44] Authors, he argues, adopted practices that were widely understood to be illegitimate – namely, forgery – in order to claim authority for their positions and, thus, to delegitimize their opponents' positions. Ehrman is careful to acknowledge the fact that authors may have a number of reasons for writing pseudepigraphically – polemics need not be the exclusive motivator – and this is certainly the case for the author of the Pseudo-Ignatian epistles.[45] Regarding Pseudo-Ignatius, in particular, Ehrman observes, "scholars have worked hard to identify the author's

---

44. Ehrman, *Forgery*, 3.

45. Christine Trevett suggests that the Long Recension was created, in part, to answer questions that the Middle Recension did not answer: "The creation of the additional letters in the so-called *Long Recension* and its interpolations were, of course, one response to the unanswered questions, though this was not the only reason for their appearance. In these later, spurious 'Ignatian' letters the bishop *did* write to Antioch (*To the Antiochenes*), as he wrote also to Euodius his predecessor as bishop,

theological alignments without asking why he may have wanted to create the forged materials in the first place."[46] I have argued, in this vein, that our author appears to be engaged in a struggle with rigorous ascetics, and he writes epistles in Ignatius's name in order to bolster his own mediating position. But why write in *Ignatius's* name? If we agree with Ehrman that pseudepigraphy is often motivated by polemics, we still must inquire whether the author's choice of Ignatius as a pen name is significant.

Ehrman suggests that Pseudo-Ignatius bolsters "his own theological position by putting it on the lips of a great proto-orthodox leader of the faith, the famed martyr bishop Ignatius."[47] Surely this is correct, but it does not quite answer my question: Why *Ignatius*? Ignatius was not, after all, a well-established subapostolic authority.[48] Indeed, the first church father to mention Ignatius's writings was Eusebius. The choice of Ignatius, therefore, is not obvious. While we cannot know with certainty what motivated our author to write in the name of Ignatius, it may be that the connection with Antioch was an incentive. James David Smith has argued that Pseudo-Ignatius's community rediscovered Ignatius's remains in the cemetery at Antioch and utilized the serendipitous find to counter their opponents' (i.e., the Meletians') claims to St. Antony and the local holy men Babylus, Aphraates, and Julian.[49] The church in Antioch might

according to some versions. *The Epistle to Hero* took care of the silence of the *Middle Recension* about his successor in the See" (Christine Trevett, *A Study of Ignatius of Antioch in Syria and Asia* [Lewiston: Edwin Mellen, 1992], 2).

46. Ehrman, *Forgery*, 467.

47. Ibid., 468.

48. Smith writes, "In summarizing the literary evidence before Eusebius, one may safely say that, aside from the *Ephesians* 19 passage which became a patristic favorite, the allusions to the Ignatian letters (MR, of course) are often marginal and, except for Origen, no writer between Polycarp and Eusebius gives any biographical note at all. Neither is there any archaeological evidence for a remembered Ignatius from this era." James David Smith, "The Ignatian Long Recension and Christian Communities in Fourth Century Syrian Antioch" (PhD diss., Harvard University, 1986), 15. For a list of references to Ignatius before 400 CE, see Lightfoot, *Apostolic Fathers*, 2.1:135–68.

49. Smith, "Long Recension," 27. Smith writes (13–14), "The Arian party in Antioch located the remains of the venerable martyr-bishop Ignatius in the Christian cemetery ca. A.D. 364–373. As noted, this coincides with the period to which Pseudo-Ignatius is usually ascribed. The 'rediscovery' of the Ignatian relics and the 'redaction' of the Ignatian literary corpus belong together, as products of the same community. This community, in a time of need, sought to appropriate Ignatius as their own saint and advocate. They had the opportunity because of his relative obscurity – his persona was a field not yet cultivated."

be more likely than other churches to remember this martyr-bishop and, thus, claiming his authority could be compelling.

A close analysis of the Long Recension, however, may suggest that Pseudo-Ignatius is staking an equal claim to both Pauline authority and Ignatian authority when he writes in Ignatius's name.[50] Ignatius mentions Paul explicitly only twice in the Middle Recension.[51] Pseudo-Ignatius, notably, adds numerous references to Paul in the letters.[52] This may indicate a concerted effort by Pseudo-Ignatius to recall Pauline teaching and, thereby, to appropriate Pauline authority. Sometimes the references to the apostle introduce quotes from his epistles, while at other times they serve as exhortations to imitation. Of particular importance for us here is a reference that advances the author's moderating position vis-à-vis rigorous asceticism. In *Philadelphians* 4, in connection with the *Haustafel* discussed above, Pseudo-Ignatius comments on Paul's marital status:

> Virgins, have only Christ before your eyes, and his father in your prayers, being instructed by the spirit. May I profit from your holiness, as that of Elijah, or Joshua son of Nun, or Melchizedek, or Elisha, or Jeremiah, or John the Baptist, or the beloved disciple, or Timothy, or Titus, or Euodius, or Clement, all of whom departed from life in chastity (ἀγνείᾳ). I do not find fault with the other blessed ones who had intercourse in marriage (γάμοις προσωμίλησαν), [the type of] which I just mentioned. For I pray, having been found worthy of God, I may be found at their feet in the kingdom, as Abraham and Isaac and Jacob, as Joseph and Isaiah and the rest of the

50. In *Const. ap.*, our author claims that Ignatius was ordained by Paul (7.4.46). Also in *Const. ap.*, "Paul" urges unmarried slaves to "enter into lawful marriage" (8.4.32).

51. In *Eph.* 12.2, Ignatius refers to the Ephesians as "fellow-initiates in the mysteries" (συμμύσται) with Paul; and in *Rom.* 4.3, Ignatius subordinates himself to the pillars of the Roman church, Peter and Paul: "I do not order you as did Peter and Paul; they were apostles, I am condemned; they were free, I am even now a slave." Ignatius's appropriation of Pauline authority – and the ways in which his letters extend beyond Pauline thought – has been studied. See, for instance Andreas Lindemann, "Paul's Influence on 'Clement' and Ignatius," in *The New Testament and the Apostolic Fathers*. Vol. 2, *Trajectories Through the New Testament and the Apostolic Fathers*, ed. Andrew F. Gregory and Christopher M. Tuckett (Oxford: Oxford University Press, 2005), 9–24, and, in the same volume, David M. Reis, "Following in Paul's Footsteps: *Mimesis* and Power in Ignatius of Antioch," 287–306; Harry O. Maier, "The Politics and Rhetoric of Discord and Concord in Paul and Ignatius," 307–324.

52. Pseudo-Ignatius includes explicit reference to Paul in *Philadelphians* 4, 7; *Ephesians* 3, 6, 10, 11, 12, 14, 15; *Trallians* 5, 7; *Tarsians* 2, 3; *Antiochians* 7; *Philippians* 1; *Mary* 4; *Magnesians* 10.

prophets, as Peter and Paul and the rest of the apostles who had intercourse in marriage (τῶν γάμοις προσομιλησάντων). For their acts were not out of desire (προθυμίας) but with the thought of bearing offspring.

As we should expect given Pseudo-Ignatius's repeated emphasis on moderation, the biblical world he sketches includes blessed men on both sides of the celibacy divide: many chose to live in chastity but many others – including, according to Pseudo-Ignatius, Paul – are representatives of the choice of marriage for the sake of procreation. Lightfoot notes that this characterization of Paul is founded on "misinterpretations" of 1 Cor 9:5 – in which Paul asks if he and those with him "have the right to be accompanied by a believing wife" (ἀδελφὴν γυναῖκα) – and Phil 4:3 – in which Paul asks his "loyal companion" (γνήσιε σύζυγε) to help Euodia and Syntyche.[53] If Pseudo-Ignatius has inherited this view of Paul – as opposed to having simply invented it for the sake of his argument – he is not the only Christian to have "misunderstood" Paul's letters in this way.[54] Clement of Alexandria testifies to understanding 1 Cor 9 as a literal question rather than merely a rhetorical one. In a section of *Stromateis*, Clement uses Paul as an example of the married life: "Even Paul did not hesitate in one letter to address his consort... Accordingly he says in a letter: 'Have we not a right to take about with us a wife that is a sister like the other apostles?'" (3.6.53).[55] Clement's means of refuting his stridently ascetic opponent is similar to Pseudo-Ignatius's: not all sexual relationships are impure, Clement argues, "for I hold that even the seed of the sanctified is holy" (3.6.46). Origen also demonstrates knowledge of traditions that Paul was married, this time based on the Philippians passage cited above. In his *Commentary on the Epistle to the Romans*, Origen writes, "Paul, then, if certain traditions are true, was called while in possession of a wife, concerning whom he speaks

53. Lightfoot, *Apostolic Fathers*, 2.1:209. The translation of 1 Corinthians follows NRSV.

54. It is possible that Pseudo-Ignatius purposefully includes Paul in a group of married men, as opposed to having received this belief. Lightfoot suggests that the "virginity of Euodius appears not to be noticed elsewhere, and was probably a venture of our Ignatian writer" (Lightfoot, *Apostolic Fathers*, 2.1:209). If Pseudo-Ignatius can freely invent the virginity of one person in his letter, surely he could freely invent the marriage of another.

55. The translation of *Stromateis* is from Henry Chadwick, ed., *The Library of Christian Classics*. Vol. 2, *Alexandrian Christianity* (Philadelphia: Westminster, 1954).

when writing to the Philippians, 'I ask you also, my loyal mate, help these women'" (1.1).[56] But Origen also betrays knowledge of competing traditions about Paul's marital status when he immediately writes, "But if, as others think, he had no wife, nonetheless he who was free when he was called is yet a slave of Christ" (1.1).[57] Lightfoot also notes that some Latin copies of the Pseudo-Ignatian epistles omit the words *et Paulus* from *Philadelphians* 4, indicating some disagreement in the tradition relating to Paul's marital status.[58] It may be some of these manuscripts that the Reformer Thomas James has in mind when he accuses "papists" of attempting – unsuccessfully – to expunge the words *"Paulus"* and *"Apostoli"* from *Philadelphians* 4. But, James wryly notes, "as in 'common burglaries, (it is Tertullian's observation) there is oft-times left a hat, glove, weapon, or some such thing, which doth bewray the doers thereof': so here, they have left such marks of the letters behind them (the ink of so ancient time taken deep impression in the parchment) that, if you hold the book against the light, you shall easily discern the words which were thought to be razed out."[59]

The reference to Paul as an important biblical representative of marriage, intertwined as it is in a household code that focuses on the good of both virginity and procreation, serves to underscore the mediating argument Pseudo-Ignatius makes elsewhere. Our author is negotiating polarized positions regarding asceticism. Throughout his epistles, he acknowledges virginity as a praiseworthy choice. But respect for the virginal life does not lead, he argues forcefully, to rejection of Christian marriage or to other rigorous ascetic practices.

If Pseudo-Ignatius wants to claim Pauline authority for his mediating position, however, why not merely write in Paul's name? We find ourselves circling back to the question: Why Ignatius? Pseudo-Ignatius has already demonstrated his comfort in writing in the apostles' names, having previously penned *Apostolic Constitutions*. The final piece to our pseudepigraphic puzzle, then, must examine the benefit of claiming Pauline authority *by means of* Ignatius. It may be that untethered Pauline

---

56. Trans. Thomas P. Scheck, *Origen: Commentary on the Epistle to the Romans, Books 1–5*, Fathers of the Church 103 (Washington, DC: Catholic University of America Press, 2001), 62.

57. Ibid., 62.

58. Lightfoot, *Apostolic Fathers*, 2.1:209.

59. Thomas James, *A Treatise on the Corruptions of Scripture, Councils, and Fathers: By the Prelates, Pastors, and Pillars of the Church of Rome, for the Maintenance of Popery* (London: John W. Parker, 1843), 127–28.

tradition could have been perceived as a liability.[60] After all, some of the most notorious heretics claimed Pauline authority for their views.[61] Thus asserting Pauline authority vis-à-vis Ignatius may provide a safe-guard for our author: by forging in the name of Ignatius, Pseudo-Ignatius can safely trace his genealogical roots to a particular construction of Paul. Significantly, the Ignatius/Paul connection allows Pseudo-Ignatius a doubly strong association with Antioch, which, as Carl Smith notes, was "a center for Pauline activity."[62] If Pseudo-Ignatius is engaged in a battle for his community in Antioch, appropriating the combined authority of two powerhouses of the past might be an especially effective rhetorical move.

Concluding Remarks

I have argued that Pseudo-Ignatius is, at least in part, engaged in a battle with rigorous ascetics who claim that marriage and procreation – along with certain foods and drinks – are abominations. Our author strenuously rejects this position without simultaneously rejecting certain modified ascetic practices and, furthermore, without rejecting the virtues of Christian celibacy. By arguing for a moderating ethic, by refusing to concede to arguments for the degradation of marriage, and by the prolif-eration of household codes, Pseudo-Ignatius mounts a three-pronged attack – an attack of moderation in all things – against a more strenuous ethic being promulgated in his community. He does this by claiming the epistolary power of two important men in the history of Antioch: the martyr-apostle, Paul, and the martyr-bishop, Ignatius. Like his forefathers, Pseudo-Ignatius writes in the hope of peace and unity in his church.

60. Here, though he writes in Paul's name, his "Paul" is restricted by associa-tion with Peter and the other disciples. Thus elsewhere this author has also tethered Pauline authority to orthodox voices.

61. David K. Rensberger argues that Paul was not – as is commonly believed – "ignored and mistrusted during the second century" because of heretics' appropriation of his letters. Rather, the evidence suggests that Paul was used by all sides of eccle-siastical debates. Such a conclusion may make associating Paul with another church father even more telling. See Rensberger, "The Use of Paul's Letters in Second-Century Christianity," in *The Writings of St. Paul*, ed. Wayne A. Meeks and John T. Fitzgerald, 2nd ed. (New York: W. W. Norton, 2007), 343.

62. Carl Smith, "Ministry, Martyrdom, and Other Mysteries: Pauline Influence on Ignatius of Antioch," in Bird and Dodson, eds., *Paul and the Second Century*, 40. Smith describes Ignatius as "a creative mind engaged with the apostolic tradition and unafraid to amplify it for his ecclesiastical and personal purposes." Smith, "Ministry, Martyrdom, and Other Mysteries," 41.

I do not intend this contribution to be a final statement on the use of Paul in Pseudo-Ignatius. Instead, I would like to open avenues of exploration. The epistles of Pseudo-Ignatius are fascinating but, even more, they are important. They have been undervalued and, thus, understudied in terms of their contributions to understanding the ethical conflicts in fourth-century Antioch. In recent decades, the study of early Christianity and late antiquity has begun to embrace texts that reflect concerns of ordinary life rather than solely the development of doctrine. While the place of Pseudo-Ignatius in the Arian controversy has been examined, the way it reflects life-on-the-ground conflicts in fourth-century Antioch await us.

Chapter 11

POLYCARP'S RECEPTION OF PAUL AND
RHETORICAL STRUCTURE:
CAN ONE INFORM THE OTHER?*

David E. Wilhite

Introduction

Two of the major concerns for scholars studying Polycarp's letter to the
Philippians are: (1) Polycarp's use of literary sources, especially what
would become the Christian Scriptures, and (2) the textual and rhetorical
unity of the letter. Understanding how Polycarp's use of Paul and Pauline
texts contribute to our understanding of Polycarp's rhetorical aim(s)
requires further attention.

Aside from these two major concerns in Polycarpology, there are the
standard questions about context. It will be helpful, therefore, to review
briefly the pertinent items that historians can and cannot affirm about
Polycarp. The reason for focusing both on what should and should not be
understood to be Polycarp's context is that the data in Polycarp's letter are
slight, and much depends on the assumed communities from which and
to which Polycarp's letter corresponds (as with Paul and his letters).[1] In
particular, two areas will be proscribed, or at least heavily qualified. The
first is Polycarp's alleged tutelage under the Apostle John, and the second
is Polycarp's alleged polemic against Marcion. In both cases I will argue
that no evidence of direct contact between Polycarp and these two persons
exists in this letter. Moreover, to assume either John or Marcion to be

* I would like to thank Paul Hartog for reading this essay. I interact with Hartog in
what follows, and so he is obviously not to be faulted for any weaknesses that remain,
especially in my attempt to engage with his work. His feedback, however, certainly
improved the following discussion.
1. Peter Steinmetz, "Polykarp von Smyrna über die Gerechtigkeit," *Hermes* 100,
no. 1 (1972): 65.

directly in view would wrongly skew any reading of Polycarp's letter to the Philippians. However, I will also show that disentangling Polycarp's letter from both John and Marcion is not simply a matter of leaving both unmentioned. In both cases Polycarp's letter is better understood as proximate to Johannine and Marcionite Christianity (however defined); in other words, much can be learned from what is not said in this letter in that this letter is probably one step removed from each.

After Polycarp's context is identified, or at least not misidentified, then the two major concerns mentioned above can be addressed in turn with the aim to show how they intersect. While Polycarp's use of Paul (et al.) and Polycarp's rhetorical aim(s) are rarely studied in isolation from each other, no one to my knowledge has identified how (or if) the two subjects can be integrated to answer some of the lingering questions about this letter. While many issues will remain unresolved in this current essay due to space constraints, I do hope to illustrate how closely aligned these two issues are and point the way forward for future work in this area.

Polycarp in Context

Polycarp's letter is usually dated to the 120s, but a wider range is certainly possible. The recent trend to push back the date of Ignatius' letters prohibits an earlier dating.[2] Likewise, any later dating is less likely since there is no apparent awareness of a monepiscopate, collections of Gospel texts, nor explicitly Marcionite teachings – all of which are often taken to be hallmarks of extant mid- to late second-century Christian texts, and the latter of which requires further discussion below. Within this range of possible dates also belong a wide range of possible sources that can help us locate Polycarp.

There are several texts that allegedly record facts about Polycarp's life and context, but which are in fact later and anachronistic, and so should not be used to inform Polycarp's letter to the Philippians.[3] The first of these is

---

2. Those arguing for later dates include the following: for theological reasons, see Paul Foster, "The Epistles of Ignatius of Antioch," in *The Writings of the Apostolic Fathers*, ed. Paul Foster (London: T&T Clark, 2007), esp. 84–89; for cultural-political terms, see Allen Brent, *Ignatius of Antioch and the Second Sophistic: A Study of an Early Christian Transformation of Pagan Culture* (Tübingen: Mohr Siebeck, 2006), 317–18; and for anti-Ptolemean terms, T. D. Barnes, "The Date of Ignatius," *ExpTim* 120, no. 2 (2008): 119–30, who dates Ignatius' letters as most probably after 138.

3. Space does not allow for incorporation of the recent attempts to identify Irenaeus' "elder" and the author of *Ad Diognetum* to Polycarp; see Charles E. Hill, *From the Lost Teaching of Polycarp: Identifying Irenaeus' Apostolic Presbyter and*

the *Martyrdom of Polycarp*. This account has enjoyed a remarkable status among the majority of scholars who deem it an authentic record, if not an eyewitness account of Polycarp's death. Even if the miraculous elements are dismissed as narratival theologizing, the *Martyrdom* has been almost unanimously understood by historians as recording reliable information. While this view need not be rejected entirely, the recent work of Candida Moss has to my mind demonstrated that the account is later than previously thought, perhaps as late as the 250s.[4]

The next two texts that must be excluded from directly informing our discussion are the *Vita Polycarpi* and the Harris Fragments.[5] The consensus of scholarly opinions rejects the authenticity of these two texts in which Polycarp was later remembered and utilized polemically and which are freighted with anachronisms. These texts, however, while proscribed, are not entirely dismissed as uninformative. They are some of the first interpreters of Polycarp himself. There is an interesting comparison with how the *Vita* and the Fragments portray Polycarp and how Polycarp can be interpreted in his letter to the Philippians by scholars today.

In the *Vita* Polycarp is shown to be the ideal bishop (whereas Polycarp refers to himself as a presbyter – probably indicative of the early second century wherein the monepiscopate had yet to emerge outside of Antioch).[6] More precisely, Polycarp is portrayed as exhibiting all of the virtues of a

---

the Author of Ad Diognetum (Tübingen: Mohr Siebeck, 2006), who also credits Pier Fanco Beatrice, "Der Presbyter des Irenäus, Polykarp von Smyrna und der Brief an Diognet," in *Pléroma: Salus Carnis: Homenaje a Antonio Orbe, S.J.*, ed. Eugenio Romero-Pose (Santiago de Compostella: Aldecoa, 1990), 179–202. Most reviewers, it should be added, are not entirely convinced: Irenaeus' elder probably is Polycarp while the author of *Ad Diognetum* only possibly is. However, if this author is not Polycarp, but is located in Smyrna (see Hill's prosopographic evidence about Diognetus), then this weakens the case for Irenaeus' presbyter being identified with Polycarp, for there was more than one such qualified person that Irenaeus could cite. Most importantly for the present study, Hill stipulates that Polycarp would only become anti-Marcionite after coming to Rome (ca. 155, see p. 81), and so Hill's view has no direct bearing on our discussion of the earlier Polycarp's *Philippians* (ca. 135, if not earlier).

4. Candida R. Moss, "On the Dating of Polycarp: Rethinking the Place of the *Martyrdom of Polycarp* in the History of Christianity," *Early Christianity* 1 (2010): 539–74.

5. See Alistair Stewart-Sykes, *The Life of Polycarp: An Anonymous Vita from Third-Century Smyrna* (Sydney: St. Pauls, 2002); and Frederick W. Weidmann, *Polycarp and John: The Harris Fragments and Their Challenge to the Literary Traditions* (Notre Dame: University of Notre Dame Press, 1999).

6. Stewart-Sykes, *The Life of Polycarp*, 32, 41, and cf. 48–55.

bishop listed in the Pastoral Epistles.[7] This Pauline depiction of Polycarp stands in sharp relief to Polycarp's alleged connection to the Apostle John, for the *Vita* reveals no knowledge of such a connection.

The other text, the Harris Fragments, find a different interpretation. Instead of the ideal Pauline bishop, Polycarp is portrayed as the successor to John. The source even goes so far as to claim that Polycarp must be martyred vicariously for John, the only one of the twelve apostles not to experience such a death.[8] Irenaeus's account is likely the source behind these fragments' connection of Polycarp and the apostle John, and this connection – even if Irenaeus exaggerated it – need not be rejected.[9] What does stand in sharp contrast is how Polycarp's letter makes no mention or explicit attempt to invoke John at all.[10] What is noteworthy for our present purpose is how Polycarp's letter to the Philippians has direct dependence on Johannine material.[11] This tension between Pauline and Johannine motifs will be important for our understanding of the unity, or lack thereof, of Polycarp's letter below.

7. Boudewijn Dehandschutter, "The Epistle of Polycarp," in *The Apostolic Fathers: An Introduction* (ed. Wilhelm Pratscher; Waco, TX: Baylor University Press, 2009), 118; cf. idem, "Images of Polycarp: Bibliography and Hagiography about the Bishop of Smyrna," in *Polycarpiana: Studies on Martyrdom and Persecution in Early Christianity*, ed. Boudewijn Dehandschutter and Johan Leemans (Leuven: Leuven University Press, 2007), 275.

8. Text and trans. in Weidmann, *Polycarp and John*, 35, 47.

9. On this exaggeration, see A. H. McNeile, *An Introduction to the Study of the New Testament*, rev. ed. (Oxford: Clarendon, 1927), 269–70; William R. Schoedel, *The Apostolic Fathers: A New Translation and Commentary*. Vol. 5, *Polycarp, Martyrdom of Polycarp, Fragments of Papias*, ed. Robert M. Grant (New York: T. Nelson, 1964), 3, concurs.

10. Pierre-Thomas Camelot, *Ignace d'Antioche, Polycarpe de Smyrne: Lettres, Martyre de Polycarpe*, rev. ed., SC 10 (Paris: Cerf, 2007), 184 n. 3, reads the reference to "the apostles who preached the gospel to us" as Polycarp's relation to John and the Philippians' relation to Paul. As evidence, Camelot offers the "Au témoignage de saint Irénée, Polycarpe avait été disciple des apôtres, et spécialement de saint Jean (*Adv. Haer*. III, 3, 4; *Ep. ad Flor.*, dans Eus. *H. E.*, V, 20;…),'' which is an uncritical acceptance of what is most likely an overstatement on Irenaeus's part.

11. See especially Pol. *Phil.* 7, which, if not directly from 1 and 2 John, is at least Johannine oral tradition. See further discussion in Paul A. Hartog, "The Opponents of Polycarp, *Philippians*, and 1 John," in *The New Testament and the Apostolic Fathers*. Vol. 2, *Trajectories Through the New Testament and the Apostolic Fathers*, ed. Andrew F. Gregory and Christopher M. Tuckett (Oxford: Oxford University Press, 2005), 380–84 (and bibliography in 375–76).

One last item that must be rejected as directly informing our discussion of Polycarp's letter is Marcionism. Marcion is traditionally dated as arriving in Rome ca. 140 and then rejected by the elders of Rome in 144.[12] Originally from Pontus in Asia Minor, Marcion has sometimes been thought to inform Ignatius and Polycarp and the Christian communities addressed by these authors[13] – the assumption being that Marcion taught his heresy for years if not decades before arriving in Rome. The problem with such an assumption is a complete lack of evidence to support it.[14]

Marcion's unique doctrines are usually said to include (1) a theological dualism wherein the truly good God of Christ is contrasted with the Demiurge of the "Old Testament"; (2) a rejection of the Old Testament and a radical editing of the New Testament wherein any references to the Old are excised, and the only remaining texts are Luke and ten of Paul's letters; and (3) Christological docetism, denying the real flesh of Christ and teaching him to have been a phantasm.

Two things must be said about Marcionism for our purposes: our understanding of Marcionism per se must be revised in general; and in particular the data found in Polycarp's letter provide no basis for understanding Marcion or Marcionites to be the opponents countered by Polycarp. Even if one does not accept the revisionist view of Marcion, there is little to no plausibility for these doctrines as being referenced by Polycarp in his letter. Since space does not allow for a discussion of the former, I will assume the latter for a brief review of the possibilities.

---

12. Recent discussions include Paul Foster, "Marcion: His Life, Works, Beliefs, and Impact," *ExpTim* 121, no. 6 (2010): 269–80; and Sebastian Moll, *The Arch-Heretic Marcion*, WUNT 250 (Tübingen: Mohr Siebeck, 2010).

13. Those in favor of Marcion as the opponent in Polycarp's *Philippians* include Peter Meinhold, "Polykarpos (1)," in *Realencyclopädie der classischen Altertumswissenschaft* 21 (1952): 1685–87 (Christoph Markschies in the latest edition of the *Realencyclopädie* also suggests that Marcion is in view); and Tashio Aono, *Die Entwicklung des paulinischen Gerichtsgedankens bei den Apostolischen Vätern* (Bern: Peter Lang 1979), 384–97, who provides an extensive discussion of all the evidence. See also Markus Vinzent, *Christ's Resurrection in Early Christianity and the Making of the New Testament* (Farnham: Ashgate, 2011), 107–10.

14. P. N. Harrison, *Polycarp's Two Epistles to the Philippians* (Cambridge: Cambridge University Press, 1936), and those who hold his view must explain this by arguing that Marcion had not fully developed his teachings while still in Asia Minor.

As for theological dualism, which is the most secure teaching of Marcion, there is no mention in Polycarp's letter whatsoever.[15]

For Marcion's second alleged doctrine – rejection of the canon and revising of Luke and Paul – there are two possible references. Polycarp (in 7.1) mentions those who "twist (μεθοδεύειν) the sayings of the Lord."[16] However, the idea of "twisting" (as Holmes translates) is far from Marcion's alleged work, which according to Tertullian, was that of editing with "a sword, instead of a stylus (*machaera, non stilo*)."[17] It should also be noted that the stated motive for said twisting of the Lord's teachings is the culprit's "lusts" (ἐπιθυμίας) (7.1, my trans.); however, "The accusation does not seem to fit Marcion, because he was known as a 'severe ascetic' rather than as a libertine."[18] The other possible reference is Polycarp's statements about "the apostles who preached the gospel to us, and the prophets who announced in advance the coming of our Lord."[19] However, Lightfoot's and Holmes's translations ("proclaimed beforehand" and "announced in advance") say more than Polycarp's Greek requires: the "prophets" who "have proclaimed" the coming[20] of the Lord may reflect

15. This point convinced Adolf von Harnack to reverse his earlier opinion that Marcion was the target of this letter (see *Marcion: Das Evangelium vom fremden Gott*, rev.; *Neue Studien zu Marcion* (Darmstadt: Wissenschaftliche Buchgesellschaft, 1960 [orig. 1921/1923; rev. 1924]), 5*–6* n. 4).

16. Helmut Koester, *An Introduction to the New Testament: History and Literature of Early Christianity* (Philadelphia: Fortress, 1982 [repr. Berlin: de Gruyter, 2000]), 2:310, believes this passage in Polycarp simply refers to Marcion's editorial work.

17. *Praescr.* 38.9 (Dietrich Schleyer, *De praescriptione haereticorum*, Fontes Christiani 42 [Turnhout: Brepols, 2002], 310 [my trans.]). Harrison, *Polycarp's Two Epistles*, 180, believed that this passage in Polycarp implies that Marcion first "twisted" the scriptures (in Asia Minor?) before arriving in Rome where he began editing them. C. M. Nielsen, "Polycarp and Marcion: A Note," *Journal of Theological Studies* 47 (1986): 297, has to admit that Harrison's explanation is "simply another way of saying that the false teacher at Philippi cannot be identified with Marcion."

18. Hartog, *Polycarp's* Epistle to the Philippians *and the* Martyrdom of Polycarp: *Introduction, Text, and Commentary*, OAF (Oxford: Oxford University Press, 2013), 130.

19. Pol. *Phil.* 6.3: οἱ εὐαγγελισάμεν οι ἡμας ἀπόστολοι καὶ προφῆται οἱ προκηρύξαντες τὴν ἔλεθσιν τοῦ κυρίου ἡμῶν.

20. For ἔλευσις, cf. Mark 14:62; Acts 1:11, etc.; as well as Pol. *Phil.* 2.1, "Jesus Christ...who is coming as judge" (Ἰησοῦν Χριστὸν...ὃς ἔρχαται κριτὴς). The fact that the second advent of Christ is in view, rather than the first (cf. Acts 7:52), is also supported by the previous statement (in Pol. *Phil.* 6.2) regarding the future "judgment seat of Christ." Those against this view include Kenneth Berding, *Polycarp and Paul:*

the kinds of "apostles and prophets" named in the *Didache* (11.3) as still present (i.e. not Old Testament prophets).[21] Moreover, as Schoedel observes, if this statement about the prophets was part of an anti-Marcion polemic, "…it would represent a remarkably anemic attack…it is by no means clear evidence of Marcionite heresy."[22]

As for the third doctrine, docetic Christology – a claim about Marcion which to my mind needs further reconsideration[23] – the discussion in Polycarp is far from what one would expect. For one thing, Marcion is not named.[24] Furthermore, the statement against antichrists (7.1) is so general that it could refer to any number of heretical groups beside Marcion.[25] The identity of the docetists attacked by Polycarp lies beyond the scope of this essay, but with Marcion himself demonstrated as an unlikely candidate

An Analysis of their Literary and Theological Relationship in Light of Polycarp's Use of Biblical and Extra-Biblical Literature, VCSup 62 (Leiden: Brill, 2002), 159 n. 10; and Hartog, *Polycarp's* Epistle, 126.

21. The view of Camelot, *Ignace d'Antioche*, 183 n. 1: "Rien n'empêche d'ailleurs d'entendre *apôtres* et *prophètes* dans un sens plus large, et de voir ici des prédicateurs de l'Évangile, doués des charismes d'*apostolat* et de *prophétie* (cf. Rom. 12, 6–7; I Cor. 12, 10; et surtout Éphés. 4,11). La *Didache* connaît encore des *docteurs*, des *apôtres* et des *prophètes* (11,1–3)."

22. Schoedel, *Polycarp*, 23.

23. David E. Wilhite, "Rhetoric and Theology in Tertullian: What Tertullian Learned from Paul," *StPatr* 65 (2013): 295–312.

24. The one possible identification comes in Polycarp's label for the opponent as "the firstborn of Satan" (7.1; cf. the anecdote in Irenaeus, *Haer.* 3.3.4; and Eusebius, *Hist. eccl.* 4.14.7). However, cf. Nils Alstrup Dahl, "Der Erstgeborene Satans und der Vater des Teufels (Polyk. 7.1 und Joh 8.44)," in *Apophoreta: Festschrift für Ernst Haenchen*, ed. Walther Eltester et al. (Berlin: Töpelmann, 1964), 70–84. Hartog, *Polycarp and the New Testament: The Occasion, Rhetoric, Theme, and Unity of the Epistle to the Philippians and Its Allusions to New Testament Literature*, WUNT 2/134 (Tübingen: Mohr Siebeck, 2002), 92, contends that if Polycarp ever encountered Marcionism proper, it would have been after he visited Rome (ca. 155).

25. Those who reject Marcion as the heretic of Pol. *Phil.* 7 include J. B. Lightfoot, *Apostolic Fathers* (London: Macmillan, 1889), 2.2:918; L.W. Barnard, "The Problem of St Polycarp's Epistle to the Philippians," in *Studies in the Apostolic Fathers and their Background* (Oxford: Blackwell, 1966), 33–35; Schoedel, *Polycarp*, 23–26; Dehandschutter, "The Epistle of Polycarp," 121; Henning Paulsen, *Die Briefe des Ignatius von Antiochia und der Brief des Polykarp von Smyrna* (Tübingen: Mohr Siebeck, 1985), 120–21; Berding, *Polycarp and Paul*, 18–25; Peter Oakes, "Leadership and Suffering in the Letters of Polycarp and Paul to the Philippians," in Gregory and Tuckett, eds., *Trajectories through the New Testament and the Apostolic Fathers*, 358.

we can at least proceed with a view to various forms of Paulinism in Polycarp's context.[26]

While Marcionism proper, as taught and led by Marcion, is most likely not in Polycarp's purview, "Marcionism" as an extreme form of Paulinism does need to be considered in a wider sense. Were we to accept recent revisions to our understanding of Marcionism, then Marcion is a product, not the architect, of an expression of Christianity that is far removed from the synagogue and its scriptures.[27] In such communities in which the Hebrew scriptures (including the LXX) are foreign, it comes as no surprise that Luke's Gospel is the text of choice, given Luke's connection to the apostle to the Gentiles.[28] The debate about whether or not Marcion rejected Acts, or whether Acts is late and in response to Marcion cannot be addressed here.[29] I would simply point out that these choices may be

26. Cerinthus could be a likely candidate for the docetist in Philippi, since he is said to be Marcion's predecessor and known to Polycarp (see Irenaeus, *Haer.* 3.3.4); see Hill, "Cerinthus: Gnostic or Chiliast? A New Solution to an Old Problem," *Journal of Early Christian Studies* 8, no. 2 (2000): 135–72.

27. For bibliography, see Heikki Räisänen, "Marcion," in *A Companion to Second-Century Christian "Heretics,"* ed. Antti Marjanen and Petri Luomanen (Leiden: Brill, 2005), 100–24; Judith M. Lieu, "'As Much my Apostle as Christ is Mine': The Dispute over Paul between Tertullian and Marcion," *Early Christianity* 1 (2010): 41–59; idem, "Marcion and the Synoptic Problem," in *New Studies in the Synoptic Problem* (Leuven: Peeters, 2011), 731–51; Todd Still, "Shadow and Light: Marcion's (Mis) Construal of the Apostle Paul," in *Paul and the Second Century*, ed. Michael F. Bird and Joseph R. Dodson, LNTS 412 (London: T&T Clark, 2011), 91–107; and John W. Marshall, "Misunderstanding the New Paul: Marcion's Transformation of the Sonderzeit Paul," *Journal of Early Christian Studies* 20 (2012): 1–29.

28. After all, if Marcion(ites) knew other Gospels, then Mark would have been a more natural fit: no birth narrative, and no resurrection appearances. On the relation between churches and synagogues in the region of Asia Minor, only a few points need be made here: as far as the specific region of Pontus, there must have been a Jewish community there, but the evidence is slim (see Aquila of Acts 18:2; cf. 1 Pet 1:1, and the convert to Judaism, Aquila the Sinope; discussed in Räisänen, "Marcion," 102); the wider region of Asia Minor with a lower percentage of its population consisting of Jews (than say Alexandria, Antioch and even Rome; cf. Josephus, *Ant.* 14.7.2) birthed forms of Christianity less familiar with and certain of the Jewish scriptures. Additionally, Pliny the Younger (*Ep.* 10.96) reports various kinds of Christians in the province. So, even if some Christians in Asia Minor in general and Sinope of Pontus in particular had a wider "canon" than Luke and Paul, others may not have.

29. E.g. John Knox, *Marcion and the New Testament: An Essay in the Early History of the Canon* (Chicago: University of Chicago Press, 1942); Joseph Tyson, *Marcion and Luke-Acts: A Defining Struggle* (Columbia: University of South Carolina Press, 2006); John T. Townsend, "Date of Acts," in *Luke–Acts: New Perspectives*

a false dichotomy: whoever de-Judaized Luke for Marcion's community could just as easily have dropped Acts for the same reason. Pauline texts, like Luke, are the natural choice for a mission to Gentile regions like Pontus, if one is simply wishing to distribute Christian teachings to supplement the *Euangelion*.[30] This set of assumptions, while not proven, offers a better starting point than the uncritical reading of the heresiologists who claimed that Marcion uniquely demolished a pre-established canon and then whittled down what remained with no apparent editorial consistency. The revised view simply offers more heuristic promise since it can explain all the data.

With this understanding we can now appreciate why some scholars have understood Polycarp not as writing against Marcion, but as a (quasi-)Marcionite.[31] The label, of course, only works in the older way of thinking in which "Marcionism" was a clearly defined movement led by Marcion himself. If this is sufficiently destabilized so as to allow for Polycarp and/or Polycarp's audience to belong to a Gentile form of Christianity that has little to no appreciation or even knowledge of the synagogue's scriptures, then much in Polycarp can be explained.[32] For

---

from the Society of Biblical Literature, ed. Charles Talbert (New York: Crossroad, 1984), 47–62; and cf. Richard Pervo, *Dating Acts: Between the Evangelists and the Apologists* (Santa Rosa, CA: Polebridge, 2006), 24.

30. For the fluidity of Gospel texts in particular during this period, see Helmut Koester, "Gospel and Gospel Traditions in the Second Century," in Gregory and Tuckett, eds., *Trajectories through the New Testament and the Apostolic Fathers*, 27–44.

31. Nielsen, "Polycarp and Marcion," 297–99. While tenuous as direct evidence, the circumstances of Smyrna commonly point to tension between Christians and Jews (cf. Rev 2:9, against the "synagogue of Satan"); and the *Martyrdom of Polycarp*, the Harris Fragments, and the *Vita* all indict Jews for their role in Polycarp's death, indicating tension between the two communities.

32. Too little attention has been given to this aspect of Polycarp's community. For example, Florinus, addressed by Irenaeus (see Eusebius, *Hist. eccl.* 5.20), was said to have been an admirer of Polycarp but later had fallen into Marcion's ditheism. The most straightforward stance is to assume that Florinus did not hear Polycarp speak against Marcion, but instead could have endorsed the kind of Paulinism or quasi-Marcionism described here. Similarly, there is the widely known fact that the *Martyrdom of Polycarp* originally contained accounts of other martyrs. It is usually assumed that these were shorter narratives and of less interest when compared to that of Polycarp and as such were simply dropped from the text. However, there is a curious statement by Eusebius about one of the martyrs originally in this text: a certain "Metrodorus, who appears to have been a proselyte of the Marcionitic sect" (Eusebius, *Hist. eccl.* 4.15.46 [NPNF[2] 1:192]). If this implies conversion to the

example, Polycarp seems to know our Old Testament, or at least several parts of it, but he refrains from referencing this source in any way.[33] Moreover, whereas Polycarp may know multiple Gospels, and whereas he probably knows 1 Peter, and almost certainly knows Johannine material, he only names two sources: sayings of the Lord (2.3; 6.3; 7.1–2) and Paul.[34] This, it must be admitted, is an uncanny comparison with Marcion, and yet this in no way makes Polycarp or the Philippian audience "Marcionite" formally. Understanding some form of Pauline Christianity to be addressed helps to explain how prominent Paul is in Polycarp's letter and how important Pauline texts are to Polycarp's rhetorical aims.[35]

Now that we have excluded certain texts and persons from directly informing our reading of Polycarp, let us turn to the texts explicitly invoked in this letter.

Marcionite sect, then, like the case of Florinus, this instance raises the question: if Polycarp was a noted anti-Marcionite, how could his community have appended a martyrdom of a Marcionite to Polycarp's own martyrdom? The answer, of course, is they did not. Metrodorus appeared to be Marcionite to the later eyes of Eusebius (and probably to whoever edited the final form of our copy of *Martyrdom of Polycarp*). Metrodorus himself may have appeared Marcionite for several reasons: perhaps because he held to two sources of creation, like Florinus; or perhaps he only utilized the New Testament writers (perhaps only the Gospels/Paul) and had no use for the Old Testament, like Polycarp.

33. Scholars range in their view of Polycarp's use of the Old Testament: the Committee of the Oxford Society of Historical Theology (hereafter OSHT) responsible for the publication of *The New Testament in the Apostolic Fathers* (Oxford: Clarendon, 1905), 84, finds him to use Jeremiah and Tobit "undoubtedly." A. Bovon-Thurneysen, "Ethik und Eschatologie im Philipperbrief des Polycarp von Smyrna," *Theologische Zeitschrift* 29, no. 4 (1973): 243, admits that the Old Testament material in Polycarp could be from previous Christian accommodation. R. M. Grant, "Polycarp of Smyrna," *Anglican Theological Review* 28, no. 3 (1946): 145, rehearses Polycarp's impressive "library," only then to conclude, "But the Old Testament was practically unknown to him." Schoedel, *Polycarp*, 5, finds Psalms, Proverbs, Isaiah, Jeremiah, Ezekiel, and Tobit to be attested, although his "use of the Old Testament is slight." Hartog, *Polycarp and the New Testament*, 199–202, offers ten reasons why Polycarp did know the Old Testament but hardly used Old Testament texts.

34. Hartog, "The Opponents of Polycarp," 382 n. 44, criticizes Berding, *Polycarp and Paul* (Chapter 4), for downplaying the non-Pauline sources. For our purposes, the explicit use of Paul over (probable) implicit use of Petrine and Johannine texts will be of central importance while no attempt is made to deny the others.

35. On Pauline Christianity/ies more generally, see the discussion and bibliography in Mark W. Elliott, "The Triumph of Paulinism by the Mid-Third Century," in *Paul and the Second Century*, ed. Michael F. Bird and Joseph A. Dodson, LNTS 412 (London: T&T Clark, 2011), 244–56.

Polycarp, His Literary Sources, and Paul

In general, Polycarp seems to be aware of and indebted to many sources. Trying to identify unambiguous references to said sources, however, is nearly impossible. Much of the difficulty lies in the question of whether Polycarp cites a text from memory and so alters it slightly, or whether Polycarp simply utilizes common tradition.[36] Another problem is that,

36. Scholarly opinions as to what constitutes a quotation, allusion, etc. range widely. For methodological considerations and what constitutes "reception," see Andrew Gregory, *The Reception of Luke and Acts in the Period before the Irenaeus: Looking for Luke in the Second Century*, WUNT 2/169 (Tübingen: Mohr Siebeck, 2003), 5–20; and Gregory and Christopher M. Tuckett, "Reflections on Method: What Constitutes the Use of the Writings That Later Formed the New Testament in the Apostolic Fathers?," *The New Testament and the Apostolic Fathers*. Vol. 1, *The Reception of the New Testament in the Apostolic Fathers*, ed. Andrew F. Gregory and Christopher M. Tuckett (Oxford: Oxford University Press, 2005), 61–82. With Polycarp in particular, two major tendencies have been labeled "thin" and "thick" approaches. In the former, even extensive verbal similarity is not enough to establish definitive "reception," since common tropes appear in various Christian texts without requiring linear dependency. In the latter, verbal similarity or even similarity on unique notions is enough to conclude a literary relationship of some sort. These generalizations do not negate the fact that scholars using either approach also apply a great deal of nuance when deciding on any particular instance. Also, many studies utilize some sort of rating spectrum that helps to indicate how many sources are "possibly" present in Polycarp's *Philippians* and how many texts are thought to be "probably" present. Influential studies using the rigorous standard include the OSHT (*The New Testament in the Apostolic Fathers*), and Michael W. Holmes ("Polycarp's *Letter to the Philippians* and the Writings That Later Formed the New Testament," in Gregory and Tuckett, eds., *Trajectories Through the New Testament and the Apostolic Fathers*, 188–227; and idem, *The Apostolic Fathers: Greek Texts and English Translations*, 3rd ed. [Grand Rapids: Baker, 2006]). Influential studies using the generous standard include Hartog (*Polycarp and the New Testament*) and Berding (*Polycarp and Paul*). According to Andrew Gregory (review of Berding and Hartog in *JTS* 2003), the more generous approach is flawed in that it does not account for Helmut Koester's work, which insists that the final form of a text must be established to qualify as "reception," not simply including common material, even when this common material is verbatim sentences. Alternatively, Berding ("Polycarp's Use of 1 Clement: An Assumption Reconsidered," *Journal of Early Christian Studies* 19 [2011]: 131 n. 11) classifies Hartog as a "lesser degree" of skeptical than the thin approach and himself more "moderate" than the thick approach. Berding (*Polycarp and Paul*, 29) unapologetically states his own methodology: "Probabilities rather than certainties form the basis upon which this study proceeds." For Hartog, I detect a shift to a more tentative approach in his 2013 monograph; this may be due, however, to the nature of that work as a "Commentary" (see pp. 91–161).

with rare exceptions, Polycarp does not name the source to whom he is indebted. Polycarp does name Ignatius,[37] two otherwise unknown martyrs named Zosimus and Rufus, and finally Paul. The only other named source is "the Lord," whose sayings are referenced as such and may or may not derive from written Gospels. In addition to some of Ignatius' letters, Polycarp shows some awareness of *1 Clement*.[38] Given the scarcity of data, no certainty can be reached for texts like *1 Clement* and Ignatius's letters. The same is true for the texts of 1 Peter and 1 John, which brings us to Polycarp's use of texts that would later become the Christian scriptures.

Despite Polycarp's silence about other sources, many verbal parallels exist which suggest he is dependent on additional sources from our New Testament. Here are some of the more recent and influential investigations on this subject.

- Schoedel[39]
  - attested – Matthew, Luke, Acts, Romans, 1 and 2 Corinthians, Galatians, Ephesians, Philippians, 1 and 2 Timothy, 1 Peter, 1 John
  - doubtful – Acts, 1 John [*sic*]
- Berding[40]
  - certainly – Matthew, Romans, 1 and 2 Corinthians, Galatians, Ephesians, Philippians, 1 and 2 Timothy, 1 Peter, 1 John
  - probably – Luke, Acts, 2 Thessalonians
  - possibly – Mark, John, Colossians, 1 Thessalonians, and Hebrews
- Hartog[41]
  - certainly – Romans, 1 Corinthians, Galatians, Ephesians, Philippians, 1 Timothy, and 1 Peter
  - probably – Matthew, 2 Corinthians, 2 Timothy, 1 John
  - possibly – Luke, Acts, 2 Thessalonians

---

37. When Polycarp mentions (13.2) the "letters" (plural) sent by Ignatius "to us," we can assume the letter of Ignatius to the Smyrnaeans and to Polycarp. When Polycarp then frustratingly generalizes about the "other [letters]" he has and is forwarding to the Philippians, we are left with little to no basis on which to guess how many.

38. For parallels, see J. B. Bauer, *Polykarpbriefe* (Göttingen: Vandenhoeck & Ruprecht, 1995), 28–30.

39. Schoedel, *Polycarp*, 5.

40. Berding, *Polycarp and Paul*, 187.

41. Hartog, *Polycarp and the New Testament*, 195.

- Holmes[42]
  - no reasonable doubt – 1 Corinthians, Ephesians, 1 Peter
  - high degree of probability – 1 and 2 Timothy, 1 John
  - lower degree of probability – Romans, Galatians, Philippians
  - possibility only – Matthew, Mark, Luke, John, Acts, 2 Corinthians, Colossians, 2 Thessalonians, Hebrews, 2 John
  - no evidence – 1 Thessalonians, Titus, Philippians, James, 2 Peter, 3 John, Jude, Revelation

Usually, texts are deemed more or less probable/possible because the citation in view could also be derived from several other sources, including oral tradition. Demonstrating clear dependency, therefore, is difficult. While texts like 1 Peter and others should not be ignored in Polycarp, they cannot compare to the certainty that can be attained for Pauline texts found in Polycarp's letter. The matter still debated about Paul in Polycarp is how to decide whether any given Pauline letter is directly referenced, even though Paul himself is clearly ubiquitous (see the table appended to the end of this essay).[43]

---

42. Holmes, "Polycarp's *Letter*."

43. The table appended to this essay charts the opinions of the following significant studies as to what Pauline texts can be identified in Polycarp's *Philippians*. The weakness of such a spreadsheet is obviously that no comparison is available with other of Polycarp's sources (not even the few possible references to Hebrews), and often texts are only "possible" because of parallels with other such sources. Nevertheless, this chart can be used as a reference for further investigation.

OSHT, *The New Testament in the Apostolic Fathers*, is provided along with its rating system. Schoedel, *Polycarp*; Schoedel notes almost every word that could be attributed to earlier writers; only those deemed "direct contact with the texts" (i.e. using quotation marks; see Schoedel's explanation in the introduction, p. 5) are listed here, while texts he simply identifies with possible "indebtedness" have regrettably had to be omitted. Hartog, *Polycarp and the New Testament*; also, Hartog has more recently offered a complete commentary (*Polycarp's* Epistle, 96–161), which, while helpful, has not been fully incorporated into the chart, since he frequently notes instances that are "reminiscent" of New Testament sources but "not necessarily dependent"; only changes or supplementations to his previous work have been noted. See Berding, *Polycarp and Paul*; for Berding's rankings and categories, see pp. 31–32; the table reflects his appendix, unless otherwise noted. See also Bauer, *Die Polykarpbriefe*; Bart D. Ehrman, *The Apostolic Fathers*, LCL (Cambridge, MA: Harvard University Press, 2003); Holmes, "Polycarp's *Letter*," 187–227; and idem, *The Apostolic Father*; the texts given are from his 2006 edition, while any comments are taken from his 2005 essay. See further Camelot, *Ignace d'Antioche*.

Since so much work has been done recently on which of Paul texts are found in Polycarp, I will attempt to highlight when Paul himself is invoked by Polycarp and for what purpose – something that can only be seen fully at the end of the next section when Polycarp's rhetorical aims and structure have been analyzed.[44] At this point, we can begin by simply noting the importance of the person of Paul in Polycarp's letter.

Paul himself is named four times by Polycarp. They are as follows. After introductory remarks, Polycarp states,

> For neither I nor anyone like me can keep pace with the wisdom of the blessed and glorious Paul. When he was with you in the presence of the people of that time, he accurately and reliably taught the word concerning the truth. And when he was absent he wrote you letters (ἐπιστολάς).[45]

Later, Polycarp recounts martyrs known to the Philippians (mentioned above), including "Paul himself and the rest of the apostles" (9.1).

The last two explicit mentions of Paul come after Polycarp has addressed the former Philippian presbyter, Valens. Polycarp recalls Paul's teaching: "Or do we not know that the saints will judge the world, as Paul teaches?" (*Aut nescimus, quia sancti mundum iudicabunt, sicut Paulus docet?*, 11.2). Then he mentions Paul's missionary work and letter writing:

> But I have not observed or heard of any such thing among you, in whose midst the blessed Paul labored, and who are praised in the beginning of his letter. For he boasts about you in all the churches – the ones that at that time had come to know the Lord, for we had not yet come to know him. (11.3)

The obvious reason for Polycarp devoting so much attention to Paul in these statements is that Paul was seen as the founder and patron of the Philippian church. It is tempting, however, to think that Polycarp's indebtedness to and use of Paul runs deeper.

Polycarp goes beyond name-dropping by introducing Pauline material with a unique expression. At several points Polycarp introduces a source with the phrase, "knowing that…" (εἰδότες ὅτι). While many commentators

---

44. Berding, "Polycarp's Use of *1 Clement*," 138: "One of the reasons that Paul is often minimized in discussions of literary influence upon Polyc. *Phil.* is that the focus is often on sources rather upon authors… [T]he primary author that has influenced Polycarp in his letter to the Philippians is Paul."

45. Pol. *Phil.* 3.2–3. As to whether or not Polycarp's implies multiple "letters" to the Philippians and whether he knew the contents of Paul's Philippians, see Hartog, *Polycarp's* Epistle, 113–14; and Holmes, "Polycarp's *Letter*," 212. The statement could refer to 2 Thess 1:4.

have observed this formula as introductory in general, I would add that it is an expression which introduces Paul's letters in particular: Pol. *Phil.* 1.3 refers to Eph 2:8–9; Pol. *Phil.* 4.1 to 1 Tim 6:7; Pol. *Phil.* 5.1 to Gal 6.7; and finally Pol. *Phil.* 6.1, which requires more explanation.[46]

The occurrence of εἰδότες ὅτι in 6.1 is explained by the OSHT as a quote, but with no known source.[47] Likewise, Holmes notes this expression in 1.3, 4.1, and 5.1 and the Pauline references, but he does not elaborate on exactly how Paul in particular is "considered authoritative by Polycarp, at least, and perhaps also his audience."[48] Holmes then agrees with the OSHT on 6.1, because the following phrase is unknown in any other Christian writing.[49] It should be noted, however, that the expression is sometimes εἰδότες οὖν ὅτι (4.1, 5.1), but in 6.1 the οὖν does not arise until the next line (6.2),[50] which is a Pauline expression (cf. Rom 14:10; 12:2; 2 Cor 5:10). Moreover, the statement about everyone's indebtedness to sin (in 6.1) immediately following Polycarp's εἰδότες ὅτι is itself a Pauline axiom.[51] Another instance of this introductory formula often unnoticed by scholars in relation to the previous instances is found when Polycarp offers the rhetorical question, "Or do we not know that the saints will judge the world, as Paul teaches?"[52] The last phrase ("as Paul teaches") is suspiciously redundant in the Latin given the fact that the Pauline teaching

46. Lightfoot, *Apostolic Fathers*, 2.2:907–8, notes that Polycarp uses this expression to introduce a quotation and most commentators have agreed. Andreas Lindemann, *Paulus im ältesten Christentum: Das Bild des Apostles und die Rezeption der paulinischen Theologie in der frühchristlichen Literatur bis Marcion*, BHT 58 (Tübingen: Mohr Siebeck, 1979), 222–23, is aware of the uniquely Pauline referent of this expression, at least in some instances: "Wenn Polykarp diese offenbar als charakteristisch paulinisch geltende Aussage hier anführt, so signalisiert er damit, daß er als in paulinischer Tradition stehend verstanden werden will."

47. OSHT, *The New Testament in the Apostolic Fathers*, 84.

48. Holmes, "Polycarp's *Letter*," 188.

49. Pol. *Phil.* 6.1: "...knowing that we are all in debt with sin" (Εἰδότες ὅτι πάντες ὀφειλέται ἐσμὲν ἁμαρτίας).

50. Schoedel, *Polycarp*, 22 n. 58, believes this is an introductory formula meant to signal apostolic material, and he acknowledges R. M. Grant's claim that this formula in 6.1 could refer forward to 6.2. Schoedel, however, believes the expression in 6.1 "echoes" Synoptic material.

51. Hartog, *Polycarp and the New Testament*, 190, sees the personification of sin as "Pauline but cannot be traced to any specific quotation." Cf. Lindemann, "Paul in the Writings of the Apostolic Fathers," in *Paul and the Legacies of Paul*, ed. William S. Babcock (Dallas: Southern Methodist University Press, 1990), 43.

52. Pol. *Phil.* 11.2: *Aut nescimus, quia sancti mundum iudicabunt, sicut Paulus docet?*

is introduced with the preparatory phrase "*Aut nescimus, quia...*", a translation of Polycarp's εἰδότες οὖν ὅτι in an interrogative form.[53] Therefore, this
formula is used in all five instances to introduce Pauline statements, and
so must be seen as Polycarp's way of restating accepted Pauline teachings
which are probably recognized as such by Polycarp's audience. The phrase
itself, it should be noted, is Pauline.[54] The difference, however, is that Paul
(and 1 Peter) uses the expression to introduce concepts commonly known,
while Polycarp uses the expression to cite Paul in particular.[55] Hartog also
finds less explicit formulae in Polycarp to introduce scripture: "for" (γὰρ,
Pol. *Phil.* 5.3, with ref. to 1 Pet 2:11 and/or 1 Cor 6:9–10); "being assured
that" (πεπεισμένους ὅτι, Pol. *Phil.* 9.2, with ref. to Phil 2:16); and "do we
not know that...?" (*nescimus, quia*, Pol. *Phil.* 11.2 with ref. to 1 Cor 6:2
[discussed above]). In other words, Polycarp's explicit introduction of
authoritative texts is strictly in reference to Paul.[56]

In addition to the references to Paul by name, specific citations of
Pauline texts, and introductory formulae that signal Pauline writings as
authoritative, Polycarp's letter to the Philippians also evinces a pattern

53. Boudewijn Dehandschutter, "Polycarp's Epistle to the Philippians: An Early
Example of 'Reception,'" in *The New Testament in Early Christianity*, ed. Jean-Marie
Sevrin (Leuven: Leuven University Press, 1989), 281, and see n. 29 for further bibliography. It should be noted that Lightfoot's reconstructed Greek (*Apostolic Fathers*,
2.2:926) differs only to the extent that he is conforming the statement to 1 Cor 6:2
rather than to Polycarp's own practice.

54. See Bauer, *Die Polykarpbriefe*, 42, for complete list of instances, including
James 3.1 and 1 Pet 1:18.

55. For a more direct statement on Paul's writings as authoritative, see Pol. *Phil.*
12.1, "as it is said in these scriptures" (*ut his scripturis dictum est*); with reference to
Eph 4:26; cf. Ps 4:5). For the sake of space, I leave aside the question as to whether
or not Polycarp had a technical category of "scripture" and whether he applied this
to Paul; see Schoedel, *Polycarp*, 5, who insists, "There is no evidence that any of the
New Testament books are regarded as Scripture"; and see Nielsen, "Polycarp, Paul and
the Scriptures," *Anglican Theological Review* 47, no. 2 (1965): 199–216, who argues
the Polycarp does in fact view Pauline texts as sacred scriptures. For discussion and
bibliography, see Hartog, *Polycarp and the New Testament*, 203–7; idem, "Polycarp,
Ephesians, and 'Scripture,'" *WTJ* 70 (2008): 255–75; Berding, *Polycarp and Paul*,
159–62; and Holmes, "Polycarp's *Letter*," 210 n. 99.

56. As for the exclusive focus on Paul compared to other New Testament writers,
Koester, *Introduction*, 2:309, notes, "Indeed, for Polycarp there is no other apostolic
authority other than Paul..." Likewise, Berding, *Polycarp and Paul*, 135, argues,
"Whereas clear references to 1 Peter exist in the letter, Polycarp never uses an introductory formula before a quotation from 1 Peter. These formulae and their primary
use for sayings from Paul strongly indicates conscious connection to the teaching and
letters of Paul."

when using Pauline texts. Berding examines what he calls "clusters" of citations.[57] The pattern of clustering Pauline and Johannine texts is especially clear when accounting for both probable and possible citations: Paul in Pol. *Phil.* 3, 9, and 11 (and in each case he mentions Paul by name), to *1 Clement* in Pol. *Phil.* 4.2–3, and to 1 John in Pol. *Phil.* 7.1.

The *1 Clement* "cluster," however, is largely in relation to the *Haustafeln* of Pol. *Phil.* 4–6, which is admittedly not only Pauline, but Petrine and possibly also Ignatian. I, however, still stipulate that Paul is the explicit source mentioned by Polycarp (3.2) immediately prior. Alternatively, the Johannine "cluster" (in 7.1–2) is explicitly aimed at docetic teaching, the "speculation of the crowd," which will be important in interpreting the rhetorical aims of the letter. It is also worth noting that the Petrine passages are less clustered and more scattered (and often less certain). Therefore, Berding's clusters can be outlined as follows, when accounting for how Paul is explicitly invoked:

A. 3   Paul
B. 4–6 Paul
C. 7   Not Paul (John)
D. 9   Paul
E. 11   Paul

This pattern of clustering Pauline texts with a Johannine cluster at the crux of the chiasm will neatly align with the structure found in the letter when applying rhetorical analysis, and so this passage's significance needs further consideration.

The (Dis-)Unity and Aim(s) of Polycarp's Letter

One of the questions that has proven problematic for studies of Polycarp is the unity of the letter. At the textual level, scholars have disagreed about the existence of interpolations until Zahn's and Lightfoot's compelling arguments for the authenticity of the middle recension of Ignatius's letters.[58] Then, after Harrison's hypothesis, scholars have disagreed about whether our current text of Polycarp's *Philippians* should be understood as one text or a compilation of two letters.[59]

---

57. Berding, "Polycarp's Use of 1 Clement," see esp. 138–39; cf. his earlier *Polycarp and Paul*, 142–55, with helpful charts on 153.

58. See Camelot, *Ignace d'Antioche*, 250.

59. Cf. Polycarp's knowledge of Ignatius (Pol. *Phil.* 9 and 13.2). Full discussion and bibliography can be found in Hartog, *Polycarp's* Epistle, 27–40.

Whether one follows the single- or the two-letter hypothesis, the parallel question about the unity of the letter (or at least Pol. *Phil.* 1–12 = "Letter 2") remains. Did Polycarp write with one underlying purpose in mind, so that all points of the letter somehow tie together around a theme, or is this letter filled with multiple aims and agendas?

While the default position must be that ancient authors could write letters with multiple aims, perhaps even answering multiple questions from the Philippians, there has been a recurring impulse among scholars to find an underlying unity to the different issues that arise in the letter.[60] I will first outline these different issues and then illustrate various attempts to unify them:

- *Inscriptio*, salutation and thanksgiving (1).
- A. *Exordium*, occasion and subject: "leave behind the empty and meaningless chatter of the error of the crowd (τῶν πολλῶν)," (2.1).[61] Polycarp follows this statement with much to say about Jesus' resurrection and imminent judgment (2.1), the hope of those who avoid "unrighteousness" (ἀδικίας, 2.2), and then "righteousness" (δικαιοσύνη, 3.1 and passim).
- B. First Admonition: an elaborate list of household codes (4.1–6.2).
- C. Second Admonition: Polycarp denounces "everyone who does not confess that Jesus Christ has come in the flesh" as "antichrist" (6.3–7.1). This admonition is followed by another exhortation to "leave behind the worthless speculation of the crowd (τῶν πολλῶν) and their false teachings" (7.2), echoing almost verbatim the earlier admonition (in 2.1).

---

60. E.g. Harry O. Maier, "Purity and Danger in Polycarp's Epistle to the Philippians: The Sin of Valens in Social Perspective," *Journal of Early Christian Studies* 1, no. 3 (1993): 238. Maier, however, does not take this rhetorical unity far enough for Hartog, because he does not adequately account for the underlying logic uniting resurrection and righteousness. See Hartog, *Polycarp and the New Testament*; idem, "The Opponents"; and idem, "The Relationship between Paraenesis and Polemic in Polycarp, *Philippians*," *StPatr* 65 (2013): 27–37.

61. Walter Bauer, *Orthodoxy and Heresy in Earliest Christianity*, 2nd ed. (Philadelphia: Fortress, 1971), 72–73, reads "the crowd" to mean that docetism was "the overwhelming majority" Christology in Philippi. Camelot, *Ignace d'Antioche*, 178 n. 2, contends, "Il s'agit non pas du grand nombre de chrétiens, mais de la 'masse' a des paiens, auxquels Polycarpe ajoute sans doute les heretiques dont les vaines spéculations (ματαιολογίαν, cf. 1 Tim. 6; Tit. 3, 9; Ign. Ad Philad., I, 1, et ci-dessous, VII, 2) risquent de seduire les croyants."

D. Third Admonition and *paradeigmata*: "Christ Jesus" is offered as
   our example to be imitated (8.1–2), along with others who suffered
   and died because they "did not love the present world (αἰῶνα)"
   (9.1–2). Once more the "Lord" is offered as an example (10.1–2)
   with a warning against "those through whom the name of the Lord is
   blasphemed" (10.3).

E. The Case of Valens: This last phrase seems to be a transition to Valens
   (11.1), and in contrast the Philippians are warned to avoid avarice
   and many other sins. The obvious implication seems to be that
   Valens committed the sin of avarice, because Polycarp asks how one
   can preach self-control without practicing it (11.2). The Philippians'
   reputation is still intact, due to Paul's famous letter (11.3), and so
   hope is offered for Valens' repentance (11.4). The Philippians are
   commended for knowing the "sacred scriptures" (*sacris literis*, 12.1).

- Benediction: Polycarp then offers what looks suspiciously like a
  benediction (12.2), along with a call for further prayer (12.3).

- [In the final two sections of the modern editions (i.e. what may be
  a separate letter) Polycarp promises to forward all correspondence
  (13), and he acknowledges a certain Crescens along with Crescens'
  sister (14).]

The outline given here is intentionally weighted so as to highlight the
parallel structure with the Pauline and Johannine clusters outlined in the
previous section. Obviously, enumerations such as these can be manipu-
lated and so are of very limited value on their own.[62] Nevertheless, all
scholarly interpretations reviewed below attempt to identify the place and
function of ch. 7 in relation to the rest of Polycarp's letter. The question
at issue is whether or not the docetism mentioned therein is a primary or
secondary issue for Polycarp.

   To summarize the points of controversy in Polycarp's letter, scholars
debate the relationship between the following three items: righteousness,
denial of Christ's flesh, and Valens' moral failure. The "crowd" is contrasted
with righteousness (in 2.1–2), and the (same?) "crowd" is denounced for
denying Christ's flesh (in 7.1–2). No mention is made of the crowd when
speaking of Valens' failure, but there does seem to be an implicit, if not

---

62. This rhetorical outline follows Hartog, *Polycarp's* Epistle, 46, only expanded
and with the following changes: I have combined the *inscriptio* and section 1, the
exordium and section 3, and the "closing paranesis (10)" with the third admonition.
Also, Hartog includes 13–14 in his "Letter Closing." It should be noted that my alter-
ations do not change the centrality of section 7 for Hartog's outline.

explicit, contrast of Valens with righteousness (in 11.1–2), which echoes the things said of the crowd (in 2.1–2).

Valens' unrighteousness – to conflate the first and third points of controversy[63] – seems to have no explicit ties to the second point of controversy, docetic Christology, and yet many have tried to subordinate one issue to the other in order to read a more coherent and unified aim in the letter. For example, those who formerly understood the docetism in view to be Marcion's tended to see the Valens' controversy and the concern with unrighteousness as secondary to Polycarp's real concern, heresy.[64] Even some who deny Marcion as the heretic in view agree that the issues of unrighteousness are symptomatic of heresy generically and so subordinate the former point to the latter.[65] More recently, however, there has been a tendency by those denying Marcion is in view to downplay the mention of docetism in light of the concrete problem faced by Valen's unrighteousness, since no specific heretic is named by Polycarp.[66] In this trend, the

---

63. As does Maier, "Purity and Danger" (cited above), contending that the "love of money" applied particularly to Valens, not to docetists. The docetic threat served Polycarp's aim for social cohesion. Maier's work is largely indebted to Steinmetz, "Polykarp von Smyrna," 65, who calls the relationship between these two points "das Grundproblem der Interpretation dieses Briefes."

64. E.g. Meinhold, "Polykarpos," 1686, argued for unity of purpose throughout the letter so that Pol. *Phil.* 6.3–7.2 is anti-Marcionite and Pol. *Phil.* 11 about Valens must be interpreted as Valens accepting a bribe from Marcion (as Marcion famously tried to do soon after in Rome [see Tertullian, *Praescr.* 30.2]).

65. E.g. Bauer, *Orthodoxy and Heresy*, 71–74, believes heresy is the major crisis in Polycarp's letter, so that even Valens' failure cannot be addressed simply by appeal to a bishop for the Philippian bishop was a docetist.

66. Steinmetz, "Polykarp von Smyrna," 68–74, interpreted Polycarp's statement on docetism as illustrative of the theological underpinnings of righteousness, which was the Philippians' concrete problem in the aftermath of Valens's moral failure. Likewise, Lindemann, "Paul in the Writings," 43, believes that Polycarp's letter "is simply his response to the Philippians' question concerning the problem of *dikaiosyne*. In either case, Polycarp did not set out to write an important theological work..." Similarly, Berding, *Polycarp and Paul*, 26: "It seems, instead [of docetism being the primary concern], that the primary purpose of the letter is found in Polycarp's statement of purpose (Pol. *Phil.* 3.1). He is responding to the Philippians' request that he write to them about the problem of righteousness... Since righteousness for Polycarp includes fidelity to 'the word delivered to us from the beginning' (7.2) and centers on ethics, including greed, the anti-docetic theme and the issue of greed should be considered sub-themes under the greater discussion of 'righteousness.'" Later, Berding adds, "...'righteousness' (3.1), this is very evidently the item of most concern for Polycarp" (*Polycarp and Paul*, 170).

rhetorical aim of the letter unites the various points by subordinating the docetic controversy as secondary to the real issue at hand, unrighteousness. Are such attempts to find an underlying rhetorical unity valid?

Of course we need not require singularity of purpose in ancient epistolary writing, and so one might argue that the burden of proof lies on those who would see a coherent theme uniting all the motifs of Polycarp's *Philippians*.[67] On the other hand, the fruitful results of rhetorical analysis have shown that Polycarp (and other Christian writers, including Paul) did tend to follow the norms of rhetorical speech.[68] Therefore, it is assumed, especially in paraenetic speech like Polycarp's *Philippians*, that there is an underlying aim in the given text and all other items found in the letter implicitly help the author accomplish that aim.[69] In this approach, no burden of proof is necessary; instead, a given text should be assessed in terms of the rhetorical aims and any potential connections detectable between given points are to be emphasized.[70]

67. Schoedel, *Polycarp*, 17: "It seems likely to me that the two issues [docetism and righteousness] were more or less separate in the letter from the Philippians."

68. For general bibliography on rhetorical analysis of early Christianity, see Wilhite, "Rhetoric." For Polycarp in particular, see Dehandschutter, "Polycarp's Epistle," 279–81; and Hartog, *Polycarp and the New Testament*, 121–34. Apparently, even Schoedel (cited above) is dissatisfied with the two issues being too separate; he explains (*Polycarp*, 17) Polycarp's use of Valens as a warning to the Philippians lest others fall by avarice into heresy (i.e. the two are connected in Polycarp's rhetorical aim). Schoedel sees the issues as truly distinct in Philippi, but as rhetorically aligned by Polycarp in his letter. Therefore, both the potential for docetism and the actual failure of Valens are understood by Schoedel (*Polycarp*, 31), as Polycarp's way of addressing the deeper problems with unrighteousness within the community. He also credits Meinhold (cited above) "as a predecessor in the effort to uncover the inner coherence of Polycarp's letter" (*Polycarp*, 4) even though he disagrees with Meinhold regarding the textual unity of the letter.

69. Hartog, *Polycarp and the New Testament*, 199, agreeing with Steinmetz (see esp. "Polykarp von Smyrna," 74–75), states, "The analysis of Polycarp's rhetorical response to the Valens scandal portrays a unifying purpose throughout the letter."

70. Even so, the rhetorical analysis cannot exclude the likelihood of an author's multifaceted aim. Holmes, "Polycarp of Smyrna," in *Dictionary of the Later New Testament and Its Developments*, ed. Ralph P. Martin and Peter H. Davids (Downers Grove: InterVarsity, 1997), 935, describes Polycarp's *Philippians* as a "complex hortatory" which combines paraenesis, advice and admonition, as well as containing sermonic elements. Hartog, *Polycarp and the New Testament*, 137, rightly stipulates that the question is not one of proof, but one of heuristic promise: "These insights [i.e. righteousness as the theme uniting the various elements in the letter] help us explain much more of the seemingly disjointed Polycarpian material."

To my knowledge, no one has done more to contribute to this line of inquiry than Paul Hartog, and while Hartog rightly strives to identify the underlying logic of Polycarp's rhetoric, he also notes the diverse elements in the letter. Both the diversity of issues and the rhetorical unity can be retained by differentiating the context/occasion from the rhetorical structure/aim.[71] I am convinced that more could be found in this letter to help demonstrate a unified rhetorical aim. This will be briefly illustrated, but it must be noted that the following point is suggestive, and problems remain. I will conclude on a more somber and skeptical note.

If we accept that the docetic heresy is not the primary concern – the concern is Valens, whose failure suggests to Polycarp that the social chaos in Philippi has exposed the flock as prey for heresy generally (not to a particular heretic) – then more must be said to explain how some of the topics and persons mentioned by Polycarp relate to the Valens' unrighteousness. Although not directly contributing to the rhetorical analysis of the letter, Peter Oakes' study is helpful in illustrating the possibilities in this line of thought.[72]

Oakes notes the emphasis on φιλαργυρία in Polycarp's *Philippians* – which incidentally is a theme also found in Paul's letter to the Philippians. Oakes's main argument involves the change in leadership structure since Paul's time. More pertinent to our present purposes, however, is when Oakes explains how righteousness (the opposite of φιλαργυρία) relates Paul to the other themes in Polycarp's *Philippians*: the martyrs (9.1) loved Christ and not "the present world (αἰῶνα)" (9.2). Moreover, two *personae* have been lovers of money, the present world, etc., and are thereby "enemies of the cross" (12.3): Valens (recently, in the Philippian experience) and the heretics (notoriously, in the polemical construction of early Christian writers).

71. Hartog, *Polycarp and the New Testament*, 81, insists: "It is negligent to suppose that the Philippians could only have had had one request in mind per letter, and therefore we must separate differing issues into separate letters." He lists the requests of the Philippians as follows: "(1) They asked that Polycarp send their letter of congratulations on to Syria (13.1). (2) They requested a copy of Polycarp's collection of Ignatian letters (13.1). (3) And they sought advice 'concerning righteousness' (3.1), which I will interpret within the context caused by Valens' action." Hartog, nevertheless, aims to undertake a reading of Polycarp's *Philippians* which assumes unity of purpose: "The following chapter will attempt to discover the threads woven throughout *Phil* through an analysis of recurrent topics." He then adds: "Many agree that a theme (if not *the* theme) of *Phil* is 'righteousness'" (135, original emphasis) For more on Polycarp's rhetorical purpose opposed to the Philippian occasion, see Hartog, *Polycarp's* Epistle, 50–51; cf. Hartog, *Polycarp and the New Testament*, 145.

72. Oakes, "Leadership and Suffering."

To press Oakes's point further than he explicitly takes it,[73] the martyrs serve as *exampla positiva* to counter Valens' and the docetists' *exempla negativa*. Oakes finds that the economic suffering is the key to understanding the letter. I would be inclined to see his contribution as broadening the letter's concern from Valens singularly to all forms of pressures put on the Philippians, and thereby illustrating how there could be an underlying rhetorical unity to the letter. Polycarp, it can be assumed, has been asked about Valens, but he is able to counterbalance the Valens problem with a wider horizon:

- on the one side there are lovers of the world, which includes
  - οἱ πολλοί (note the economic and spiritual overtones),[74] and
  - antichrists (7.1) who reject the flesh and future judgment of Christ;
- on the other side there are the lovers of Christ, which includes
  - the saints (1.1; 11.2; 12.2, 3), and
  - the martyrs (9.1), and Paul (see outline above),[75] who embody abandonment of the world.

Even if this generation of Philippian Christians has lost the presbyter Valens and thereby experienced suffering, they can remember the apostle Paul and thereby experience joy. In this understanding, the docetists – who are not so much the crux of the argument as they are simply in contrast to the heroes of the faith – can now be seen as foils for Polycarp's wider aim and are not truly in the purview of the Philippian audience.

Now that such a hypothesis has been articulated, a word of caution is in order. This explanation is a conjecture born from an attempt to find rhetorical unity. The hypothesis, it must be admitted, is at the least questionable when this rhetorical analysis is compared with Polycarp's use of Paul.

---

73. Ibid., 368–69, is careful to claim φιλαργυρία as "the prominent, but not overwhelmingly dominant" theme, noting that the issue "markedly disappears when Polycarp actually writes about heresy (chapter 7)." What Oaks does insist upon is that Valens is not "the letter's overriding focus" (368 n. 26), but is instead indicative of how φιλαργυρία impacts the community.

74. Hartog, *Polycarp and the New Testament*, 104, "While οἱ πολλοί is more pejorative than statistical, Polycarp evidently is not singling out one heretic." For the first clause Hartog cites (n. 89) Schoedel, *Polycarp*, 12, and then adds, "For Greek writers, the οἱ πολλοί are those 'to whom intelligence normally is denied.'"

75. Cf. Steinmetz, "Polykarp von Smyrna," 70–74.

Conclusion: Comparing Pauline Reception and Rhetorical Analysis

The proposed rhetorical unity offered here requires further attention because it only tentatively explains why Polycarp switches from Pauline to Johannine material when addressing docetism and therefore does not meet the burden of heuristic promise completely.[76] While there is possible coherence (esp. if one explores the content of 7.2 related to righteousness), the anti-heretical material may still be more than a rhetorical device to be subsumed under a larger aim to address righteousness.[77] The need for Polycarp to switch from Pauline material, clearly used (in either the maximalist or the minimalist readings) against Valens and unrighteousness, to the Johannine material against the docetic teaching, begs for further explanation.[78]

Polycarp's *Phil.* 7 proves significant both in the study of reception history and in rhetorical analysis.[79] The limitations of focusing solely on Paul as has been done here should be obvious. Nevertheless, it is hoped that such a focus has made salient the need for further investigation as to how Polycarp's statements against docetism (with its complete absence of Pauline material) may or may not fit within the overarching rhetorical aim(s) of Polycarp, for whom Paul features so prominently.

---

76. Cf. Berding, "Polycarp's Use of *1 Clement*," 138–39; idem, *Polycarp and Paul*, 142–55. I note that the references to Paul and the use of Pauline "clusters" align with Polycarp's discussion of "righteousness" in *Phil.* 3, of whom Paul is an example, not loving the present world in *Phil.* 9, of which Paul et al. are examples, and Valens' love of money in *Phil.* 11, for which "as Paul teaches" the saints will judge the world. And yet the Johannine cluster in 7.1 is the only place in the letter that addresses docetism.

77. The two-fold subject matter is even reflected in Irenaeus, *Haer.* 3.3.4: "There exists also a very forceful letter of Polycarp written to the Philippians. From it those who wish and are concerned about their salvation can learn both the standard of his faith and the preaching of the truth" (trans. Matthew C. Steenberg and Dominic J. Unger, *St. Irenaeus of Lyons: Against the Heresies [Book 3]*, ACW 64 [New York: Paulist, 2012]); and *apud* Eusebius, *Hist. Eccl.* 4.14.8). The "standard of his faith" very precisely echoes the subject of righteousness vs. Valens' unrighteousness, while the "preaching of the truth" very precisely speaks to the subject of proper Christology. The former is almost entirely Pauline while the latter is almost exclusively Johannine in Polycarp's *Philippians*. Also, Irenaeus next emphasizes the dual influences of Paul and John at Ephesus. Irenaeus's remembrance of both Paul and John recalls the point made in the first section about how Polycarp was connected with each apostle respectively in the *Vita* and the Harris Fragments.

78. Paulsen, *Die Briefe*, 120, on *Phil.* 7.1: "folgt eine Kennzeichnung der Gegner, bei der zunächst auffallig ist, daß sie sich aus höchst unterschiedlicher Topik (z. T. wohl auch literarisch verbittelter Polemik!) zusammenfügt."

79. Berding, *Polycarp and Paul*, 24, finds *Phil.* 7.1 to be the "fulcrum" of the letter.

Pol. Phil.	OSHT	Schoedel	Hartog	Berding	Ehrman	Bauer	Holmes	Camelot
1.1	Phil 2:17; 4:10 B.d. cf. 2 Thess		Phil 2:17 "prob." (177) "perhaps" (2013: 98)	Phil 2:17; 4:10 poss.				
1.2	Col 1:5–6 D.d.					1 Cor 15:3		
1.3	Eph. 2:8 B.b.	Eph 2:5, 8–9	Eph 2 "certainly" cf. 2:5, 8–9 (2013: 103)		Eph 2:5, 8–9	Eph 2:5, 8–9	Eph 2:5, 8–9	Eph 2:5, 8–9
2.1	Phil 2:10 B.c. cf. Phil 3:21 1 Cor 15:28 A.d.		Phil 2:10, "prob." (177)	Phil 2:20; 3:21 poss.	Eph 6:14 poss. cf. 1 Cor 15:28; Phil 2:10; 3:21	cf. Phil 3:21; 2:10; 2 Tim 4:1	cf. 1 Cor 15:28; Phil 3:21; Phil 2:10 only "poss." (2005: 213)	cf. Phil 2:10; 3:21
2.2	2 Cor 4:14 B.b.	2 Cor 4:14; cf. 1 Cor 6:14	2 Cor 4:14, "prob." (177) cf. Rom 8:11; 1 Cor 6:14; "difficult to pin down an exact literary source" (2013: 105)	2 Cor 4:14 poss.	cf. 2 Cor 4:14	cf. Rom 8:11; 1 Cor 6:14; 2 Cor 4:14	2 Cor 4:14 "no more than a possibility" (2005: 208)	2 Cor 4:14

Pol. *Phil.*	OSHT	Schoedel	Hartog	Berding	Ehrman	Bauer	Holmes	Camelot
3.2–3	2 Cor 10:1 B.d. 1 Cor 13:13 A.c. 1 Cor 8:10 A.d Rom 13:8; Gal 5:14 B.d. Gal 4:26 B.b.	1 Cor 13:13	"Pauline but cannot be traced to any specific quotation" (190). 1 Cor 13:13 preferred (2013: 115)	Phil 1:27 poss. 1 Cor 13:13 prob. Rom 13:8–10; Gal. 5:14 prob. Gal 4:26 poss.	Gal 4:26	cf. Gal 4:26; 1 Cor 13:13; Rom 13:10	Gal 4:26, "c" (2005: 210) Faith, hope, and love occur several times in Paul (2005: 206)	cf. 1 Cor 13–14
4.1–6.2			"Pauline" (190)	1 Tim prob.				"est un écho des épitres pastorales de saint Paul" (184 n. 2)
4.1	1 Tim 6:7; 6:10 B.b. Rom 13:12; 6:13; 2 Cor 6:7; Eph 6:13 B.d.	1 Tim 6:10; 6:7 2 Cor 6:7 (cf. Rom 6:13)	1 Tim 6:10; 6:7 2 Cor 6:7 "prob." (177– 78) "limited evidence" (2013: 116–17 n. 203)	1 Tim 6:10; 6:7 alm. cert. 2 Cor 6:7 prob.	cf. 1 Tim 6:10; 6:7	cf. 1 Tim 6:10; 6:7 cf. 2 Cor 6:7	cf. 1 Tim 6:10, 6:7 2 Cor 6:7; Rom 6:13 Yet, "sufficiently common" (2005: 207)	cf. 1 Tim 6:10; 1 Tim 6:7 cf. 2 Cor 6:7
4.2								"écho" (Eph 5:21ff.; 6:4; Col 3:18ff., etc.)

Pol. *Phil.*	OSHT	Schoedel	Hartog	Berding	Ehrman	Bauer	Holmes	Camelot
4.3	1 Tim 5:5 B.c. 1 Cor 14:3 A.d.	1 Cor 14:25	1 Tim 5:5 "may be an allusion" (179 n. 57) cf. 1 Cor 14:25 (2013: 118)	Phil 2:17; 4:18 poss. 1 Cor 14:25 prob.	1 Cor 14:25	cf. 1 Tim 5:5 cf. 1 Cor 14:25	1 Cor 14:25	cf. 1 Tim 5:3–16; Titus 2:3–4 cf. 1 Cor 14:25
5.1	Gal 6:7 B.b.	Gal 6:7	Gal 6:7 "Echoing" (2013: 119)	Gal 6:7 alm. cert.		cf. Gal 6:7	Gal 6:7 "b" or even a "c" (2005: 208–209)	Gal 6:7
5.2	1 Tim 3:8 B.c. cf. Eph 4:32 Phil 1:27 B.d. 2 Tim 2:11 B.c.		1 Tim 3:8 "relatively weak" (178) Phil 1:27 "prob." (177)	Phil 1:27 prob. 2 Tim 2:12 prob.	cf. 1 Tim 3:8–13; 2 Tim 2:12	cf. 2 Tim 2:12	cf. 1 Tim 3:8–13; Phil 1:27 2 Tim 2:11–12, is rated "d" (2005: 218)	2 Tim 2:12
5.3	Gal 5:17 B.d. 1 Cor 6:9 A.a.	1 Cor 6:9–10	1 Cor 6; Gal 5:16–21 "may be traced… possibly influenced by" (2013: 122)	Gal 5:17 poss. 1 Cor 6:9–10 alm. cert.	1 Cor 6:9	cf. 1 Cor 6:9–10	1 Cor 6:9	1 Cor 6:9–10
6.1	2 Cor 8:21 B.d. cf. Rom 12:17		2 Cor 8:21 "prob." (177–78) "Pauline" (190)	2 Cor 8:21 poss. 1 Tim 5:19 poss.	cf. 2 Cor 8:21	cf. Rom 12:17; 2 Cor 8:21	cf. 2 Cor 8:21	cf. Rom 12:17; 2 Cor 8:21

Pol. Phil.	OSHT	Schoedel	Hartog	Berding	Ehrman	Bauer	Holmes	Camelot
6.2	Rom 14:10, 12 B.b. cf. 2 Cor 5:10	Rom 14:10; 14:12	Rom 14:10 "clearly used" (177) 2 Cor 5:10 "prob." (177–78) "probably a conflation" (2013: 125)	Rom 14:10, 12 alm. cert. 2 Cor 5:10 prob.	cf. Rom 14:10; 12:2; 2 Cor 5:10	cf. Rom 14:10; 14:12 cf. 2 Cor 5:10	Rom 14:10, 12; 2 Cor 5:10 Rom as "d" (2005: 202–4) 2 Cor 5:10, denied (2005: 207 n. 83)	cf. Rom 14:10–12
6.3	Titus 2:14 "poss."						cf. Titus 2:14	cf. Rom 12:6–7; 1 Cor 12:10; Eph 4:11
7.1–2			2 Tim 2:18 shares the same content					
8.1	1 Tim 1:1 B.c.			1 Tim 1:1; Col 1:27 prob. cf. 1 Cor 1:22; 5:5; Eph 1:14				cf. 1 Tim 1:1; Col 1:27
9.1				Phil 1:29–30 poss.				
9.2	Phil 2:16 B.b. cf. Gal 2:2 Rom 8:17 B.d. 2 Tim 4:10 B.b.	Phil 2:16 2 Tim 4:10	Phil 2:16, "prob." (177) "may echo" (2013: 137) 2 Tim 4:10 "not decisive" (179)	Phil 2:16 prob. Rom 8:17 poss. 2 Tim 4:10 alm. cert. 2 Cor 5:15 poss.	Phil 2:16 cf. 2 Tim 4:10	cf. Gal 2:2; Phil 2:16 cf. 2 Tim 4:10; Rom 4:25; 2 Cor 5:15	Phil 2:16, "prob. ...c" (2005: 212) cf. Rom 12:10 2 Tim 4:10 "probability" (2005: 218)	Phil 2:16; Gal 2:2 cf. 2 Tim 4:10

Pol. *Phil.*	OSHT	Schoedel	Hartog	Berding	Ehrman	Bauer	Holmes	Camelot
10.1	1 Cor 15:58 A.d. cf. Col 1:23 Rom 12:10 B.d.		"echoes Pauline thought… (cf. especially Rom. 12:10; 1 Cor. 15:58; Col. 1.23)" (2013: 139)	1 Cor 15:58 or Col 1:23 prob. Rom 12:10 prob. 2 Cor 12:10 poss.		1 Cor 15:58/ Col 1:23 cf. 2 Cor 10:1	cf. 1 Cor 15:58 cf. Rom 12:10 denied (2005: 204–205)	Col 1:23; 1 Cor 15:58; Rom 13:8 "un certain nombre de textes" (188–89 n. 2)
10.2				Eph 5:21 poss.		cf. Eph. 5:21; Rom 2:24	cf. Eph 5:21	
10.3				Rom 2:24 poss.				
11.1				1 Thess 5:22 poss.	cf. 1 Thess 5:22	cf. 1 Thess 5:22	1 Thess 5:22	
11.2	1 Tim 3:5 B.d. Eph 5:5 B.c. cf. Col 3:5 1 Cor 6:2 A.b.		1 Tim 3:5 "relatively weak" (178) 1 Cor 6:2 "clearly referred to" (177)	1 Tim 3:5 poss. Eph 5:5; Col 3:5 poss. 1 Cor 6:2 alm. cert.	cf. 1 Tim 3:5 1 Cor 6:2	cf. 1 Tim 3:5 cf. 1 Cor 6:2	1 Tim 3:5 1 Cor 6:2	Eph 5:5; Col 3:5 cf. 1 Cor 6:2
11.3	2 Cor 3:2 B.d. 2 Thess 1:4 B.b.		Phil 4:15 2 Thess 1:4 "weaker evidence" (178)	Phil 4:15 or 2 Cor 3:2 poss. 2 Thess 1:4 prob.		cf. 2 Thess 1:4	1 Thess 1:4 "d" (2005: 214)	cf. 2 Thess 1.4 Also notes (190 n. 1) Phil 4:5; 2 Cor 3:2; Phil 1:3–9

Pol. *Phil.*	OSHT	Schoedel	Hartog	Berding	Ehrman	Bauer	Holmes	Camelot
11.4	2 Tim 2:25 B.c. 2 Thess 3:15 B.c. 1 Cor 12:26 A.d. 1 Cor 14:10 [*sic*] A.d.		2 Thess 3:15 "weaker evidence" (178)	2 Tim 2:25 poss. 2 Thess 3:15 prob. Pauline metaphor (1 Cor 12:12–27; Rom 14:4–8; Eph 4:4–13) prob.		cf. 2 Tim 2:25 cf. 2 Thess 3:15	2 Thess 3:15 "unlikely" (2005: 214–15)	cf. 2 Tim 2:25 cf. 2 Thess 3:15
12.1	Eph 4:26 B.b. cf. Ps 4:5 2 Tim 1:5 B.d.	Ps 4:5 as quoted in Eph 4:26		Ps 4:5a "with awareness of" Eph 4:26b prob.	Eph 4:26; Ps 4:5	Ps 4:5; Eph 4:26	Eph 4:26–27, quoting Ps 4:5	Ps 4:5; Eph 4:26
12.2	cf. Rom 4:24; 10:9; 1 Cor 14:10 [*sic*]; Gal 1:1; Col 2:12; "etc."			Gal 1:1 poss.		cf. Col 1:12 cf. 1 Tim 1:16 [*sic*]	Gal 1:1	cf. Col 1:12 Also notes 1 Cor 6:1; 2 Cor 1:1; Eph 2:19; 3:8; Phil 4:22 (192 n. 3)
12.3	Eph 6:18 B.d. 1 Tim 2:2 B.c. Phil 3:18 B.c. 1 Tim 4:15 B.d.	Eph 6:18	1 Tim 2:2 "relatively weak" (178) Phil 3:18, "prob." (177)	Eph 6:18 poss. 1 Tim 2:2 poss. Phil 3:18 prob.	cf. Eph 6:18	cf. Eph 6:18 cf. 1 Tim 2:1–2 cf. Phil 3:18 cf. 1 Tim 4:15; 1 Tim 2:2	cf. Eph 6:18 Phil 3:18 "c" (2005: 213)	Notes 1 Tim 2:2; 4:15; Col 2:10; Phil 3:18 (193 n. 4) cf. Phil 3:18
13								
14								

AFTERWORD:
SOME REFLECTIONS ON METHODS
AND APPROACHES

Andrew Gregory

This volume is published in the context of a range of recent studies on the reception of Paul. There have been at least three collections of essays on this topic in the four years before I wrote this chapter,[1] as well as a number of significant articles or monographs that touch directly or indirectly on the reception of Paul in the early Church.[2] Underpinning and giving impetus to much of this recent discussion is the realization that Paul's influence was very widespread, even if a significant number of early Christian authors neither mention him by name nor make demonstrable use of letters attributed to the apostle. Here the work of Andreas Lindemann[3] has been of

---

1. See M. F. Bird and J. R. Dodson, eds., *Paul and the Second Century*, LNTS 412 (London: T&T Clark, 2011), which considers a wide range of second century texts, including from among the Apostolic Fathers Ignatius and Polycarp; K. Liljeström, ed., *The Early Reception of Paul*, PFES 99 (Helsinki: Finnish Exegetical Society, 2011), which focuses mainly on NT texts that it dates to the late first century, although it includes one essay, by David Lincicum, which takes in *1 Clement* and *2 Clement*, and argues that in both texts Pauline influence may be seen in each author's citations from Jewish Scripture; T. Nicklas et al., eds., *Ancient Perspectives on Paul*, NTOA 102 (Göttingen: Vandenhoeck & Ruprecht, 2013), which considers authors later than the Apostolic Fathers, and compares their theological outlook with key Pauline themes that are important for the new perspective on Paul.

2. E.g. W. Arnal, "The Collection and Synthesis of 'Tradition' and the Second-Century Invention of Christianity," *MTSR* 23 (2011): 193–215; R. I. Pervo, *The Making of Paul: Constructions of the Apostle in Early Christianity* (Minneapolis: Fortress, 2010); J. M. Lieu, "The Battle for Paul in the Second Century," *ITQ* 75 (2010): 3–14. Many others are noted elsewhere in this volume.

3. A. Lindemann, *Paulus im ältesten Christentum: Das Bild des Apostels und die Rezeption der paulinischen Theologie in der frühchristlichen Literatur bis Marcion*, BZHT 58 (Tübingen: Mohr Siebeck, 1979). Note also E. Dassmann, *Der Stachel im Fleisch: Paulus in der frühchristlichen Literatur bis Irenäus* (Münster: Aschendorff,

particular significance; there is no longer any reason to suppose that Paul's influence dissipated quickly after his death, either because the communities that he had founded faded away, or because "orthodox" theologians were reluctant to quote an author whom "heretics" or "gnostics" had made their own.[4] Thus it need come as no surprise that although some Apostolic Fathers clearly make explicit or unambiguous use of at least some Pauline letters, others make no explicit reference either to the apostle or to his letters, and may demonstrate little or no acquaintance with characteristic or distinctive Pauline theology. This need not mean, of course, that the latter were not familiar either with Paul's letters or the ideas that they contain, or that they were unaware of his reputation as an authoritative teacher. Nor need it mean that they had no interest in Paul, let alone that they opposed him, because they may simply have felt no need to cite or to refer to Paul, even in contexts where later readers might suppose that they would. Nevertheless, given the widespread influence of Paul in the early church, it is intriguing that some texts show little if any evidence that his letters were of any significance for the authors of these post-Pauline texts or the likely audiences for whom they wrote.

What sets this volume apart from many of these other works is its focus on a particular body of texts, the Apostolic Fathers, most of which are dated conventionally somewhere from the end of the first century CE to around the middle of the second century CE. This means some of them may have been written at the same time or shortly after the time at which some letters attributed to Paul and now included in the New Testament were written, or during the period in which letters attributed to Paul were gathered together in the collection or collections that would become part of canonical Scripture,[5] and possibly edited in the process.[6] It may even be the case that those among or for whom some of the Apostolic Fathers wrote influenced the formation or preservation of the collection of Paul's letters. If so, they themselves may have shaped and influenced how Paul was understood in their own day and beyond, just as the ideas contained in Paul's letters, or other traditions concerning his life, may have influenced them.

1991); D. K. Rensberger, "As the Apostle Teaches: The Development of the Use of Paul's Letters in Second-Century Christianity" (PhD diss., Yale University, 1981).

4. For a brief and convenient overview, see J. Carleton Paget, "Paul and the Epistle of Barnabas," *NovT* 38 (1996): 359–81, on 359–63.

5. S. E. Porter, "When and How Was the Pauline Canon Compiled?," in *The Pauline Canon*, ed. S. E. Porter, PAST 1 (Leiden: Brill, 2004), 95–127, on 95.

6. Pervo, *The Making of Paul*.

Questions about how the impact of Paul as apostle to the Gentiles, itinerant herald of the gospel, planter of churches, and writers of letters, continued to be felt cannot be reduced to the simple question of which later authors may be shown to have known and used which of his letters, or with what degree of probability we may conclude that they did so. Thus, for example, Andreas Lindemann has made the distinction between the image of Paul as he may have been remembered and the influence of his letters and theology,[7] François Bovon has written about the difference between Paul as document (i.e. Paul read as a text) and Paul as monument (i.e. Paul remembered as a figure),[8] and Daniel Marguerat has distinguished between the documentary Paul (remembered as a writer, as mediated through his collected letters), the biographical Paul (remembered and celebrated as a herald of the gospel, as reflected in the Acts of the Apostles and in the *Acts of Paul*), and the doctoral Paul (invoked and imitated as a doctor or teacher of the Church, as exemplified in the Pastoral Epistles and other Deutero-Pauline letters).[9] Any or all of these Pauls may be the Paul whose influence may be seen in the writings of the Apostolic Fathers and in other texts, so the question of which Paul an author may know, remember, revere (or even revile?) raises wider issues than simply which Pauline letters, if any, they may have known.

Nevertheless the particular question of which Pauline letters later authors knew still remains an issue that cannot be ignored; much may rest upon it, even if its importance can be overstated. It does not follow, however, that it needs to be addressed again at length, for there is wide agreement on the broad outlines of the answer to this question. This may be seen from a comparison of the results presented in the 2005 volume, *The Reception of the New Testament in the Apostolic Fathers*,[10] with the

7. A. Lindemann, *Paulus im ältesten Christentum*, and idem, "Paul in the Writings of the Apostolic Fathers," in *Paul and the Legacies of Paul*, ed. W. S. Babcock (Dallas: Southern Methodist University Press, 1990), 25–45, on which see also, in the same volume, M. De Boer, "Comment: Which Paul?," 45–54.

8. F. Bovon, "Paul as Document and Paul as Monument," in *New Testament and Christian Apocrypha: Collected Studies II*, ed. G. E. Snyder, WUNT 237 (Tübingen: Mohr Siebeck, 2009), 307–17.

9. D. Marguerat, "Paul After Paul: A (Hi)story of Reception," in *Paul in Acts and Paul in His Letters*, WUNT 310 (Tübingen: Mohr Siebeck, 2013). Also in D. P. Moessner et al., eds., *Paul and the Heritage of Israel*, LNTS 452 (London: T&T Clark, 2012), first published in French as "Paul après Paul: une histoire de reception," *NTS* 54 (2008): 317–37.

10. A. F. Gregory and C. M. Tuckett, eds., *The Reception of the New Testament in the Apostolic Fathers* (Oxford: Oxford University Press, 2005).

results presented in the 1905 volume, *The New Testament in the Apostolic Fathers*,[11] as well as in other recent studies of one or more Apostolic Fathers. As contributors to the 2005 volume make clear, no new evidence has emerged to shake the general consensus that the author of *1 Clement* certainly knew 1 Corinthians and likely knew Romans, that Ignatius certainly knew 1 Corinthians, very likely Ephesians, and probably 1 and 2 Timothy, and that Polycarp very likely knew 1 Corinthians, Ephesians, 1 and 2 Timothy, and probably knew Romans, Galatians and Philippians, but that other Apostolic Fathers show less evidence for their demonstrable use of Paul's letters. (Neither the 1905 nor the 2005 volume included the *Epistle of Diognetus* but, as Michael Bird has shown, its author also drew on Romans and 1 Corinthians, and probably also Titus.[12])

Given the broad consensus on this particular issue, it is possible to identify at least two ways in which to advance the study of the Paul and the Apostolic Fathers. One is to look again at texts where it has not been possible to demonstrate dependence on a particular Pauline letter or concept at any point, and to ask if there is any other way in which any likely Pauline influence on the text may be discerned. The other is to return to texts where some form of dependence is not in doubt, but to ask wider questions about other ways in which further Pauline influence might be discerned elsewhere in the text. In principle, the approach to be taken to the latter need not differ significantly from the sort of questions that we might ask of the former, but scholars addressing wider questions to the latter may perhaps draw comfort from the fact that since some Pauline influence is already clear, there may be good reason to ask if more may be discerned. The fact that some influence on these texts has already been established means that there is nothing about the form or context of these texts that may have led their authors consciously to pass over in silence or even to suppress their knowledge of Paul, even if they do not necessarily acknowledge every way in which his legacy may have influenced them. Consequently, they may warrant further attention.

---

11. A Committee of the Oxford Society of Historical Theology, *The New Testament in the Apostolic Fathers* (Oxford: Clarendon, 1905).

12. M. F. Bird, "The Reception of Paul in the *Epistle to Diognetus*," in Bird and Dobson, eds., *Paul and the Second Century*, 70–90. See also the relevant sections in H. E. Lona, ed., *An Diognet*, KFA 8 (Freiburg: Herder, 2001), and C. N. Jefford, ed., *The Epistle to Diognetus (with the Fragment of Quadratus)*, OAF (Oxford: Oxford University Press, 2013).

Paul Ignored?

Texts that are usually thought to show little or no Pauline influence are the *Epistle of Barnabas*, *2 Clement*, the *Didache*, the *Martyrdom of Polycarp*, the writings of Papias, and the *Shepherd of Hermas*. They may also include *Diognetus* 11–12 if it is considered to have originated separately from the rest of that letter. These are the subjects of essays in this volume by Clayton Jefford, Paul Foster and James Carleton Paget, and I shall consider each in turn.

Jefford ranges most widely, and considers the *Didache*, the *Epistle to Diognetus* 11–12, the *Martyrdom of Polycarp*, the writings of Papias, and the *Shepherd of Hermas*. As Jefford shows, a range of reasons may be given to explain the apparent absence of any clear or demonstrable direct Pauline influence, or to suggest that more Pauline influence should be acknowledged than is often the case. Thus he posits a number of reasons why it may come as no surprise that the *Didache* shows little evidence of Pauline influence (though perhaps not none whatsoever) if it may be read as evidence for a conservative Christian Jewish perspective, even if it postdates the writing and circulation of Paul's letters. He also gives reasons why it may not be possible to see much influence of Paul in the fragmentary remains of Papias, or in the *Martyrdom of Polycarp*, which clearly draws mainly on narratives of the death of Jesus, without recourse to any claim that their authors were either unfamiliar with Paul's letters or opposed to Pauline theology.

Jefford's approach to *Epistle to Diognetus* 11–12 (which he holds to derive from a different author and context than the rest of the letter) is quite different, for he argues that it should be considered distinctively unPauline, despite the clearly Pauline outlook of *Diognetus* 1–10, and the presence of an explicit citation of Paul (named as "the apostle") at 12.5. (This citation, he argues, might be explained as an editorial insertion designed precisely to make chs. 11–12 fit more closely with the Pauline feel of chs. 1–10.) This is an intriguing hypothesis that is difficult to test, not only because of the lack of manuscript witnesses for the *Epistle to Diognetus*, but also because of the short length of chs. 11–12. Is it really the case that it should be considered "unPauline" because the influence of Johannine traditions may be prominent at this point, or might an early Christian theologian such as the author of this text not draw upon different authorities and traditions at different times, depending on the ideas that he wished to develop or the situation that he wished to address? Modern scholars may make clear distinctions between Pauline and Johannine theology, but it is neither clear that early Christians did the same, nor that they could not draw on both traditions at once, as the example of Polycarp clearly shows.

Finally, Jefford's approach to the *Shepherd of Hermas* is altogether different. Rather than accept the view that it shows little if any evidence of Pauline influence, he instead offers a sample of potential parallels with Romans, and argues that there is more evidence for its author's familiarity with Paul than is often allowed. Unfortunately he does not develop this line of argumentation beyond listing the possible parallels that he identifies, and noting why in principle it seems likely that this author (writing from Rome) would have been familiar with at least some of the letters of Paul. Thus Jefford prepares the way for others to do more work on this topic, and to ask if it is possible to provide a methodologically more secure basis for the combined cumulative evidence of a number of possible literary parallels, none of them probative by itself, and the common sense view that an author writing from Rome "must" have been aware of or familiar with at least some letters by Paul.

Whereas Jefford discusses a number of texts, Foster and Carleton Paget each focus on one alone, and approach it in a sustained and detailed way. For Foster, this means considering a number of potential parallels between *2 Clement* and the letters of Paul, with a view to whether careful close reading can demonstrate the direct literary dependence of the former on the latter. His discussion is more extensive than that of many scholars who have surveyed a similar range of evidence, but he confirms the conclusions that they have reached rather than breaking new ground: "there is no decisive evidence for establishing literary dependence between that text and any of the Pauline letters, or even of the author's knowledge of Paul"[13] – which is not to say that the author knew neither of Paul nor of his writings. However elsewhere in this volume David Eastman presents the case for literary dependence at one particular point,[14] so there is by no means unanimity on this question.

Carleton Paget's approach to *Barnabas* is very different, and allows him to argue very persuasively for the likelihood of Pauline influence, even though clear literary dependence on Paul cannot be demonstrated. His study is a carefully considered discussion in which he draws on and refines arguments that he has presented elsewhere, and advances discussion on a methodological level by showing how sustained attention to a range of factors much wider than "an over-reliance on precise verbal parallels, or the replication of so-called Pauline opinions"[15] may result in a much more nuanced and sophisticated appreciation of the possible influence of one author on the work of another than would otherwise be

13. Foster, above, 77.
14. Eastman, above, 17–18.
15. Carleton Paget, above, 82.

the case. Thus his contribution is a model of scholarship which shows how Paul may have been a shadowy but influential presence for the author of this letter, even if the direct literary dependence of the latter on the former cannot be proven on the basis of the evidence available to us. Carleton Paget not only enumerates *a priori* reasons why it seems likely that this pseudonymous letter would surely have some reference to Paul, but also shows how it likely did, even if his demonstration falls short of proof.

Paul Remembered

Other contributors discuss *1 Clement*, Polycarp or Ignatius, the three Apostolic Fathers who not only mention Paul by name (*1 Clem.* 5.5–7; 47.1–4; Ign. *Eph.* 12.2; *Rom.* 4.3; Pol. *Phil.* 3.2; 9.1; 11.2–3) but also draw unambiguously on one or more of the letters that he wrote. All begin from the position that each of those authors clearly knew at least something of Paul and his letters, and each offers different ways in which to build on that foundation.

Rothschild, for example, takes as her starting point the widely held belief that the author of *1 Clement* demonstrably drew on 1 Corinthians, and focuses on the question of how he did so. Thus she shows how the later author drew both on structural elements of 1 Corinthians, mapping its own argument on to Paul's argument, in order (like Paul) to address the problem of division between fellow believers, and demonstrates how particular allusions contribute to this over-arching goal. Her case is well made, quite apart from whether we read *1 Clement* in the particular historical context of further factionalism in Corinth or (as Rothschild argues) as an "allegorical" letter intended to address the general and widespread problem of division and difference between those who claim Paul's legacy rather than particular divisions in one specific community at one specific time. Either way, she shows how reading *1 Clement* in the light of its author's use of Paul makes a helpful contribution to our under-standing of the later text, and demonstrates the authority and influence that some post-Pauline Christians attributed to the apostle and at least the letter that we know today as 1 Corinthians.

Another contributor who adopts a similar approach to Rothschild, but achieves quite different results, is David Wilhite. Polycarp clearly knew at least some Pauline letters, and he too addressed his letter – *Philippians* – to a church in a city to which Paul had previously written. Thus Wilhite can assume Polycarp's knowledge of Paul, and (like Rothschild) focus on the question of how Polycarp used Paul in order to deal with the situation that his letter addresses. Like Rothschild, he succeeds in showing how attention to Polycarp's use of Paul contributes to our own understanding of Polycarp's rhetorical aims – but as well as note that Polycarp makes extensive use of Paul, he also observes that Polycarp makes significant use of Johannine tradition too. Polycarp, in other words, is not constrained by the Pauline tradition on which he draws, but uses it alongside other strands of earlier teaching that he considers authoritative in order to sustain the claims that he wishes to make, and to address the issue that he believes to be important (whether it be the specific problem of Valens, or more general concerns that his example raises). As Wilhite shows, it is certainly helpful to note how Polycarp used Paul. His key finding is that Polycarp used Paul not only as an authority to whom he could appeal, but also insofar as he found his teaching one helpful resource alongside other helpful resources for the particular situation that he faced.

Just as *1 Clement* and Polycarp may each be read in the light of Paul, so too they may be compared with each other in their appropriation of Paul. Thus Paul Hartog notes a number of parallels between them. These include their reference to Paul by name, their mention of a letter or letters that he wrote, and their labelling of him as "the blessed Paul." He also notes how each text refers to the ancient foundation of the churches that they address (for *1 Clement*, Corinth, and for Polycarp, Philippi) which may be an allusion to each having been founded by Paul. In addition, he notes how Polycarp may suggest that the church at Smyrna was founded at a later date, and argues that this militates against the assumption of some New Testament scholars that it, like other Asian churches addressed in Revelation, must have been founded by Paul while he was in Asia Minor. Thus, he observes, scholars who read only canonical texts miss evidence that is available elsewhere, and so fail to draw on the full range of historical evidence that is available in early Christian texts outside as well as inside the New Testament. Or, to put it in positive terms, he presents the case that evidence from the Apostolic Fathers can have a bearing on how we understand texts that happened to be included in the canon, just as canonical texts such as the letters of Paul may shed light on those other texts. Comparative studies may be beneficial in more than one direction, and later texts may shed light on earlier texts just as earlier texts may shed light on those written later. Given the relatively scant evidence that there is for the early development of the Christian church, it follows that scholars who work within a historical framework need to look past later theological distinctions, such as those drawn between canonical and non-canonical texts, and instead make full use of all the evidence that is available.

The third Apostolic Father who was clearly familiar with at least some of Paul's letters was Ignatius, who is in some sense the most Pauline of the Apostolic Fathers. He also gives scholars most to work with, since he refers to Paul in a number of his letters, so it is not surprising that he is the Apostolic Father who receives most attention in the present volume, both in three chapters devoted to him, and also in two other chapters that each range more widely.

As David J. Downs, observes, there is no doubt that Ignatius was influenced not only by Paul's writings but also by the memory of the apostle, even if the nature and extent of this influence is unclear. Thus he takes for granted not only that Ignatius knew certain letters by Paul, but also that he was aware of traditions of his martyrdom. His main interest, however, is in the wider question of the extent to which Paul's influence may be seen in Ignatius's theological thinking. The test case that he considers is the theme of union with Christ. It is a well-chosen topic, not only because the theme is prominent both in Paul and in Ignatius, which gives enough scope for a comparative approach, but also because the idea of participation in or union with Christ is not restricted to Paul and Ignatius but is found also in John. Thus Downs acknowledges that parallels or similarities between Paul and Ignatius do not in themselves demonstrate dependence, and sets himself the challenge of asking a genealogical as well as a comparative question. His conclusions are modest, but perhaps significant: although there is "a fairly high level of conceptual correspondence between Paul and Ignatius on the theme of union with Christ,"[16] it is very difficult to demonstrate that Ignatius depends on Paul for this concept, even if such a suggestion is plausible. Thus Downs offers a comparative study in which differences between Paul and Ignatius help to show what is distinctive about each author's understanding of union with Christ, as well as outlining what they have in common. This casts light not only on Paul but also on Ignatius, and emphasizes that no matter how significant Paul's influence may have been, he was not the only theologian on whom later authors could draw. Likewise, his conclusion suggests that were Ignatius to have drawn on Paul, it would hardly be surprising if he had reshaped his teaching in order to address the particular circumstances he himself faced, or drawn on Pauline teaching only in part, not least if he were drawing on Paul from memory and writing or dictating letters at speed as he travelled towards his fate in Rome.

16. Downs, above, 160.

Downs's comparative study may be compared with the studies by Maier and by Still, neither of whom seeks to articulate any form of genealogical explanation for similar material in Paul and in Ignatius. For Still, this is because his comparison of Paul's and Ignatius's respective attitudes to the prospect of their own deaths finds more evidence for difference than similarity. Both authors may write of their openness to death, but whereas he understands Paul to approach the prospect of his death in the context of eschatological salvation that lies beyond, Still understands Ignatius to see death not only as imitating the example of Jesus and of Paul, but as a redemptive end in itself. Thus although he acknowledges similarities between Ignatius and Paul, he claims (quite reasonably!) that Ignatius's perspective is shaped less by a full appreciation of the range of views that Paul expresses in different letters than by his own impending fate. Consequently, Still argues that while it is important to acknowledge Paul's influence in general terms on Ignatius's presentation of his desire to suffer and to die, it is also important to note those points at which he differs from Paul, and the importance of Ignatius's own particular context in shaping what Still takes to be Ignatius's own distinctive view. Once again, a careful comparison of the letters of these two different authors, albeit with much in common, can point to differences as well as to similarities between them.

For Maier, the difference is much more radical than it was for Still. For whereas Still, like Downs, proceeds by comparing particular passages of Paul and of Ignatius that touch on a similar topic, he distances himself from the sort of approach that considers Ignatius's letters from a strictly theological point of view, or with a view to literary influences on his thought by New Testament authors. Instead, his starting point is theoretically informed: he draws on the socio-geographical concept of Thirdspace, and uses the framework that it offers to ask how each of Paul and Ignatius conceptualise and articulate their experience of being part of religious communities that met in particular urban spaces that each of them imbued with theological significance, drawing on both widespread civic vocabulary as well as distinctively Judaeo-Christian understandings and practices in the process. Thus although Maier explicitly affirms that Ignatius drew on a Pauline legacy and almost certainly knew 1 Corinthians, his chosen method of reading each author from a theoretical perspective allows him to point to similarities and differences that may be explained by each author addressing similar issues in different contexts, rather than by the degree of faithfulness (or otherwise) that Ignatius exhibits towards Paul (either as Ignatius, or indeed others, understood him). Thus, argues Maier, Ignatius's understanding of his social world has "a Pauline imprint," but in a form that is more similar to the Paul of the Pastoral

Epistles than of 1 Corinthians (which is not to say that Ignatius's affinities with those deutero-pauline texts need mean that he drew on them; it may be that each is the result of similar historical and social pressures and arose independently of the other, but in a similar historical context).

David Eastman's study on Paul as a martyr touches on themes that Still and Downs each consider in their respective treatments of Ignatius. But Eastman ranges more widely and analyzes material that relates to the portrayal of Paul as a martyr that may be found in *1 Clement*, Ignatius, Polycarp and (he argues) *2 Clement*. His comparative approach across four texts helps to provide his discussion with breadth and texture, and his topic means that his study, more than any other in the book, focuses on an aspect of what Marguerat has called the biographical Paul. Yet even in this context he finds himself noting how later authors drew on imagery from letters attributed to Paul to articulate their understanding of Paul as a martyr. This can be seen in *1 Clement* (which, as Eastman reminds us, is the earliest evidence – or should it be explicit evidence? – for the tradition that Paul died as a martyr) where the author draws on 1 Corinthians and shows affinities with 1 Timothy (which might be earlier or later than *1 Clement*) in his description of Paul as a martyr. Similarly, he also draws on details found also in Philippians and in 2 Corinthians when he refers to hardships that Paul suffered before he died, and on a claim that might be inferred from Romans when he writes of Paul having travelled "even to the limit of the West." It is difficult to determine the extent to which *1 Clement* may have used traditions drawn directly or indirectly from Paul's letters (and possibly Acts, if it is an earlier text) to give flesh to his belief, independent of these texts, that Paul had died as a martyr, or whether that tradition might have been inferred in no small part from other texts associated with Paul. Similar issues may be noted in the letters of Ignatius; he too seems to know the tradition that Paul was a martyr (*Eph.* 12.2), and clearly wishes that he too will die as a martyr, although I am not convinced that his reference to following in Paul's footsteps need mean that Ignatius knew of Paul's death in Rome, and wanted to follow him there in order to die because that is where Paul was martyred. If that is the case, his understanding of Rome as the place of Paul's death may be compared with the same belief in *1 Clement*, which may be implicit in the ending of Acts, but it can hardly be traced to any letter attributed to Paul. By contrast, however, everything that Polycarp appears to imply about Paul's death may be paralleled in letters attributed to Paul, despite Polycarp most likely having known the text of *1 Clement*,[17] and having

---

17. K. Berding, "Polycarp's Use of *1 Clement*: An Assumption Reconsidered," *JECS* 19 (2011): 127–39.

received a letter from Ignatius, and perhaps having been familiar with some of Ignatius's other letters.[18] Even if the author of *1 Clement* or Ignatius may have known traditions that did not depend on Paul's letters, such traditions are all but subsumed by the time that Polycarp wrote within a tradition shaped by words attributed to Paul.

If Polycarp may have known the letters of Ignatius, one author who certainly did was Pseudo-Ignatius, who was probably active in Syrian Antioch in the late fourth-century, and wrote a number of letters in the name of Ignatius. These later letters make significant use of Paul whom, as Stephanie Cobb demonstrates, their author presents as "a proponent of marriage," whom he enlists to counter the rigorous asceticism that he sets out to oppose. Quite clearly, the Paul whom he enlists is Paul as known through the reading of his letters – the same epistolary Paul whom those who favoured asceticism could also enlist in their support, albeit through reference to other passages in his letters than those that their opponents used.[19] By the fourth century, the written Paul was the only Paul to whom later generations could make any sort of direct appeal, whether through letters attributed to him, or texts written about him. But even his own letters could be read in different ways, according to the needs or convictions of those who read them.

Conclusion

As contributors to this volume have shown, it can be fruitful either to take a comparative approach to Paul and to the various texts included among the Apostolic Fathers, for any such comparison may help to shed light on a period in the history of early Christianity about which we know so little, or to seek to investigate the influence of the former upon the latter. Since everything that we know of these ancient authors is mediated to us through written texts, many of them written as letters addressed to particular situations, it should come as no surprise that later readers who ask questions that the ancient authors did not address may need to approach their evidence in a variety of ways, and to read them against, as well as with, the grain. What may be surprising, however, is the extent to which the discussion depends on comparisons between what ancient authors may

18. For a list of parallels, some of which might suggest dependence, see K. Berding, *Polycarp and Paul: An Analysis of their Literary and Theological Relationship in Light of Polycarp's Use of Biblical and Extra-Biblical Literature*, VCSup 62 (Leiden: Brill, 2002), 203.

19. On which see Elizabeth Clark, *Reading Renunciation: Asceticism and Scripture in Early Christianity* (Princeton, NJ: Princeton University Press, 1999), 259–73.

have known of Paul from some of the letters attributed to him, and what they may have known of Paul from other sources. For although Paul's significance as a herald of the gospel and as church-planter and pastor can hardly be over-estimated, it is striking how little of the "historical Paul" or "Paul as he really was" may be established from the writings of the Apostolic Fathers (and indeed from many other early Christian texts). Even those authors who claim to remember Paul, and appeal to him as an authoritative teacher, or testify to his death as a martyr, record very little that does not reflect and likely depend on the Paul that they knew from one or more his letters. Thus although both the author of *1 Clement* and Ignatius may each provide independent evidence of the belief that Paul died as a martyr, which is not mentioned explicitly in any of the letters attributed to him (even if some of his letters – like Acts – might imply his imminent death), each moves very quickly from referring to Paul's death to describing it in terms drawn from Paul's own letters. Polycarp, who may have known the work of both authors, as well as a wider selection of Pauline letters than they did, also does the same.[20] Their remembered Paul is largely, if not entirely, an epistolary Paul. Consequently it is difficult, if not impossible, to extract any further biographical information about Paul from the Apostolic Fathers that is clearly independent of letters that he wrote or that other people attributed to him, and that other people collected and circulated among those who continued to look to Paul as some sort of authority, however they may have understood his role.

According to Richard Pervo, the only Paul whom later generations may meaningfully encounter is the dead Paul, all knowledge of whom depends on the book (i.e. the collection of letters attributed to Paul) that was put together by other people after Paul's death.[21] We do not know to what extent any of the Apostolic Fathers may have played a role in putting together the collection of Paul's letters, but already in their writings the process of relating to Paul primarily as known through one or more of his letters is clearly underway. That is certainly the case for the author of *1 Clement*, for Ignatius, or for any others whose demonstrable or likely knowledge of Paul is confined only to what may be found in a small number of letters. It is also true for Polycarp, who may have known most, if not demonstrably all, of the letters in the entire Pauline collection as it would emerge clearly by the late second century.

20. On the remembered Paul of these three authors, see further M. D. Holmes, "Paul and Polycarp," in Bird and Dodson, eds., *Paul and the Second Century*, 57–69, on 63–65.

21. Pervo, *The Making of Paul*.

BIBLIOGRAPHY

A Committee of the Oxford Society of Historical Theology. *The New Testament in the Apostolic Fathers*. Oxford: Clarendon, 1905.

Aageson, James W. *Paul, the Pastoral Epistles, and the Early Church*. LPS. Peabody, MA: Hendrickson, 2008.

Adams, Edward. "Paul's Story of God and Creation: The Story of How God Fulfils His Purpose in Creation." Pages 19–43 in *Narrative Dynamics in Paul: A Critical Assessment*. Edited by Bruce W. Longenecker. Louisville: Westminster John Knox, 2002.

Allison, Dale C. *James*. ICC. London: Bloomsbury T&T Clark, 2014.

———. "James 2:14–26: Polemic Against Paul, Apology for James." Pages 123–49 in *Ancient Perspective on Paul*. Edited by T. Nicklas, A. Merkt and J. Verheyden; Göttingen: Vandenhoeck & Ruprecht, 2013.

———. "The Pauline Epistles and the Synoptic Gospels: The Pattern of the Paralllels." *NTS* 28 (1982): 1–32.

Aono, Tashio. *Die Entwicklung des paulinischen Gerichtsgedankens bei den Apostolischen Vätern*. Bern: Lang, 1979.

Arnal, W. "The Collection and Synthesis of 'Tradition' and the Second-Century Invention of Christianity." *MTSR* 23 (2011): 193–215.

Ascough, Richard S. *Religious Rivalries and the Struggle for Success in Sardis and Smyrna*. Studies in Christianity and Judaism 15. Waterloo: Wilfrid Laurier University Press, 2005.

Aune, David E. *Revelation 1–5*. WBC 52A. Dallas: Word, 1997.

Aus, Roger D. "Paul's Travel Plans to Spain and the 'Full Number of the Gentiles' of Rom XI 25." *NovT* 21, no. 3 (1979): 242–46.

Babcock, W. ed. *Paul and the Legacies of Paul*. Dallas: Southern University Methodist Press, 1990.

Backus, Irena. *Historical Method and Confessional Identity in the Era of the Reformation (1378 1615)*. Studies in Medieval and Reformation Thought. Leiden: Brill, 2003.

Balabanski, Vicky. *Eschatology in the Making*. SNTSMS 97. Cambridge: Cambridge University Press, 1997.

Balch, David L. *Let Wives Be Submissive: The Domestic Code in 1 Peter*. SBL Monograph Series 26. Chico: Scholars Press, 1981.

Baldry, H. C. *The Unity of Mankind in Greek Thought*. Cambridge: Cambridge University Press, 1965.

Bammel, C. P. H. "Ignatian Problems." *JTS* 33 (1982): 62–63.

Bardenhewer, Otto. *Geschichte der altkirchlichen Literatur*. vol. 1. 2nd ed. Freiburg: Herder, 1913.

Barker, Margaret. *The Revelation of Jesus Christ*. Edinburgh: T&T Clark, 2000.

Barnard, L. W. "The Problem of St Polycarp's Epistle to the Philippians." Pages 31–39 in *Studies in the Apostolic Fathers and Their Background*. Oxford: Blackwell, 1966.

Barnes, T. D. "The Date of Ignatius." *ExpTim* 120 (2008): 119–30.

Barnett, A. E. *Paul Becomes a Literary Influence.* Chicago: University of Chicago Press, 1941.

Barr, David L. *Tales of the End: A Narrative Commentary on the Book of Revelation.* Santa Rosa: Polebridge, 1998. 21.

Barrett, C. K. *The Acts of the Apostles: A Shorter Commentary.* London: T & T Clark, 2002. 292.

———. *Critical and Exegetical Commentary on the Acts of the Apostles.* Vol. 2. ICC. Edinburgh: T&T Clark, 1998. 906.

———. "Things Sacrificed to Idols." Pages 41–42 in *Essays on Paul.* Philadelphia: Westminster, 1982.

Bartsch, Hans W. *Gnostisches Gut und Gemindetradition bei Ignatius von Antiochien.* Gütersloh: Bertelsmann, 1940.

Batten, Alicia. "The Moral World of Greco-Roman Associations." *Studies in Religion* 36 (2007): 135–51.

Bauer, J. B. *Die Polykarpbriefe.* KAV 5. Göttingen: Vandenhoeck & Ruprecht, 1995.

Bauer, Walter. *Die Briefe des Ignatius von Antiochia und der Polykarpbrief.* HNT: Apostolischen Väter 2. Tübingen: Mohr Siebeck, 1920.

———. *Orthodoxy and Heresy in Earliest Christianity.* Edited by Robert A. Kraft and Gerhard Krodel. Philadelphia: Fortress, 1971.

Baumeister, Theofried. "Zur Datierung der Schrift an Diognet." *VC* 42 (1988): 105–11.

Beale, G. K. *The Book of Revelation: A Commentary on the Greek Text.* NIGTC. Grand Rapids: Eerdmans, 1999.

Beasley-Murray, G. R. *The Book of Revelation.* NCB. London: Oliphants, 1974.

Beatrice, Pier Fanco. "Der Presbyter des Irenäus, Polykarp von Smyrna und der Brief an Diognet." Pages 179–202 in *Pléroma: Salus Carnis: Homenaje a Antonio Orbe, S.J.* Edited by Eugenio Romero-Pose. Santiago de Compostella, 1990.

Bell, Albert A. Jr. "The Date of John's Apocalypse: The Evidence of Some Roman Historians Reconsidered." *NTS* 25 (1978): 93–102.

Bence, Philip A. *Acts.* Indianapolis: Wesleyan Publishing, 1998.

Berding, "John or Paul? Who Was Polycarp's Mentor." *TynBul* 59 (2008): 140.

———. *Polycarp and Paul: An Analysis of Their Literary and Theological Relationship in Light of Polycarp's Use of Biblical and Extra-Biblical Literature.* VCSup 62. Leiden: Brill, 2002.

———. "Polycarp of Smyrna's View of the Authorship of 1 and 2 Timothy." *VC* 53 (1999): 349–60.

———. "Polycarp's Use of 1 Clement: An Assumption Reconsidered." *Journal of Early Christian Studies* 19 (2011): 127–39.

Bergamelli, Ferdinando. "L'unione a Cristo in Ignazio di Antiochia." Pages 73–109 in Vol. 1 of *Cristologia e catechesi patristica: Convegno di studio e aggiornamento, Pontificium Institutum Altioris Latinitatis (Facoltà di lettere cristiane e classiche), Roma, 17–19 febbraio 1979.* Edited by S. Felici. 2 vols. BibScRel 31. Rome: Libreria Ateneo Salesiano, 1980.

Betz, Hans Dieter. *Galatians: A Commentary on Paul's Letter to the Churches in Galatia.* Hermeneia. Philadelphia: Fortress, 1979.

Billings, Bradly S. "From House Church to Tenement Church: Domestic Space and the Development of Early Urban Christianity: The Example of Ephesus." *JTS* 62 (2011): 541–69.

Bird, Michael F. "The Reception of Paul in the Epistle to Diognetus." Pages 70–90 in *Paul and the Second Century.* Edited by M. F. Bird and J. R. Dodson. LNTS 412. London: T&T Clark, 2011.

Bird, M. F., and J. R. Dodson, eds. *Paul and the Second Century.* LNTS 412. London: T&T Clark, 2011.

Blackwell, Ben C. *Christosis: Pauline Soteriology in Light of Deification in Irenaeus and Cyril of Alexandria.* WUNT 2/314; Tübingen: Mohr Siebeck, 2011.

Blakeney, E. H. *The Epistle to Diognetus.* London: SPCK. New York: Macmillan, 1943.

Blanco, A. González. "Alusiones a España en las obras de san Juan Crisóstomo." *HAnt* 4 (1974): 352–62.

Bock, Darrell L. *Acts.* BECNT. Grand Rapids: Baker, 2007.

Bornkamm, G. "The History of the Origin of the So-called Second Letter to the Corinthians." *NTS* 8 (1961–62): 258–64.

———. *Die Vorgeschichte des sogenannten Zweiten Korintherbriefes.* SHAW 2. Heidelberg: Winter, 1961. Repr. with Addendum on pages 162–94 of Gesammelte Aufsätze. IV. Geschichte und Glaube. BevT 53. Munich: Kaiser, 1971.

Bovon, F. "Paul as Document and Paul as Monument." Pages 307–17 in *New Testament and Christian Apocrypha: Collected Studies II.* Edited by G. E. Snyder. WUNT 237. Tübingen: Mohr Siebeck.

Bovon-Thurneysen, A. "Ethik und Eschatologie im Philipperbrief des Polycarp von Smyrna." *TZ* 29 (1973): 241–56.

Bowe, Barbara E. Review of David G. Horrell, *The Social Ethos of the Corinthian Correspondence: Interest and Ideology from 1 Corinthians to 1 Clement.* SNTIW (Edinburgh: T&T Clark, 1996). *CBQ* 60 (1998): 566–68.

Bower, Richard A. "The Meaning of EPITUCHEIN in the Epistles of St. Ignatius of Antioch." *VC* 28 (1974): 1–14.

Brent, Allen. "History and Eschatological Mysticism in Ignatius of Antioch." *ETL* 65 (1989): 309–29.

———. *Ignatius of Antioch and the Second Sophistic: A Study of an Early Christian Transformation of Pagan Culture.* Studien und Texte zu Antike und Christentum 36. Tübingen: Mohr Siebeck, 2006.

———. *The Imperial Cult and the Development of Church Order: Concepts and Images of Authority in Paganism and Early Christianity Before the Age of Cyprian.* Leiden: Brill, 1999.

Brock, S. P. "Early Syrian Asceticism." *Numen* 20 (1973): 1–19.

Brown, Eric. "Hellenistic Cosmopolitanism." Pages 549–58 in *A Companion to Ancient Philosophy.* Edited by Mary Louise Gill and Pierre Pellegrin. Oxford: Blackwell, 2006.

Brown, Milton P. Jr. "Notes on the Language and Style of Pseudo-Ignatius." *JBL* 83 (1964): 146–52.

Brown, Peter. "The Rise and Function of the Holy Man in Late Antiquity." *JRS* 61 (1971). 80–101.

Brown, R. E. *An Introduction to the New Testament.* ABRL. New York: Doubleday, 1997.

Bruce, F. F. *Book of the Acts.* Rev. ed. NICNT. Grand Rapids: Eerdmans, 1988.

Bultmann, Rudolf. "Ignatius and Paul." Pages 267–77 in *Existence and Faith: Shorter Writings of Rudolf Bultmann.* Edited and translated by Schubert M. Ogden. London: Hodder & Stoughton, 1961.

Buri, Fritz. *Clemens Alexandrinus und der Paulinische Freiheitsbegriff.* Zurich: Max Niehans, 1939.

Cadoux, Cecil John. *Ancient Smyrna.* Oxford: Blackwell, 1938. 310.

Caird, G. B. *The Revelation of St. John.* Peabody, MA: Hendrickson, 1993.

Calhoun, Robert Matthew. "The Resurrection of the Flesh in 3 Corinthians." Pages 235–57 in *Christian Body, Christian Self: Concepts of Early Christian Personhood.* Edited by C. K. Rothschild and T. W. Thompson. Tübingen: Mohr Siebeck, 2011.

Calvin, John. *Institutes of the Christian Religion.* Translated by Henry Beveridge. Edinburgh: Edinburgh Printing, 1845.

Camelot, P. T. *Ignace d'Antioche, Polycarpe de Smyrne: Lettres, Martyre de Polycarpe.* 4th ed. SC 10. Paris: Cerf, 1998.

———. *Ignace d'Antioche, Polycarpe de Smyrne: Lettres, Martyre de Polycarpe.* Rev. ed. SC 10. Paris: Cerf, 2007.

Campbell, Constantine R. *Paul and Union with Christ: An Exegetical and Theological Study.* Grand Rapids: Zondervan, 2012.

Campenhausen, Hans von. *Ecclesiastical Authority and Spiritual Power in the Churches of the First Three Centuries.* Translated by J. A. Baker. London: A. & C. Black, 1969.

———. "Polykarp von Smyrna und die Pastoralbriefe." Pages 196–252 in *Aus der Frühzeit des Christentums.* Tübingen: Mohr Siebeck, 1963.

Capelle, D. B. "La 1a Clementis et l'épitre de Polycarpe." *RBén* 37 (1925): 283–87.

Carlyle, A. J. *The New Testament in the Apostolic Fathers.* Oxford: Clarendon, 1905.

Certeau, Michel de. *The Practice of Everyday Life.* Translated by Steven Rendall. Berkeley: University of California Press, 1984.

Chadwick, Henry. *The Church in Ancient Society.* OHCC. Oxford: Oxford University Press, 2001.

———, ed. *The Library of Christian Classics.* Vol. 2, *Alexandrian Christianity.* Philadelphia: Westminster, 1954.

———. "The Silence of Bishops in Ignatius." *HTR* 43 (1950): 169–72.

Charles, R. H. *A Critical and Exegetical Commentary on the Revelation of St. John.* Vol. 1. ICC. Edinburgh: T&T Clark, 1920.

———. *The Old Testament Pseudepigrapha and the New Testament.* Cambridge: Cambridge University Press, 1985.

Chilton, David. *The Days of Vengeance: An Exposition of the Book of Revelation.* Fort Worth: Dominion, 1987.

Clark, Elizabeth A. "Antifamilial Tendencies in Ancient Christianity." *Journal of the History of Sexuality* 5 (3 1995): 356–80.

———. *Founding the Fathers: Early Church History and Protestant Professors in Nineteenth-Century America.* Philadelphia: University of Pennsylvania Press, 2011.

———. "From Patristics to Early Christian Studies." Pages 7–41 in *The Oxford Handbook to Early Christian Studies.* Edited by Susan Ashbrook Harvey and David G. Hunter. Oxford: Oxford University Press, 2008.

———. *Reading Renunciation: Asceticism and Scripture in Early Christianity.* Princeton: Princeton University Press, 1999.

Collins, A. Y. *Crisis and Catharsis: The Power of the Apocalypse.* Philadelphia: Westminster, 1984.

Conzelmann, Hans. *Acts of the Apostles.* Hermeneia. Philadelphia: Fortress, 1987.

Court, John M. *Myth and History in the Book of Revelation.* London: SPCK, 1979.

———. *Revelation.* NTG. Sheffield: Sheffield Academic, 1999.

Crouch, J. E. *The Origin and Intention of the Colossian Haustafel.* FRLANT 109. Göttingen: Vandenhoeck & Ruprecht, 1972.

Cullmann, Oscar. *Peter: Disciple, Apostle, Martyr: A Historical and Theological Study.* Translated by Floyd V. Filson. 2nd ed. London: SCM, 1962.

Cureton, William. *The Ancient Syriac Version of the Epistles of Saint Ignatius to Saint Polycarp, the Ephesians, and the Romans.* London: Rivingtons, 1845.

Dahl, Nils Alstrup. "Der Erstgeborene Satans und der Vater des Teufels (Polyk. 7.1 und Joh 8.44)." Pages 70–84 in *Apophoreta: Festschrift für Ernst Haenchen*. Edited by Walther Eltester et al. Berlin: Töpelmann, 1964.

Dassmann, E. *Der Stachel im Fleisch: Paulus in der frühchristlichen Literatur bis Irenäus*. Münster: Aschendorff, 1991.

Dassmann, Ernst. *Der Stachel im Fleisch*. Munster: Aschendorff, 1979.

Davies, W. D. *Paul and Rabbinic Judaism*. London: SPCK, 1948. Repr., Philadelphia: Fortress, 1980.

De Boer, M. "Comment: Which Paul?" Pages 45–54 in *Paul and the Legacies of Paul*. Edited by W. S. Babcock. Dallas: Southern Methodist University Press, 1990.

Dehandschutter, Boudewijn. "The Epistle of Polycarp." Pages 117–33 in *The Apostolic Fathers: An Introduction*. Edited by Wilhelm Pratscher. Waco, TX: Baylor University Press, 2009.

———. "Images of Polycarp: Bibliography and Hagiography About the Bishop of Smyrna." Pages 271–77 in *Polycarpiana: Studies on Martyrdom and Persecution in Early Christianity*. Edited by B. Dehandschutter and Johan Leemans. Leuven: Leuven University Press, 2007.

———. *Martyrium Polycarpi*. BETL 52; Leuven: Leuven University Press, 1979.

———. "Polycarp's Epistle to the Philippians: An Early Example of 'Reception.'" Pages 275–91 in *The New Testament in Early Christianity*. Edited by Jean-Marie Sevrin. Louvain: Leuven University Press, 1989.

———. "Some Notes in 1 Clement 5, 4–7." *IP* 19 (1989): 83–89.

DeMar, Gary, and Francis X. Gumerlock. *The Early Church and the End of the World*. Powder Springs: American Vision, 2006.

Dibelius, Martin, and Hans Conzelmann. *The Pastoral Epistles*. Edited by Helmut Koester. Translated by Philip Buttolph and Adela Yarbro. Hermeneia; Philadelphia: Fortress, 1972.

Donaldson, James. *The Apostolical Fathers: A Critical Account of their Genuine Writings and of their Doctrines*. London: Macmillan, 1874.

Downs, David J. "Justification, Good Works, and Creation in Clement of Rome's Appropriation of Romans 5–6." *NTS* 59 (2013): 415–32.

Droge, Arthur J. "Mori Lucrum: Paul and Ancient Theories of Suicide." *NovT* 30 (1988): 263–86.

Drummond, James. "Shepherd of Hermas." In *The New Testament in the Apostolic Fathers*. Oxford: Clarendon, 1905.

Dungan, David L. *The Sayings of Jesus in the Churches of Paul*. Philadelphia: Fortress. Oxford: Blackwell, 1971.

Dunn, James D.G. *The Parting of the Ways: Between Christianity and Judaism and Their Significance for the Character of Christianity*. 2nd ed. London: SCM, 2006.

Eastman, David L. "Ignatius, pseudo-Ignatius, and the Art of Pauline Reception," *Early Christianity* 7 (2016): 1–16.

———. "Jealousy, Internal Strife, and the Deaths of Peter and Paul: A Reassessment of 1 Clement." *ZAC* 18 (2014): 34–53.

———. "Paul: An Outline of His Life." Pages 34–56 in *All Things to All Cultures: Paul Among Jews, Greeks, and Romans*. Edited by Mark Harding and Alanna Nobbs. Grand Rapids: Eerdmans, 2013.

———. *Paul the Martyr: The Cult of the Apostle in the Latin West*. WGRWSup 4. Atlanta: Society of Biblical Literature. Leiden: Brill, 2011.

Eckhardt, Karl. *August. Der Tod des Johannes als Schlüssel zum Verständnis der Johanneischen Schriften.* Berlin: de Gruyter, 1961.

Edwards, Mark J. "Ignatius and the Second Century: An Answer to R. Hübner." *ZAC* 2 (1998): 214–26.

Ehrman, Bart, ed. and trans. *The Apostolic Fathers.* 2 vols. LCL 25. Edited by Jeffrey Henderson. Cambridge, MA: Harvard University Press, 2003.

———. *Forgery and Counterforgery: The Use of Literary Deceit in Early Christian Polemics.* New York: Oxford University Press, 2013.

Elliott, John H. *A Home for the Homeless: A Social-Scientific Criticism of 1 Peter, Its Situation and Strategy.* Minneapolis: Fortress, 1981.

Elliott, Mark W. "The Triumph of Paulinism by the Mid-Third Century." Pages 244–56 in *Paul and the Second Century.* LNTS 412. Edited by Michael F. Bird and Joseph R. Dodson. London: T&T Clark, 2011.

Evans, Robert. *Reception History, Tradition and Biblical Interpretation Gadamer and Jauss in Current Practice.* London: Bloomsbury, 2014.

Farkasfalvy, Denis. "'Prophets and Apostles': The Conjunction of the Two Terms Before Irenaeus." Pages 109–34 in *Texts and Testaments.* Edited by W. Eugene March and Stuart Dickson Currie. San Antonio: Trinity University Press, 1980.

Farrer, Austin. *The Revelation of St. John the Divine.* Oxford: Clarendon, 1964.

Feuillet, André. *L'Apocalypse: état de la question.* Paris: Desclée, 1963.

Fitzgerald, John. "Haustafeln." *ABD* 3:1980–81.

Ford, J. Massyngberde. *Revelation.* AB 38. Garden City: Doubleday. 1975.

Foster, P. "Christ and the Apostles in the Epistles of Ignatius." Forthcoming.

Foster, Paul. "The Epistles of Ignatius of Antioch." Pages 81–107 in *The Writings of the Apostolic Fathers.* Edited by Paul Foster. London: T&T Clark, 2007.

———. "The Epistles of Ignatius of Antioch (Part 2)." *ExpTim* 118 (2006): 2–11.

———. "The Epistles of Ignatius of Antioch and the Writings That Later Formed the New Testament." Pages 159–86 in *The Reception of the New Testament in the Apostolic Fathers.* Edited by Andrew F. Gregory and Christopher M. Tuckett. Vol. 1 of *The New Testament and the Apostolic Fathers.* Oxford: Oxford University Press, 2005.

———. "Justin and Paul." Pages 108–25 in *Paul and the Second Century.* Edited by M. F. Bird and J. R. Dodson. LNTS 412. London: Continuum, 2011.

———. "Marcion: His Life, Works, Beliefs, and Impact." *ExpTim* 121 (2010): 269–80.

———. "Who Wrote 2 Thessalonians? A Fresh Look at an Old Problem." *JSNT* 35 (2012). 150–75.

Foucault, Michel. "Of Other Spaces." *Diacritics* 16 (1986): 22–27.

Frend, W. H. C. *Martyrdom and Persecution in the Early Church: A Study of a Conflict from the Maccabees to the Donatists.* Garden City: Anchor, 1965.

———. *The Rise of Christianity.* Philadelphia: Fortress, 1984.

Frid, A. "The Enigmatic ΑΛΛΑ in 1 Cor. 2.9." *NTS* 31 (1985): 603–11.

Friesen, Steven J. *Imperial Cults and the Apocalypse of John.* Oxford: Oxford University Press, 2001.

Funk, Franz X. *Die apostolischen Konstitutionen. Eine litterar-historische Untersuchung.* Rottenburg: Bader, 1891.

Furnish, Paul. "Paul the MARTUS." Pages 73–88 in *Witness and Existence: Essays in Honor of Schubert M. Ogden.* Edited by Philip E. Devenish and George L. Goodwin. Chicago: University of Chicago Press, 1989.

Galli, Mark. *The Apostolic Fathers.* Chicago: Moody, 2009.

Garrow, Alan J. P. "The Eschatological Tradition behind 1 Thessalonians: Didache 16."
    JSNT 32 (2009): 191–213.
———. *The Gospel of Matthew's Dependence on the Didache.* JSNTSup 254. London:
    T&T Clark, 2004.
Gathercole, S. *The Composition of the Gospel of Thomas: Original Languages and
    Influences.* Cambridge: Cambridge University Press, 2012.
Gaventa, Beverly Roberts. *The Acts of the Apostles.* ANTC. Nashville: Abingdon, 2003.
Gentry, Kenneth L. *Before Jerusalem Fell: Dating the Book of Revelation.* Tyler: Institute
    for Christian Economics, 1989.
Giesen, Heinz. *Die Offenbarung des Johannes. Regensburger Neues Testament.*
    Regensburg: Pustet, 1997.
Glimm, Francis X., Joseph Marie-Felix Marique, and Gerald Groveland Walsh. *The
    Apostolic Fathers.* FC 1. New York: Cima, 1947.
Gorman, Michael J. *Inhabiting the Cruciform God: Kenosis, Justification, and Theosis in
    Paul's Narrative Soteriology.* Grand Rapids: Eerdmans, 2009.
Grant, Robert M. "The Apostolic Fathers' First Thousand Years." *Church History* 57
    (1988): 20–28.
———. "Polycarp of Smyrna." *Anglican Theological Review* 28, no. 3 (1946): 137–48.
Grant, Robert M., and Holt H. Graham. *The Apostolic Fathers.* Vol. 2. *First and Second
    Clement.* New York: Thomas Nelson & Sons, 1965.
Gregory, Andrew F. "1 Clement and the Writings That Later Formed the New Testament."
    Pages 129–57 in *The Reception of the New Testament in the Apostolic Fathers.* Edited
    by Andrew F. Gregory and Christopher M. Tuckett. Vol. 1 of *The New Testament and
    the Apostolic Fathers.* Oxford: Oxford University Press, 2005.
Gregory, Andrew. *The Reception of Luke and Acts in the Period Before the Irenaeus:
    Looking for Luke in the Second Century.* WUNT 2/169; Tübingen: Mohr Siebeck,
    2003.
Gregory, Andrew F., and Christopher M. Tuckett. "2 Clement and the Writings That Later
    Formed the New Testament." Pages 251–92 in *The Reception of the New Testament
    in the Apostolic Fathers.* Edited by Andrew F. Gregory and Christopher M. Tuckett.
    Vol. 1 of *The New Testament and the Apostolic Fathers.* Oxford: Oxford University
    Press, 2005.
———. "Reflections on Method: What Constitutes the Use of the Writings That Later
    Formed the New Testament in the Apostolic Fathers?" Pages 61–82 in *The Reception
    of the New Testament in the Apostolic Fathers.* Edited by Andrew F. Gregory and
    Christopher M. Tuckett. Vol. 1 of *The New Testament and the Apostolic Fathers*;
    Oxford: Oxford University Press, 2005.
Guthrie, Donald. *New Testament Introduction.* Rev. ed. Downers Grove: InterVarsity,
    1990.
Hagedorn, Dieter. *Der Hiobkommentar des Arianers Julian.* PTS 14. Berlin: de Gruyter,
    1973.
Hagner, Donald A. *The Use of the Old and New Testaments in Clement of Rome.* NovTSup
    34. Leiden: Brill, 1973.
Hammond, C. E. *Liturgies Eastern and Western: Being the Texts Original or Translated of
    the Principal Liturgies of the Church.* Oxford: Clarendon, 1965.
Hannah, Jack W. "The Setting of the Ignatian Long Recension." *JBL* 79 (1960): 221–38.
Hanson, R. P. C. *The Life and Writings of the Historical Saint Patrick.* New York: Seabury,
    1983.

Harland, Philip. *Associations, Synagogues, and Congregations: Claiming a Place in Ancient Mediterranean Society.* Minneapolis: Fortress, 2003.

———. *Dynamics of Identity in the World of the Early Christians.* London: Continuum, 2009.

Harnack, Adolf von. *The History of Dogma.* Translated by Neil Buchanan. 3rd ed. New York: Dover, 1961.

———. *Die Chronologie der Literatur bis Irenäus nebst einleitenden Untersuchungen.* Leipzig: Hinrichs, 1958.

———. *Die Lehre der zwölf Apostel nebst Untersuchungen zur Geschichte der Kirchenverfassung und des Kirchenrechts.* Leipzig: Hinrichs, 1844.

———. *Die Pfaff'schen Irenäus-Fragmente als fälschungen Pfaffs nachgewiesen.* TUGAL 5/3. Leipzig: Hinrichs, 1900.

———. *Die Zeit des Ignatius und die Chronologie der Antiochenischen Bischöfe bis Tyrannus nach Julius Africanus und den späteren Historikern.* Leipzig: Hinrichs, 1878.

———. *Einführung in die alte kirchengeschichte: Das schreiben der Römischen Kirche an die Korinthische aus der zeit Domitians (I. Clemensbrief).* Leipzig: Hinrichs, 1929.

———. *Marcion: Das Evangelium vom fremden Gott.* 2nd ed. Leipzig: Hinrichs, 1924.

Harris, Horton. *Tübingen School.* Oxford: Clarendon, 1975.

Harrison, P. N. *Polycarp's Two Epistles to the Philippians.* Cambridge: Cambridge University Press, 1936.

Hartog, Paul A. "The Opponents of Polycarp, Philippians, and 1 John." Pages 375–91 in *Trajectories Through the New Testament and the Apostolic Fathers.* Edited by Andrew F. Gregory and Christopher M. Tuckett. Vol. 2 of *The New Testament and the Apostolic Fathers.* Oxford: Oxford University Press, 2005.

———. "Philippians." Pages 475–88 in *The Blackwell Companion to the New Testament.* Edited by David E. Aune. Blackwell Companions to Religion. Chichester: Wiley-Blackwell, 2010.

———. *Polycarp and the New Testament: The Occasion, Rhetoric, Theme, and Unity of the Epistle to the Philippians and Its Allusions to New Testament Literature.* WUNT 2/134. Tübingen: Mohr Siebeck, 2002.

———. "Polycarp, Ephesians, and 'Scripture.'" *WTJ* 70 (2008): 255–75.

———. *Polycarp's Epistle to the Philippians and the Martyrdom of Polycarp: Introduction, Text, and Commentary.* Oxford: Oxford University Press, 2013.

———. "The Relationship Between Paraenesis and Polemic in Polycarp, Philippians." *StPatr* (2012): 27–38.

Harvey, Susan Ashbrook. *Asceticism and Society in Crisis: John of Ephesus and the Lives of the Eastern Saints: The Transformation of the Classical Heritage.* Berkeley: University of California Press, 1990.

Hatfield, Gary. "Kant on the Perception of Space (and Time)." Pages 77–82 in *The Cambridge Companion to Kant and Modern Philosophy.* Edited by Paul Guyer. Cambridge: Cambridge University Press, 2006.

Hays, Richard B. *Echoes of Scripture in the Letters of Paul.* New Haven: Yale University Press, 1989.

———. "What Is 'Real Participation in Christ': A Dialogue with E. P. Sanders on Pauline Soteriology." Pages 336–51 in *Redefining First-Century Jewish and Christian Identities: Essays in Honor of Ed Sanders.* Edited by Fabian E. Udoh et al. Notre Dame: University of Notre Dame Press, 2008.

Hemer, Colin J. *The Letters to the Seven Churches of Asia in Their Local Setting.* Sheffield: JSOT Press, 1986.

Hengel, Martin. *The Johannine Question.* London: SCM, 1989.

Heuvel, Gerd van den. "Cosmopolite, Cosmopolitisme." Pages 41–55 in *Handbuch politisch-sozialer Grundbegriffe in Frankreich 1680–1820.* Edited by Rolf Reichardt and Eberhard Schmidt. Munich: Oldenbourg, 1986.

Hilgenfeld, Adolf. *Ignatii Antiocheni et Polycarpi Smyrnaei epistulae et martyria.* Berlin: Schwetschke, 1902.

Hill, Charles. "Cerinthus: Gnostic or Chiliast? A New Solution to an Old Problem." *JECS* 8, no. 2 (2000): 135–72.

———. *From the Lost Teaching of Polycarp: Identifying Irenaeus' Apostolic Presbyter and the Author of Ad Diognetum.* Tübingen: Mohr Siebeck, 2006.

———. "Papias of Hierapolis." *ExpTim* 117 (2006): 309–15.

———. *Regnum Caelorum.* 2nd ed. Grand Rapids: Eerdmans, 2001.

———. *Who Chose the Gospels? Proving the Great Gospel Conspiracy.* Oxford: Oxford University Press, 2010.

Hitchcock, Roswell D. "Origin and Growth of Episcopacy." *American Presbyterian and Theological Review* 5 (1867): 133–59.

Holland, Henry Scott. *The Apostolic Fathers.* London: SPCK, 1897.

Holmes, Michael W. *The Apostolic Fathers: Greek Texts and English Translations.* 3rd ed. Grand Rapids: Baker, 2007.

———. "Ignatius of Antioch." *DLNT* (1997): 530–33.

———. "The Martyrdom of Polycarp and the New Testament Passion Narratives." Pages 407–32 in *Trajectories Through the New Testament in the Apostolic Fathers.* Edited by Andrew F. Gregory and Christopher M. Tuckett. Vol. 2 of *The New Testament and the Apostolic Fathers.* Oxford: Oxford University Press, 2005.

———. "A Note on the Text of Polycarp Philippians 11,3." *VC* 51 (1997): 207.

———. "Paul and Polycarp." Pages 57–69 in *Paul and the Second Century.* Edited by M. F. Bird and J. R. Dodson. LNTS 412. London: T&T Clark, 2011.

———. "Polycarp of Smyrna, Epistle to the Philippians." Pages 108–25 in *The Writings of the Apostolic Fathers.* Edited by Paul Foster. London: T&T Clark, 2007.

———. "Polycarp's Letter to the Philippians and the Writings That Later Formed the New Testament." Pages 188–227 of *The Reception of the New Testament in the Apostolic Fathers.* Edited by Andrew F. Gregory and Christopher M. Tuckett. Vol. 1 of *The New Testament and the Apostolic Fathers.* Oxford: Oxford University Press, 2005.

Horbury, W. "Jewish–Christian Relations in Barnabas and Justin Martyr." Pages 315–45 in *Jews and Christians in Contact and Controversy.* Edinburgh: T&T Clark, 1998.

Horrell, David. "Domestic Space and Christian Meetings at Corinth: Imagining New Contexts and the Buildings East of the Theatre." *NTS* 50 (2004): 349–69.

———. *The Social Ethos of the Corinthian Correspondence: Interest and Ideology from 1 Corinthians to 1 Clement.* SNTIW. Edinburgh: T&T Clark. 1996.

Horton, Michael S. *Covenant and Salvation: Union with Christ.* Louisville: Westminster John Knox, 2007.

Howell, Kenneth J. *Ignatius of Antioch and Polycarp of Smyrna.* Rev. ed. Early Christian Fathers Series 1. Zanesville: CHResources, 2009.

Hughes, R. Kent. *Acts: The Church Afire.* Preaching the Word. Wheaton: Crossway, 1996.

Hunter, David. *Augustine: Marriage and Virginity.* WSA I/9. Hyde Park, NY: New City Press, 1999.

Hurd, John. Review of David G. Horrell, *The Social Ethos of the Corinthian Correspondence: Interest and Ideology from 1 Corinthians to 1 Clement*, SNTIW (Edinburgh: T&T Clark, 1996). *JBL* 118 (1999): 768–69.

Hurtado, Larry. "Interactive Diversity: A Proposed Model of Christian Origins." *JTS* 64 (2013): 445–62.

Hurtado, Larry W. *Lord Jesus Christ: Devotion to Jesus in Earliest Christianity.* Grand Rapids: Eerdmans, 2003.

Hvalvik, Reidar. *The Struggle for Scripture and Covenant: The Purpose of the Epistle of Barnabas and Jewish-Christian Competition in the Second Century.* WUNT 2/82. Tübingen: Mohr Siebeck, 1996.

Inge, W. R. "Ignatius." Pages 61–83 in *The New Testament in the Apostolic Fathers.* Oxford Society of Historical Theology. Oxford: Clarendon, 1905.

Isbell, A. C. "The Dating of Revelation." *Restoration Quarterly* 9 (1966): 107–17.

James, Thomas. *A Treatise on the Corruptions of Scripture, Councils, and Fathers: By the Prelates, Pastors, and Pillars of the Church of Rome, for the Maintenance of Popery.* London: Parker, 1843.

Jaubert, A., ed. *Clément de Rome: Épître aux Corinthiens.* SC 167. Paris: Cerf, 1971.

Jefford, Clayton N. *The Apostolic Fathers and the New Testament.* Peabody, MA; Hendrickson, 2006.

———. "Conflict at Antioch: Ignatius and the Didache at Odds." *StPatr* 36 (2001): 262–69.

———, ed. *The Epistle to Diognetus (with the Fragment of Quadratus).* Oxford Apostolic Fathers. Oxford: Oxford University Press, 2013.

———. "The Milieu of Matthew, the Didache, and Ignatius of Antioch: Agreements and Differences." Pages 35–47 of *Matthew and the Didache.* Edited by Huub van de Sandt. Minneapolis: Fortress. Assen: Van Gorcum, 2005.

———. "Reflections on the Role of Jewish-Christianity in Second-Century Antioch." Pages 147–67 in *Actes du colloque international.* Edited by Simon C. Mimouni with F. Stanley Jones. Lectio Divina, Hors Série. Paris: Cerf, 2001.

———. *The Sayings of Jesus in the Teachings of the Twelve Apostles.* VCSup 11. Leiden: Brill, 1989.

———. "Social Locators as a Bridge Between the Didache and Matthew." Pages 245–64 of *Trajectories Through the New Testament and the Apostolic Fathers.* Edited by Andrew F. Gregory and Christopher M. Tuckett. Vol. 2 of *The New Testament and the Apostolic Fathers.* Oxford: Oxford University Press, 2005.

Jervell, Jacob. *Die Apostelgeschichte.* KEK 3. Göttingen: Vandenhoeck & Ruprecht, 1998.

Johnson, Luke Timothy. *The Acts of the Apostles.* Sacra Pagina 5. Collegeville: Liturgical Press, 1992.

Joly, Robert. *Le dossier d'Ignace d'Antioche.* Université libre de Bruxelles. Faculté de Philosophie et Lettres 69. Brussels: Éditions de l'Université de Bruxelles, 1979.

Jones, C. P. *The Roman World of Dio Chrysostom.* Cambridge, MA: Harvard University Press, 1978.

Karrer, Martin. *Die Johannesoffenbarung als Brief.* Göttingen: Vandenhoeck & Ruprecht, 1986.

Kayser, C. L., ed. *Flavii Philostrati Opera.* Vol. 1. Leipzig: Teubner, 1870.

Kelhoffer, James A. "Suffering as Defense of Paul's Apostolic Authority in Galatians and 2 Corinthians 11." *SEÅ* 74 (2009): 127–43.

Kent, Homer A. *Jerusalem to Rome: Studies in the Book of Acts.* Grand Rapids: Baker, 1972.

Kirk, Alexander N. "Ignatius' Statements of Self-Sacrifice: Intimations of an Atoning Death or Expressions of Exemplary Suffering?" *JTS* 64 (2013): 66–88.

———. "Paul's Approach to Death in His Letters and in Early Pauline Effective History." PhD diss., Oxford University, 2013.

Kleist, James A. *The Didache; the Epistle of Barnabas; the Epistles and the Martyrdom of St. Polycarp; the Fragments of Papias; the Epistle to Diognetus.* ACW 6. Westminster: Newman, 1948.

Klek, J. *Symbuleu-tui qui dicitur sermoms historia critica.* Kirchhain: Schmersow, 1919.

Knox, John. *Marcion and the New Testament: An Essay in the Early History of the Canon.* Chicago: University of Chicago Press, 1942.

Koester, Helmut. "The Apostolic Fathers and the Struggle for Christian Identity." *ExpTim* 117 (4 2006): 133–39.

———. "Gospel and Gospel Traditions in the Second Century." Pages 27–44 of *Trajectories Through the New Testament and the Apostolic Fathers.* Edited by Andrew F. Gregory and Christopher M. Tuckett. Vol. 2 of *The New Testament and the Apostolic Fathers.* Oxford: Oxford University Press, 2005.

———. *Introduction to the New Testament: History and Literature of Early Christianity.* Berlin: de Gruyter, 2000.

———. *Synoptische Überlieferung bei den Apostolischen Vätern.* TU 65. Berlin: Akademie Verlag, 1957.

Kok, M. "The True Covenant People: Ethnic Reasoning in the Epistle of Barnabas." *Studies in Religion/Science religieuses* 40 (2011): 81–97.

Körtner, Ulrich H. J. *Papias von Hierapolis.* Göttingen: Vandenhoeck & Ruprecht, 1985.

Kramer, H. *Quid valeat homonoia in littens graecis.* PhD diss., Göttingen University, 1915.

Krodel, Gerhard. *Acts.* ACNT. Minneapolis: Augsburg, 1986.

Krüger, Gustav. "Briefe des Ignatius und Polykarp." Pages 190–200 in *Handbuch zu den neutestamentlichen Apokryphen.* Edited by Edgar Hennecke. Tübingen: Mohr Siebeck, 1904.

Ladd, George Eldon. *A Commentary on the Revelation of John.* Grand Rapids: Eerdmans, 1972.

Lake, Kirsopp. *Apostolic Fathers.* LCL. Boston: Harvard University Press, 1985.

———. *Apostolic Fathers*, Vol. 1. LCL. Cambridge, MA: Harvard University Press, 1912.

Lampe, G. W. H., ed. *A Patristic Greek Lexicon.* Oxford: Clarendon, 1961.

Lanfranchi, P., and J. Verheyden. "Jacob and Esau: Who are They? The Use of Romans 9:10–13 in Anti-Jewish Literature of the First Centuries." Pages 297–316 in *Ancient Perspective on Paul.* Edited by T. Nicklas, A. Merkt and J. Verheyden. Göttingen: Vandenhoeck & Ruprecht, 2013.

Larkin, William J. Jr. *Acts.* IVPNTC. Downers Grove: InterVarsity, 1995.

Layton, Bentley. *Gnostic Scriptures.* ABRL; New York: Doubleday, 1987.

———. "The Sources, Date and Transmission of Didache 1.3b–2.1." *HTR* 61 (1968): 343–83.

Lechner, Thomas. *Ignatius Adversus Valentinianos? Chronologische und theologischicht-liche Studien zu den Briefen des Ignatius von Antiochien.* VCSup 47. Leiden: Brill, 1999.

Lefebvre, Henri. *The Production of Space.* Translated by Donald Nicholson Smith. Oxford: Blackwell, 1991.

Lieu, Judith. "'As Much My Apostle As Christ Is Mine': The Dispute Over Paul Between Tertullian and Marcion." *Early Christianity* 1 (2010): 41–59.

———. 'The Battle for Paul in the Second Century.' *ITQ* 75 (2010): 3–14.

———. *Image and Reality: The Jews in the World of the Christians in the Second Century.* London: T&T Clark, 1996.

———. "Marcion and the Synoptic Problem." Pages 731–51 of *New Studies in the Synoptic Problem.* Leuven: Peeters, 2011.

———. "'The Parting of the Ways,': Theological Construct or Historical Reality?" *JSNT* 56 (1994): 101–19.

Lightfoot, J. B. *The Apostolic Fathers: Clement, Ignatius, and Polycarp.* Peabody, MA: Hendrickson, 1989.

Liljeström, K. ed. *The Early Reception of Paul.* PFES 99. Helsinki: Finnish Exegetical Society, 2011.

Lindemann, Andreas. "Antwort auf die 'Thesen zur echtheit und Datierung der sieben Briefe des Ignatius von Antiochien.'" *ZAC* 1 (1997): 185–94.

———. *Die Clemensbriefe.* HNT 17. Tübingen: Mohr Siebeck, 1992.

———. "Paul in the Writings of the Apostolic Fathers." Pages 25–45 of *Paul and the Legacies of Paul.* Edited by W. S. Babcock. Dallas: Southern Methodist University Press, 1990.

———. "Paulinische Theologie im Brief an Diognet." Pages 337–50 in *Kerygma and Logos.* Edited by A. M. Ritter. Göttingen: Vandenhoeck & Ruprecht, 1979.

———. "Paul's Influence on 'Clement' and Ignatius." Pages 11–24 in *Trajectories Through the New Testament and the Apostolic Fathers.* Edited by Andrew F. Gregory and Christopher M. Tuckett. Vol. 2 of *The New Testament and the Apostolic Fathers.* Oxford: Oxford University Press, 2005.

———. "Paulus im zweiten Jahrhundert." Pages 294–322 in *Paulus Apostel und Lehrer derKirche.* Tübingen: Mohr, 1999.

———. "Paulus in den Schriften der Apostolischen Väter." Pages 252–79 in *Paulus Apostel und Lehrer der Kirche.* Tübingen: Mohr, 1999.

———. *Paulus im ältesten Christentum: das Bild des Apostels und die Rezeption der paulinischen Theologie in der frühchristlichen Literatur bis Marcion.* BHT 58. Tubingen: Mohr, 1979.

Lindemann, Andreas, and Henning Paulsen. *Die Apostolischen Väter.* Tübingen: Mohr Siebeck, 1992.

Lipinski, E. "L'apocalypse et le martyre e Jean à Jérusalem." *NovT* 11 (1969): 225–32.

Lona, Horacio E. ed., *An Diognet.* KFA 8; Freiburg: Herder, 2001.

———. *Der erste Clemensbriefe.* KAV 2. Göttingen: Vandenhoeck & Ruprecht, 1998.

———. "'Petrus in Rom' und der erste Clemensbrief." Pages 221–46 in *Petrus und Paulus in Rom.* Edited by Stefan Heid. Freiburg: Herder, 2011.

Lotz, John-Paul. *Ignatius and Concord: The Background and Use of the Language of Concord in the Letters of Ignatius of Antioch.* Patristic Studies 8. New York: Lang, 2007.

Lüdemann, Gerd. *The Acts of the Apostles: What Really Happened in the Earliest Days of the Church.* Amherst: Prometheus, 2005.

———. *Paul: The Founder of Christianity.* New York: Prometheus, 2002.

Lull, David J. "Paul and Empire." *RelSRev* 36 (2010): 252–62.

MacDonald, Dennis R. *Two Shipwrecked Gospels.* ECIL 8. Atlanta: Society of Biblical Literature, 2012.

Maier, Harry O. *Picturing Paul in Empire: Imperial Image, Text and Persuasion in Colossians, Ephesians and the Pastoral Epistles*. London: T&T Clark, 2013.

———. "The Politics and Rhetoric of Discord and Concord in Ignatius and Paul." Pages 307–24 in *Trajectories through the New Testament and the Apostolic Fathers*. Edited by Andrew F. Gregory and Christopher M. Tuckett. Vol. 2 of *The New Testament and the Apostolic Fathers*. Oxford: Oxford University Press, 2005.

———. "Purity and Danger in Polycarp's Epistle to the Philippians: The Sin of Valens in Social Perspective." *JECS* 1 (1993): 229–47.

———. *The Social Setting of the Ministry as Reflected in the Writings of Hermas, Clement, and Ignatius*. Studies in Christianity and Judaism/Études sur le christanisme et le judaisme 12. Waterloo, ON: Wilfred Laurier University Press, 2002.

Malherbe, A. J. *Ancient Epistolary Theorists*. SBL 19. Atlanta: Scholars, 1988.

Mangina, Joseph. *Revelation*. Brazos Theological Commentary on the Bible. Grand Rapids: Brazos, 2010.

Marguerat, D. "Paul After Paul: A (Hi)story of Reception." In *Paul in Acts and Paul in His Letters*. WUNT 310. Tübingen: Mohr Siebeck, 2013.

———. "Paul après Paul: une histoire de reception." *NTS* 54 (2008): 317–37.

Marrou, Henri I. *A Diognète*. 2nd ed. SC 33. Paris: Cerf, 1965.

Marshall, I. Howard. *Acts*. TNTC 5. Downers Grove: InterVarsity, 2008.

———. *The Pastoral Epistles*. ICC. Edinburgh: T&T Clark, 1999.

Marshall, John W. "Misunderstanding the New Paul: Marcion's Transformation of the Sonderzeit Paul." *Journal of Early Christian Studies* 20 (2012): 1–29.

———. "Parables of the War: Reading the Apocalypse Within Judaism and During the Judaean War." 2 vols. PhD diss., Princeton University, 1997.

Marshall, Peter. *Enmity in Corinth: Social Conventions in Paul's Relations with the Corinthians*. WUNT 2/23. Tübingen: Mohr Siebeck, 1987.

Martin, Dale B. *The Corinthian Body*. New Haven: Yale University Press, 1995.

McNeile, A. H. *An Introduction to the Study of the New Testament*. Rev. ed. Oxford: Clarendon, 1927.

Meggitt, Justin. *Paul, Poverty and Survival*. Studies in the New Testament and Its World. Edinburgh: Clark, 1998.

Meinhold, P. "Geschichte und Exegese im Barnabasbrief." *ZKG* 59 (1940): 255–303.

———. "Polykarpos (1)." *Realencyclopädie der classischen Altertumswissenschaft 21* (1952): 1685–87.

———. *Studien zu Ignatius von Antiochien*. Veröffentlichungen des Insituts für europäische Geschichte Mainz 97. Wiesbaden: Steiner, 1979.

Mellink, A. O. "Death as Eschaton: A Study of Ignatius of Antioch's Desire for Death." PhD diss., University of Amsterdam, 2000.

———. "Ignatius' Road to Rome: From Failure to Success or in the Footsteps of Paul?" Pages 127–65 in *Recycling Biblical Figures*. Edited by Athalya Brenner and Jan Willem van Henten. Leiden: Deo, 1999.

Middleton, Arthur. *Fathers and Anglicans: The Limits of Orthodoxy*. Hertfordshire: Gracewing, 2001.

Milavec, Aaron. *The Didache*. New York: Newman, 2003.

———. "The Saving Efficacy of the Burning Process in Didache 16.5." Pages 133–55 in *The Didache in Context*. Edited by Clayton N. Jefford. NovTSup 77. Leiden: Brill, 1995.

Mitchell, Margaret M. *Paul and the Rhetoric of Reconciliation: An Exegetical Investigation of the Language and Composition of 1 Corinthians*. Louisville: Westminster John Knox, 1992.

Mitchell, Matthew W. "In the Footsteps of Paul: Scriptural and Apostolic Authority in Ignatius of Antioch." *JECS* 14 (1 2006): 27–45.

Moberly, Robert B. "When Was Revelation Conceived?" *Bib* 73 (1992): 376–93.

Moessner, D. P. et al., eds. *Paul and the Heritage of Israel*. LNTS [JSNTS] 452. London: T&T Clark, 2012.

———. "Paul après Paul: une histoire de reception." *NTS* 54 (2008): 317–37.

Moles, J. L. "Cynic Cosmopolitanism." Pages 105–20 in *The Cynics: The Cynic Movement in Antiquity and Its Legacy*. Edited by R. Bracht Branham and Marie-Odile Goulet-Cazé. Berkeley: University of California Press, 1996.

Moll, Sebastian. *The Arch-Heretic Marcion*. WUNT 250. Tübingen: Mohr Siebeck, 2010.

Morris, Leon. *Revelation*. 2nd ed. TNTC 20. Downers Grove: InterVarsity, 1987.

Moss, C. "On the Dating of Polycarp: Rethinking the Place of the Martyrdom of Polycarp in the History of Christianity." *EC* 1, no. 4 (2010): 539–74.

———. *The Other Christs: Imitating Jesus in Ancient Christian Ideologies of Martyrdom*. New York: Oxford University Press, 2010.

Mounce, Robert H. *The Book of Revelation*. Rev. ed. NICNT. Grand Rapids: Eerdmans, 1997.

Mounce, W. D. *The Pastoral Epistles*. WBC 46. Nashville: Thomas Nelson, 2000.

Muddiman, J. B. "The Church in Ephesians, 2 Clement, and Hermas." Pages 107–21 in *Trajectories Through the New Testament and the Apostolic Fathers*. Edited by Andrew F. Gregory and Christopher M. Tuckett. Vol. 2 of *The New Testament and the Apostolic Fathers*. Oxford: Oxford University Press, 2005.

Murray, John. *Redemption—Accomplished and Applied*. Grand Rapids: Eerdmans, 1955.

Nicklas, T. et al., eds. *Ancient Perspectives on Paul*. NTOA 102. Göttingen: Vandenhoeck & Ruprecht, 2013.

Niederwimmer, Kurt. *The Didache*. Edited by Harold W. Attridge. Translated by Linda M. Maloney. Hermeneia. Minneapolis: Fortress, 1998.

Nielsen, C. M. "The Epistle to Diognetus: Its Date and Relationship to Marcion." *AThR* 52 (1970): 82–83.

———. "Polycarp and Marcion: A Note." *Journal of Theological Studies* 47 (1952): 297–99.

———. "Polycarp, Paul and the Scriptures." *Anglican Theological Review* 47 (1965). 199–216.

Oakes, Peter. "Leadership and Suffering in the Letters of Polycarp and Paul to the Philippians." Pages 353–70 in *Trajectories Through the New Testament and the Apostolic Fathers*. Edited by Andrew F. Gregory and Christopher M. Tuckett. Vol. 2 of *The New Testament and the Apostolic Fathers*. Oxford: Oxford University Press, 2005.

———. *Philippians: From People to Letter*. SNTSMS 110. Cambridge: Cambridge University Press, 2001.

———. *Reading Romans in Pompeii*. London: SPCK; Minneapolis: Fortress, 2009.

———. "Urban Structure and Patronage: Christ Followers in Corinth." Pages in *Understanding the Social World of the New Testament*. Edited by Dietmar Neufeld and Richard E. DeMaris. London: Routledge, 2010.

O'Connor, Jerome Murphy. *St Paul's Corinth: Texts and Archaeology*. 3rd ed. Collegeville, MN: Liturgical Press, 2002.

O'Loughlin, Thomas. *The Didache*. Grand Rapids: Baker; London: SPCK, 2010.

Osborne, Grant R. *Revelation*. BECNT. Grand Rapids: Baker, 2002.

Osiek, Carolyn. *The Shepherd of Hermas*. Hermeneia. Minneapolis: Fortress, 1999.

Oxford Society of Historical Theology. *The New Testament in the Apostolic Fathers*. Oxford: Clarendon, 1905.

Pagels, E. *The Gnostic Paul: Gnostic Exegesis of the Pauline Letters.* London: Continuum, 1975.

———. *Revelations: Visions, Prophecy, and Politics in the Book of Revelation.* New York: Viking, 2012.

Paget, Carleton. "Barnabas 9.4: A Peculiar Verse on Circumcision." Pages 77–89 of *Jews, Christians, and Jewish Christians in Antiquity.* Tübingen: Mohr Siebeck, 2010.

———. "Barnabas and the Outsiders: Jews and Their World in the Epistle of Barnabas." In *Communities in the Second Century: Between Ideal and Reality.* Edited by M. Grundeken and J. Verheyden; Tübingen: Mohr Siebeck, 2015.

———. "The Epistle of Barnabas and the Writings That Later Formed the New Testament." Pages 222–49 in *The Reception of the New Testament in the Apostolic Fathers.* Edited by Andrew F. Gregory and Christopher M. Tuckett. Vol. 1 of *The New Testament and the Apostolic Fathers.* Oxford: Oxford University Press, 2005.

———. *The Epistle of Barnabas: Outlook and Background.* WUNT 2/64. Tubingen: Mohr, 1994.

———. "Paul and the Epistle of Barnabas." *NovT* 38 (1996): 359–81.

———. "Pseudo-Clementine Homilies 4–6: Rare Evidence of a Jewish Literary Source from the Second Century CE." Pages 427–92 of *Jews, Christians, and Jewish Christians in Antiquity.* Tübingen: Mohr Siebeck, 2010.

Palmer, D. V. "To Die Is Gain (Philippians 1:21)." *NovT* 17 (1975): 203–18.

Parvis, P. "2 Clement and the Meaning of the Christian Homily." Pages 32–41 in *The Writings of the Apostolic Fathers.* Edited by P. Foster. London: T&T Clark, 2007.

Paulsen, Henning. *Die Briefe des Ignatius von Antiochia und der Brief des Polykarp von Smyrna.* HNT: Apostolischen Väter 2. Tübingen: Mohr Siebeck, 1985.

Pearson, John. *Vindiciae epistolarum S. Ignatii.* Cambridge: Hayes, 1672.

Peretto, Elio. *Clemente Romano: Lettera ai Corinzi.* Bologna: Dehoniane, 1999.

Perkins, Judith. "The 'Self' as Sufferer." *HTR* 85 (1992): 245–72.

Pervo, Richard I. *Acts: A Commentary.* Edited by Harold W. Attridge. Hermeneia. Minneapolis: Fortress, 2009.

———. *Dating Acts: Between the Evangelists and the Apologists.* Santa Rosa, CA: Polebridge, 2006.

———. *The Making of Paul: Constructions of the Apostle in Early Christianity.* Minneapolis: Fortress, 2010.

Peterson, David G. *The Acts of the Apostles.* PNTC. Grand Rapids: Eerdmans, 2009.

Pfleiderer, O. *Paulinismus: ein Beitrag zur Geschichte der urchristlichen Theologie.* 2nd ed. Leipzig: J. Hinrichs, 1890.

Polhill, John B. *Paul and His Letters.* Nashville: Broadman & Holman, 1999.

Porter, Stanley E. 'When and How Was the Pauline Canon Compiled?' Pages 95–127 of *The Pauline Canon.* PAST 1. Leiden: Brill, 2004.

Porter, Stanley E., and Thomas H. Olbricht, eds. *Rhetoric and the New Testament.* JSNTSup 90. Sheffield: Sheffield Academic, 1993.

Pratscher, Wilhelm, ed. *The Apostolic Fathers: An Introduction.* Waco, TX: Baylor University Press, 2010.

Preiss, Theo. "La mystique de l'imitation de Christ et de l'unité chez Ignace d'Antioch." *RHPR* 18 (1938): 197–241.

Prigent, Pierre. "Au temps de l'Apocalypse." *RHPR* 54 (1974): 455–83; 55 (1975): 215–35.

Prostmeier, Ferdinand R. "Antijüdische Polemik im Rahmen christlicher Hermeneutik. Zum Streit über christliche Identität in der Alten Kirche. Notizen zum Barnabasbrief." *ZAC* 6 (2002): 38–58.

———. *Der Barnabasbrief.* Göttingen: Vandenhoeck & Ruprecht 1999.

Radt, Stefan, ed. *Strabons Geographika.* Vol. 1. Göttingen: Vandenhoeck & Ruprecht, 2002.

Räisänen, H. "'The Hellenists': A Bridge Between Jesus and Paul?" Pages 149–202 of *Jesus, Paul and Torah: Collected Essays.* Sheffield: JSOT Press, 1992.

———. "Marcion." Pages 100–124 in *A Companion to Second-Century Christian "Heretics."* Edited by Antti Marjanen and Petri Luomanen. Leiden: Brill, 2005.

Rathke, Heinrich. *Ignatius von Antiochien und die Paulusbriefe.* TU 99. Berlin: Akadamie, 1967.

Reis, David M. "Following in Paul's Footsteps: Mimesis and Power in Ignatius of Antioch." Pages 287–305 in *Trajectories through the New Testament and the Apostolic Fathers.* Edited by Andrew F. Gregory and Christopher M. Tuckett. Vol. 2 of *The New Testament and the Apostolic Fathers.* Oxford: Oxford University Press, 2005.

Rensberger, D. K. "As the Apostle Teaches: The Development of the Use of Paul's Letters in Second-Century Christianity." PhD diss., Yale University, 1981.

———. *The New Testament in the Apostolic Fathers.* Edited by A. J. Carlyle, for the Committee of the Oxford Society of Historical Theology. Oxford: Clarendon, 1905.

———. "The Use of Paul's Letters in Second-Century Christianity." In *The Writings of St. Paul.* Edited by Wayne A. Meeks and John T. Fitzgerald. 2nd ed. New York: W. W. Norton, 2007.

Resch, D. Alfred. *Der paulinismus und die Logia Jesu.* TUGAL 27, Bd. 12. Edited by Oscar de Gebhardt and Adolf von Harnack. Leipzig: Hinrichs, 1904.

Reumann, John. *Philippians: A New Translation with Introduction and Commentary.* AYB. New Haven: Yale University Press, 2008.

Rhodes, James. "Barnabas 4.6B: The Exegetical Implications of a Textual Problem." *VC* 58 (2004): 365–92.

———. *The Epistle of Barnabas and the Deuteronomic Tradition.* WUNT 2/188. Tübingen: Mohr Siebeck, 2004.

Richardson Cyril C., ed. *Early Christian Fathers.* LCC 1. London: SCM, 1953.

Ritter, A. M. "De Polycarpe à Clément: Aux origines d'Alexandrie chrétienne." Pages 151–72 in *ΑΛΕΞΑΝΔΡΙΝΑ: Hellénisme, judaïsme et christianisme à Alexandrie.* Edited by P. Claude Mondésert. Paris: Cerf, 1987.

Rius-Camps, J. *The Four Authentic Letters of Ignatius, the Martyr.* Christianismos 2. Rome: Pontificium Institutum Orientalium Studiorum, 1979.

Robinson, John A. T. *Redating the New Testament.* Philadelphia: Westminster, 1976.

Robinson, Thomas A. *Ignatius of Antioch and the Parting of the Ways: Early Jewish-Christian Relations.* Grand Rapids: Baker Academic, 2009.

Rothschild, Clare K. *Hebrews as Pseudepigraphon: The History and Significance of the Pauline Attribution of Hebrews.* WUNT 1/235; Tübingen: Mohr Siebeck, 2009.

Rowland, Christopher. *The Open Heaven: A Study in Apocalyptic in Judaism and Early Christianity.* New York: Crossroad, 1982.

Rowland, Christopher. *Revelation.* Epworth Commentaries. London: Epworth, 1993.

Ruinart, Thierry. *Acta primorum martyrum sincera et selecta.* Paris: Muguet, 1689.

Runesson, Anders. "Inventing Christian Identity: Paul, Ignatius, and Theodosius I." Pages 59–92 in *Exploring Early Christian Identity.* Edited by Bengt Holmberg. WUNT 226. Tübingen: Mohr Siebeck, 2008.

Sack, Robert David. *Homo Geographicus: A Framework for Action, Awareness, and Moral Concern*. Baltimore: Johns Hopkins University Press, 1997.

———. *Human Territoriality: Its Theory and History*. Cambridge Studies in Historical Geography. Cambridge: Cambridge University Press, 1986.

Sampley, J. Paul, and Peter Lampe. eds. *Paul and Rhetoric*. Edinburgh: T&T Clark, 2010.

Sanders, E. P. *Paul and Palestinian Judaism: A Comparison of Patterns of Religion*. Minneapolis: Fortress, 1977.

Scheck, Thomas P. *Origen: Commentary on the Epistle to the Romans, Books 1–5*. Fathers of the Church 103. Washington, DC: Catholic University of America Press, 2001.

Schleyer, Dietrich. *De praescriptione haereticorum*. Fontes Christiani 42. Turnhout: Brepols, 2002.

Schmithals, Walter. "The Pre-Pauline Tradition in 1 Corinthians 15:20–28." *PRSt* 20 (1993): 357–80.

Schoedel, William R. *Ignatius of Antioch: A Commentary on the Letters of Ignatius of Antioch*. Hermeneia. Philadelphia: Fortress, 1985.

———. *Polycarp, Martyrdom of Polycarp, Fragments of Papias*. Vol. 5 of Robert M. Grant, *The Apostolic Fathers: A New Translation and Commentary*. New York: Nelson, 1964.

Schofield, Malcolm. *The Stoic Idea of the City*. Cambridge: Cambridge University Press, 1991.

Schwartz, D. R. *Studies in the Jewish Background of Christianity*. WUNT 1/60. Tübingen: Mohr Siebeck, 1992.

Schweitzer, Albert. *The Mysticism of Paul the Apostle*. Translated by William Montgomery. Baltimore: Johns Hopkins University Press, 1998.

Schweizer, Eduard. "Der zweite Thessalonicherbrief ein Philipperbrief?" *TZ* 1 (1945): 90–105.

Siegert, Folker. "Unbeachtete Papiaszitate bei armenischen Schriftstellern." *NTS* 27 (1981): 605–14.

Skarsaune, O. *The Proof from Prophecy: A Study in Justin Martyr's Proof-Text Tradition: Text Type, Provenance, Theological Profile*. Leiden: Brill, 1987.

Smith, Carl B. "Ministry, Martyrdom, and Other Mysteries: Pauline Influence on Ignatius of Antioch." Pages 37–56 of *Paul and the Second Century*. Edited by Michael F. Bird and Joseph R. Dodson. LNTS 412. London: T&T Clark, 2011.

Smith, James David. "The Ignatian Long Recension and Christian Communities in Fourth Century Syrian Antioch." PhD diss., Harvard University, 1986.

Smith, Johnathan Z. *To Take Place: Toward a Theory in Ritual*. Chicago: University of Chicago Press, 1992.

Soja, Edward W. *Thirdspace: Journeys to Los Angeles and Other Real-and-Imagined Places*. Oxford: Blackwell, 1996.

Son, Sang-Won. *Corporate Elements in Pauline Anthropology: A Study of Selected Terms, Idioms, and Concepts in the Light of Paul's Usage and Background*. AnBib 148. Rome: Pontifical Biblical Institute, 2001.

Sproul, R. C. The Last Days According to Jesus. Grand Rapids: Baker, 1998.

Staniforth, Maxwell, and Andrew Louth. *Early Christian Writings: The Apostolic Fathers*. Rev. ed. London: Penguin, 1987.

Steenberg, Matthew C., and Dominic J. Unger. *St. Irenaeus of Lyons: Against the Heresies (Book 3)*. ACW 64. New York: Paulist, 2012.

Steinmetz, Peter. "Polykarp von Smyrna über die Gerechtigkeit." *Hermes* 100 (1972): 63–75.

Steward, Eric. "New Testament Space/Spatiality." *Biblical Theology Bulletin* 42 (2012): 139–50.

Stewart-Sykes, Alistair. *The Life of Polycarp: An Anonymous Vita from Third-Century Smyrna.* Sydney: St. Pauls, 2002.

Still, Todd D. *Philippians & Philemon.* Smyth & Helwys Bible Commentary 22. Macon: Smyth & Helwys, 2011.

———. "Shadow and Light: Marcion's (Mis)Construal of the Apostle Paul." Pages 91–107 of *Paul and the Second Century.* Edited by Michael F. Bird and Joseph R. Dodson. London: T&T Clark, 2011.

Stolt, Jan. "Om dateringen af Apokalypsen." *DTT* 40 (1977): 202–7.

Stoops, Robert Jr. "If I Suffer… Epistolary Authority in Ignatius of Antioch." *HTR* 80 (1987): 161–78.

Streeter, B. H. *The Four Gospels.* London: Macmillan, 1924.

———. *The Primitive Church.* London: Macmillan, 1929.

Sullivan, F. A. *From Apostles to Bishops: The Development of the Episcopacy in the Early Church.* Mahwah, NJ: Newman, 2001.

Swartley, Willard M. "The Imitatio Christi in the Ignatian Letters." *VC* 27 (1973): 81–103.

Sweet, J. P. M. *Revelation.* Philadelphia: Westminster, 1979.

Tajra, Harry. *The Martyrdom of St. Paul: Historical and Judicial Context, Traditions, and Legends.* WUNT 2/67. Tübingen: Mohr Siebeck, 1994.

The Oxford Society of Historical Theology. *The New Testament in the Apostolic Fathers.* Oxford: Clarendon, 1905.

Theissen, Gerd. "Soziale Integration und sakramentales Handeln: Eine Analyse von 1 Cor. 11:17–34." *Novum Testamentum* 16 (1974): 145–74.

Thiselton, A. C. *The First Epistle to the Corinthians.* NIGTC. Grand Rapids: Eerdmans. Carlisle: Paternoster, 2000.

Thomas, Robert L. *Revelation 1–7: An Exegetical Commentary.* Chicago: Moody, 1992.

Thompson, Leonard L. *The Book of Revelation: Apocalypse and Empire.* New York: Oxford University Press, 1990.

Thompson, Michael B. *Clothed with Christ.* JSNTSup 59. Sheffield: JSOT, 1991.

Thompson, Trevor W. "As if Genuine: Interpreting the Pseudepigraphic Second Thessalonians." Pages 471–88 of *Pseudepigraphie und Verfasserfiktion in frühchrist-lichen Briefen.* Edited by J. Frey et al. WUNT 246. Tübingen: Mohr Siebeck, 2009.

———. "Writing in Character: Claudius Lysias to Felix as a Double Pseudepigraphon." Pages 393–407 in *The Interface of Orality and Writing: Seeing, Speaking, Writing in the Shaping of New Genres.* Edited by A. Weissenrieder and R. B. Coote. WUNT 260. Tübingen: Mohr Siebeck, 2010.

Torrance, Thomas F. *The Doctrine of Grace in the Apostolic Fathers.* Edinburgh: Oliver & Boyd, 1948.

Torrey, Charles. *The Apocalypse of John.* New Haven: Yale University Press, 1958.

Towner, P. H. *The Letters to Timothy and Titus.* NICNT. Grand Rapids Eerdmans, 2006.

Townsend, John T. "Date of Acts." Pages 47–62 in *Luke–Acts: New Perspectives from the Society of Biblical Literature.* Edited by Charles Talbert. New York: Crossroad, 1984.

Trevett, Christine. *A Study of Ignatius of Antioch in Syria and Asia.* Lewiston: Edwin Mellen, 1992.

Trümper, Monika. "Material and Social Environment of Greco-Roman Households in the East: The Case of Hellenistic Delos." Pages 19–43 in *Early Christian Families in Context: An Interdisciplinary Dialogue.* Edited by Carolyn Osiek and David L. Balch. Ann Arbor, MI: Eerdmans, 2003.

Tuckett, C. *2 Clement: Introduction, Text, and Commentary*. Oxford: Oxford University Press, 2012.

Tugwell, S. *The Apostolic Fathers*. London: Chapman, 1989.

Turner, Cuthbert H., ed. *Ecclesiae occidentalis monumenta iuris antiquissima*. Oxford: Clarendon, 1899–1939.

Tyson, Joseph. *Marcion and Luke–Acts: A Defining Struggle*. Columbia, SC: University of South Carolina Press, 2006.

Ubieta, Carmen Bernabé. "'Neither Xenoi nor paroikoi, sympolitai and oikeioi tou theou' (Eph 2.19): Pauline Christian Communities, Defining a New Territoriality." Pages 260–80 in *Social Scientific Models for Interpreting the Bible: Essays by the Context Group in Honor of Bruce J. Malina*. Edited by John J. Pilch. Leiden: Brill, 2001.

Van der Waal, C. "The Last Book of the Bible and the Jewish Apocalypses." *Neot* 12 (1981): 111–32.

Van Unnik, W. C. *Studies over de zogenaamde eerste brief van Clemens I Het littéraire genre*. Amsterdam: N. V. Noord-Hollandsche Uitgevers Maatschappij, 1970.

Varner, William. *The Way of the Didache*. Lanham, MD: University Press of America, 2007.

Vega, Angel Custudio. "La venida de San Pablo a Espana y los Varones Apostólicos." *BRAH* 154 (1964): 7–78.

Verheyden, Joseph. "Eschatology in the Didache and the Gospel of Matthew." Pages 193–216 in *Matthew and the Didache*. Edited by Huub van de Sandt. Assen: Van Gorcum; Minneapolis: Fortress, 2005.

———. "The Shepherd of Hermas and the Writings That Later Formed the New Testament." Pages 293–329 in *The Reception of the New Testament in the Apostolic Fathers*. Edited by Andrew F. Gregory and Christopher M. Tuckett. Vol. 1 of *The New Testament and the Apostolic Fathers*. Oxford: Oxford University Press, 2005.

Vielhauer, P. *Geschichte der urchristlichen Literatur: Einleitung in das Neue Testament, die Apokryphen und die Apostolischen Väter*. Berlin: de Gruyter, 1975.

Villada, Zacarías García. *Historia eclesiástica de España*. Madrid: Compañía Ibero-americana de Publicaciones, 1929.

Vinzent, Markus. *Christ's Resurrection in Early Christianity and the Making of the New Testament*. Farnham: Ashgate, 2012.

Wagner, Georg. "Zur Herkunft der Apostolischen Konstitutionen." Pages 525–37 in *Mélanges liturgiques offerts au R. P. dom Bernard Botte à l'occasion du cinquantième anniversaire de son ordination sacerdotale (4 juin 1472)*. Louvain, Abbaye du Mont César, 1972.

Walaskay, Paul W. *Acts*. Westminster Bible Companion. Louisville: Westminster John Knox, 1998.

Wall, Robert W. *Revelation*. NIBC 18. Peabody, MA: Hendrickson, 1991.

Wallace-Hadrill, Andrew. "Domus and Insulae in Rome: Families and Housefuls." Pages in 3–18 *Early Christian Families in Context: An Interdisciplinary Dialogue*. Edited by Carolyn Osiek and David L. Balch. Ann Arbor: Eerdmans, 2003.

Watson, Francis R., ed. *Diodorus Siculus: Library of History*, vol. 11. LCL 409. Cambridge, MA: Harvard University Press, 1957.

Watt, William Smith. ed. *Vellei Paterculi Historiarum ad M. Vinicium Consulem libri duo*. Stuttgart: Teubner, 1998.

Weidmann, Frederick W. *Polycarp and John: The Harris Fragments and Their Challenge to the Literary Traditions*. Notre Dame: University of Notre Dame Press, 1999.

Weinandy, Thomas G. "The Apostolic Christology of Ignatius of Antioch: The Road to Chalcedon." Pages 71–84 in *Trajectories through the New Testament and the Apostolic Fathers*. Edited by Andrew F. Gregory and Christopher M. Tuckett. Vol. 2 of *The New Testament and the Apostolic Fathers*. Oxford: Oxford University Press, 2005.

Welborn, Laurence L. "Clement, First Epistle of." *ABD* 1:1056.

———. "On the Date of 1 Clement." BR 29 (1984): 35–54.

———. "On the Discord in Corinth: 1 Corinthians 1–4 and Ancient Politics.'" *JBL* 106 (1987): 85–111.

———. "The Preface to 1 Clement: The Rhetorical Situation and the Traditional Date." Pages 197–216 in *Encounters with Hellenism: Studies on the First Letter of Clement*. Edited by Cilliers Breytenbach and Laurence L. Welborn. Leiden: Brill, 2004.

Wengst, K. *Schriften des Urchristentums: Didache, Barnabasbrief, zweiter Klemensbrief, Schriften an Diognet*. Darmstadt: Wissenschaftliche Buchgesellschaft, 1984.

Wengst, Klaus. *Schriften des Urchristentums*. Munich: Kösel-Verlag, 1984.

Wenham, D. *Paul: Follower of Jesus or Founder of Christianity?* Grand Rapids: Eerdmans, 1995.

Werline, R. "The Transformation of Pauline Arguments in Justin Martyr's 'Dialogue with Trypho.'" *HTR* 92 (1999): 79–93.

Whitenton, Michael R. "After ΠΙΣΤΙΣ ΚΡΙΣΤΟΥ: Neglected Evidence from the Apostolic Fathers." *JTS* 61, no. 1 (2010): 82–109.

Wiles, M. *The Divine Apostle: The Interpretation of St Paul's Epistles in the Early Church*. Cambridge: Cambridge University Press, 1967.

Wilhite, David. "Rhetoric and Theology in Tertullian: What Tertullian Learned from Paul." *StPatr* 65 (2013): 295–312.

Wilken, R. L. *John Chrysostom and the Jews: Rhetoric and Reality in the Late 4th Century*. Berkeley: University of California Press, 1983.

Wilkins, Michael J. "The Interplay of Ministry, Martyrdom, and Discipleship in Ignatius of Antioch." Pages 294–315 in *Worship, Theology and Ministry in the Early Church: Essays in Honor of Ralph P. Martin*. JSNTSup 87. Sheffield: Sheffield Academic, 1992.

Williams, David J. *Acts*. NIBC. Peabody, MA: Hendrickson, 1990.

Wilson, J. Christian. "The Problem of the Domitianic Date of Revelation." *NTS* 39 (1993): 587–605.

Windisch, H. "Der Branbasbrief." Pages 219–343 of *Handbuch zum NT Ergänzungsband: Die Apostolischen Väter III*. Tübingen: Mohr, 1920.

Witherington, Ben III. *The Acts of the Apostles: A Socio-Rhetorical Commentary*. Grand Rapids: Eerdmans, 1998.

Woollcombe, K. J. "The Doctrinal Connexions of the Pseudo-Ignatian Letters." *StPatr* 6 (1962): 269–83.

Zahn, Theodor. *Ignatii et Polycarpi: Epistulae, martyria, fragmenta. Patrum Apostolicorum Opera*. Leipzig: Hinrichs, 1876.

———. *Ignatius von Antiochen*. Gotha: Perthes, 1873.

Zetterholm, Magnus. "The Didache, Matthew, James – and Paul: Reconstructing Historical Developments in Antioch." Pages 73–90 in *Matthew, James, and Didache*. SBLSymS 45. Edited by Huub van de Sandt and Jürgen K. Zangenberg. Atlanta: Society of Biblical Literature, 2008.

———. *The Formation of Christianity in Antioch*. RECM. London: Routledge, 2003.

Zwierlein, Otto. *Zwierlein, Petrus in Rom: Die literarischen Zeugnisse*. 2nd ed. Berlin: de Gruyter, 2010.

INDEX OF REFERENCES

INDEX OF AUTHORS

CPSIA information can be obtained
at www.ICGtesting.com
Printed in the USA
LVOW13s2307290618
582305LV00007B/99/P